SKEPTICISM
A Contemporary Reader

D0223998

Edited by

Keith DeRose
and
Ted A. Warfield

New York   Oxford
OXFORD UNIVERSITY PRESS
1999

For Peter Klein and Peter Unger

Oxford University Press

Oxford New York
Athens Auckland Bangkok Bogotá Buenos Aires Calcutta
Cape Town Chennai Dar es Salaam Delhi Florence Hong Kong Istanbul
Karachi Kuala Lumpur Madrid Melbourne Mexico City Mumbai
Nairobi Paris São Paulo Singapore Taipei Tokyo Toronto Warsaw

and associated companies in
Berlin Ibadan

Copyright © 1999 by Oxford University Press, Inc.

Published by Oxford University Press, Inc.
198 Madison Avenue, New York, New York 10016

Library of Congress Cataloging-in-Publication Data
Skepticism : a contemporary reader / edited by Keith DeRose and Ted A.
   Warfield.
      p. cm.
   Includes bibliographical references and index.
   ISBN-13 978-0-19-511826-1; 978-0-19-511827-8 (pbk.)
   ISBN 0-19-511826-X; 0-19-511827-8 (pbk.)
   1. Skepticism.   I. DeRose, Keith, 1962– . II. Warfield, Ted
A., 1969– .
B837.S566   1999
149'.73--dc21
                                                      98-22393
                                                      CIP

Printing (last digit) : 9 8 7 6

Printed in the United States of America
on acid-free paper

CONTENTS

Contents

CONTRIBUTORS

Anthony Brueckner is Professor of Philosophy at the University of California, Santa Barbara.

Keith DeRose is Associate Professor of Philosophy at Yale University

Fred Dretske is Professor of Philosophy at Stanford University

Graeme Forbes is Professor of Philosophy at Tulane University

Christopher S. Hill is Professor of Philosophy at the University of Arkansas, Fayetteville

David Lewis is Professor of Philosophy at Princeton University

Thomas Nagel is Professor of Philosophy and Law at New York University

Robert Nozick is Professor of Philosophy at Harvard University

Hilary Putnam is Professor of Philosophy Emeritus at Harvard University

Ernest Sosa is Professor of Philosophy at Brown University

Gail Stine was Professor of Philosophy at Wayne State University

Barry Stroud is Professor of Philosophy at the University of California, Berkeley

Peter Unger is Professor of Philosophy at New York University

Ted A. Warfield is Assistant Professor of Philosophy at the University of Notre Dame

CHAPTER 1

Introduction: Responding to Skepticism

Keith DeRose

1. THE ARGUMENT BY SKEPTICAL HYPOTHESIS

For almost anything you might think you know, there are powerful skeptical arguments that threaten to establish that you know no such thing. Take, for instance, your belief that you have hands. (Those who don't have hands should change the example.) Surely there is something you not only believe, but also know! What kind of skeptical argument could possibly undermine that solid piece of knowledge?

Well, skeptical arguments come in many varieties, but some of the most powerful of them proceed by means of *skeptical hypotheses.* Hypotheses explain. What does a skeptical hypothesis explain? It explains how you might be going wrong about the very things you think you know.

Consider, to use an old example, the scenario Descartes describes in the First Meditation, in which he is the victim of a very powerful and very deceitful "evil genius" who "has directed his entire effort to misleading" Descartes. This hypothesis could explain how Descartes has come to have any number of false beliefs. On this supposition, "the heavens, the air, the earth, colors, shapes, sounds, and all external things" are, Descartes writes, "nothing but the deceptive games of my dreams, by which [the evil genius] lays snares for my credulity." What becomes of Descartes's supposed knowledge of the existence of his hands? Descartes makes it clear that his evil genius hypothesis has cast this belief into doubt when, in keeping with his resolution to regard as false anything for which he finds a reason to doubt, he reacts: "I will regard myself as having no hands, no eyes, no flesh, no blood, no senses, but as nevertheless falsely believing that I possess all these things" (Descartes 1980, p. 60).

Much the same effect can be attained by means of the more up-to-date skeptical hypothesis according to which you are a bodiless brain in a vat who has been electrochemically stimulated to have precisely those sensory experiences you have had, perhaps because you are appropriately hooked up to an immensely powerful computer, which, taking into account the "output" of the brain which is you, has seen to it that you receive appropriate sensory "input."

Other old favorites include the hypothesis that one is dreaming—which Descartes considers in Meditation I before getting to the evil genius hypothesis—and Bertrand Russell's proposal that the earth came into existence only five minutes ago, but was created complete with all the evidence of great age (including our apparent "memories") that it actually contains. As these illustrate, some skeptical hypotheses are designed to target more limited ranges of beliefs than the evil genius or brain in a vat hypotheses. Descartes seems to believe the dream hypothesis undermines a narrower range of beliefs than does his evil genius hypothesis, and Russell's hypothesis seems to target only our supposed knowledge of the past.

By what reasoning can these skeptical hypotheses be used to undermine our supposed knowledge? The skeptic's argument, at least in its most basic form, is as simple as it is powerful. The skeptic begins by asserting, and asking us to agree, that it is in *some* way an open question whether or not the situation described in her hypothesis is our actual situation. This may take the form of a premise to the effect that we *can't rule out* her hypothesis, that it's *possible* that her hypothesis is true, or that we *don't know* that her hypothesis is false. (It is of course not necessary to her argument that the skeptic should profess to believe, or ask us to believe, that her hypothesis is true, or even that it is at all probable.) The skeptic then concludes that since we cannot rule out her hypothesis, and must admit that it may be correct, or anyway that we don't *know* it isn't, we don't after all know the thing we originally supposed we did know.

A skeptical thesis is typically a claim that a certain range of beliefs lack a certain status. In addition, then, to varying in their *scope*—which specifies the range of beliefs being targeted—skeptical theses, and the arguments used to establish them, also differ in their *force*—which specifies precisely what lack the skeptic alleges befalls the targeted beliefs. Some skeptics may claim that the beliefs in the targeted range *aren't justified,* or that they're *possibly false,* or that they *aren't known with complete certainty,* and so forth. But one of the most popular skeptical claims is that the targeted beliefs *aren't known* to be true. Keeping our focus on knowledge, the above argument can be rendered as follows, where O is a proposition one would *or*dinarily think one knows, and H is a suitably chosen skeptical *hy*pothesis:

The Argument by Skeptical Hypothesis

1. I don't know that not-H.
2. If I don't know that not-H, then I don't know that O.

So,

C. I don't know that O.

Though there are very different skeptical arguments, we will here focus on responses to this form of skeptical argument. (Many of the responses, or analogues of them, will also apply to other forms of skeptical arguments.) Before describing lines of response that are represented by the essays to follow in this anthology, we will begin by discussing one of the most popular responses this argument, and skeptical arguments generally, meet with in philosophy classes, and a very influential response given by G. E. Moore that is very similar in spirit to the popular response, and which raises important issues about how to approach the topic of skepticism.

2. "AW, COME ON!"

In *The Significance of Philosophical* Scepticism, Barry Stroud describes one common reaction to arguments by skeptical hypotheses as follows:

> I think that when we first encounter the sceptical reasoning outlined in the previous chapter we find it immediately gripping. It appeals to something deep in our nature and seems to raise a real problem about the human condition.[1]

When arguments by skeptical hypotheses are first presented to students in philosophy classes, some do have roughly the reaction that Stroud describes. But many have a very different reaction, finding the arguments far-fetched, ridiculously weak, and quite unthreatening; such a reaction is often accompanied by an exclamation somewhat along the lines of, "Aw, come on!" Those inclined to react in this latter way probably grew increasingly impatient of my repeated description, in section 1, above, of the Argument by Skeptical Hypothesis as "powerful," thinking instead that the argument hasn't a chance in the world of establishing its absurd conclusion.

Well, the skeptical argument really is powerful—at least fairly powerful—and is certainly not absurdly weak. The argument is clearly valid—its premises imply its conclusion—and each of its premises, considered on its own, enjoys a good deal of intuitive support. For however improbable, far-fetched, or even bizarre it seems to suppose that you are a brain in a vat, it also seems that you don't *know* that you're not one. How *could* you possibly know such a thing? And it also seems that if, for all you know, you are a brain in a vat, then you don't know that you have hands. How could you know you have hands if, for all you know, you're bodiless, and therefore handless?

The reaction that the skeptical argument is weak is probably best refined to the claim that, however strong the argument may be, it's not strong *enough* to adequately support such a counterintuitive conclusion. And the reaction that the skeptical argument is *absurdly* weak is probably best refined to the claim that, however strong the argument may be, it's *nowhere near* to being strong enough to support such a counterintuitive conclusion. This would still make sense of the objector's sense that the argument is unthreatening and doesn't have a chance in the world of establishing its conclusion. Such an objector could be feeling that our knowledge that we have hands is, as David Lewis puts it in chapter 12 of this collection, "a Moorean fact. . . . It is one of those things that we know better than we know the premises of any philosophical argument to the contrary" (p. 220). In looking at G. E. Moore's own reaction to the skeptical argument, we can find strong reasons for even those in the "Aw, come on!" crowd to have ample interest in the skeptical argument. (Those who instead react in the way Stroud describes will of course be well motivated to study the argument.)

3. MOORE'S RESPONSE

In "Four Forms of Scepticism," Moore considers a skeptical argument of Bertrand Russell's to the conclusion that he does not know "that this is a pencil or that you are conscious."[2] After identifying and numbering four assumptions on which Russell's argument rests, Moore writes:

> And what I can't help asking myself is this: Is it, in fact, as certain that all four of these assumptions are true, as that I *do* know that this is a pencil or that you are conscious? I cannot help answering: It seems to me *more* certain that I *do* know that this is a pencil and that you are conscious, than that any single one of these four assumptions are true, let alone all four. That is to say, though, as I have said, I agree with Russell that (1), (2), and (3) *are* true; yet of no one even of these three do I feel *as* certain as that I do know for certain that this is a pencil. Nay more: I do not think it is *rational* to be as certain of any one of these four propositions, as of the proposition that I do know that this is a pencil.
>
> (Moore 1959, p. 226)

This reaction of Moore's may be attractive to the "Aw, Come on!" crowd. Rather than having to identify one of the premises of the skeptical argument as positively implausible, one can, like Moore, make the more modest—and more reasonable—claim that however plausible those premises may be, they are not as certain or as plausible as is the thought that we do know the things in question, and thus those premises don't have enough power to overturn that thought. Indeed, as we see in the above quotation, Moore *agrees* with Russell's first three assumptions, so he certainly finds *them* plausible, though Moore makes it clear that if it came down to it, he'd reject any of those three premises before he'd accept Russell's skeptical conclusion. And though Moore will ultimately reject it, there's no indication that Moore finds Russell's fourth assumption, considered by itself, to be initially implausible.

Indeed, if the premises of a valid skeptical argument are all plausible, then those who judge that the fact that we're knowers to be a Moorean fact should find great value in the study of skeptical arguments: Such arguments show that some premise that we are tempted to accept must be false, because if it were true, we wouldn't know what we clearly do know. Such is the fate of Russell's fourth assumption in Moore's hands. Skeptical arguments should in that case be seen as a rich source of information about what is, and what is not, necessary in order to know something to be the case.

Though the skeptical argument of Russell's that Moore is countering above is quite different from our Argument by Skeptical Hypothesis, the basic type of maneuver Moore makes above is applicable to our argument; indeed, Moore himself, in his essay *Certainty*, wrestles in a similar way with a form of the Argument by Skeptical Hypothesis. The skeptical hypothesis that obsessed Moore throughout his career was the dreaming hypothesis. Moore provocatively argues:

> I agree, therefore, with that part of the argument which asserts that if I don't know that I'm not dreaming, it follows that I *don't* know that I'm standing up, even if I both actually am and think that I am. But this first part of the argument is a consideration which cuts both ways. For, if it is true, it follows that it is also true that if I *do* know that I am standing up, then I do know that I'm not dreaming. I can therefore just as well argue: since I do know that I'm standing up, it follows that I do know that I'm not dreaming; as my opponent can argue: since you don't that you're not dreaming, it follows that you don't know that you're standing up. The one argument is just as good as the other, unless my opponent can give better reasons for asserting that I don't know that I'm not dreaming, than I can give for asserting that I do know that I'm standing up.
>
> (Moore 1959, p. 247)

Here Moore agrees with premise 2 of the Argument by Skeptical Hypothesis (at least in its dream argument version). But rather than accepting the skeptic's conclusion that he doesn't know that he's standing up, Moore instead holds fast to the position that he knows that he's standing up, and uses that, together with premise 2, to reach the conclusion that he does indeed know that he's not dreaming. Thus, while the skeptic argues

1; 2; therefore, C,

Moore argues

2; not-C; therefore, not-1,

and claims that his argument is just as good as the skeptic's (though one cannot help but suspect, especially given the first quotation from Moore above, that Moore considers it more rational to follow his line of argument than it is to draw the skeptic's conclusion).

What is one to do if a powerful argument is presented toward a conclusion the negation of which one finds very plausible—plausible enough to (at least) rival the plausibility of the premises? In the quotations above, Moore motions toward two suggestions. In the first quotation, it is suggested that we make a choice according to what seems most certain to us. What we face in the situation imagined is a puzzle—a set of statements (the premises of the argument in question together with the negation of the argument's conclusion) all of which we find plausible, but such that they can't all be true. If we want to have consistent beliefs,[3] we'll want to reject, or at least suspend belief in, at least one of the members of that set. Moore apparently finds Russell's (4) to be the least certain, and so, presumably, it's that member of the set he denies. If no further progress on the problem can be made, then perhaps making such a "Moorean" choice is the best we can do. Better to reject what seems less certain to us than what seems more certain, after all. To be sure, such a "solution" is not very satisfying. Rejecting something on the grounds that other propositions one finds plausible imply its falsity is not very fulfilling when what one rejects is itself plausible. Still, Moore rightly points out that in the situation in question there are alternatives to accepting the skeptical conclusion—alternatives that many will and perhaps should find preferable.

Can we hope for a better solution to our puzzle? In the second quotation above, Moore suggests that the parties to the dispute look for positive reasons in support of the puzzle members they support.[4] Of course, if that can be done, it would certainly help. But since each of the puzzle members will be very plausible, it may be difficult to find arguments for them whose premises are even more certain than are the puzzle members themselves.

There is an alternative, and perhaps more promising, avenue of possible progress that Moore seems to overlook: One can hope for an *explanation* of how we fell into the puzzling conflict of intuitions in the first place. Perhaps we can explain how premises that together imply a conclusion we find so incredible can themselves seem so plausible to us. Such an explanation can take the form of explaining, for the member of the set that one seeks to deny, why it *seems* to us to be true, though it's in fact false. The game then would not be one of producing more positive support for the aspects of one's position that are already plausible anyway, so much as it is a game of *damage control*—of providing a deflationary explanation for why we have the misleading intuition we do have about the plausible statement that one chooses to deny.

4. THE RESPONSE FROM SEMANTIC EXTERNALISM

We can distinguish between two types of "Moorean" responses to skeptical arguments. One such type of response is any reaction according to which one claims that it's more certain or more plausible that the skeptic's conclusion is false than it is that her premises are true, and one therefore takes the argument not to successfully support its conclusion, but to rather show that one of its premises is mistaken. This type of response can be made to any skeptical argument, whether it's of the form we're focusing on or not. (In fact, one can make this general kind of response to any argument for a counterintuitive conclusion, whether or not that conclusion is a skeptical thesis.) And, if it is applied to the Argument by Skeptical Hypothesis, an executor of this type of "Moorean" maneuver needn't follow Moore in fingering the first premise of the argument as the problem—the second premise can also be denied. But sometimes, when a response to skepticism is described as "Moorean," what is meant is something quite different: that the responder, like Moore, denies the first premise of the Argument by Skeptical Hypothesis.

A line of response that's "Moorean" in this latter sense and that has been very influential—largely due to the work of Hilary Putnam (see chapter 2 of this collection)—is the Response from Semantic Externalism. According to semantic externalism, the contents of at least some of one's thoughts are not completely determined by "internal" facts about what is going on inside one's head, but are at least partially determined by such "external" facts as the nature of the items one has been in contact with. In particular, according to Putnam, you cannot think about, say, trees, if you haven't been causally connected with trees in the proper way. Thus, a brain in a vat (henceforth, a BIV), if it hasn't been in contact in the proper way with real trees, cannot refer to or think about trees. When such a BIV thinks such thoughts as those she expresses via the sentences, "There's a tree," or "Here's a hand," or "I'm not a BIV," then, it is not thinking the same thing that those words would express in *our* mouths/minds (given that we're not BIVs), since the BIV is not causally connected with trees, hands, vats, etc., in the way needed to have such thoughts. What *does tree*, as used by a BIV (in "vat-English"), refer to? Putnam lists several different suggestions: "[I]t might refer to trees in the image, or to the electronic impulses that cause tree experiences, or to the features of the program that are responsible for those electronic impulses." All of these suggestions are in the spirit of semantic externalism, because, as Putnam writes, "there is a close causal connection between the use of the word 'tree' in vat-English" and each of these suggested referents (pp. 36–37). Importantly, on any of these suggestions, the BIV ends up thinking something *true* when it thinks "There's a tree," or "Here's a hand," or even "I'm not a BIV," for, to take the "in the image" reading, the BIV is indeed indicating a tree-in-the-image and a hand-in-the-image, and it indeed is not a BIV-in-the-image (it's just a BIV).[5]

A semantic externalist, as such, needn't commit himself to any of these positive suggestions about what "tree," and so on, refers to in vat-English, only to the negative thesis that it doesn't refer to real trees. Indeed, Putnam not only doesn't commit himself to any particular positive proposal, he doesn't even commit himself to the thought that *any* positive proposal on which the BIVs end up thinking largely true thoughts is correct. In fact, Putnam seems unsure that the BIVs succeed in meaning anything at all; he writes that if we are BIVs, then "what we now mean by 'we are not brains in a vat' is that *we are not brains in a vat in the image* or something of the kind (*if we mean anything at all*)."[6] What Putnam seems committed to is just this: That *if* the BIVs succeed in meaning anything true or false by their relevant thoughts involving "tree," "hand," "vat," and so on, they mean one of the three above proposals, or some closely related other thing, on which the relevant thoughts turn out to be true.

Putnam himself seems largely uninterested in the potential such results have for the problem of skepticism.[7] But Putnam does claim that semantic externalism furnishes "an argument we can give that shows we are not brains in a vat" (p. 32), and whether or not *he* is interested in using this argument for antiskeptical purposes, understandably enough, others have thought that such an argument may be of use against the skeptic. If we can use semantic externalism to prove that we're not BIVs, after all, it seems we can, by means of this proof, come to know that we're not BIVs, and this would block the first premise of the Argument by Skeptical Hypothesis, at least in its BIV form.

But how might such an argument proceed? There are two quite different ways that have been proposed, both as promising antiskeptical strategies in their own right and as interpretations of Putnam.

The main idea of the first type of argument is this. If we are BIVs, then by, "I am not a BIV," one means that one is not a BIV-in-the-image (or some closely related true thing), which is in that case true. On the other hand, if we are not BIVs, then by "I am not a BIV," one means that one is not a BIV, which is in *that* case true. Thus, whether we are BIVs or whether we are not, our use of "I am not a BIV" is true. Either way, it's true; so, it's true.

A problem that quickly emerged for this type of strategy is that it seems to yield only the conclusion that

(a) My utterance of "I am not a BIV" is true,

while what we seem to need, and what Putnam seemed to promise, was an argument to the quite different conclusion that

(b) I am not a BIV.[8]

Chapter 4 in this collection by Graeme Forbes is set up as an attempt to take the crucial last step from what this strategy has yielded (a) to what is needed (b).

Another problem is that this first type of strategy seems to require the strong, positive externalist thesis that by her use of such sentences as, "I am not a BIV," a BIV means some true thought such as that she is not a BIV-in-the-image, and it's unclear whether the thought experiments used to support semantic externalism support such a conclusion. Putnam himself, we saw, only claimed the weaker, negative results about what a BIV could *not* mean.

The second strategy, employed by both Brueckner and Warfield in their essays in this collection, seems to avoid that problem. The externalist thesis used on this second strategy is only a negative claim about what a BIV cannot mean or think—that by "tree," "hand," "vat," and so on, the BIV does not refer to trees, hands, vats, and so on, due to her lack of causal contact with such items. This negative externalist thesis is then combined with a positive claim to the effect that *we* do have the thoughts in question—the thoughts that the BIVs cannot have. These together imply that we are not BIVs.[9]

This strategy immediately raises the issue of whether such an antiskeptic has any right to his second claim—the positive claim that he does have the thoughts in question. Since he does not have such thoughts if he is a BIV, he seems, in claiming to have such thoughts, to be helping himself to a question-begging assumption that he is not a BIV. Ted Warfield seeks to defend his use of this second strategy from this charge in chapter 5 of this collection.

There are other potential problems/limitations that inflict both types of response from semantic externalism. Many of these are dealt with in the chapters by Brueckner, Forbes, and Warfield in this collection. Each of these essays is, in its own way, quite sensitive to the potential problems of Putnam-style responses to skepticism. (Forbes, while he thinks the strategy does yield a proof that one is not a BIV, thinks that such a proof fails to provide the needed relief from skepticism. Brueckner and Warfield, while sensitive to the apparent problems, express a hope—more confident in the case of Warfield than in the case of Brueckner—that these problems are only apparent, and that the antiskeptical strategy can succeed.)[10] Here, we'll bring up only two such problems/limitations.

The first is an often-noted potential problem, first noted in an early paper by Brueckner,[11] that both Forbes and Warfield discuss in their essays in this collection: To solidify his externalist claim that the BIVs he was imagining were not capable of thinking about trees, hands, vats, etc., Putnam imagined a very special scenario in which the BIVs have always been BIVs. In fact, he went further and supposed that all sentient beings had always been BIVs, the universe, by accident, just happening "to consist of automatic machinery tending a vat full of brains" (p. 31). But what of other scenarios? What if I am a brain who has only very recently been envatted, after many years of normal embodiment and causal contact with real trees, hands, vats, etc.? Then, it seems, and it seems consistent with externalism, that I do mean tree by "tree," vat by "vat," and so on, and so I *am* falsely thinking, "I am not a BIV." In short, the response by semantic externalism seems to be effective only against a quite limited number of skeptical hypotheses, while, in order to pack much antiskeptical power, it must work against them all. (Perhaps it's precisely this problem that made Putnam himself hesitant in using his argument for antiskeptical purposes.)

The second is a less often noted problem, which the authors of the essays in the collection don't bring up. As opposed to Moore, who settles for the claim that he feels more certain that he does know that he's standing up than that he doesn't know that the relevant skeptical hypothesis is false, the Putnam-style response to skepticism attempts—leaving open the question of whether it succeeds—to provide a nonquestion-begging argument that one is not a BIV. In this way, it is a very aggressive antiskeptical strategy. (Which explains the placement of the section on this type of response in the present collection: We have sought to order the types of response from the most aggressively antiskeptical to the most conciliatory to skepticism.) But in another respect, this strategy seems to concede much to the skeptic. By proving that one is not a BIV, one seeks, it seems, in following this strategy, to *make* it the case that the first premise of the Argument by Skeptical Hypothesis is false, as applied to oneself. In this respect, this strategy is "heroic" in the way Descartes's response to the evil genius argument is: the Putnam-style arguer, like Descartes, seeks by constructing a proof against the obtaining of the relevant hypothesis, to *gain* knowledge, for himself and all that would follow him, that the hypothesis is false. Externalist semantics has replaced Descartes's God as the slayer of skeptical hypotheses. Presumably, though, the proof only helps those who follow the hero—who know and understand the argument. But what of people who have never encountered this complicated argument that one is not a BIV? Do such folks fail to know that *they* have hands? Other strategies, which attempt not to show how to regain knowledge in the face of the skeptical argument, but rather to show how the skeptical argument never worked in the first place, by protecting the knowledge of the unphilosophical, seem in that respect at least to be more aggressively antiskeptical.

Forbes's strategy, by which he argues that there are no relevant alternative situations in which one's belief that one is not a BIV is false, seems, if it works at all, to secure the knowledge of even the nonphilosophical that they're not BIVs, and thereby promises to block the skeptic's first premise, even as it is applied to those who don't know the proof. In that respect, Forbes's use of the Putnam-style strategy is unusual; other uses of the strategy at least seem not to share that virtue with Forbes's.

There may be ways, other than Forbes's, in which the Putnam-type strategy could be used to show how, in the face of the skeptical argument, we all knew all along.[12] But, to initial appearances, a proof that the BIV hypothesis is false is of help against the skeptic's first premise only to those who possess the proof, and, at the very least, those engaging in the externalist strategy haven't done much to tell us how it is of value in securing the knowledge of those who don't possess the proof against the onslaughts of the skeptical argument.[13]

5. RESPONSES FROM EPISTEMIC EXTERNALISM

As opposed to the *semantic* externalism discussed in the previous section, *epistemic* externalism is not a thesis about the content of one's beliefs. Rather, it concerns the conditions under which a belief is justified or constitutes knowledge.

According to the externalist's rival, the epistemic *internalist*, these matters depend primarily on factors internal to the believer's point of view and/or factors to which the believer has special access. Most internalists admit that the external matter of whether the belief is true is relevant to the issue of whether it constitutes knowledge, so on the issue of knowledge, internalism is usually the position that only or primarily internal factors are relevant to whether *true* beliefs constitute knowledge. The epistemic externalist, on the other hand, claims that issues of knowledge and/or justification depend exclusively or primarily on such factors as how the belief was caused or how reliable is the faculty or mechanism by which the subject came to hold the belief—matters that are not in the requisite way "internal" to the subject's point of view, as can be seen by the fact that you can imagine two subjects whose cognitive lives are identical with respect to what they can tell from their own point of view, but whose beliefs diverge with respect to the matters in question. The internalist about justification will have to hold that the beliefs of such subjects have the same justificatory status, and the internalist about knowledge will have to hold that, where the beliefs of such "twins" don't diverge in their truth values, they also don't diverge on the matter of whether they constitute knowledge.

The above characterization of the distinction between epistemic internalism and externalism should strike you as rather murky. How exactly to distinguish "internal" from "external" factors is a very difficult matter, and probably varies greatly from writer to writer.

The paradigm case of an externalist theory, though, is *process reliabilism,* according to which the justificatory status of a belief and/or the issue of whether a true belief constitutes knowledge hinges on whether the process by which the belief was formed and/or maintained is reliable. The champion of reliabilism is Alvin Goldman, in whose hands process reliabilism has been developed through many stages and has been very ably defended.

Goldman, however, has not done much to apply his reliabilism to the problem of skepticism. And the interaction between process reliabilism or most other forms of externalism on the one hand, and the issue of skepticism on the other can be fascinating. For it's difficult to see how most skeptical arguments could ever gain a foothold if reliabilism were correct, since they, for the most part, seem to have no tendency to show that our beliefs are formed by an unreliable process. Consider the BIV argument. Arguably, if we were BIVs, then our belief-forming processes would not be very reliable (though the *semantic* externalist would contest that judgment). But the skeptical argument doesn't endeavor to show merely that we *wouldn't* know much about the physical world *if* we were BIVs, but that we *don't* know. But there's nothing in that argument with any tendency to show that our belief-forming processes are in fact unreliable. The BIV skeptic would probably happily admit that, for all she knows, we are hooked up to the world in a reliable way. But she'll still insist that we don't know we're not BIVs and that if we don't know that, then we don't know such things as that we have hands. All this without impugning the reliability of the processes by which our beliefs are formed.

One might conclude that externalism promises an antidote to skepticism. If we can establish epistemic externalism, then the skeptic is in trouble, for then her arguments can only work if they establish that our beliefs are unreliable, or false, or that they suffer from some other "external" malady. But most of the weapons in the skeptic's arsenal seem ill suited for any such task.

But those more pessimistic about externalism and/or more taken by skepticism will probably draw a different conclusion. The fact that skeptical arguments that don't even begin to show that the processes by which our beliefs are formed are unreliable can nevertheless be so intuitively powerful (whether or not the skeptical arguments are ultimately sound), they'll claim, shows that externalism is wrong. How could we find skeptical arguments that don't address reliability so powerful if our concept of knowledge were that of true, reliably formed belief? The persuasiveness of skepticism can in this way be seen as constituting an objection to reliabilism. (Other forms of epistemic externalism would have similar interactions with the issue of skepticism.)

In chapter 7 of this collection, Christopher Hill seeks to meet this objection on behalf of process reliabilism. Hill argues that the process reliabilist can explain the persuasiveness of the skeptical arguments, and thereby disarm this objection. But, according to Hill, while the persuasiveness of the skeptical arguments is explained, it's not explained in such a way as to vindicate the arguments. Thus, Hill concludes that it's skepticism that is threatened by externalism, not the other way around.

A common reaction to such externalist responses is to change the subject. Maybe we *know* various things, for all the skeptic can show, but we might still fall short of epistemic ideals in other ways. Perhaps the lesson of skepticism is that we *don't know that we know* the things in question, or that we *can't show that we know* them, or some other such thing. This move sets up an interesting dynamic. For the externalist will perhaps be able to employ his tricks on some of the other alleged shortcomings. For instance, it's not clear that externalism can't secure knowledge of one's knowing as well as first-order knowledge. But the externalist may concede some of the alleged shortcomings—particularly the ones that involve epistemic concepts that are clearly internalist in character—but argue that it's not so interesting or important that we fall short in the ways in question. The search, for the skeptic, becomes one to find a conclusion that is both interesting and established by the skeptical arguments, slightly revised to make them suitable for establishing their new targets. The antiskeptic responds to each proposal by either showing that it's no great shortcoming that we fail in the way alleged, or that the skeptical argument cannot establish that particular shortcoming.

Ernest Sosa, in chapter 6 of this collection, pursues the antiskeptical side of this dialectic. Sosa argues that externalism, and in particular reliabilism, can provide an escape from *philosophical skepticism,* but by *philosophical skepticism* he does not just mean the claim that we don't know this or that, but means rather the following thesis: "There is no way to attain full philosophical understanding of our knowledge. A fully general theory of knowledge is impossible" (p. 93). Sosa argues that there's no reason to suppose that an externalist theory of knowledge—in particular, a reliabilist theory—would fall short of such full generality. Sosa does admit that externalism will fall short of meeting certain requirements some might want a theory of knowledge to meet, but argues that it's misguided to want a theory of knowledge to meet such requirements. In particular, Sosa admits that a fully general *legitimating* account of our knowledge is indeed impossible, where a legitimating account "specifies the sorts of inferences that justify one's beliefs . . . without circularity or endless regress" (p. 96). But when we're seeking a fully general account—an account of *all* our knowledge—we *of course* are not going be able to make it at the same time a legitimating account. We can provide legitimating account of limited stretches of our presumed knowledge, because we can appeal to knowledge from outside of that limited stretch to construct our account. But if the account is to be fully general, it will have to draw its starting point from beliefs that are among those in question, and the account will then suffer from circularity. If reliabilism can provide a fully general account, then it's giving us everything we can reasonably desire. To ask for an account that is at the same time legitimating is to ask for the obviously impossible.

It should be noted that externalism is quite popular these days, and several of the papers in this collection other than Hill's and Sosa's are externalist in character. We've collected Hill's and Sosa's paper together under the heading of "Responses from Epistemic Externalism" because each, while defending a particular version of externalism with respect to its handling of skepticism, does so in such a way as to bring to the fore issues of general importance to the relation of externalism to skepticism.

6. RELEVANT ALTERNATIVES AND DENYING CLOSURE

According to what is known as the "Closure Principle" for knowledge, if you know some proposition P, and you know that P entails some second proposition Q, then you also know that Q.[14]

This principle looks like it describes how knowledge can be *expanded* by means of inference: If you know something you can come to know anything it entails by coming to know the entailment. But, in the Argument by Skeptical Hypothesis, the skeptic uses the principle to *attack* the thesis that we know. For the skeptic seeks to argue that since you don't know that her hypothesis, H, is false, and since, given closure, you would be able to know that the hypothesis is false if you knew O (the proposition you would ordinarily think you know [e.g., that you have hands]), you must *not* know that O. Thus, the Closure Principle has come to be seen as underwriting skepticism. In chapter 8 of this collection, Fred Dretske goes so far as to write that "Almost all skeptical objections trade on it" (p. 135). In particular, this Principle supports premise 2 of our Argument by Skeptical Hypothesis.

As we saw in section 3, above, the Argument by Skeptical Hypothesis can be profitably viewed as presenting us with a puzzle consisting of three individually plausible but jointly inconsistent theses: the first premise of the argument (I don't know that not-H); the second premise (If I don't know that not-H, then I don't know that O), and the negation of the argument's conclusion (I do know that O). The skeptic, in accepting the argument's skeptical conclusion, of course, rejects that conclusion's negation. The Moorean rejects the first premise of the argument. It was only a matter of time before the puzzle was dealt with by denying the second premise. That time was the 1970s and 1980s, and the most prominent of the deniers of closure were Fred Dretske and Robert Nozick. Of course, it's easy enough to simply deny the second premise and the Closure Principle that underwrites it; what's more difficult is to give a plausible rationale for taking that approach to the puzzle. Both Dretske and Nozick sought to provide an account of what knowledge is that backed that maneuver.

Nozick, following earlier work by Dretske,[15] advances an account of knowledge that rests heavily on *subjunctive conditionals*. On this account, what is needed for S to know that P, in addition to the usual requirements that (1) P is true and that (2) S believes that P, is that both of the following subjunctive conditionals hold:

(3) If P weren't true, S wouldn't believe that P

(4) If P were true, S would believe that P

The star of Nozick's show is condition (3),[16] which plays a pivotal role in Nozick's application of his account of knowledge to the Argument by Skeptical Hypothesis. For your belief that you're not a BIV fails to meet that condition: If that belief weren't true (if you were a BIV), you would still believe it was true (you would believe you weren't a BIV). For, remember, the BIV has had all the sensory experiences you've had, and would thus believe everything you believe, including, presumably, that he's not a BIV. But, Nozick argues, the likes of your belief that you have hands *does* satisfy this condition for knowledge, as well as the other conditions Nozick posits. Thus, if Nozick's account of knowledge is correct, you do know you have hands, but you don't know that you're not a BIV. The skeptic's first premise is true, but her second premise, and the Closure Principle that underwrites it, is false.

As I've already indicated, Dretske had also proposed that subjunctive conditionals be used in the analysis of knowledge, but Dretske's "Epistemic Operators" (chapter 8 of this collection), especially toward its end, provides an early statement of another approach to knowledge that became quite popular in subsequent years—the "Relevant Alternatives" theory of knowledge. On this theory, the main ingredient that must be added to true belief to make knowledge is that one be in a position to rule out all the *relevant alternatives* to what one believes. The important implication here is that some alternatives to what one believes are *not* relevant, and so one can know in the face of some uneliminated possibilities of error. Thus, in one of his examples (pp. 138–139), you can know that the animals in a cage are zebras, according to Dretske, without knowing that they are not cleverly painted mules, because the alternative that the animals are merely cleverly painted mules is, in any normal context, an irrelevant alternative to their being zebras. Thus, you can know that the animals are zebras without knowing that they're not painted mules. Thus, closure does not hold in general. You can know that P without knowing everything that you know that P entails, for P will entail the falsity of *all* the contraries or alternatives to P, but you need only know the falsity of the *relevant* alternatives to P in order to know that P. Dretske attempts to support this thesis by means of analogies with "operators" other than "S knows that . . ." (see especially pp. 139–144). Thus, for example, that Brenda didn't order dessert entails that she didn't order dessert and throw it at the waiter; still, some proposition R (e.g., Brenda was on a diet) might explain why Brenda didn't order dessert, while failing to explain why Brenda didn't order dessert and throw it at the waiter. Thus, Dretske concludes, "explains that . . ." is importantly like "knows that . . .": Just as you can know that P without knowing everything that you know P entails, so can a proposition explain another proposition without explaining everything that that second proposition is known to entail. The skeptic, Dretske concludes, is right to claim that we don't know her skeptical hypothesis to be false, but, since her hypothesis is not a relevant alternative to O, she is wrong to think that we therefore fail to know O.

The primary problem for the strategies of both Nozick and Dretske involves the powerful intuitions most of us have supporting closure.[17] Many, in fact, consider the anticlosure implications of Dretske's and Nozick's theories to be *reductios* of those theories. To their credit, both Dretske and Nozick admit the intuitive power of closure. Dretske admits that producing examples in which closure seems violated will not suffice to support his thesis of nonclosure because "the thesis itself is sufficiently counterintuitive to render controversial most of the crucial examples" (p. 139). And Nozick goes so far as to compare closure, with respect to its "intuitive appeal," to a steamroller (p. 170). Whether either philosopher's theory of knowledge and/or Dretske's analogies with other "operators" are sufficiently convincing to warrant accepting the counterintuitive results of their views is a matter we must leave to each reader to decide.

Gail Stine, in chapter 9 of this collection, which is largely a response to Dretske, offers a Relevant Alternatives approach to skepticism that does not involve denying closure. Stine agrees that, at least typically, we're correctly described as knowing various Os despite our inability to rule out various skeptical hypotheses that are alternatives to those Os. And she agrees that this is because those skeptical hypotheses typically fail to be *relevant* alternatives to the Os we ordinarily think we know. How, then, does Stine avoid denying closure on this Relevant Alternatives approach? By claiming that what the range of relevant alternatives is varies with conversational context, and that this amounts to a change in the *meaning* of knowledge-attributing sentences. She then claims that in testing closure, we should hold constant the range of relevant alternatives, and thereby avoid changing the meaning of the relevant sentences and committing "some logical sin akin to equivocation" (p. 151). And, according to Stine, closure does not fail so long as the range of relative alternatives is held constant. In extraordinary contexts, even the hypotheses of philosophical skeptics may be relevant.[18] Stine labels the standards that allow these hypotheses as relevant "extreme" (p. 149), "very peculiar" p. 152), and even "very perverse" (p. 149), but, apparently, they're allowable. In those contexts, you don't count as knowing that the skeptical hypotheses are false, but you also don't count as knowing such things as that you have hands. In more ordinary, and presumably less "perverse" contexts, you do count as knowing you have hands, but you also count as knowing that the skeptical hypotheses are false. Since in such an ordinary context the skeptical hypotheses are irrelevant, Stine concludes that you "simply know" (p. 154) that they're false, with no need for any evidence to that effect: "If the negation of a proposition in not a relevant alternative, then I know it—obviously, without needing to provide evidence—and so obviously that it is odd, misleading even, to give utterance to my knowledge" (p. 153). Part of the explanation for the oddity of saying you know, say, you're not a BIV is that there's a presupposition that not-P is a relevant alternative when it's knowledge of P that's in question (p. 151). But Stine claims that this presupposition can be canceled, and one can truthfully (though perhaps oddly) claim to know such a thing as that one is not a BIV.

7. CONTEXTUALIST RESPONSES

When students are first presented with skeptical arguments like the Argument from Skeptical Hypothesis, it's quite common for some of them to react by positing two senses of "know" and claiming that the argument shows only that in some "high" or "philosophical" sense we don't know we have hands, while, for all the argument shows, we retain knowledge in the "low" or "ordinary" sense of "know." The skeptic's argument has induced us to switch over to the "high" sense of "know," which is why the argument is so persuasive. But the truth of our ordinary claims to know is not threatened by the skeptic's attack. Some philosophers have developed this type of idea in their treatments of skepticism; see, for example, Norman Malcolm's distinction between "strong" and "weak" knowledge (1952), and Stroud's distinction between "internal" and "external" varieties of knowledge (1984).[19] Such "Two Senses of 'Knows'" approaches to skepticism are limiting cases of a more general type of approach that have come to be called the "contextualist" approach to knowledge and skepticism.

A problem with such "Two Senses of 'Know'" theories is that, to avoid making their approach to the problem of skepticism ad hoc, we'd like to find, in ordinary, nonphilosophical uses of knowledge-attributing sentences, support for the view that different standards for knowledge govern different contexts. The problem here is not that we find no such variation, but rather that we find more such variation than can be handled by such "Two Senses" theories. A wide variety of different standards for knowledge seem actually to be used in different contexts.

Current contextualists posit such a wide variety of different standards; they look for rules by which what is said in a conversation can change the standards that are in place; and they typically try to (at least partially) explain the intuitive pull of skeptical arguments by claiming that the skeptic, in presenting her argument, exploits one of these rules, raising the standards for knowledge, and thereby *making* her conclusion that we "don't know" true. If this is how the skeptic's argument works, then the truth values of our ordinary claims to know are protected, for the fact that the skeptic can install very high standards that we don't meet has no tendency to show that we don't know according to the lower standards that govern our ordinary, nonphilosophical conversations.

Such contextualist strategies also seem to provide a tighter tie between the skeptic's and the ordinary use of 'know,' than do "Two Senses of 'Know'" theories, which may help them to explain why skeptical arguments can seem to threaten our knowledge ordinarily so-called. For if these current theories are correct, the standards for knowledge are variable even in ordinary, nonphilosophical settings. It's not as if we had always used a single set of standards and the skeptic is now introducing some new and different standards in an unprecedented way. Rather, the skeptic is making use of a feature of "know" that shows itself in nonphilosophical contexts, and is employing rules we're already accustomed to.

Both of our contextualist authors, Keith DeRose and David Lewis, follow Stine (see section 6, above) in upholding closure, relative to any set standard for knowledge. Both follow Stine in seeing the skeptic as employing higher standards than are usual, though neither follows Stine in describing the skeptic's standards as "perverse."[20] And both seek to view the skeptic as employing a rule for the raising of standards that is common in nonphilosophical discussion.

Lewis, maintaining closer ties with the relevant alternatives tradition than does DeRose, gives the following account of knowledge:

> S knows proposition P iff S's evidence eliminates every possibility in which not-P—Psst!—except for those possibilities that we are properly ignoring.[21]

Here, the "possibilities that we are properly ignoring" amount to what, on the relevant alternatives approach, are the *irrelevant* alternatives to P. On Lewis's account, the relevant alternatives—the alternatives that our evidence must eliminate if we're to be knowers—are the possibilities in which not-P that we're either paying attention to or else are ignoring, but improperly so. Much of Lewis's paper consists in spelling out the rules that govern what possibilities are properly ignored. The skeptic, on Lewis's account, exploits the "Rule of Attention," according to which those alternatives to which we're paying attention are relevant. By calling attention to various possibilities that we typically (and properly) ignore, the skeptic *makes* those alternatives relevant. Thus, if our evidence fails to eliminate them—and the skeptic's hypotheses are always carefully chosen to be such that our evidence doesn't eliminate them—the skeptic succeeds in creating a context in which we don't count as knowers. However, that doesn't mean we speak falsely when we claim to know those very same Os in contexts in which no skeptics are calling our attention to those hypotheses. Even if our evidence doesn't eliminate those possibilities, we can still be correctly attributed with knowledge, on Lewis's account, if those who are calling us knowers are properly ignoring those uneliminated possibilities.

DeRose, seeking to hold on to what he finds correct in Nozick's subjunctive conditionals account while avoiding its pitfalls, claims that the conversational rule that the skeptic exploits in the Argument by Skeptical Hypothesis is the "Rule of Sensitivity." Where a belief that P is called "sensitive" if it meets Nozick's third condition for knowledge—where it's true that you would not have believed that P if P had been false—this rule states:

> When it asserted that some subject S knows (or does not know) some proposition P, the standards for knowledge tend to be raised, if need be, to such a level as to require S's belief in that particular P to be sensitive for it to count as knowledge. (pp. 205–206)

Since, as DeRose argues, you must be in a *very* strong epistemic position before any belief you might have that a skeptical hypothesis is false can be sensitive, the skeptic's assertion of her first premise ("I don't know that not-H") will, by the Rule of Sensitivity, raise the standards for knowledge to a level at which you count as knowing neither that not-H, nor that O. The Rule of Sensitivity, DeRose argues, explains why we won't call someone a knower if we think his or her belief is not sensitive, and thus explains why Nozick's account of knowledge can seem so attractive. But, DeRose argues, his contextualist account accomplishes this without licensing the counterintuitive violations of the Closure Principle that Nozick's noncontextualist account is committed to.

A major problem for contextualist solutions, at least in the eyes of many, is that they concede much to the skeptic, since these strategies allow that we don't know, according to the high standards that are put in place by the presentation of the skeptical argument, the Os we usually take ourselves to know. How much of a concession is this? Much will depend on how important one thinks it is to have such "high" knowledge. At one extreme, if one, like Stine, thinks of the skeptic's standards as "perverse," one probably won't mind our failing to meet them. On the other extreme, it will seem to some that it's the issue of whether we have the "high" knowledge put into play by the skeptic that's been the important issue all along. To these folks, the contextualist is conceding everything of value to the skeptic, and the fact that the contextualist protects our "low" ("vulgar"?) knowledge is of little importance. Middle positions, according to which there is interest both in what the skeptic is granted and in what she is denied by the contextualist approach, are of course possible, and will seem to many to be quite sensible.

The above potential problem involves how significant the contextualist response would be if it were successful. Another problem for these approaches, which will be developed in section 8 below, threatens to show that they won't be successful in the first place. It involves the presence of a rival theory, which threatens to handle all the phenomena contextualism seeks to explain, while holding the standards for knowledge constant in all contexts.[22]

8. CONCESSIVE RESPONSES

In important work on skepticism in the early and mid 1970s, which culminated in his book *Ignorance: A Case for Scepticism*,[23] Peter Unger argued that, in order to really know something, one must be in a *very* strong epistemic position with respect to that proposition—so strong, in fact, that it would be impossible for anyone ever to be better positioned with respect to any matter than he or she is now with respect to the matter in question. Unger admitted that varying standards for knowledge govern our use of sentences of the form "S knows that P," but did not endorse contextualism, because Unger claimed that these varying standards were standards for whether it was *appropriate* to say that S knows; the truth conditions for the sentence—the conditions under which what the sentence expresses would be *true*—were, according to Unger, constant, and *very* high. Thus, the skeptic is right when she says we don't know, and we are saying something false (though perhaps appropriate) when, even in ordinary, nonphilosophical discussions, we claim to know this or that. This is the rival to contextualism mentioned in the above paragraph. The "rival" came first, however: It was largely in response to this "invariantist" theory of Unger's that the early contextualist views of the late 1970s and early 1980s—like that expressed by David Lewis (1979) and in contextualist versions of the Relevant Alternatives approach[24]—were developed.

Unger's 1984 book *Philosophical Relativity*, the guts of which constitutes chapter 13 of the present collection, contained what was at that time—and for some time to come, for that matter—easily the most complete exposition of the contextualist view. But while this book represented a change of mind for Unger from his skeptical writings of his *Ignorance* period, he was not advocating contextualism in *Philosophical Relativity*. Instead, he defended the "relativist" conclusion that contextualism and his earlier invariantist views that led to skepticism were equally good theories, and that there simply is no fact as to which view is correct. Unger's relativism, defended, as it is, by parity considerations, according to which the advantages and disadvantages of contextualism and invariantism balance each other out in such a way that there is no winner, is a precarious view to defend: Any contextualist who succeeds in defeating invariantism will conquer Unger's relativism as an automatic corollary, and the same will happen for any invariantist who produces a successful argument against contextualism. But here Unger laid out very carefully the rival to contextualism, together with an argument that it was, while not superior to contextualism, at least an equal of it. In sections 15 and especially 16 of chapter 11, DeRose attempts to show why, in the face of Unger-like considerations, contextualism is superior to invariantism.

Contextualism, as we saw in the previous section, can already be viewed as quite concessive to the skeptic. Unger's relativism, which straddles contextualism and out-and-out skepticism, is even more concessive—enough to make the "Concessive Responses" section of this book.

Though the general drift of recent discussions of skepticism has been fairly antiskeptical, there has also been an undercurrent of writing, other than Unger's, more friendly to the skeptic, a couple of important examples of which we've included in this collection.

In chapter 14, Thomas Nagel argues that skeptical doubt is the natural result of a realist picture of the world and our place in it—a picture according to which "there is a real world in which we are contained, and . . . appearances result from our interaction with the rest of it" (p. 272). This picture naturally leads us to wonder which aspects of the appearances reflect the way the world really is, and which are misleading results of our interaction with the world. As we pursue greater objectivity—a view that relies "less and less on certain individual aspects of our point of view" (p. 272)—we will not be able to leave skeptical doubts behind. For as we develop a more objective account of our place in the world, an account that explains why the world appears to us as it does, this new picture will also be the result of our interaction with the world, though a more complicated interaction. Nagel argues: "If the initial appearances cannot be relied upon because they depend on our constitution in ways that we do not fully understand, this more complex idea should be open to the same doubts, for whatever we use to understand certain interactions between ourselves and the world is not itself the object of that understanding. However often we may try to step outside of ourselves, something will have to stay behind the lens, something in us will determine the resulting picture, and this will give grounds for doubt that we are really getting any closer to reality" (p. 273).

Here Nagel raises some of the problems that arise from attempting to develop what Sosa, in chapter 6, called "a fully general philosophical understanding of our knowledge." The question naturally arises: Which epistemic achievements are blocked by our inability to get completely outside of ourselves in the way Nagel outlines? Does that prevent us from having *knowledge* of what the world is like? Some of Nagel's remarks appear to indicate that knowledge is thereby undermined. For instance, he writes: "Skepticism is really a way of recognizing our situation, though it will not prevent us from continuing to pursue *something like* knowledge" (pp. 277–278, emphasis added), hinting that knowledge itself is not in the cards. But Nagel also writes that "definitions of knowledge cannot help us" with our problem, for, "The central problem of epistemology is the first-person problem of what to believe and how to justify one's beliefs—not the impersonal problem of whether, given my beliefs together with some assumptions about their relation to what is actually the case, I can be said to have knowledge" (p. 274). Here Nagel indicates that knowledge isn't the real issue. But what if knowledge itself, correctly defined, and not just "something like" knowledge, could be attained without our getting fully outside of ourselves in the way

Nagel says we cannot? What if even loftier epistemic states, like, say, *knowing for certain*, properly defined, could survive the lack Nagel alleges? After all, it's in no way obvious that getting fully outside of oneself in the way Nagel claims we cannot should be construed as a necessary condition for knowing for certain that one has (real, objective) hands.

We'd then be left with the question of how significant *in its own right* is the result that we cannot get fully outside of ourselves if that result doesn't lead to any of the more familiar shortcomings that we might have feared are shown by skeptical arguments. Some (perhaps Sosa?) would urge us to see the attempt to meet such an impossible demand as misguided: "*Of course* we can't attain a fully objective view of ourselves if *that's* what you mean by a fully objective view. Who would have ever thought we could have?"

But some otherwise inclined will urge that, though it does follow fairly automatically from a realist picture, the lack Nagel points to is an important result, for it is the inevitable outcome of pursuit of objectivity, a pursuit deeply embedded within us. Even if it is somehow inevitable that this will lead to the disappointment, doesn't that only intensify the worry? That the realist picture and the resulting search for greater objectivity lead inevitably to our inability to complete the task we set out on is a deep problem, however inevitable it was that this would be the result.

One may well wonder whether, not too far down this dialectical path, there will be much of a *real* disagreement between skeptics and antiskeptics. Perhaps there will be agreement about which epistemic states are undermined by skepticism and which aren't, the only differences being over the significance of the lacks established by skepticism.

In chapter 15, Barry Stroud seems to reach such a point in his debate with Sosa, whose essay in chapter 6 is Stroud's primary target. Stroud writes:

> Here, perhaps, we approach something that Sosa and I can agree about. What I have tried to identify as a dissatisfaction that the epistemological project will always leave us with is for him something that simply has to be accepted if we are going to have a fully general theory of knowledge at all. He appears to think, as I do, that it is endemic to the epistemological project itself. We differ in what moral we draw from that thought. (pp. 302–303)

The lack in question is roughly that, in any fully general account of our knowledge, we'll have to rely on a starting point that we simply must accept to be true without a noncircular reason for thinking it true. In Sosa's terminology (see section 5, above), no fully general account of our knowledge could succeed in also being a legitimating account. But though Stroud does draw a different moral from this than does Sosa, he doesn't think the lack necessarily leads to skepticism. At the close of his essay, he indicates that skepticism will be the winner *if* we pursue epistemological theories in the traditional way. The moral Stroud draws is that *if* skepticism is to be successfully resisted, "the resistance has to start farther back" (p. 303)—with a reexamination of the traditional epistemological project itself.

Sosa, however, could claim to have already proposed the needed revision to that project. The problem with the traditional project is that it seeks a fully general, legitimating account of our knowledge. Sosa's advise would be: You can seek a fully general account or you can try for a legitimating account. You can in fact pursue both types of account separately. What you can't have, and shouldn't seek, is an account of our knowledge that is, at the same time, both fully general and legitimating. Stroud, apparently, would reject this as the revision he was seeking, but it's difficult to say exactly what's wrong with it as such a revision.

But we shouldn't assume that we are destined to reach a point where there's agreement about what skeptical results can be established and disagreement only over the significance of the skepticism that holds. Skeptics and antiskeptics should strive to make precise exactly what are the lacks shown by skeptical arguments, and to investigate exactly what consequences such lacks may have for familiar issues of knowledge, certain knowledge, justification, and so on. We'll then be better positioned to evaluate the shortcomings that philosophical skepticism really establishes.[25]

NOTES

1. Stroud 1984, p. 39. The "sceptical reasoning" to which Stroud refers, and which was presented in his first chapter, is Stroud's rendition of Descartes's dream argument.

2. As the quotations in the text are about to show, Moore vacillates freely between knowing and knowing *for certain*, sometimes presenting the skeptical arguments as attempts to reach the conclusion that we don't know the things in question for certain, and sometimes as urging the conclusion that we don't know them. This vacillation is explained by Moore's belief that knowing and knowing for certain are the same thing—that there is no knowing that isn't knowing for certain. Throughout, we treat Moore as addressing the issue of knowledge, but the reader should be aware that Moore was also writing about certain knowledge, which he thought was the same thing.

3. It's not to be automatically assumed that we should maintain consistent beliefs in such a situation, especially where the members of the set all seem to have about the same high degree of plausibility. The option of continuing to believe all of them, while, of course, realizing that they can't all be true, and so tempering the degree of one's belief in each, seems to some an attractive possibility. It's where one member of the set is, while somewhat plausible, not nearly as plausible as the other members that a rejection of a belief seems the best choice. For arguments that one can rationally hold beliefs one knows to be inconsistent, see Klein 1985 and chapter 4 of Foley 1993.

4. Though Moore writes, "The one argument is just as good as the other, unless my opponent can give better reasons for asserting that I don't know that I'm not dreaming, than I can give for asserting that I do know that I'm standing up," indicating that both he and the skeptic will be presenting such a positive case, in what follows in "Certainty," he merely looks at what case the skeptic might give, arguing that the skeptic's argument won't be convincing, and never gives any reasons for his position that he does know that he's standing up.

5. This aspect of these responses to skepticism was anticipated in Bouwsma 1949. Bouwsma argues that a victim of Descartes's evil genius would not be fooled into holding false beliefs, but would in fact be thinking thoughts that were largely true.

6. Page 37, emphasis added. Along the same lines, Putnam writes, "So, if we are brains in a vat, then the sentence 'We are brains in a vat' says something false (*if it says anything*)" (p. 37, emphasis added).

7. Of the BIV scenario, Putnam writes early in his essay: "When this sort of possibility is mentioned in a lecture on the Theory of Knowledge, the purpose, of course, is to raise the classical problem of scepticism with respect to the external world in a modern way. (*How do you know you aren't in this predicament?*) But this predicament is also a useful device for raising issues about the mind/world relationship" (p. 31). And in what follows, Putnam's own interest seems confined to the "mind/world relationship," for the "classical problem of scepticism" is hardly ever again mentioned.

8. See especially Brueckner 1986a.

9. See note 11 of chapter 3 in this collection, where Brueckner relates some of the advantages of this second strategy.

10. In his more recent 1996 (see especially section 9), Brueckner reverses his judgment, deciding the strategy won't work after all.

11. See again Brueckner 1986a. In chapter 3 of this collection, Brueckner rehearses this objection to the first type of strategy in note 10.

12. For instance, as Brueckner construes the skeptical argument, it depends on a premise that the BIV hypothesis is logically possible (see p. 43 of this volume). And at places Robert Nozick seems to construe the skeptic as relying upon the claim that her hypotheses are logically possible or coherent (see pp. 156–157). The externalist strategy could then be seen as undermining that premise. But that premise at least *seems* unnecessary. As I've been formulating the argument here, there is no such premise, and Nozick sometimes ignores this premise, construing the skeptic as proceeding merely from her true (according to Nozick) insight that we don't know the hypothesis to be false, together with her "short step" (short, but mistaken!) from that insight to her conclusion that we don't know such things as that we have hands. But maybe, for reasons I can't see, that premise really is needed by the skeptic. Or maybe there is some other way the Putnam-style approach can derail the skeptical argument even as it applies to the nonphilosophical.

13. For further critique of this type of response to skepticism, see section 2 (pp. 275–278) of Thomas Nagel's essay in chapter 14 of this collection.

14. The Principle, so formulated, is not exactly correct: One could know that P, and know that P entails Q, without ever having put these two pieces of knowledge together in order to infer that Q. In such a case, you might not even believe that Q, much less know it. The details may be difficult to get exactly right, but the following formulation of the principle may at least come close: If you know that P, and you know that P entails Q, and you believe that Q based on an inference from your beliefs that P and that P entails Q, then you know that Q. Such a fancier principle seems equally useful to the skeptic, who can argue that if you really knew that O, you could, given that principle, come to know that not-H, provided that you knew that O entails that not-H. Given that more complicated version of the second premise of the Argument by Skeptical Hypothesis, the first premise would also have to be doctored up a bit, but not, it seems, in such a way as to diminish its plausibility. The skeptic can claim that you don't know that not-H, *and* can't come to know it by means of an inference from your "knowledge" that O. Thus, you must not really know that O, after all. Unfortunately, I suspect even the fancier version of the Principle is not correct. Just as I think one can just barely know that P and just barely know that Q, yet just barely fall short of knowing the conjunction of P and Q—even when holding constant the standards for knowledge—because of the accumulation of doubt, so also can one know that P and know that P entails Q, while falling short of knowing that Q, even if one's belief that Q is based on one's knowledge of P and knowledge of the fact that P entails Q.

15. Nozick was apparently unaware of Dretske's much earlier work until after writing a draft of the relevant portion of his book; see note 33 of Nozick's essay in this collection. For an example of the precursors of Nozick's treatment, see especially Dretske 1971, where Dretske advances an account of knowledge in which subjunctive conditionals loom large. See also note 4 of Dretske's essay in this collection, where Dretske explains how any account of knowledge in subjunctive conditionals play such a role will result in failures of closure.

16. Condition (4) is problematic. Many—perhaps most—students of subjunctive conditionals believe that where the antecedent and the consequent of such a conditional are both true, then so is the conditional. Thus, where Nozick's first two conditions for knowledge hold, condition (4) will *always* be met. Thus, (4) can do no work. Anyone who meets conditions (1) and (2) will automatically meet (4) as well. Others, noticing how odd is to use the subjunctive ("If P *were* true") in (4) if P is true, may conclude that if P is true, then (4) cannot be met. This would make knowledge impossible, since in that case nobody could ever meet both (1) and (4). What Nozick needs is an account of "true-true subjunctives"—subjunctive conditionals whose antecedent and consequent are both true—which makes them neither always true nor always false. Such an account is controversial at best. Alternatively, Nozick could perhaps give up on formulating his fourth condition in terms of subjunctive conditionals, and instead put it directly in terms of possible worlds, as follows: "In all of the possible worlds very close to the actual world in which P is true, S believes that P." This could give rise to problems for Nozick, however. First, how close is close enough to count as "very" close? Our understanding of subjunctive conditionals cannot in any obvious way answer this question if we've given up on expressing the fourth condition in terms of subjunctive conditionals. Second, such a strategy would involve Nozick in a more serious use of the apparatus of possible worlds than he seems to want (see p. 160 and note 9 of Nozick's essay in chapter 10 in this collection).

17. For more on this, especially as it applies to Nozick, see section 9 (pp. 200–201) of DeRose's essay in chapter 11 of this collection and Forbes 1984. For a good general discussion of the antiskeptical approach of denying closure, see Brueckner 1985.

18. Stine writes, "But the skeptic has an entering wedge, and rightly so. It is an essential characteristic of our concept of knowledge that tighter criteria are appropriate in different contexts. It is one thing in a street encounter, another in a classroom, another in a court of law—and who is to say it cannot be another in a philosophical discussion? And this is directly mirrored by the fact we have different standards for judging that there is some reason to think an alternative is true, i.e., relevant. We can point out that some philosophers are very perverse in their standards (by *some* extreme standard, there is some reason to think there is an evil genius, after all)—but we cannot legitimately go so far as to say that their perversity has stretched the concept of knowledge out of all recognition—in fact they have played on an essential feature of the concept" (p. 149). I assume Stine would say the same thing about the BIV hypothesis that she says above of the evil genius possibility.

19. Warning: Stroud treats different historical figures in each chapter of his book, and the labels "internal" and "external" seem to mean something different—though perhaps tied together by some hard-to-describe common thread—in each of these chapters. But in some of those chapters, the distinction seems to amount to a difference between two senses of "know."

20. In his earlier 1979b, Lewis warns against the opposite mistake of thinking that the skeptic's standards are better or more legitimate than the lower, ordinary standards, or that what's true relative to the skeptic's standards is somehow more true than what is true relative to ordinary standards (p. 355, see also p. 353).

21. Page 225; "iff" is an abbreviation for "if and only if."

22. For further critique of the contextualist approach to skepticism, see Schiffer 1996.

23. Unger 1975. This book incorporates, with some improvements, Unger's important journal articles from the early 1970s, while adding new material as well.

24. For a discussion of the relation between the Relevant Alternatives approach and contextualism, and, in particular, of when a Relevant Alternatives theory is a contextualist view, see section 2 of DeRose 1992.

25. Thanks to Anthony Brueckner, Graeme Forbes, and Ted Warfield for helpful comments

PART ONE

The Response from Semantic Externalism

CHAPTER 2   # Brains in a Vat

Hilary Putnam

An ant is crawling on a patch of sand. As it crawls, it traces a line in the sand. By pure chance the line that it traces curves and recrosses itself in such a way that it ends up looking like a recognizable caricature of Winston Churchill. Has the ant traced a picture of Winston Churchill, a picture that *depicts* Churchill?

Most people would say, on a little reflection, that it has not. The ant, after all, has never seen Churchill, or even a picture of Churchill, and it had no intention of depicting Churchill. It simply traced a line (and even *that* was unintentional), a line that *we* can 'see as' a picture of Churchill.

We can express this by saying that the line is not 'in itself' a representation[1] of anything rather than anything else. Similarity (of a certain very complicated sort) to the features of Winston Churchill is not sufficient to make something represent or refer to Churchill. Nor is it necessary: in our community the printed shape 'Winston Churchill', the spoken words 'Winston Churchill', and many other things are used to represent Churchill (though not pictorially), while not having the sort of similarity to Churchill that a picture—even a line drawing—has. If *similarity* is not necessary or sufficient to make something represent something else, how can *anything* be necessary or sufficient for this purpose? How on earth can one thing represent (or 'stand for', etc.) a different thing? one thing represent another not thru similarity

The answer may seem easy. Suppose the ant had seen Winston Churchill, and suppose that it had the intelligence and skill to draw a picture of him. Suppose it produced the caricature *intentionally*. Then the line would have represented Churchill. Intention needed to represent thing

On the other hand, suppose the line had the shape WINSTON CHURCHILL. And suppose this was just accident (ignoring the improbability involved). Then the 'printed shape' WINSTON CHURCHILL would *not* have represented Churchill, although that printed shape does represent Churchill when it occurs in almost any book today. words don't represent either

So it may seem that what is necessary for representation, or what is mainly necessary for representation, is *intention*.

How thoughts represent external?

But to have the intention that *anything*, even private language (even the words 'Winston Churchill' spoken in my mind and not out loud), should *represent* Churchill, I must have been able to *think about* Churchill in the first place. If lines in the sand, noises, etc., cannot 'in themselves' represent anything, then how is it that thought forms can 'in themselves' represent anything? Or can they? How can thought reach out and 'grasp' what is external?

thoughts have intentionality that physical objects don't

Some philosophers have, in the past, leaped from this sort of consideration to what they take to be a proof that the mind is *essentially non-physical in nature*. The argument is simple; what we said about the ant's curve applies to any physical object. No physical object can, in itself, refer to one thing rather than to another; nevertheless, *thoughts in the mind* obviously do succeed in referring to one thing rather than another. So thoughts (and hence the mind) are of an essentially different nature than physical objects. Thoughts have the characteristic of *intentionality*—they can refer to something else; nothing physical has 'intentionality', save as that intentionality is derivative from some employment of that physical thing by a mind. Or so it is claimed. This is too quick; just postulating mysterious powers of mind solves nothing. But the problem is very real. How is intentionality, reference, possible?

MAGICAL THEORIES OF REFERENCE

meaning / connection / name

We saw that the ant's 'picture' has no necessary connection with Winston Churchill. The mere fact that the 'picture' bears a 'resemblance' to Churchill does not make it into a real picture, nor does it make it a representation of Churchill. Unless the ant is an intelligent ant (which it isn't) and knows about Churchill (which it doesn't), the curve it traced is not a picture or even a representation of anything. Some primitive people believe that some representations (in particular, *names*) have a necessary connection with their bearers; that to know the 'true name' of someone or something gives one power over it. This power comes from the *magical connection* between the name and the bearer of the name; once one realizes that a name *only* has a contextual, contingent, conventional connection with its bearer, it is hard to see why knowledge of the name should have any mystical significance.

mental + physical pics are subject to same things

What is important to realize is that what goes for physical pictures also goes for mental images, and for mental representations in general; mental representations no more have a necessary connection with what they represent than physical representations do. The contrary supposition is a survival of magical thinking.

Perhaps the point is easiest to grasp in the case of mental *images*. (Perhaps the first philosopher to grasp the enormous significance of this point, even if he was not the first to actually make it, was Wittgenstein.) Suppose there is a planet somewhere on which human beings have evolved (or been deposited by alien spacemen, or what have you). Suppose these humans, although otherwise like us, have never seen *trees*. Suppose they have never imagined trees (perhaps vegetable life exists on their planet only in the form of molds). Suppose one day a picture of a tree is accidentally dropped on their planet by a spaceship which passes on without having other contact with them. Imagine them puzzling over the picture. What in the world is this? All sorts of speculations occur to them: a building, a canopy, even an animal of some kind. But suppose they never come close to the truth.

For *us* the picture is a representation of a tree. For these humans the picture only represents a strange object, nature and function unknown. Suppose one of them has a mental image which is exactly like one of my mental images of a tree as a result of having seen the picture. His mental image is not a *representation of a tree*. It is only a representation of the strange object (whatever it is) that the mysterious picture represents.

Still, someone might argue that the mental image is *in fact* a representation of a tree, if only because the picture which caused this mental image was itself a representation of a tree to begin with. There is a causal chain from actual trees to the mental image even if it is a very strange one.

But even this causal chain can be imagined absent. Suppose the 'picture of the tree' that the spaceship dropped was not really a picture of a tree, but the accidental result of some spilled paints. Even if it looked exactly like a picture of a tree, it was, in truth, no more a picture of a tree than the ant's 'caricature' of Churchill was a picture of Churchill. We can even imagine that the spaceship which dropped the 'picture' came from a planet which knew nothing of trees. Then the humans would still have mental images qualitatively identical with my image of a tree, but they would not be images which represented a tree any more than anything else.

The same thing is true of *words*. A discourse on paper might seem to be a perfect description of trees, but if it was produced by monkeys randomly hitting keys on a typewriter for millions of years, then the words do not refer to anything. If there were a person who memorized those words and said them in his mind without understanding them, then they would not refer to anything when thought in the mind, either.

Imagine the person who is saying those words in his mind has been hypnotized. Suppose the words are in Japanese, and the person has been told that he understands Japanese. Suppose that as he thinks those words he has a 'feeling of understanding'. (Although if someone broke into his train of thought and asked him what the words he was thinking *meant*, he would discover he couldn't say.) Perhaps the illusion would be so perfect that the person could even fool a Japanese telepath! But if he couldn't use the words in the right contexts, answer questions about what he 'thought', etc., then he didn't understand them.

By combining these science fiction stories I have been telling, we can contrive a case in which someone thinks words which are in fact a description of trees in some language *and* simultaneously has appropriate mental images, but *neither* understands the words *nor* knows what a tree is. We can even imagine that the mental images were caused by paint-spills (although the person has been hypnotized to think that they are images of something appropriate to his thought—only, if he were asked, he wouldn't be able to say of what). And we can imagine that the language the person is thinking in is one neither the hypnotist nor the person hypnotized has ever heard of—perhaps it is just coincidence that these 'nonsense sentences', as the hypnotist supposes them to be, are a description of trees in Japanese. In short, everything passing before the person's mind might be qualitatively identical with what was passing through the mind of a Japanese speaker who was *really* thinking about trees—but none of it would refer to trees.

All of this is really impossible, of course, in the way that it is really impossible that monkeys should by chance type out a copy of *Hamlet*. That is to say that the probabilities against it are so high as to mean it will never really happen (we think). But it is not logically impossible, or even physically impossible. It *could* happen (compatibly with physical law and, perhaps, compatibly with actual conditions in the universe, if there are lots of intelligent beings on other planets). And if it did happen, it would be a striking demonstration of an important conceptual truth; that even a large and complex system of representations, both verbal and visual, still does not have an *intrinsic,* built-in, magical connection with what it represents—a connection independent of how it was caused and what the dispositions of the speaker or thinker are. And this is true whether the system of representations (words and images, in the case of the example) is physically realized—the words are written or spoken, and the pictures are physical pictures—or only realized in the mind. Thought words and mental pictures do not *intrinsically* represent what they are about.

THE CASE OF THE BRAINS IN A VAT

Here is a science fiction possibility discussed by philosophers: imagine that a human being (you can imagine this to be yourself) has been subjected to an operation by an evil scientist. The person's brain (your brain) has been removed from the body and placed in a vat of nutrients which keeps the brain alive. The nerve endings have been connected to a super-scientific computer which causes the person whose brain it is to have the illusion that everything is perfectly normal. There seem to be people, objects, the sky, etc; but really all the person (you) is experiencing is the result of electronic impulses travelling from the computer to the nerve endings. The computer is so clever that if the person tries to raise his hand, the feedback from the computer will cause him to 'see' and 'feel' the hand being raised. Moreover, by varying the program, the evil scientist can cause the victim to 'experience' (or hallucinate) any situation or environment the evil scientist wishes. He can also obliterate the memory of the brain operation, so that the victim will seem to himself to have always been in this environment. It can even seem to the victim that he is sitting and reading these very words about the amusing but quite absurd supposition that there is an evil scientist who removes people's brains from their bodies and places them in a vat of nutrients which keep the brains alive. The nerve endings are supposed to be connected to a super-scientific computer which causes the person whose brain it is to have the illusion that . . . *Brain in a vat: no way of telling you're not in a BIV*

When this sort of possibility is mentioned in a lecture on the Theory of Knowledge, the purpose, of course, is to raise the classical problem of scepticism with respect to the external world in a modern way. (*How do you know you aren't in this predicament?*) But this predicament is also a useful device for raising issues about the mind/world relationship. *Skeptical about external world*

Instead of having just one brain in a vat, we could imagine that all human beings (perhaps all sentient beings) are brains in a vat (or nervous systems in a vat in case some beings with just a minimal nervous system already count as 'sentient'). Of course, the evil scientist would have to be outside—or would he? Perhaps there is no evil scientist, perhaps (though this is absurd) the universe just happens to consist of automatic machinery tending a vat full of brains and nervous systems. *powerful force that controls brains*

This time let us suppose that the automatic machinery is programmed to give us all a *collective* hallucination, rather than a number of separate unrelated hallucinations. Thus, when I seem to myself to be talking to you, you seem to yourself to be hearing my words. Of course, it is not the case that my words actually reach your ears—for you don't have (real) ears, nor do I have a real mouth and tongue. Rather, when I produce my words, what happens is that the efferent impulses travel from my brain to the computer, which both causes me to 'hear' my own voice uttering those words and 'feel' my tongue moving, etc., and causes you to 'hear' my words, 'see' me speaking, etc. In this case, we are, in a sense, actually in communication. I am not mistaken about your real existence (only about the existence of your body and the 'external world', apart from brains). From a certain point of view, it doesn't even matter that 'the whole world' is a collective hallucination; for you do, after all, really hear my words when I speak to you, even if the mechanism isn't what we suppose it to be. (Of course, if we were two lovers making love, rather than just two people carrying on a conversation, then the suggestion that it was just two brains in a vat might be disturbing.) *minds exist & same reality", but lack body*

I want now to ask a question which will seem very silly and obvious (at least to some people, including some very sophisticated philosophers), but which will take us to real philosophical depths rather quickly. Suppose this whole story were actually true. Could we, if we were brains in a vat in this way, *say* or *think* that we were? *If BIV, can we have BIV thoughts?*

I am going to argue that the answer is 'No, we couldn't.' In fact, I am going to argue that the supposition that we are actually brains in a vat, although it violates no physical law, and is perfectly consistent with everything we have experienced, cannot possibly be true. *It cannot possibly be true,* because it is, in a certain way, self-refuting. *Putnam: impossible to be BIV & have BIV thoughts*

The argument I am going to present is an unusual one, and it took me several years to convince myself that it is really right. But it is a correct argument. What makes it seem so strange is that it is connected with some of the very deepest issues in philosophy. (It first occurred to me when I was thinking about a theorem in modern logic, the 'Skolem—Löwenheim Theorem', and I suddenly saw a connection between this theorem and some arguments in Wittgenstein's *Philosophical Investigations*.)

A 'self-refuting supposition' is one whose truth implies its own falsity. For example, consider the thesis that *all general statements are false*. This is a general statement. So if it is true, then it must be false. Hence, it is false. Sometimes a thesis is called 'self-refuting' if it is *the supposition that the thesis is entertained or enunciated* that implies its falsity. For example, 'I do not exist' is self-refuting if thought by *me* (for any '*me*'). So one can be certain that one oneself exists, if one thinks about it (as Descartes argued).

What I shall show is that the supposition that we are brains in a vat has just this property. If we can consider whether it is true or false, then it is not true (I shall show). Hence it is not true. *[handwritten: BIV not true b/c self-refuting supposition]*

Before I give the argument, let us consider why it seems so strange that such an argument can be given (at least to philosophers who subscribe to a 'copy' conception of truth). We conceded that it is compatible with physical law that there should be a world in which all sentient beings are brains in a vat. As philosophers say, there is a 'possible world' in which all sentient beings are brains in a vat. (This 'possible world' talk makes it sound as if there is a *place* where any absurd supposition is true, which is why it can be very misleading in philosophy.) The humans in that possible world have exactly the same experiences that *we* do. They think the same thoughts we do (at least, the same words, images, thought-forms, etc., go through their minds). Yet, I am claiming that there is an argument we can give that shows we are not brains in a vat. How can there be? And why couldn't the people in the possible world who really *are* brains in a vat give it too? *[handwritten: BIV can't have BIV thoughts]*

The answer is going to be (basically) this: although the people in that possible world can think and 'say' any words we can think and say, they cannot (I claim) *refer* to what we can refer to. In particular, they cannot think or say that they are brains in a vat (*even by thinking 'we are brains in a vat'*).

[handwritten: referring to something (function) ≠ structure]

TURING'S TEST

Suppose someone succeeds in inventing a computer which can actually carry on an intelligent conversation with one (on as many subjects as an intelligent person might). How can one decide if the computer is 'conscious'?

The British logician Alan Turing proposed the following test:[2] let someone carry on a conversation with the computer and a conversation with a person whom he does not know. If he cannot tell which is the computer and which is the human being, then (assume the test to be repeated a sufficient number of times with different interlocutors) the computer is conscious. In short, a computing machine is conscious if it can pass the 'Turing Test'. (The conversations are not to be carried on face to face, of course, since the interlocutor is not to know the visual appearance of either of his two conversational partners. Nor is voice to be used, since the mechanical voice might simply sound different from a human voice. Imagine, rather, that the conversations are all carried on via electric typewriter. The interlocutor types in his statements, questions, etc., and the two partners—the machine and the person—respond via the electric keyboard. Also, the machine may *lie*—asked 'Are you a machine', it might reply, 'No, I'm an assistant in the lab here.')

The idea that this test is really a definitive test of consciousness has been criticized by a number of authors (who are by no means hostile in principle to the idea that a machine might be conscious). But this is not our topic at this time. I wish to use the general idea of the Turing test, the general idea of a *dialogic test of competence,* for a different purpose, the purpose of exploring the notion of *reference.*

Imagine a situation in which the problem is not to determine if the partner is really a person or a machine, but is rather to determine if the partner uses the words to refer as we do. The obvious test is, again, to carry on a conversation, and, if no problems arise, if the partner 'passes' in the sense of being indistinguishable from someone who is certified in advance to be speaking the same language, referring to the usual sorts of objects, etc., to conclude that the partner does refer to objects as we do. When the purpose of the Turing test is as just described, that is, to determine the existence of (shared) reference, I shall refer to the test as the *Turing Test for Reference.* And, just as philosophers have discussed the question whether the original Turing test is a *definitive* test for consciousness, i.e. the question of whether a machine which 'passes' the test not just once but regularly is *necessarily* conscious, so, in the same way, I wish to discuss the question of whether the Turing Test for Reference just suggested is a definitive test for shared reference.

The answer will turn out to be 'No'. The Turing Test for Reference is not definitive. It is certainly an excellent test in practice; but it is not logically impossible (though it is certainly highly improbable) that someone could pass the Turing Test for Reference and not be referring to anything. It follows from this, as we shall see, that we can extend our observation that words (and whole texts and discourses) do not have a necessary connection to their referents. Even if we consider not words by themselves but rules deciding what words may appropriately be produced in certain contexts—even if we consider, in computer jargon, *programs for using words*—unless those programs themselves *refer to something extra-linguistic* there is still no determinate reference that those words possess. This will be a crucial step in the process of reaching the conclusion that the Brain-in-a-Vat Worlders cannot refer to anything external at all (and hence cannot say *that* they are Brain-in-a-Vat Worlders).

Suppose, for example, that I am in the Turing situation (playing the 'Imitation Game', in Turing's terminology) and my partner is actually a machine. Suppose this machine is able to win the game ('passes' the test). Imagine the machine to be programmed to produce beautiful responses in English to statements, questions, remarks, etc. in English, but that it has no sense organs (other than the hookup to my electric typewriter), and no motor organs (other than the electric typewriter). (As far as I can make out, Turing does not assume that the possession of either sense organs or motor organs is necessary for consciousness or intelligence.) Assume that not only does the machine lack electronic eyes and ears, etc., but that there are no provisions in the machine's program, the program for playing the Imitation Game, for incorporating inputs from such sense organs, or for controlling a body. What should we say about such a machine?

To me, it seems evident that we cannot and should not attribute reference to such a device. It is true that the machine can discourse beautifully about, say, the scenery in New England. But it could not recognize an apple tree or an apple, a mountain or a cow, a field or a steeple, if it were in front of one. *Can't recognize things, only say things*

What we have is a device for producing sentences in response to sentences. But none of these sentences is at all connected to the real world. *If one coupled two of these machines and let them play the Imitation Game with each other, then they would go on 'fooling' each other forever, even if the rest of the world disappeared!* There is no more reason to regard the machine's talk of apples as referring to real world apples than there is to regard the ant's 'drawing' as referring to Winston Churchill. *words w/ no meaning / understanding of external world*

What produces the illusion of reference, meaning, intelligence, etc., here is the fact that there is a convention of representation which *we* have under which the machine's discourse refers to apples, steeples, New England, etc. Similarly, there is the *illusion* that the ant has caricatured Churchill, for the same reason. But we are able to perceive, handle, deal with apples and fields. Our talk of apples and fields is intimately connected with our *nonverbal* transactions with apples and fields. There are 'language entry rules' which take us from experiences of apples to such utterances as 'I see an apple', and 'language exit rules' which take us from decisions expressed in linguistic form ('I am going to buy some apples') to actions other than speaking. Lacking either language entry rules or language exit rules, there is no reason to regard the conversation of the machine (or of the two machines, in the case we envisaged of two machines playing the Imitation Game with each other) as more than syntactic play. Syntactic play that *resembles* intelligent discourse, to be sure; but only as (and no more than) the ant's curve resembles a biting caricature. *words refer to action + not just illusion of word / physical representation*

In the case of the ant, we could have argued that the ant would have drawn the same curve even if Winston Churchill had never existed. In the case of the machine, we cannot quite make the parallel argument; if apples, trees, steeples and fields had not existed, then, presumably, the programmers would not have produced that same program. Although the machine does not *perceive* apples, fields, or steeples, its creator—designers did. There is *some* causal connection between the machine and the real world apples, etc., via the perceptual experience and knowledge of the creator—designers.

But such a weak connection can hardly suffice for reference. Not only is it logically possible, though fantastically improbable, that the same machine *could* have existed even if apples, fields, and steeples had not existed; more important, the machine is utterly insensitive to the *continued* existence of apples, fields, steeples, etc. Even if all these things *ceased* to exist, the machine would still discourse just as happily in the same way. That is why the machine cannot be regarded as referring at all. *can still say things that don't exist (dependent on creator) transpire to actual existence*

The point that is relevant for our discussion is that there is nothing in Turing's Test to rule out a machine which is programmed to do nothing *but* play the Imitation Game, and that a machine which can do nothing *but* play the Imitation Game is *clearly* not referring any more than a record player is.

BRAINS IN A VAT (AGAIN)

Let us compare the hypothetical 'brains in a vat' with the machines just described. There are obviously important differences. The brains in a vat do not have sense organs, but they do have *provision* for sense organs; that is, there are afferent nerve endings, there are inputs from these afferent nerve endings, and these inputs figure in the 'program' of the brains in the vat just as they do in the program of our brains. The brains in a vat are *brains*; moreover, they are *functioning* brains, and they function by the same rules as brains do in the actual world. For these reasons, it would seem absurd to deny consciousness or intelligence to them. But the fact that they are conscious and intelligent does not mean that their words refer to what our words refer. The question we are interested in is this: do their verbalizations containing, say, the word 'tree' actually refer to *trees*? More generally: can they refer to *external* objects at all? (As opposed to, for example, objects in the image produced by the automatic machinery.) *even tho intelligent, can BIV refer to external at all!*

To fix our ideas, let us specify that the automatic machinery is supposed to have come into existence by some kind of cosmic chance or coincidence (or, perhaps, to have always existed). In this hypothetical world, the automatic machinery itself is supposed to have no intelligent creator—designers. In fact, as we said at the beginning of this chapter, we may imagine that all sentient beings (however minimal their sentience) are inside the vat.

This assumption does not help. For there is no connection between the *word* 'tree' as used by these brains and actual trees. They would still use the word 'tree' just as they do, think just the thoughts they do, have just the images they have, even if there were no actual trees. Their images, words, etc., are qualitatively identical with images, words, etc., which do represent trees in *our* world; but we have already seen (the ant again!) that qualitative similarity to something which represents an object (Winston Churchill or a tree) does not make a thing a representation all by itself. In short, the brains in a vat are not thinking about real trees when they think 'there is a tree in front of me' because there is nothing by virtue of which their thought 'tree' represents actual trees.

If this seems hasty, reflect on the following: we have seen that the words do not necessarily refer to trees even if they are arranged in a sequence which is identical with a discourse which (were it to occur in one of our minds) would unquestionably *be about trees* in the actual world. Nor does the 'program', in the sense of the rules, practices, dispositions of the brains to verbal behavior, necessarily refer to trees or bring about reference to trees through the connections it establishes between words and words, or *linguistic* cues and *linguistic* responses. If these brains think about, refer to, represent trees (real trees, outside the vat), then it must be because of the way the 'program' connects the system of language to *non-verbal* input and outputs. There are indeed such non-verbal inputs and outputs in the Brain-in-a-Vat world (those efferent and afferent nerve endings again!), but we also saw that the 'sense-data' produced by the automatic machinery do not represent trees (or anything external) even when they resemble our tree-images exactly. Just as a splash of paint might resemble a tree picture without *being* a tree picture, so, we saw, a 'sense datum' might be qualitatively identical with an 'image of a tree' without being an image of a tree. How can the fact that, in the case of the brains in a vat, the language is connected by the program with sensory inputs which do not intrinsically or extrinsically represent trees (or anything external) possibly bring it about that the whole system of representations, the language-in-use, *does* refer to or represent trees or anything external?

The answer is that it cannot. The whole system of sense-data, motor signals to the efferent endings, and verbally or conceptually mediated thought connected by 'language entry rules' to the sense-data (or whatever) as inputs and by 'language exit rules' to the motor signals as outputs, has no more connection to *trees* than the ant's curve has to Winston Churchill. Once we see that the *qualitative similarity* (amounting, if you like, to qualitative identity) between the thoughts of the brains in a vat and the thoughts of someone in the actual world by no means implies sameness of reference, it is not hard to see that there is no basis at all for regarding the brain in a vat as referring to external things.

THE PREMISES OF THE ARGUMENT

I have now given the argument promised to show that the brains in a vat cannot think or say that they are brains in a vat. It remains only to make it explicit and to examine its structure.

By what was just said, when the brain in a vat (in the world where every sentient being is and always was a brain in a vat) thinks 'There is a tree in front of me', his thought does not refer to actual trees. On some theories that we shall discuss it might refer to trees in the image, or to the electronic impulses that cause tree experiences, or to the features of the program that are responsible for those electronic impulses. These theories are not ruled out by what was just said, for there is a close causal connection between the use of the word 'tree' in vat-English and the presence of trees in the image, the presence of electronic impulses of a certain kind, and the presence of certain features in the machine's program. On these theories the brain is *right*, not *wrong* in thinking 'There is a tree in front of me.' Given what 'tree' refers to in vat-English and what 'in front of' refers to, assuming one of these theories is correct, then the truth-conditions for 'There is a tree in front of me' when it occurs in vat-English are simply that a tree in the image be 'in front of' the 'me' in question—in the image—or, perhaps, that the kind of electronic impulse that normally produces this experience be coming from the automatic machinery, or, perhaps, that the feature of the machinery that is supposed to produce the 'tree in front of one' experience be operating. And these truth-conditions are certainly fulfilled.

By the same argument, 'vat' refers to vats in the image in vat-English, or something related (electronic impulses or program features), but certainly not to real vats, since the use of 'vat' in vat-English has no causal connection to real vats (apart from the connection that the brains in a vat wouldn't be able to use the word 'vat', if it were not for the presence of one particular vat—the vat they are in; but this connection obtains between the use of *every* word in vat-English and that one particular vat; it is not a special connection between the use of the *particular* word 'vat' and vats). Similarly, 'nutrient fluid' refers to a liquid in the image in vat-English, or something related (electronic impulses or program features). It follows that if their 'possible world' is really the actual one, and we are really the brains in a vat, then what we now mean by 'we are brains in a vat' is that *we are brains in a vat in the image* or something of that kind (if we mean anything at all). But part of the hypothesis that we are brains in a vat is that we aren't brains in a vat in the image (i.e. what we are 'hallucinating' isn't that we are brains in a vat). So, if we are brains in a vat, then the sentence 'We are brains in a vat' says something false (if it says anything). In short, if we are brains in a vat, then 'We are brains in a vat' is false. So it is (necessarily) false.

The supposition that such a possibility makes sense arises from a combination of two errors: (1) taking *physical possibility* too seriously; and (2) unconsciously operating with a magical theory of reference, a theory on which certain mental representations necessarily refer to certain external things and kinds of things.

There is a 'physically possible world' in which we are brains in a vat—what does this mean except that there is a *description* of such a state of affairs which is compatible with the laws of physics? Just as there is a tendency in our culture (and has been since the seventeenth century) to take *physics* as our metaphysics, that is, to view the exact sciences as the long-sought description of the 'true and ultimate furniture of the universe', so there is, as an immediate consequence, a tendency to take 'physical possibility' as the very touchstone of what might really actually be the case. Truth is physical truth; possibility physical possibility; and necessity physical necessity, on such a view. But we have just seen, if only in the case of a very contrived example so far, that this view is wrong. The existence of a 'physically possible world' in which we are brains in a vat (and always were and will be) does not mean that we might really, actually, possibly *be* brains in a vat. What rules out this possibility is not physics but *philosophy*.

Some philosophers, eager both to assert and minimize the claims of their profession at the same time (the typical state of mind of Anglo-American philosophy in the twentieth century), would say: 'Sure. You have shown that some things that seem to be physical possibilities are really *conceptual* impossibilities. What's so surprising about that?'

Well, to be sure, my argument can be described as a 'conceptual' one. But to describe philosophical activity as the search for 'conceptual' truths makes it all sound like *inquiry about the meaning of words*. And that is not at all what we have been engaging in.

What we have been doing is considering the *preconditions* for *thinking about, representing, referring to,* etc. We have investigated these preconditions *not* by investigating the meaning of these words and phrases (as a linguist might, for example) but by *reasoning a priori.* Not in the old 'absolute' sense (since we don't claim that magical theories of reference are *a priori* wrong), but in the sense of inquiring into what is *reasonably* possible *assuming* certain general premises, or making certain very broad theoretical assumptions. Such a procedure is neither 'empirical' nor quite 'a priori', but has elements of both ways of investigating. In spite of the fallibility of my procedure, and its dependence upon assumptions which might be described as 'empirical' (e.g. the assumption that the mind has no access to external things or properties apart from that provided by the senses), my procedure has a close relation to what Kant called a 'transcendental' investigation; for it is an investigation, I repeat, of the *preconditions* of reference and hence of thought—preconditions built in to the nature of our minds themselves, though not (as Kant hoped) wholly independent of empirical assumptions.

One of the premises of the argument is obvious: that magical theories of reference are wrong, wrong for mental representations and not only for physical ones. The other premiss is that one cannot refer to certain kinds of things, e.g. *trees,* if one has no causal interaction at all with them,[3] or with things in terms of which they can be described. But why should we accept these premises? Since these constitute the broad framework within which I am arguing, it is time to examine them more closely.

THE REASONS FOR DENYING NECESSARY CONNECTIONS BETWEEN REPRESENTATIONS AND THEIR REFERENTS

I mentioned earlier that some philosophers (most famously, Brentano) have ascribed to the mind a power, 'intentionality', which precisely enables it to *refer.* Evidently, I have rejected this as no solution. But what gives me this right? Have I, perhaps, been too hasty?

These philosophers did not claim that we can think about external things or properties without using representations at all. And the argument I gave above comparing visual sense data to the ant's 'picture' (the argument via the science fiction story about the 'picture' of a tree that came from a paint-splash and that gave rise to sense data qualitatively similar to our 'visual images of trees', but unaccompanied by any *concept* of a tree) would be accepted as showing that *images* do not necessarily refer. If there are mental representations that necessarily refer (to external things) they must be of the nature of *concepts* and not of the nature of images. But what are *concepts?*

When we introspect we do not perceive 'concepts' flowing through our minds as such. Stop the stream of thought when or where we will, what we catch are words, images, sensations, feelings. When I speak my thoughts out loud I do not think them twice. I hear my words as you do. To be sure it feels different to me when I utter words that I believe and when I utter words I do not believe (but sometimes, when I am nervous, or in front of a hostile audience, it feels as if I am lying when I know I am telling the truth); and it feels different when I utter words I understand and when I utter words I do not understand. But I can imagine without difficulty someone thinking just these words (in the sense of saying them in his mind) and having just the feeling of understanding, asserting, etc., that I do, and realizing a minute later (or on being awakened by a hypnotist) that he did not understand what had just passed through his mind at all, that he did not even understand the language these words are in. I don't claim that this is very likely; I simply mean that there is nothing at all unimaginable about this. And what this shows is not that concepts *are* words (or images, sensations, etc.), but that to attribute a 'concept' or a 'thought' to someone is quite different from attributing any mental 'presentation', any introspectible entity or event, to him. Concepts are not mental presentations that intrinsically refer to external objects for the very decisive reason that they are not mental presentations at all. Concepts are signs used in a certain way; the signs may be public or private, mental entities or physical entities, but even when the signs are 'mental' and 'private', the sign itself apart from its use is not the concept. And signs do not themselves intrinsically refer.

We can see this by performing a very simple thought experiment. Suppose you are like me and cannot tell an elm tree from a beech tree. We still say that the reference of 'elm' in my speech is the same as the reference of 'elm' in anyone else's, viz. elm trees, and that the set of all beech trees is the extension of 'beech' (i.e. the set of things the word 'beech' is truly predicated of) both in your speech and my speech. Is it really credible that the difference between what 'elm' refers to and what 'beech' refers to is brought about by a difference in our *concepts?* My concept of an elm tree is exactly the same as my concept of a beech tree (I blush to confess). (This shows that the determination of reference is social and not individual, by the way; you and I both defer to experts who *can* tell elms from beeches.) If someone heroically attempts to maintain that the difference between the reference of 'elm' and the reference of 'beech' in *my* speech is explained by a difference in my psychological state, then let him imagine a Twin Earth where the words are switched. Twin Earth is very much like Earth; in fact, apart from the fact that 'elm' and 'beech' are interchanged, the reader can suppose Twin Earth is exactly like Earth. Suppose I have a *Doppelganger* on Twin Earth who is molecule for molecule identical with me (in the sense in which two neckties can be 'identical'). If you are a dualist, then suppose my *Doppelganger* thinks the same verbalized thoughts I do, has the same sense data, the same dispositions, etc. It is absurd to think his psychological state is one bit different from mine: yet his word 'elm' represents *beeches*, and my word 'elm' represents elms. (Similarly, if the 'water' on Twin Earth is a different liquid—say, XYZ and not H_2O—then 'water' represents a different liquid when used on Twin Earth and when used on Earth, etc.) Contrary to a doctrine that has been with us since the seventeenth century, *meanings just aren't in the head.*

We have seen that possessing a concept is not a matter of possessing images (say, of trees—or even images, 'visual' or 'acoustic', of sentences, or whole discourses, for that matter) since one could possess any system of images you please and not possess the *ability* to use the sentences in situationally appropriate ways (considering both linguistic factors—what has been said before—and non-linguistic factors as determining 'situational appropriateness'). A man may have all the images you please, and still be completely at a loss when one says to him 'point to a tree', even if a lot of trees are present. He may even have the image of what he is supposed to do, and still not know what he is supposed to do. For the image, if not accompanied by the ability to act in a certain way, is just a *picture*, and acting in accordance with a picture is itself an ability that one may or may not have. (The man might picture himself pointing to a tree, but just for the sake of contemplating something logically possible; himself pointing to a tree after someone has produced the—to him meaningless—sequence of sounds 'please point to a tree'.) He would still not know that he was supposed to point to a tree, and he would still not *understand* 'point to a tree'.

I have considered the ability to use certain sentences to be the criterion for possessing a full-blown concept, but this could easily be liberalized. We could allow symbolism consisting of elements which are not words in a natural language, for example, and we could allow such mental phenomena as images and other types of internal events. What is essential is that these should have the same complexity, ability to be combined with each other, etc., as sentences in a natural language. For, although a particular presentation—say, a blue flash—might serve a particular mathematician as the inner expression of the whole proof of the Prime Number Theorem, still there would be no temptation to say this (and it would be false to say this) if that mathematician could not unpack his 'blue flash' into separate steps and logical connections. But, no matter what sort of inner phenomena we allow as possible *expressions* of thought, arguments exactly similar to the foregoing will show that it is not the phenomena themselves that constitute understanding, but rather the ability of the thinker to *employ* these phenomena, to produce the right phenomena in the right circumstances.

The foregoing is a very abbreviated version of Wittgenstein's argument in *Philosophical Investigations*. If it is correct, then the attempt to understand thought by what is called 'phenomenological' investigation is fundamentally misguided; for what the phenomenologists fail to see is that what they are describing is the inner *expression* of thought, but that the *understanding* of that expression—one's understanding of one's own thoughts—is not an *occurrence* but an *ability*. Our example of a man pretending to think in Japanese (and deceiving a Japanese telepath) already shows the futility of a phenomenological approach to the problem of *understanding*. For even if there is some introspectible quality which is present when and only when one *really* understands (this seems false on introspection, in fact), still that quality is only *correlated* with understanding, and it is still possible that the man fooling the Japanese telepath have that quality too and *still* not understand a word of Japanese.

On the other hand, consider the perfectly possible man who does not have any 'interior monologue' at all. He speaks perfectly good English, and if asked what his opinions are on a given subject, he will give them at length. But he never thinks (in words, images, etc.) when he is not speaking out loud; nor does anything 'go through his head', except that (of course) he hears his own voice speaking, and has the usual sense impressions from his surroundings, plus a general 'feeling of understanding'. (Perhaps he is in the habit of talking to himself.) When he types a letter or goes to the store, etc., he is not having an internal 'stream of thought'; but his actions are intelligent and purposeful, and if anyone walks up and asks him 'What are you doing?' he will give perfectly coherent replies.

This man seems perfectly imaginable. No one would hesitate to say that he was conscious, disliked rock and roll (if he frequently expressed a strong aversion to rock and roll), etc., just because he did not think conscious thoughts except when speaking out loud.

What follows from all this is that (a) no set of mental events—images or more 'abstract' mental happenings and qualities—*constitutes* understanding; and (b) no set of mental events is *necessary* for understanding. In particular, *concepts cannot be identical with mental objects of any kind*. For, assuming that by a mental object we mean something introspectible, we have just seen that whatever it is, it may be absent in a man who does understand the appropriate word (and hence has the full blown concept), and present in a man who does not have the concept at all.

Coming back now to our criticism of magical theories of reference (a topic which also concerned Wittgenstein), we see that, on the one hand, those 'mental objects' we *can* introspectively detect—words, images, feelings, etc.—do not intrinsically refer any more than the ant's picture does (and for the same reasons), while the attempts to postulate special mental objects, 'concepts', which *do* have a necessary connection with their referents, and which only trained phenomenologists can detect, commit a *logical* blunder; for concepts are (at least in part) *abilities* and not occurrences. The doctrine that there are mental presentations which necessarily refer to external things is not only bad natural science; it is also bad phenomenology and conceptual confusion.

NOTES

1. In this [essay] the terms 'representation' and 'reference' always refer to a relation between a word (or other sort of sign, symbol, or representation) and something that actually exists (i.e. not just an 'object of thought'). There is a sense of 'refer' in which I can 'refer' to what does not exist; this is not the sense in which 'refer' is used here. An older word for what I call 'representation' or 'reference' is *denotation.*

Secondly, I follow the custom of modern logicians and use 'exist' to mean 'exist in the past, present, or future'. Thus Winston Churchill 'exists', and we can 'refer to' or 'represent' Winston Churchill, even though he is no longer alive.

2. Turing 1950.

3. If the Brains in a Vat will have causal connection with, say, trees *in the future,* then perhaps they can *now* refer to trees by the description 'the things I will refer to as "trees" at such-and-such a future time'. But we are to imagine a case in which the Brains in a Vat *never* get out of the vat, and hence *never* get into causal connection with trees, etc.

CHAPTER 3

Semantic Answers to Skepticism

Anthony Brueckner

Semantic theses are sometimes invoked in the attempt to refute epistemological skepticism. In this paper, I will reexamine a kind of semantic answer to skepticism. In other papers, I have criticized this semantic answer, which is found in the work of Putnam and Davidson, and I now wish to reevaluate the semantic anti-skeptical strategy in the light of recent work on self-knowledge and further reflection on the workings of the strategy.[1] In the end, I will offer a roundabout defense of the strategy.

1. Let us first discuss the Cartesian skeptical argument which the semantic strategy takes as its target. Let us say that Q is a *counterpossibility* to P iff P and Q are logically possible but logically incompatible propositions. Then the first component of the skeptical argument is the principle that if I know that P and I know that Q is a counterpossibility to P, then I know that Q is not the case. This counterpossibility principle is not importantly different from the principle that knowledge is closed under known logical implication. According to this closure principle, if I know that P and I know that P logically implies Q, then I know that Q. The second component of the skeptical argument is the claim that the following is a logically possible proposition which is known by me to be incompatible with the proposition that I am standing up:

> I am a brain in a vat with sensory evidence qualitatively indistinguishable from my actual evidence.

The third component of the argument is the claim that I do *not* know that I am *not* a brain in a vat. This is not the claim that I lack absolute certainty that

"Semantic Answers to Skepticism" from *Pacific Philosophical Quarterly* 73 (1992, pp. 200–219). © University of Southern California. Reprinted with the permission of the publisher.

I am not a brain in a vat, and neither is it the claim that my evidence fails to entail that I am not a brain in a vat. Rather, it is the claim that I fail to satisfy at least one necessary condition for knowing that I am not a brain in a vat, perhaps the justification condition. Given these three components, the skeptic can argue that I do not know that I am standing up. Such knoledge requires the knowledge that I am not a brain in a vat, which I lack.

In order to vindicate my claim to know that I am standing up, I must say something in response to the foregoing Cartesian skeptical argument. I must explain why it goes wrong. A counterintuitive but increasingly popular response is to reject the closure principle. On this approach, it is held that the skeptic has specified a genuine logical possibility. It is further admitted that I do not know that this possibility is merely possible rather than actual. That is, it is admitted that I do not know that I am not a brain in a vat. I am unjustified in rejecting the possibility in question. Yet it is held that I do know that I am standing up, even though I do not know the obviously entailed proposition that I am not a brain in a vat.[2]

Another approach, which I will not pursue here, is to accept the closure principle but deny that the skeptic has succeeded in specifying a genuine logical possibility. Verificationists and perhaps semantic anti-realists might be viewed as following this approach. The semantic strategy I will discuss here is sometimes also conceived—mistakenly—as a variant of this approach. But the strategy in fact countenances the skeptic's possibilities. The strategy is an instance of a third approach to blocking the Cartesian argument.

This is to accept that the skeptic has specified a genuine possibility, accept the closure principle, and maintain that I *do* know that I am not envatted, even though my evidence would be just the same as it is were I envatted. One way of arguing this is to hold that I am justified in rejecting the skeptic's possibility because the 'hypothesis' he sketches is somehow inferior to the ordinary 'hypothesis' that the world is largely as I take it to be. The competing hypotheses are meant to explain the evidence of my senses, it might be held, and the ordinary hypothesis is the better of the two. But better in what respect? It is wrong to say that I am justified in rejecting the skeptical hypothesis as false in the same way that I am justified in rejecting an empirically inadequate scientific hypothesis. The skeptical hypothesis can be constructed so that it is empirically indistinguishable from the ordinary one. Suppose it is said instead that the skeptical hypothesis is judged explanatorily inferior according to some sort of simplicity criterion. Then the criterion must be plausibly spelled out, and it must then be explained why a simpler hypothesis is more likely to be true than a more complex one. Unless this is explained, it is unclear why one would be justified in believing the simpler hypothesis and rejecting the more complex one.[3]

On the semantic version of the third general approach to blocking the skeptical argument, no appeal is made to simplicity considerations as licensing justified belief in the ordinary hypothesis. Instead, the falsity of the skeptical hypothesis is held to follow from a plausible semantic thesis taken together with an apparently trivial disquotation principle. The semantic thesis says, roughly, that the truth conditions of one's utterances of sentences and, correlatively, the contents of one's thoughts are, in part, determined by environmental circumstances external to one's mind. For example, in an anti-skeptical strategy I reconstructed in another paper from Putnam's book *Reason, Truth and History,* the key externalist semantic claims are these: when an envatted thinker in a rabbitless world tokens the sentence 'A rabbit is present', this utterance is true iff a rabbit is present *in the image.*[4] I take it that by *the image* Putnam means: the stream of sense-impressions had by the envatted subject of experience. So a rabbit is present in the image if one has sense-impressions as of a rabbit being present. Putnam also considers this account of truth conditions for an envatted thinker's utterances of 'A rabbit is present': his utterances are true iff the computer which stimulates his brain is in the state which typically causes him to have sense-impressions as of rabbits. Either way, it is not the case that: his utterances are true iff a rabbit is present. The utterances have strange truth conditions, according to Putnam, in virtue of plausible causal constraints on the references of the parts of the uttered sentences. Since the envatted thinker has had no causal commerce with rabbits—and, in the Putnamian version of the skeptical hypothesis, no interaction with anyone else who has had such commerce—his word 'rabbit' does not refer to rabbits. Instead, his word 'rabbit' refers to the typical cause of his uses of the word. As we have seen, Putnam seems willing to hold that sense-impressions and compter states are *both* reasonable candidates for playing this causal role in the case of the brain in a vat. Even though it seems to me that computer states are a much more plausible candidate than sense-impressions, I will sometimes use the sense-impression version of the strange Putnamian truth conditions in what follows, because it makes things somewhat simpler. Why is the computer state version preferable (though more cumbersome)? Even though both computer states and sense-impressions play a causal role in the production of an envatted thinker's utterances of 'A rabbit is present', the role of computer states is more similar to that of rabbits in the normal case than is the role of sense-impressions. After all, sense-impressions play the same causal role in both the normal and the vat cases.

So the envatted thinker's utterances of 'A rabbit is present' have non-standard truth conditions (of course, these 'utterances' are *thought tokens,* rather than acoustic or inscriptional entities). When he utters the sentence as a result of computer stimulation causing sense-impressions as of rabbits, he thinks something true, not something false, as would be the case if his sentence had the standard truth conditions, whose satisfaction requires the presence of a rabbit. So when he thinks and accepts the sentence, this does not constitute a *mistake* on his part.

Donald Davidson's theory of radical interpretation yields the same result.[5] The cornerstone of the theory is a principle of charity which, according to Davidson, precludes the possibility of correct attribution of massive error to a target of radical interpretation. It is no easy task to discern Davidson's considered intentions regarding the formulation of the principle of charity.[6]

But the basic idea seems to be that I am to interpret another's sentences in such a way as to maximize agreement in belief between the two of us. If I operate on the assumption that his sentences express mostly *mistaken* beliefs, then I cannot even begin to interpret him, since it is left open to me to attribute just about any crazy set of beliefs to him. Instead, I am to maximize agreement in belief between me and the interpretee. The problem with this construal of charity is that it would lead me to attribute to a New Guinean subject of radical interpretation beliefs which concern goings-on in America. If I am bidden to try to maximize the overlap between his beliefs and mine, then I am constrained by the fact that my beliefs largely concern my experience in America. This clearly leads to a ridiculous assignment of beliefs to the New Guinean. Suppose, instead, that we construe the principle of charity as requiring that I maximize agreement in belief between me and the New Guinean *given similar evidence.* So when I take it that the New Guinean holds a belief on the basis of evidence like mine—say, sense-impressions as of rabbits—I attribute to him the belief that I hold on the basis of my evidence. The problem with this version of charity—and with any version which somehow highlights agreement in belief—is that interpreter and interpretee may agree even though *both* are massively mistaken.[7] Also, consider how the second construal of charity—maximize agreement in belief relative to similar evidence—would affect my interpretation of an envatted counterpart of me. Suppose I interpret his English-like sentences as expressing the same beliefs expressed by my counterpart sentences, since our evidence is indistinguishable. Then I interpret him as holding massively mistaken beliefs—just the result Davidson wishes to avoid. Despite his talk about maximizing agreement in belief, Davidson apparently wants, in the end, to formulate charity roughly as follows:

In radical interpretation, assign beliefs by reference to their causes.[8]

Now we get the Putnamian verdict on the brain in a vat. His utterances of 'A rabbit is present' are typically caused by a computer state of a certain kind, not by the presence of rabbits. Thus, we interpret his utterances as having strange truth conditions and as usually expressing correct beliefs about his world, in which the strange truth conditions are usually satisfied. The brain in a vat is not massively mistaken—he is predominantly right about things.

How does any of this help with the refutation of Cartesian skepticism? Let me now state the anti-skeptical argument I reconstructed from Putnam in an earlier paper.[9] Let 'BIV' abbreviate 'Putnamian brain in a vat', i.e., a brain in a vat in a universe containing nothing but brains in a vat and the computer which tends them.

(1) Either I am a BIV or I am a non-BIV.
(2) If I am a BIV, then my utterances of 'I am a BIV' are true iff I have sense-impressions as of being a BIV.

• 46 •

(3) If I am a BIV, then I do not have sense-impressions as of being a BIV (instead, I have sense-impressions as of being a normal, embodied human).

(4) If I am a BIV, then my utterances of 'I am a BIV' are false. [(2),(3)]

(5) If I am a non-BIV, then my utterances of 'I am a BIV' are true iff I am a BIV.

(6) If I am a non-BIV, then my utterances of 'I am a BIV' are false. [(5)]

(7) My utterances of 'I am a BIV' are false. [(1),(4),(6)]

(8) My utterances of 'I am not a BIV' are true. [(7)][10]

I think that this argument is not only a charitable reconstruction of Putnam, but is also consonant with Davidson's thinking on these matters. Davidson's idea seems to be that even if *I* am a BIV, I am not massively mistaken given the formulation of charity in terms of belief causation. Even if I am a BIV, when I utter 'I am not a BIV', I express a correct belief given the causal constraints on belief attribution, which apply equally to all language users, myself included.

In the earlier paper, my first complaint about the foregoing argument was that it is incomplete. The anti-skeptical conclusion we desire is not metalinguistic in character: it is rather the conclusion that I am not a BIV, not the conclusion that my sentence 'I am not a BIV' is true. We desire that the semantic argument afford me the object language knowledge that I am not a BIV. So for this purpose we must add to the argument a disquotation principle:

My utterances of 'I am not a BIV' are true iff I am not a BIV.

Then we can move from the original argument's conclusion to the claim that I am not a BIV.

If we are going to avail ourselves of the supplementary disquotational premise, we can accordingly simplify and generalize the semantic argument. Let us first elaborate upon some terminological matters. In general, tokens of a sentence S as uttered in a given object language L will have *disquotational truth conditions relative to a metalanguage L'* iff there is a true sentence of L' which consists of S surrounded by quotation marks, followed by an L'-translation of the phrase 'is true in L iff', followed by S itself. When the tokens of a sentence as uttered in a given object language have disquotational truth conditions relative to *my* language, I will abbreviate this by saying that the tokens (or utterances) have disquotational truth conditions *tout court*, leaving implicit the relativization to my own language as metalanguage. I will say, further, that if the tokens of a sentence have truth conditions but do *not* have disquotational truth conditions, then they have *non-disquotational truth conditions*. If the utterance of a given sentence S expresses a thought content which is correctly statable in the course of formulating disquotational truth conditions for S, then the utterance expresses a *disquotational content* (and mutatis mutandis for *non-disquotational content*). Now consider what I will call the *stripped-down semantic argument:*

(I) If I am a BIV, then my utterances of sentences have non-disquotational truth conditions and express non-disquotational contents.

(II) My utterances of sentences have disquotational truth conditions and express disquotational contents.

(III) I am not a BIV. [(I), (II)][11]

In evaluating the stripped-down semantic argument, let us grant the externalist semantic views discussed above and see whether they can underwrite a successful rejection of the BIV possibility. Then the first premise of the argument appears to follow. This premise turns out to be rather problematic, though, and we will discuss this in some detail at the end of the paper. The second premise seems as good as gold: *of course* my sentences have disquotational truth conditions and express disquotational contents. My utterances of 'A rabbit is present' are true iff a rabbit is present, and they express my belief that a rabbit is present. So if we accept the externalist semantic assumptions underlying the argument, it seems that we *do* get the desired anti-skeptical conclusion that I am not a BIV.

2. The main objection I made to the original reconstructed argument in the earlier paper equally applies to the stripped-down version just stated (from now on, I will call it *the semantic argument*). The objection concerns the semantic argument's second premise. In order to claim knowledge of that premise, according to which my utterances of sentences have disquotational truth conditions, I must know that these utterances do not have strange, non-disquotational truth conditions. But according to the semantic assumptions underlying the argument's first premise, things would seem exactly as they now seem and have seemed even if I were a BIV speaking a language composed of sentences having non-disquotational truth conditions (as uttered by me) and expressing beliefs with non-disquotational contents. A normal thinker, whose utterances have disquotational truth conditions and express beliefs with disquotational contents, is phenomenologically and introspectively indistinguishable from his envatted twin. So given externalism, unless I somehow know that I am not a BIV, I fail to know that the truth conditions of my utterances are not strange, non-disquotational ones, and I fail to know that my utterances do not express strange, non-disquotational belief contents. So, unless I somehow know that I am not a BIV, I fail to know that the truth conditions of my utterances are disquotational, and I fail to know that my utterances express disquotational belief contents. So unless I somehow know that I am not a BIV, I fail to know the second premise of the semantic argument, whose *conclusion* is that I am not a BIV.

The objection, then, is that the semantic externalism underlying the anti-skeptical argument engenders a skeptical argument exactly paralleling the target Cartesian one. That Cartesian argument concerns knowledge of the external world; the parallel skeptical argument concerns knowledge of the truth conditions of one's utterances of sentences and knowledge of the contents of the beliefs expressed by one's utterances of the sentences. For brevity, let us call this *skepticism about knowledge of content*. We could save the semantic argument directed against Cartesian skepticism if we could answer skepticism about knowledge of content and thereby claim knowledge of the semantic argument's second premise. I will now consider some proposals aimed at providing such an answer.

According to semantic externalism, a thinker on twin earth, which is devoid of H_2O and replete with XYZ, thinks that twater is wet when he thinks the sentence 'Water is wet'.[12] His thought has a different content from that of his twin on plain old earth. I believe that when I think the sentence 'Water is wet', I am thinking that water is wet, not that twater is wet. I believe that my thought has disquotational content. But if I were on twin earth thinking the sentence, things would seem exactly the same to me as they now seem. So how do I know that I am not thinking that twater is wet? Knowing this would require knowledge of content-determining circumstances external to my mind. Now if I fail to know that I am *not* thinking that twater is wet, then I do not know that I *am* thinking that water is wet. This is, once again, skepticism about knowledge of content, this time generated by consideration of twin earth.

One way to answer such skepticism, whether generated by consideration of twin earth or by consideration of a vat world, is to deny the principle that knowledge is closed under known implication. This would enable me to hold that I know that I am thinking that twater is wet. I can know that my thought has its content without knowing that it does not have, instead, the pertinent twin content. Thus I can know that my thought has its content without appealing to knowledge of external circumstances which rule out the possibility that it has its twin content.

The trouble with this answer to skepticism about knowledge of content is that it is by itself sufficient to answer Cartesian skepticism about knowledge of the external world, as we noted earlier. We are looking to save knowledge of content in order to save the semantic argument directed against external world skepticism. If we save knowledge of content by denying the closure principle, we no longer need concern ourselves with the semantic argument against external world skepticism, since the denial of closure effectively answers both sorts of skepticism. That is, if it is really true that the closure principle fails, then this allows us to answer both sorts of skepticism and renders superfluous the semantic argument. Further, whether closure does fail is controversial.

A second way of answering skepticism about knowledge of content is proposed by Tyler Burge as part of a complex strategy.[13] I will discuss another, independent component of the strategy later. On the second way of answering the content-skeptic, we accept the closure principle and hold that I *do* know that my thought does not have the pertinent twin content. According to this answer, I know this without appealing to knowledge of external circumstances which preclude the twin content. But how is this epistemic situation possible? The idea is that I can know that I am thinking that water is wet without first, separately knowing that I am in an earthly and hence non-twin-earthly environment. I know that I am *not* thinking that twater is wet by inferring this from my knowledge that I *am* thinking that water is wet. I know that I am not thinking the twin thought by inference from my knowledge of what I am thinking, not by investigation of external conditions which preclude my thinking the twin thought. Further, my grounds for my belief about what I am thinking do not enable me to discriminate my thought from its twins. Still, I know that I am not thinking any of its twins by deduction from my knowledge of what I *am* thinking.

This answer suffers from the same problem as the first: it is by itself sufficient to refute external world skepticism. The position would be that I know that I am not a BIV by inferring this from my knowledge that I am standing, and I can know the latter without first, separately knowing that I am in an earthly and hence non-envatted environment. Further, the answer is controversial. Suppose that it is not required that I somehow *first*, separately rule out the skeptic's counterpossibility in order to know the proposition P that I claim to know. Still, my grounds for believing P must be strong enough to justify a belief that the skeptic's counterpossibility does not obtain. Otherwise, it will not be plausible to say that my inference from P to the denial of the counterpossibility terminates in a *warranted* rejection of that counterpossibility. Is it obvious that my grounds do have the required strength?

Another answer is found in the work of Burge and of John Heil.[14] Davidson also sees himself as giving this sort of answer, but I think it is hard to find it in his work. He sums up the answer by saying that no skeptical difficulty about knowledge of content arises from externalism because "what determines the contents of thoughts also determines what the thinker thinks the contents are."[15] Heil's version of this answer is as follows. Consider a mental state M of mine which has the content that *water is wet* in virtue of the obtaining of a state of affairs A in my environment. Next consider my second-order state M', in which I introspect on M. According to externalism, M' has its content in virtue of the obtaining of a state of affairs A' in my environment, where A' may well include A. The content of M' is that *I am thinking that water is wet*. Heil points out that on externalism, M' has this content in virtue of the obtaining of the external state of affairs A', *regardless* of whether I know or believe that A' obtains.

But the skeptic about knowledge of content will grant all this. He will readily grant that M' has its second-order content in virtue of the sheer *obtaining* of A': that is an obvious consequence of the externalist theory of content-determination whose epistemological shortcomings he is bent on exposing. All that Heil's point shows is that given externalism, I can *think* that I am thinking that water is wet without knowing that A' (or any other external state of affairs) obtains. That is, all that has been shown is that my introspective thought M' can have the content that *I am thinking that water is wet* without my knowing that A' obtains. But *thinking*, via an introspective state like M', that I am thinking that such and such does not necessarily amount to *knowing* that I am thinking that such and such, even if it is true that I am thinking that such and such. Skepticism about *knowledge* of content is not answered by Heil's way of developing the Davidsonian suggestion.[16]

Burge puts forward an answer to skepticism about knowledge of content that is consonant with that suggestion but which goes beyond it in an important way.[17] Burge focusses upon the self-referential, self-verifying character of thoughts like *I am thinking that water is wet.* According to Burge, my act of thinking a thought with the content that *I am thinking that water is wet* makes that thought true, since in order to think a thought with that content at t, I must at t think a thought with the content that *water is wet.* The content of this constituent thought is fixed by external circumstances, and the containing, second-order thought has its content fixed—and made true—by its reference to the contained thought. Unlike the Davidsonian suggestion, then, Burge focusses upon the relation between a second-order thought and the corresponding first-order thought, rather than the relation between a second-order thought and the thinker's environment.

Let us grant the claim that some second-order thoughts have this self-verifying character. Does the strategy provide an answer to skepticism about knowledge of content? As noted above in connection with Heil, it is one thing to *think* that I am thinking that water is wet, and another to *know* that I am thinking that water is wet. Similarly, it is one thing to *think correctly* that I am thinking that water is wet, and another to *know* that I am thinking that water is wet. A true thought need not amount to knowledge. But at this point Burge might well say that not only is my current second-order thought about what I am thinking a correct thought, but, further, it is *guaranteed* to be a correct thought by its self-referential character. It does not just happen to be a correct thought. In response, we may say that even a thought which is guaranteed to be correct need not amount to knowledge. For example, thinking a necessary proposition need not amount to knowing the proposition. Still, Burge can reply that in the case of self-verifying thoughts, I can come to *see* that such a thought of mine is guaranteed to be true by virtue of its self-referential character. Seeing this, I know that such thoughts are guaranteed to be true. Now the thinking of such thoughts does amount to knowledge.

The foregoing defense of Burge has the uncomfortable result that the philosophically unsophisticated fail to think knowledgeably when they think thoughts about what they are thinking. We could avoid this result by adopting some sort of reliabilist theory of knowledge, but then we are faced with a version of the earlier objection: reliabilism is by itself sufficient to block external world skepticism. If the justification condition for knowledge is either analyzed by or replaced by a reliability condition, then the skeptic is placed in a dialectically impossible position. In order to argue that I fail to satisfy some necessary condition for knowing that P, he must then argue that I fail to satisfy the reliability condition or some other condition. Which other? Surely not the belief condition, and surely not the condition requiring that known propositions are true propositions. In order to argue that I fail to satisfy the reliability condition, the skeptic would have to argue that my belief-forming mechanisms *actually* fail to produce a sufficiently high ratio of true beliefs, or that they would fail to do so in relevant counterfactual circumstances similar to the actual circumstances. This is obviously a thankless task for the skeptic.[18]

Let me briefly raise another worry about the Burge strategy. The foregoing discussion of the strategy has been conducted in the material mode. In characterizing the self-verifying nature of some of my thoughts, I should have confined myself to admissions such as this: when I think the sentence 'I am thinking that water is wet', I therein think a second-order content which is guaranteed to be true by its connection to a contained first-order content. But similar remarks apply to a BIV using the same sentence to think a different second-order content also guaranteed to be true in the same fashion. So which true second-order content am I now thinking? Is it that *I am thinking that water is wet?* Or is it that *I am thinking that twater is wet?* If I do not know which second-order thought I am thinking, then how can the thinking of such a thought amount to knowledge of the contained first-order thought? Burge can address this problem by saying that my sentence 'I think that I am thinking that water is wet' expresses a third-order content which is guaranteed to be true. So my question about which second-order content I am thinking can be answered by thinking the third-order sentence and thereby thinking something true. But which true thing am I thereby thinking? For each new question, I can get a correct answer by moving up a level and thinking the next higher level sentence. This suggests that thinking an n-order self-verifying sentence at t does not necessarily amount to the having of knowledge of $(n-1)$-order content. For that, one must think the pertinent $(n+1)$-order sentence at $(t+1)$. But the contained $(n-1)$-order thought, occurring at $(t+1)$, is numerically distinct from the $(n-1)$-order thought occurring at t. We were looking for knowledge of the content of the *latter* $(n-1)$-order thought, not the former.[19]

3. Even given the foregoing reservations, Burge's strategy has a core of intuitive attractiveness. Consider an analogue of the claim that knowledge of the contents of one's thoughts is trivial given the self-referential mechanism at work in such thoughts. This is the claim that it is a similarly trivial matter to know that one's utterances of sentences have disquotational truth conditions. It might well seem that this is guaranteed by the meanings of quotation marks and the truth predicate. It is a truth on a par with the truth that my term 'dog' refers to dogs. Now the second premise of the semantic argument—the disquotational premise—once again seems as good as gold. However, to the extent that we are impressed by the triviality and security of the argument's second premise concerning disquotation, we should begin to doubt the *first* premise even given the assumption of semantic externalism. Contrary to what one might have thought, the first premise does not unproblematically follow from semantic externalism. Thus, even if the second premise is knowable from the sorts of reasons just mentioned, the semantic argument may well be blocked because the semantic assumptions underlying the argument do not yield its first premise.

To see this, first consider why the second premise—the disquotational premise—seems right. The sentence

(*) S's utterances of 'S is a BIV' are true iff S is a BIV.

is guaranteed to express a truth so long as the metalanguage in which (*) is stated contains the object language to which the mentioned sentence belongs. The same thing holds for

(**) My utterances of 'I am a BIV' are true iff I am a BIV.

This statement of disquotational truth conditions for my utterances of 'I am a BIV' is guaranteed to express a truth so long as the metalanguage in which (**) is stated contains the object language to which my sentence 'I am a BIV' belongs.[20]

Now according to the first premise of the semantic argument, if I am a BIV, then my sentences have non-disquotational truth conditions. So this sentence follows from the premise as an instance:

(Cond) If I am a BIV, then my utterances of 'I am a BIV' are true iff I am a BIV*.

where 'I am a BIV*' formulates the Putnamian non-disquotational truth conditions, whatever they are. In order for the semantic argument to be sound, its first premise needs to express a truth, and thus the entailed (Cond) needs to express a truth. Does (Cond) say something true? Consider first its consequent:

(Cons) My utterances of 'I am a BIV' are true iff I am a BIV*.

In view of what we have just said about (**), the sentence which states disquotational truth conditions for my sentence 'I am a BIV', we can now see that (Cons) expresses a truth only if the metalanguage in which it is stated does *not* contain the object language to which the mentioned sentence 'I am a BIV' belongs. If that relation of containment did hold, then (**), rather than (Cons), would express a truth. To put the point slightly differently, the only way in which my utterance of (Cons) can express a truth is as follows: the mentioned sentence is a sentence of a language semantically different from the language I am using to state the semantic argument, some possible language different from the language I am actually using in stating the semantic argument. Therefore, my utterance of (Cons) does not express a semantic claim which is true of my actual language. I will come back to this point below.

We have been discussing, in a preliminary way, the sentence (Cons), which is the consequent of the conditional (Cond), which is in turn an instance of the semantic argument's first premise. In order to evaluate that argument, we must first ask, what sort of conditional is (Cond) supposed to be? The most natural supposition is that it is meant to be a strict conditional, since it is held to follow from semantic externalism, a thesis of philosophical semantics which, if true, is not merely contingently true. If (Cond) is a strict conditional, then if it is to express a true proposition, its consequent has to express a proposition which is true when evaluated at, or with respect to, a vat world (a world in which I am a BIV). This is because its antecedent expresses a proposition which is true when evaluated at, or with respect to, such a world. On the other hand, if (Cond) is meant to be a subjunctive conditional, then the proposition expressed by its consequent, again, needs to be true when evaluated at a vat world, if the conditional sentence is to express a truth (at least, the proposition expressed by the consequent needs to be true at the vat worlds most similar to the actual world, whichever they are). Suppose that (Cond) is read as an indicative conditional and that such conditionals are not material conditionals. The conditional's antecedent expresses a proposition which is true when evaluated at vat worlds. So if its consequent expresses a proposition which is false when evaluated at vat worlds, the conditional will not be assertible by someone who recognizes these facts. Suppose, though, that the proponent of the semantic argument maintains that it will be sufficient for his purposes if (Cond) is read as a material conditional. On this reading, if I am in fact in a non-vat world, then it expresses a truth by virtue of having an antecedent which expresses an actually false proposition, and we need not worry about evaluating at a vat world the proposition expressed by its consequent. But what if I am in fact in a vat world? In order to use (Cond), interpreted as a material conditional, in an anti-skeptical argument,[21] we must verify that the proposition expressed by its consequent is true when evaluated at a vat world, for I may be *in* a vat world. Unless we know that the proposition expressed by the consequent of (Cond) is true at a vat world, the only reason the skeptic has for accepting the material conditional reading of (Cond) is an acknowledgement that its antecedent expresses an actually false proposition. This is obviously not something the skeptic will acknowledge. So, however we read (Cond), we must ask, is the proposition expressed by its consequent, namely (Cons), true when evaluated at a vat world?

What is involved in the sort of truth value evaluation to which we have been alluding? To determine whether the proposition expressed by a sentence of mine is true when evaluated at a vat world, we first ask: what proposition is expressed by my current use of the sentence, given the meaning of the sentence in my actual language? Then, Kaplan-style, we take that proposition to a possible world, in this case a vat world. Then we ask: is the proposition true with respect to, or at, the world in question?

Now consider the sentence

(***) My utterances of 'I am a BIV' are produced in a vat.

Let us take the proposition expressed by (***) and evaluate it at a vat world. We accordingly consider the location of the utterances of the mentioned sentence produced by me in a vat world. This is because (***), as I use it, expresses the proposition that my utterances of the mentioned sentence are produced in a vat. In a vat world, these utterances *are* produced in a vat. The proposition expressed by (***), then, is true at a vat world.

Let us evaluate at a vat world the proposition expressed by (Cons), our conditional's consequent. We thus consider the utterances of the mentioned sentence which I produce in a vat world and ask whether (Cons), as I use it, correctly states the truth conditions of such envatted utterances. We have already seen that (Cons) correctly states the truth conditions for utterances of the mentioned sentence only if the object language to which that sentence belongs is a *different* language from the metalanguage I am now using to state (Cons). Thus the proposition expressed by (Cons) is true at a vat world only if my utterances of the mentioned sentence in a vat world are not utterances of sentences in the metalanguage I am currently using to state (Cons). In other words, the proposition expressed by (Cons) is true *at* a vat world only if I am not now *in* a vat world: the proposition in question is true at a vat world only if the actual world is a normal, non-vat world. If I am in a vat world—if the actual world is a vat world—then my envatted utterances of the mentioned sentence are utterances of sentences in the metalanguage, and in that case the proposition expressed by (Cons) is false at a vat world.

Let us review the dialectical situation. (Cons) is the consequent of the conditional (Cond), and (Cond) is an instance of the semantic argument's first premise

(I) If I am a BIV, then my utterances of sentences have non-disquotational truth conditions and express non-disquotational contents.

As we noted earlier, in order to use premise (I) as a premise in an anti-skeptical argument, we must be in a position to claim knowledge that the proposition expressed by (Cons), the consequent of (Cond), is true at a vat world. This requirement, we saw, holds no matter how we read the conditional. But the proposition expressed by (Cons), we have just seen, is true at a vat world only if the actual world is *not* a vat world. So unless we know that the actual world is not a vat world, we cannot claim to know that the proposition expressed by (Cons) is true at a vat world. So in view of the foregoing considerations, we apparently cannot, *without begging the question,* use premise (I) of the anti-skeptical semantic argument.

4. We are attempting to determine whether or not we can use externalist semantics as the foundation for an anti-skeptical strategy which will rule out the BIV possibility. If we deny externalism, then our semantic argument will not get off the ground. But can we consistently accept externalist semantics (as we are claiming to do for the sake of argument) and yet refrain from accepting (Cond) (due to the foregoing worry about question-begging)? Here are some considerations which seem to support a connection between (Cond) and externalist semantics. According to that thesis, the truth conditions of my sentences depend upon my external environment. This means that if I were in an environment sufficiently different from my actual environment, then my sentences, as used in that different environment, would have different truth conditions from their actual ones, even holding fixed everything 'internal' to my mind. If I were in such an environment, the language I would be speaking therein would be different from my actual language, even though everything would seem, and would have seemed, just the way it actually seems and has seemed. This much is clearly contained in externalist semantics. Now suppose I am in fact not a BIV. Then if I *were* a BIV, in a vat environment different from my actual normal environment, the language I would be speaking would be different from my actual language, even though everything would seem just the way it actually seems. In particular, my sentences, such as 'I am a BIV', would have non-disquotational truth conditions, as opposed to the disquotational truth conditions they obviously actually have. If, contrary to actual fact, I were a BIV, then my sentence 'I am a BIV' would belong to a language semantically different from the language I am actually speaking, in which the sentence of course has disquotational truth conditions.

These considerations show that (Cons) is true at a vat world, however, *only relative to the assumption that the actual world is not a vat world.* That assumption is obviously not part of semantic externalism. If we were entitled to the assumption that the actual world is not a vat world, then we could read (Cond) as a true *counterfactual* whose antecedent is false at the actual world. A similar example would be this:

> If (obviously contrary to fact) I were 1 mile north of here, then my utterances of 'I am here' would be true iff I am 1 mile north of here.[22]

This is a true counterfactual which states that some of my utterances would have strange truth conditions if I were in a counterfactual situation different from the actual situation in certain respects. I can use the counterfactual, together with the denial that the utterances in question have strange truth conditions, to argue that I am not 1 mile north of here. However, to use (Cond), read as a counterfactual with an *actually false antecedent,* in order to argue in a parallel manner that I am not a BIV is to argue in a manner which obviously begs the question aganst the skeptic.

Here is a different, and more promising, way to defend the semantic argument against the criticism I have lodged. One might argue that semantic externalism yields (Cond) as an instance of the following *strict* conditional:

($) Necessarily, for all x, if x is a BIV, then x's utterances of 'I am a BIV' are true iff x is a BIV*.

Suppose that we know that ($) expresses a true strict conditional proposition simply by virtue of knowing the truth of semantic externalism. (I will discuss the case for this claim in more detail below.) Then we know that (Cond) expresses a true strict conditional proposition. We thus know that the proposition expressed by (Cons), the consequent of (Cond), is true at a vat world, since in all worlds in which the antecedent of the strict conditional is true (these are vat worlds), the consequent is true as well. By the reasoning we considered earlier (which assumed the correctness of the disquotational premise (II)), we can conclude that the actual world is not a vat world. This is because, according to that reasoning, the proposition expressed by (Cons) is true at a vat world only if the actual world is not a vat world. (Note that this defense of the semantic argument does not depend upon a question-begging reading of (Cond) as a counterfactual with an actually false antecedent.) What of the earlier charge that the anti-skeptic cannot put forward the argument's first premise without begging the question? This appearance is seen to be misleading once ($) is highlighted: the distance from semantic externalism (via ($)) to the refutation of the BIV possibility is, so to speak, so short that the case against the skeptic tends to seem unfair.

Suppose that the skeptical opponent of the semantic argument attempts to undermine the foregoing defense of that argument as follows. He accepts semantic externalism, for the sake of argument, but he denies that the strict conditional ($) follows as a consequence. As noted above, the skeptic who accepts semantic externalism agrees that it has the consequence that the truth conditions of a being's utterances (and the contents of its thoughts) depend in certain ways upon its external environment, so that the truth conditions of its utterances can vary across possible worlds with different environments even though its 'internal' phenomenology is held fixed. Relative to various assumptions about the actual world, we have noted, acceptance of the foregoing consequence will commit the skeptic to the truth of various counterfactuals. But the skeptic rejects such *specifications* of the dependence of semantics upon environment as that given in ($).

The defender of the semantic argument will object that the skeptic is missing the simple point that strict conditionals like ($) are *constitutive* of semantic externalism. Externalism is the view that the truth conditions of one's utterances (and the contents of one's thoughts) depend upon one's environment in certain ways *such as that specified in ($)*. Necessarily, if a being is in a treeless vat environment, then, according to semantic externalism, its terms refer to the entities playing the right causal role *vis-à-vis* its uses of terms, viz., computer states and not absent trees, tables, etc. Hence the truth conditions of its utterances of sentences are non-disquotational. Necessarily, if a being is in a normal environment, then its terms refer to the obvious candidates (e.g., its tokens of 'tree' refer to trees, since these entities play the right causal role vis à vis its tokenings of 'tree'). Hence the truth conditions of its utterances of sentences are disquotational. Denying these points commits the skeptic to the position that there is a treeless possible world in which a being—call him *Skip*—is envatted (in the Putnamian way) and, even so, his term 'tree' refers to trees rather than to computer states. Hence Skip's utterances of 'tree'-sentences have disquotational truth conditions. According to semantic externalism, there is no such possible world. Contrary to what the skeptical opponent of the semantic argument at this point wishes to maintain, his condition cannot possibly be the one allegedly facing Skip. In any treeless world in which the skeptic is envatted, his term 'tree' refers to computer states and *not* to things absent from his causal environment (such as trees). In such a world, his 'tree'-sentences accordingly have non-disquotational truth conditions.[23]

5. Thus, if semantic externalism is accepted, then one can construct a simple, apparently viable argument to the conclusion that one is not a Putnamian brain in a vat. The conditional premise of the argument appears to follow straightforwardly from semantic externalism. The disquotational premise seems acceptable given the relation of containment holding between the pertinent metalanguage and object language. The simplicity of the argument might make it seem somehow question-begging, but this appearance, I have argued, is misleading.

Let us conclude by considering a final worry about the argument. In order to have anti-skeptical force, the premises of the argument must be knowable in an a priori manner. I have given reasons which support the view that the disquotational premise passes this test. Now suppose that we accept the claims of the previous section and thus acknowledge that if semantic externalism is true, then ($), (Cond) and the semantic argument's conditional premise (I) are all true strict conditionals. This still would not establish that any of them expresses something knowable a priori, since the propositions in question might be among the *metaphysical necessities* which are not knowable a priori. It might be that semantic externalism requires for its justification some justified empirical beliefs concerning actual connections between the truth conditions of utterances and their causal environment. After all, we typically come to accept the idea that semantic facts depend upon the environment while armed with what we take to be knowledge concerning the causal connections linking our environment and the use of language in this environment. Thus justified acceptance of ($), (Cond) and premise (I) might depend upon justified acceptance of some empirical considerations. Thus it might be that none of these claims is knowable a priori, and the semantic argument would in that case be unavailable for anti-skeptical use.[24]

It could be replied that the a priori method of appeal to thought experiments supports the semantic externalist view that reference and truth conditions depend upon causal environment. We consider in thought various ranges of possible worlds in which language users are ensconced in various stipulated causal environments. Without appealing to problematic empirical considerations in order to support a claim to know which sort of world we are in fact in, we still come to appreciate in thought the dependence of semantic facts upon the environment in considering such worlds. Without appealing to problematic empirical considerations concerning what our own world is like, we still come to appreciate that in a treeless, vat world, the language users do not refer to trees and hence do not produce utterances having disquotational truth conditions.

Thus, a case can be made for the a prioricity of the semantic argument's premises. Maybe I *do* know, by means of this simple argument, that I am not a Putnamian brain in a vat.[25]

NOTES

1. See Brueckner 1986a and 1986b.

2. See, e.g., Dretske (in this volume) and of Nozick (in this volume) for this strategy. For a critical discussion, see Brueckner 1985.

3. For a recent discussion of this strategy, see Vogel 1990.

4. See Putnam (in this volume). My reconstruction of Putnam is given in Brueckner 1986a.

5. See especially Davidson 1986a and 1986b.

6. See Brueckner 1986b and 1991 for discussion of how to interpret Davidson on charity.

7. See Brueckner 1991 for discussion of this problem.

8. See, e.g., Davidson 1986b, p. 322.

9. See Brueckner 1986a.

10. Note that a parallel argument cannot be directed against skeptical counterpossibilities in which the alleged victim of deception has a sort of causal contact with ordinary objects which is sufficient for reference to them. For example, consider the counterpossibility in which I am kidnapped by evil neuroscientists after leading a normal life of thirty-odd years. Then I am envatted. In such a situation, my envatted uses of 'tree' would, on semantic externalism, at first apparently refer to trees (though the references of my terms might well shift if the envatment persisted for a long time). A counterpart to the reconstructed Putnamian argument *can* be deployed against the Cartesian evil genius possibility. In Descartes's scenario, there are no physical objects whatsoever. My utterances would have nonstandard truth conditions, since my uses of 'tree', for example, would refer to the states of the evil genius with which those uses are systematically correlated, not to trees.

11. Not only is this argument attractively simple, but, further, it does not involve a specification of the truth conditions of a BIV's utterances. According to the argument, these truth conditions whatever they are are non-disquotational. There is no commitment to the view that, e.g., the causal correlation between a BIV's uses of 'tree' and computer states is *sufficient* for reference to computer states. The argument is only committed to the view that since a BIV's causal environment lacks trees, cars, etc., his terms do not refer to these missing things. Thus, his utterances of sentences do not have disquotational truth conditions. Assuming that they *do* have truth conditions, these truth conditions are non-disquotational. In what follows, however, I will usually follow Putnam in assuming that a BIV's terms do refer to computer states. Brian Loar has pointed out that a BIV's utterances might lack truth conditions altogether. The utterances would thus not have non-disquotational truth conditions, as in my formulation. A more stripped down version of the argument could accordingly be formulated which would contain the premise

If I am a BIV, then my utterances do not have disquotational truth conditions.

12. Twin Earth arrived on the philosophical scene in Putnam 1975. See also Burge 1982, for a discussion of the ramifications of Twin Earth for the theory of content.

13. See Burge 1988.

14. See Burge 1988 and Heil 1988b.

15. Davidson 1988, p. 664.

16. For an elaboration of this criticism of Heil, see Brueckner 1990.

17. See Burge 1988.

18. I discuss this problem in Brueckner 1987 and 1993.

19. For a related criticism of Burge, see Boghossian 1989.

20. Whereas Burge focusses upon the relation of containment holding between a second-order thought and a first-order thought, the current remarks focus upon the relation of containment holding between the metalanguage in which (**) is stated and the object language to which the contained mentioned sentence belongs.

21. Strictly speaking, the semantic argument employs the more general conditional premise of which (Cond) is an instance.

22. Allan Gibbard suggested this example.

23. As noted in n. 11, the semantic argument is not committed to any particular specification of truth conditions for Skip's 'tree'-sentences. All that the argument says is that these truth conditions are non-disquotational. This means that the proponent of the argument only needs to maintain that whatever Skip's tokens of 'tree' refer to, they do *not* refer to things absent from his causal environment (such as trees). Further, as also noted in n. 11, a variant of the semantic argument could be constructed in which it is not assumed that Skip's tokens of 'tree' refer.

24. For a criticism of Burge according to which his externalist views commit him to the availability of *too much* a priori knowledge, see McKinsey 1991. For a reply, see Brueckner 1992b, in which I discuss the question of how much of externalist theory is knowable a priori.

25. Versions of this paper were read at the University of Michigan, UC Riverside, California State University at Northridge, UC Santa Barbara, and the 1993 Pacific Division APA. I benefitted from the discussions. I would also like to thank Tyler Burge, Gary Ebbs, John Heil, Brian Loar, Jonathan Wilwerding and Stephen Yablo for valuable comments on the paper. Special thanks go to Christopher Hill, who argued relentlessly to get me to see that the conclusion of this paper is correct.

CHAPTER 4

Realism and Skepticism: Brains in a Vat Revisited

Graeme Forbes

One way in which the distinction between realism and antirealism can be drawn is by characterizing antirealism as the view that a statement's being true *consists in* its being one that would be accepted as a result of an idealized process of rational inquiry into its truth value. This kind of antirealism has been extensively explored by Hilary Putnam,[1] who once called it "internal realism," though he came to regard the terminology as unfortunate. I call it antirealism because it collides head-on with a central tenet of any classically realist view, the tenet that, even if it is in fact the case that (*p* is true if and only if *p* would be confirmed by a process of ideally rational inquiry), such a truth condition can work only because of a contingent, perhaps even fortunate, dovetailing of our cognitive faculties with the external environment in which they are exercised; it has little to do with what is *constitutive* of truth.

Of course, if the proposed characterization of antirealism is to mark out a defensible version, we need to be able to explain "ideally rational inquiry" without surreptitiously trading on a realist notion of truth. Though I do not believe it, I shall grant that this can be done, since I want to discuss a difficulty that arises no matter how the antirealist story goes. The difficulty is that ideally rational inquirers must themselves be able to come to know, individually or as a community, that their inquiries have what it takes to be

"Realism and Skepticism: Brains in a Vat Revisited" from *Journal of Philosophy* 92 (1995, pp. 205–222) Reprinted by permission of the publisher.

For discussion of the topic of this paper and comments on various versions of it, I am grateful to Frank Döring, Jon Oberlander, François Recanati, Jerry Seligman, Timothy Williamson, and Crispin Wright, and especially to Bruce Brower, Keith DeRose, Richard Grandy, and Carolyn Morillo.

ideally rational. For if there is a condition C on inquiry satisfaction of which is necessary for it to be ideally rational, and C may obtain yet be undetectable by all ideally rational inquirers, then the obtaining of C is a condition whose holding does not consist in its verifiability by ideally rational inquirers. But it is a standard realist objection that the requirement that all such conditions C be detectable by ideally rational inquiry severs whatever link there may have seemed to be between truth and the outcome of ideally rational inquiry. For there is the following dilemma about the condition C of *not being a brain in a vat.* If not being a brain in a vat is *not* a condition of ideally rational inquiry, then there is no link between such inquiry and truth, since the ideally rational inquiries of brains in vats may produce nothing but falsehoods, if a systematic deception about their situation is being perpetrated upon them. On the other hand, if not being a brain in a vat *is* a condition on ideally rational inquiry, then since a normally embodied person cannot detect that he is not a brain in a vat,[2] there is a condition on ideally rational inquiry that can obtain without being detectable by ideally rational inquirers. So, again, the connection between truth and verifiability by ideally rational inquiry is broken.

One use to which Putnam's justly famous discussion of the predicament of brains in vats can be put is to rebut the entire dilemma just outlined, a use Putnam may have had in mind, since in the context of that discussion he is championing the antirealist connection between rational inquiry and truth. If Putnam is right, we can say that not being a brain in a vat *is* a condition on ideally rational inquiry, because contrary to the dilemma's first horn, brains in vats, at least brains of a certain kind, are not subject to massive error; and contrary to the dilemma's second horn, ideally rational, normally embodied inquirers *can* tell that they are not brains in vats of that kind; indeed, only a moderate amount of rationality is required to establish this. Putnam argues to the following effect. In order to possess the concepts *brain, in,* and *vat,* a thinker must somehow be informationally linked to brains, instances of the spatial relation of containment, and vats. However generous we should be about the sorts of links that suffice, it is plausible that a sentient creature that is *and always has been* a brain in a vat need not stand in such links. If it does not stand in them then it cannot employ thoughts with the concepts *brain, in,* and *vat* as constituents. So, if such a brain in a vat thinks the thought it would express to itself with 'I am not a brain in a vat', it is not thinking that it is not a brain in a vat. The closest it can come to that thought with the sentence 'I am not a brain in a vat', according to Putnam, is the thought that it is not a *brain-in-a-vat-in-the-image.* But a brain in a vat is a physical thing, not an image constituent. So the thought the brain thinks with 'I am not a brain in a vat' is true (and similarly for other thoughts, so there is not massive error). On the other hand, normally embodied thinkers such as ourselves will also think something a fortiori true with 'I am not a brain in a vat'. So both brains in vats and normally embodied thinkers are right when they think 'I am not a brain in a vat'. Hence (perhaps by constructive dilemma—see section I below) we may conclude that we are not brains in vats, with the a priori guarantee of the fore-going argument that our conclusion is true.[3] If we have followed Putnam's argument in a competent way, we *know* the conclusion is true. So we have established one of the conditions that have to be satisfied for our inquiries to be ideally rational, and refuted a realist attempt to drive a wedge between truth and the outcome of ideally rational inquiry.

It is fair to say that many philosophers have found Putnam's proof un-convincing, including, initially, Putnam himself (see this volume, p. 32). I agree that the argument underwhelms, but it may for all that be a proof that we are not brains in vats, or at least not brains in vats of Putnam's kind, brains which have been and always will be envatted and which exist in a universe that contains only them and their life-support machinery. Perhaps there are versions of the brains-in-a-vat hypothesis which Putnam's argu-ment leaves untouched (my brain was removed from my body last night and is now, for the first time ever, in a vat, with appropriate virtual reality hook-ups) but this is beside the point of the intuition that Putnam's proof is un-convincing *even on its own terms*. It is that intuition which I want to explore here.

I shall begin by considering a certain objection to Putnam's proof, and shall argue against the objection that there are considerations with which Putnam's argument can be supplemented, and in this supplemented form, it does indeed prove to us that we are not brains in vats (of Putnam's kind—I shall not make this qualification again). But I shall also argue that, because of the *way* in which the supplemented argument succeeds, it undercuts its own accomplishment. Hence, my overall conclusion is that despite its technical success, the argument's appearance of ineffectiveness does not deceive.

I. THE METALINGUISTIC READING OF THE PROOF

A first objection to Putnam's proof is that it seems to show only that we can know a priori that 'I am not a brain in a vat' is true.[4] This is particularly plau-sible if the argument works by constructive dilemma (CD). The CD schema is $p \lor q, p \rightarrow r, q \rightarrow r \vdash r$. If p is 'I am normally embodied' and q is 'I am a brain in a vat', then r cannot be 'I am not a brain in a vat', since there is nothing in Putnam's argument that directly warrants the conditional $q \rightarrow r$, 'If I am a brain in a vat then I am not a brain in a vat'. But we get true conditionals if we let r be something like 'the thought I express with "I am not a brain in a vat" is true'. That constructive dilemma is being used by Putnam for a met-alinguistic conclusion is strongly suggested by the fact that he explicitly states the relevant instance of $q \rightarrow r$ as the gist of his reasoning: "In short, if we are brains in a vat, then 'We are brains in a vat' is false". On the other hand, his preliminary description of what he is aiming at is different; he says that he seeks to show that the hypothesis that I am a brain in a vat is like the hypothesis that I do not exist in being *self-refuting*: "If we can consider whether it is true or false, then it is not true . . . Hence it is not true." We shall subsequently see (cf. footnote 9) that the difference between these two accounts of what the argument is supposed to be does not have much significance vis-à-vis its effectiveness. But the metalinguistic reading raises some interesting issues.

The plausibility of the claim that Putnam's argument only establishes something metalinguistic is well brought out by the apparatus of David Kaplan's[5] logic of demonstratives. In terms of this frame-work, Putnam is considering two kinds of context, one whose agent is a normally embodied person and the other whose agent is a brain in a vat (I shall take these to be jointly exhaustive of the possibilities). Relative to the first kind of context, the sentence type 'I am not a brain in a vat' is true, since the agent is normally embodied. Relative to the second kind, 'I am not a brain in a vat' is again true since its truth condition is that the envatted brain is not a brain-in-the-image. So by constructive dilemma, 'I am not a brain in a vat' is true relative to any context (it is *logically* true in Kaplan's system, and consequently a priori). But this is as far as we get. The antirealist needs to be able to show that the *proposition* is known a priori, but all that Putnam's proof yields is a priori knowledge that the sentence type is true, whatever the context.[6] So it does nothing to show that *our* contexts are the normally embodied sort, rather than the envatted sort.[7]

This account explains and supports one reaction Putnam's proof often produces, namely, the response that it cannot do what it claims, since a brain in a vat could recite the proof, or better, the *words* of the proof, to itself, and thereby come to know what anyone who follows the proof comes to know.[8] Hence, whatever that proposition is, it is not any proposition to the effect that the agent of the context is not a brain in a vat. From the Kaplanesque considerations, we have the plausible alternative candidate, the proposition that 'I am not a brain in a vat' is true. But, though we are here going beyond Putnam's explicit discussion, an antirealist can reasonably respond that there is no need to stop the argument at the insufficient metalinguistic conclusion: the agent of the context (of whatever kind) can make a further step to reach the desired conclusion that he is not a brain in a vat. 'I am not a brain in a vat' is no doubt ambiguous over and above its indexicality, meaning one thing relative to contexts with envatted brains as agents and another relative to contexts with normally embodied agents. But all Putnam needs is that ideally rational inquirers, who are *ex hypothesi* not brains in vats, can come to know that they are not brains in vats. Putnam's proof plus the further step provides them with this knowledge.

So what exactly is the further step? Standard cases in which a subject has metalinguistic knowledge but not ground-level knowledge are suggestive. Suppose that a monolingual Frenchman ignorant of the main results of set theory is reliably informed that the sentence 'The continuum hypothesis is independent of the standard axioms of set theory' expresses a truth in English. Then the Frenchman knows that it is true in English, but just on this basis, we would not say that he knows that the continuum hypothesis is independent of the standard axioms of set theory (even if he possesses these concepts). What is missing is understanding of the sentence of whose truth value he has been informed. But granted understanding of the sentence, we can reason about him as follows:

(a) He knows that 'The continuum hypothesis is independent of the standard axioms of set theory' expresses a truth in English.

(b) He understands the English sentence 'The continuum hypothesis is independent of the standard axioms of set theory' (by knowing its translation in French and understanding that French sentence).

(c) Therefore, if he makes some elementary inferences he will come to know that the continuum hypothesis is independent of the standard axioms of set theory.

In our own case, then, one way in which the agent of a context C could move from knowing that 'I am not a brain in a vat' is true relative to C to knowing that he is not a brain in a vat is by exercising his understanding of 'true' and of the sentence 'I am not a brain in a vat'.

The realist is likely to counter, however, that Putnam is not entitled to help himself to understanding of 'I am not a brain in a vat'. For the very semantic externalism on which Putnam's constructive dilemma depends—that his envatted brains lack information links to brains and vats of a kind that would suffice for acquisition of the concepts *brain* and *vat*—threatens to entail that understanding the sentence is a condition of ideally rational inquiry which may obtain undetectably, or indeed, not obtain at all. Understanding a sentence requires knowing the meanings of its words. So does not understanding 'I am a brain in a vat' require that I know that 'brain' is satisfied in my language by brains, as opposed to brains-in-the-image, and that 'vat' is satisfied in my language by vats, as opposed to vats-in-the-image? Does it not require *discriminating* knowledge? Yet knowing that I am employing predicates with these satisfaction conditions would appear to require that I first establish that I am not a brain in a vat. So we have gone in a rather small circle.[9]

Crispin Wright[10] has suggested a response which, if successful, would show that there need be no circle. His proposal is that the agent's understanding is guaranteed just by his knowledge of two facts:

(1) that his language disquotes;

(2) that in his language, 'I am not a brain in a vat' is a meaningful sentence.

From (1) and (2) the agent of the context can infer ' "I am not a brain in a vat" is true if and only if I am not a brain in a vat', and from his knowledge of this biconditional he can proceed from the conclusion of Putnam's proof, that 'I am not a brain in a vat' is true relative to his context, to the conclusion that is needed, namely, that he is not a brain in a vat. But I do not think that this will work. To know that my language disquotes amounts to no more than this: that I know that any instance of the schema

'...' is true in my language if and only if . . .

is true in my language if it is obtained by replacing both ellipses with one and the same meaningful sentence S. Thus, Wright's strategy would at best yield only knowledge that the biconditional

'I am not a brain in a vat' is true in my language if and only if I am not a brain in a vat.

is a true sentence of my language, which does not get us off the metalinguistic level.[11] There is also a question about how an agent of a context knows fact (2), that in his language 'I am not a brain in a vat' is a meaningful sentence. The predicate 'is meaningful' is implicitly existentially quantified, like 'is married': 'S is meaningful' means "there is a meaning that S expresses." How might an agent come to know this? If he uses existential introduction, then he has to know the premise of the inference, 'S expresses the meaning . . .', that is, a statement of the specific meaning of S, if the whole chain of inference is to be knowledge preserving. But it is knowledge of this specific meaning which Wright's argument is either trying to *conclude* that the agent has, or else is trying to avoid relying on in deriving the agent's knowledge that he is not a brain in a vat. For this reason, the agent's possession of it cannot be exploited en route to the conclusion, and hence knowledge of (2) cannot come from an ∃I inference. Knowledge of (2) must then be indirect: perhaps, like our monolingual Frenchman, the agent is merely reliably informed that 'I am not a brain in a vat' is meaningful. But if that is all we assume, then it is left open that the agent stands to the words 'brain' and 'vat' in his language as the monolingual Frenchman stood to English words like 'axiom' and 'set': he does not know what they mean. In such a case, we could not use those words to make a correct knowledge attribution to the agent.[12] It looks, then, as if the semantic externalism on which Putnam's proof depends constitutes a real obstacle to getting beyond the merely metalinguistic conclusion that is as much as we have so far managed to extract from it.

II. INDEXICALITY AND UNDERSTANDING

In situating Putnam's proof within Kaplan's framework, I make a small departure from Putnam's own exposition. For Putnam (and Wright), there are two languages in play, the language of the normally embodied agent and the language of the envatted brain; the word sequence 'I am not a brain in a vat' is meaningful in both languages, but means something different in each. From the viewpoint of Kaplan's logic, on the other hand, there is only a single language, in which words like 'brain' and 'vat' are indexicals: they have a character that generates one type of content for normally embodied contexts and another for envatted contexts.[13] This contrast between two languages, on the one hand, versus indexicals in a single language, on the other, is in principle inconsequential, but the 'one language with indexicals' version has the advantage of suggesting, via comparisons with ordinary indexicals, a mechanism that allows us to get beyond the merely metalinguistic conclusion.

The issue is how the agent of the context can understand his words if he does not have discriminating knowledge of their referents, that is, if he cannot tell that he is thinking about brains rather than brains-in-the-image, vats rather than vats-in-the-image, and so on. Wright's proposal was that discriminating knowledge is not required for understanding. My proposal is that the agent *does* have discriminating knowledge, in the only sense that is appropriate for understanding the indexicals 'brain' and 'vat'. Consider an analogous case involving the ordinary indexical 'here'. Suppose that E is an explorer who is lost in a featureless sand desert. After wandering aimlessly for a short while, E notices a viper at her feet and thinks to herself *There is danger here.* It is clear that E understands her own words, or grasps her own thought. After all, E will *act* upon that thought, by moving rapidly away from the snake. This is in contrast with the monolingual Frenchman, who cannot do anything that could plausibly be regarded as acting upon the content of a sentence that he does not understand, even if he knows its truth value. Similarly, E knows such propositions as she expresses with 'By "here" I am referring to here'. How is this possible if she is lost? It is possible because the notion of being lost involves an inability to identify one's location in one way, while thinking of one's location as *here* involves an ability to identify it in a different way. To think of a place as *here* is, in the most common use, to think of it egocentrically, as *the place where I am now located,* and even someone who is lost can think of her current location in this kind of way. This is possible because thinking of a specific place as *the place where I am now located* requires only a fairly minimal amount of self-awareness. By contrast, being lost is being unable approximately to situate one's location on a mental map of the general area where one is which includes familiar landmarks.[14]

The kind of discriminating knowledge that E's use of 'here' has is manifest in such a judgment as 'By "here" I am referring to here, not somewhere else qualitatively indistinguishable from here'. This is certainly something she knows. Her knowledge of the proposition she expresses with 'By "here" I am referring to here' is a priori—she does not have to investigate the world to confirm it. Additionally, the proposition is contingent: she *could* have been referring to somewhere else. On the other hand, if the co-ordinates of her location in a system M are $\langle a,b \rangle$, say, and $\langle a',b' \rangle$ are the M-co-ordinates of a place sensorily indistinguishable from $\langle a,b \rangle$, then of course she may not know that by 'here' she refers to $\langle a,b \rangle$ rather than $\langle a',b' \rangle$, and would certainly not know it a priori. But that is not germane to her grasp of *here*-thoughts, since propositions with map co-ordinates involve a different way of thinking of places and are therefore different propositions (they are different even on a Millian

view,[15] since according to that view, I presume, 'here' would be directly referential while '⟨a,b⟩' would not be).

Failure to distinguish between thinking of one's current location egocentrically and thinking of it in other ways encourages fallacious objections
to hypotheses about when a sentence is understood or a thought grasped.
For example, it has been held that *relevant alternative* considerations threaten
such claims as that E knows the proposition she expresses with 'By "here" I
am referring to here'.[16] Suppose that ⟨a′,b′⟩ is close by, so that, given the aim-
lessness of her wandering, E might easily have been at ⟨a′,b′⟩, recoiling from
the visually indistinguishable viper located there, instead of at ⟨a,b⟩. If ⟨a′,b′⟩
had been her location, she would still have believed the proposition she
would express with 'By "here" I am referring to here', though the place
would have been different. But to *know* the proposition she expresses with
'By "here" I am referring to here', does she not, adapting an objection of Paul
Boghossian,[17] have to "be able to exclude the possibility that [she is thinking
about ⟨a′,b′⟩ rather than ⟨a,b⟩]"?

Not at all. For in order to construct a relevant alternative counterexample to knowledge claims in this context, an objector would have to use
propositions involving M-co-ordinates, or something similar, not propositions involving the egocentric *here*. A standard relevant alternative case
demonstrates that actually a proposition *p* is not known by a subject B, by
pointing out that given the way things actually are, B might easily have acquired instead a counterpart belief *p′* which is *false. p′* may be the very same
proposition as *p*, but where demonstratives and indexicals are involved, it is
likely, by the criteria of semantic externalism, to be a different thought, expressed in the same words. For example, in Alvin Goldman's basic case,
where the subject correctly thinks 'That's a barn' in a region with many false
barns, the incorrect thought 'That's a barn' which he has in a "close" possible
situation where his eye alights instead on one of the false barns, is a different
thought from his actual one, because it involves a different object. But the
case is still taken to show that the subject's actual belief 'That's a barn' is not
knowledge.

Relevant alternative examples rely on the fact that when it is a matter of
accident or good fortune that a *true* belief is acquired, the belief is not knowledge. They show that it *is* an accident that a true belief is acquired by describing a "close" world where a false belief is acquired instead. But returning now to E, that is exactly what *cannot* be done when the believed
proposition involves the *here*-type way of thinking of one's location. In particular, though there are close worlds where E is at ⟨a′,b′⟩ instead of ⟨a,b⟩, the
egocentric belief she has in those worlds, expressed in 'By "here" I am referring to here', is still true. There is therefore no proof that her actual belief is
not knowledge.[18] Things are different if we use propositions involving M-co-
ordinates, of course. If E believes 'By "here" I am referring to ⟨a,b⟩' with good
justification based on how things look to her, then since she could easily
have been at ⟨a′,b′⟩ instead but would still have believed that she was at ⟨a,b⟩,
and so would have had a false belief, her actual belief is not knowledge. But

location beliefs that involve a nonegocentric way of thinking of current location are simply not to the point.[19]

It may be objected that this only shows that one way of challenging the knowledge claim fails. Perhaps there are other ways. For example, certain extreme forms of epistemological externalism aside, accounts of knowledge typically require that one who knows that p has some sort of justification for her belief that p. A proposition like

(H) In using 'here', I am thinking of here.

is relational, and it is hard to see how E could know that a relation holds between certain things if she does not know, concerning a particular position in the relation, whether it is occupied by this object or that one, $\langle a,b \rangle$ or $\langle a',b' \rangle$. It does not seem that reflection on the particular way of thinking that is activated when 'here' is used could justify the belief, for, again in an objection of Boghossian's, "you cannot tell by mere inspection of an object that it has a given *relational* or *extrinsic* property". But I doubt that this objection is effective either. If we think of justifying (H) on the model of justifying a judgment about who the subject of a certain photograph is, then mere reflection on the way of thinking is no more helpful by itself than mere inspection of the photograph by itself (without the appropriate recognitional capacity). But in thinking (H), the second 'here' is *used* to identify a place egocentrically, and the thinker thereby knows that that place is the occupant of the relevant role in the relational fact (H) reports. Analogously, someone who is engaged in the act of photographing knows whom he is photographing, since he demonstratively identifies the subject as he looks through the viewfinder.[20]

It seems, then, that the various beliefs that embody E's grasp or understanding of the proposition she expresses with 'There is danger here' cannot be denied the status of knowledge because of relevant alternative considerations or because of a problem about their justification. Nor are they arrived at via false lemmas. Propositions like (H) are therefore things that E knows. But it is straightforward to carry these points about a case involving an ordinary indexical over to the case where the indexicals are 'brain', 'vat', and so on. In the latter case, there are two contexts to be compared, one whose agent is normally embodied and one whose agent is a Putnam-style brain in a vat. We can suppose, if we like, that the second context is counterfactual and the two contexts have the same agent. We saw that a proposition like 'By "here" I mean here, not somewhere else' is an a priori truth which E grasps even in her situation. The corresponding proposition that a normally embodied agent grasps and knows a priori is expressed by a sentence of the following sort: ' "Brain" is satisfied by brains, not brains-in-the-image'. That the proposition is grasped, or that the word 'brain' is understood by such an agent, is simply a consequence of that agent's having appropriate information links to brains, just as the content of 'here' is grasped by E in her context on account of her epistemic links to $\langle a,b \rangle$. To think in the relevant way of a location as *here* is to think of it as *the place where I am now located*, something E can do even though she is lost. Suppose that we can think of something as a brain if we think of it as an organ of the same type as *this,* where the demonstrative refers to a brain that has itself been presented to us, or represented to us in some way (this is not meant to rule out alternative ways of thinking of brains). Then the mere possibility that one is a brain in a vat does not prevent one from *actually* thinking of brains in this way. In so thinking of them, one is justified in believing that one does. Even if the possibility that I am a brain in a vat is somehow "close," I still think something true with ' "Brain" is satisfied by brains' in that possibility (see again note 18). On these grounds, given similar conclusions about 'vat', there seems to be no obstacle to my understanding 'I am not a brain in a vat', and hence my knowing that if 'I am not a brain in a vat' is true in my language relative to my context, then I am not a brain in a vat. Here I use one half of the T-sentence for 'I am not a brain in a vat', but it is the indexicality model, not disquotation, which explains my entitlement to it.[21]

III. "MANKIND AND ITS PLACE IN NATURE"

The announced goal of this paper was to explain why Putnam's "argument we can give which shows that we are not brains in a vat" seems ineffective. In the previous section, I have argued that, if the proof is supplemented with other considerations, then it is a correct proof that I am not a brain in a vat. But I do not expect my account of the proof to make it seem any more effective to the reader. There is a persistent unpersuasiveness which afflicts the general strategy, whose source we have still to identify.

Perhaps it strikes one, on first encounter, that the argument only succeeds by exploiting some kind of trick with words. It seems as if Putnam has used semantic externalism merely to deprive the realist of the means of formulating a certain epistemic possibility *in ordinary terms.* This move is of little significance if the only burden it puts on the realist is to reformulate his objection using another way of expressing the underlying point, a way which remains unaffected by Putnam's linguistic gimmickry. But it is a striking difference between the spatial case and the brains-in-vats case that only in the spatial case are other means of expression available. In the spatial case, there is a nonegocentric way of thinking of the external environment and consequently of the spatial differences between contexts, namely, by the use of map co-ordinates. Using expressions for ways of thinking of places afforded by such co-ordinates, we can formulate sentences whose truth values change across contexts in virtue of the spatial differences between the contexts, and which can easily be used to express skeptical epistemic possibilities; for example, the sentence 'I am at $\langle a',b'\rangle$'. By contrast, if we accept Putnam's argument from semantic externalism, there is no similar way of conceptualizing the difference between a context with a normally embodied agent and a context with an envatted agent, because any way of thinking of this difference is formulated from within the agent's total cognitive context, consisting in all the information links in which the agent stands to elements of his environment and the identities of those elements. Perhaps there is some minimal language with logical constants and vocabulary for qualitative features which a normally embodied agent and an envatted brain can share, but so far as I can see, we could not use this language to formulate mistaken beliefs analogous to mistakes about one's position on a map and corresponding skeptical hypotheses which presuppose realism.

None of this is inconsistent with the ability of the normally embodied agent to conceive of the *metaphysical* possibility that he is a brain in a vat, using just those concepts, even though they are anchored by his cognitive perspective, an ability no more puzzling than a spatially located agent's ability to understand the *metaphysical* possibility of being elsewhere, rather than here. But 'I am a brain in a vat' no more expresses an *epistemic* possibility for me than does 'I am elsewhere, not here'. So the trouble with the proposed criticism of Putnam's proof, that it simply obliges the realist to reformulate his examples in a perhaps unusual way, is that the constraints of cognitive perspective, unlike those of spatial perspective, seem inescapable: How could our concepts *not* be determined by the information links in which we stand in our environment to the particular objects that populate it? Even if we *can* make sense to ourselves of the possibility of a way of thinking of things in the world which is not an expression of the perspective of any particular cognitive context, the antirealist need not be concerned with the epistemological problems that might afflict users of such a scheme. His claim is only that truth for propositions of the sort that we actually employ consists in their being confirmable as the outcome of an idealized process of rational inquiry, and it would be a significant concession for the realist to allow this much.

The persistent unpersuasiveness of Putnam's proof, then, is not traceable to its depending on a merely verbal manoeuver. To end on a note of agreement with Wright, I think that it may instead be traced to a feature of the *contrast* between the situation of an envatted brain and that of a normally embodied agent, a contrast that is consistent with the normally embodied agent knowing that he is not a brain in a vat. In trying to drive a wedge between truth and verifiability by ideal inquiry, it is not necessary that it be shown to be epistemically possible that we unavoidably acquire false beliefs. For the realist's purposes, it is sufficient to establish the weaker thesis that it is epistemically possible that we are in principle *precluded* from acquiring certain *true* beliefs. To argue for this, the realist can abstract from the contrast between brains in vats and normally embodied agents to arrive at something more general. The brains in Putnam's scenario *are* precluded from knowing certain truths, for instance, that they are envatted brains. They do not even have the concepts with which to formulate this proposition, much less verify it, since in their cognitive context they cannot acquire those concepts, lacking the appropriate information links, and, as we have seen, there are no perspective-independent concepts available when "context" is understood so broadly. So the comparison between a pair of agents consisting in an envatted brain and a normally embodied person is the comparison between (A) a context in which certain truths are unknowable, even for a thinker as rational as possible in the circumstances of that context, and (B) an epistemically favored context in which ways of thinking about the cognitively deficient kind of context are available, and using which its deficiencies can be precisely delineated.

One intelligible instance of this contrast is enough to establish the intelligibility of the contrast. In the instance under discussion, *we* have the good fortune to occupy the epistemically favored type of context. But we cannot avoid raising the question for ourselves whether there may not be other instances of the same contrast differing precisely from the given one by having *us* occupy the cognitively deficient type of context, one whose agents are precluded in principle from knowing certain truths. Of course, it is no use asking what a context that is epistemically favored relative to ours would be like, or what kind of truth we might be precluded from knowing, or what feature of our circumstances might give rise to these hypothetical epistemic barriers. Such questions are as unanswerable for us as their counterparts are for the envatted brain, which cannot conceive of the cognitive context of a normally embodied agent or describe the world in terms which trace the boundaries of its own limited acquaintance with what there is. A metaphysical possibility exists, the specifics of which are beyond the envatted brain's grasp. So why should there not be such a possibility the specifics of which are beyond *our* grasp?[22]

If this question is as effective as any raised by the traditional sceptic and is not addressed by Putnam's proof, where does it leave the antirealist's dilemma about the condition of not being a brain in a vat? As should now be evident, one horn of the dilemma cannot be grasped by the antirealist: if ideally rational inquirers *can* be Putnam-style brains in a vat, then even though their beliefs are not generally false, and so may aspire to the status of knowledge, there are truths they will never know, which means that truth outstrips the reach of ideally rational inquiry. Grant, then, that just for this reason, ideally rational inquirers cannot be brains in vats. In section II of this paper, I in effect defended the proposition that this condition, if it obtains, is not one that does so undetectably by ideally rational inquirers, since a normally embodied agent can come to know that he is not a brain in a vat by Putnam's proof. But the other horn of the original dilemma is not thereby grasped, since to preserve the equation of truth and the outcome of ideally rational inquiry, we must evidently require that ideally rational inquirers not be in any situation that is relevantly *similar* to that of brains in vats. While Putnam's proof allows an ideally rational inquirer to establish that he is not a brain in a vat, it seems clear that there is no proof of the generalization that he is not in a context that is from some other inconceivable perspective as limited as the situation of brains in a vat can be seen to be from our perspective. That is, there is no proof that, in a nice phrase of Wright's, we do not occupy circumstances whose obtaining "would make a mockery of mankind and its place in nature". So the generalization of the condition of not being a brain in a vat is one which may obtain undetectably, and again we find that truth and verifiability by ideally rational inquiry come apart.[23]

This is an unhappy outcome for anyone holding the combination of views Putnam advanced in 1981. It may still be wondered, however, if I have told the whole story about the appearance of ineffectiveness of Putnam's proof. Did this appearance concern only the *realist's* use of brains in a vat to distinguish truth from the conclusions of ideally rational enquiry? Or did it also apply to the *skeptic's* use of (Putnam-style) brains in a vat against ordinary-knowledge claims about the external world? For all I have said so far, Putnam's proof refutes the skeptic, if not the realist, and this suggests that there is more to be said.

Suppose it is epistemically possible that there is a perspective upon our own circumstances from which our access to what is real can be seen to be as truncated as a brain in a vat's can be seen to be from our perspective. Does it follow from this supposition that we do not really know anything about the external world? Put in those terms, it does not follow, at least if our concept *the external world* has as its content that domain which is broadly accessible to us. There is still a distinction between knowledge and mere opinion to be drawn, even for brains in a vat, and so for us as well, regardless of the true nature of our circumstances. Indeed, the classical skeptic is wrong on two counts, by Putnam's reasoning: (a) it is not true that for all we can tell, we are (Putnam-style) brains in vats; and (b) it is not true that, if we were brains in vats, we would continue to believe what we actually believe and would therefore have massively false belief systems. A classical skeptic, however, can still get mileage out of the thought that we are perhaps relevantly *like* brains in vats. Plato's problem of distinguishing knowledge from mere opinion derives its significance and centrality in the history of philosophy from the value we place on knowledge, and ultimately from the value we place on *understanding,* for which knowledge is a prerequisite. But these concepts are emptied of significance if we are in fact relevantly like brains in vats: just as Putnam's brains in vats have no real understanding of the universe in which they exist, neither do we, if we are relevantly like them. While our inability to rule out the hypothesis that we are relevantly like them does not threaten to show that we have no knowledge, it does threaten to show that we have no assurance that knowledge is worth having: it grants us the capacity to acquire it but destroys its value. This is a cost of Putnam's strategy that dissipates the value of its outcome.

NOTES

1. Putnam 1981 [partially reprinted in this volume] and 1992.

2. I ask the reader to allow this for the sake of the argument. The claim has considerable force, as is evident from the durability of the problem of skepticism in the history of philosophy.

3. Putnam writes: "if . . . we are really . . . brains in a vat, then what we now mean by 'we are brains in a vat' is that *we are brains in a vat in the image* or something of that kind (*if we mean anything at all)*" (Putnam, in this volume, p. 37; emphasis in parentheses added). I have been unable, however, to discover a version of the argument which will work (provide us with knowledge that we are not brains in a vat) on the assumption that

brains in a vat are subject to a mere illusion of meaning. It is a nice question for an anti-private-language theorist whether a brain in a vat's cognitive development suffices to impart semantic content to the words that run through its head.

4. See Brueckner 1986a.

5. Kaplan 1989. I shall assume familiarity with Kaplan's terminology. For Kaplan, the entities that define a context C are themselves constituents of the propositions that sentences with demonstratives and indexicals express relative to C. I prefer something more Fregean, in which the indexicals and the elements of the context together fix *de re* senses as the propositional constituents. See Peacocke 1983, ch. 5, for one way of implementing this.

6. As many readers have noted (see, for example, Brueckner 1986a), Putnam seems insensitive to the distinction between knowing that I am a brain in a vat and knowing that 'I am not a brain in a vat' is true. After stating that "if we are brains in a vat, then 'We are brains in a vat' is false," Putnam continues: "So it is necessarily false," and then goes on to deny on these grounds "that we might really, actually, possibly *be* brains in a vat" (in this volume, pp. 37–38). Prima facie the reasoning exhibits the same fallacy as in moving from 'I am elsewhere now' being false in every context to the impossibility of my really, actually, possibly being elsewhere now.

7. One problem for the view that truth consists in verifiability by ideally rational inquirers is that ideally rational inquirers would surely verify the proposition that there are ideally rational inquirers. Hence the proposition that there are ideally rational inquirers is true—indeed, a priori true—according to this account of truth. For other kinds of criticism of this version of antirealism, see ch. 2.II and 2.III of Wright 1992 and Johnston 1993, pp. 87–97.

8. See Heil 1988a, p. 166.

9. This kind of criticism is developed by Brueckner 1990. It applies equally to the "self-refuting hypothesis" reading of Putnam's proof, since I can only come to know that I am not a brain in a vat by modus ponens from the known premise, 'If I am entertaining the hypothesis that I am a brain in a vat then I am not a brain in a vat,' if I also know the antecedent 'I am entertaining the hypothesis that I am a brain in a vat.' If Brueckner's objection is effective at all, it would show that to know this I must first establish that I am not a brain in a vat. It is because both readings of Putnam's argument must dispel this aura of circularity (and because they can both dispel it in the same way) that I said there was no significant difference between them.

10. Wright 1992b, p. 94.

11. Here I am in agreement with Brueckner 1986a, p. 165. But Brueckner also argues (p. 164) against the use of such biconditionals, that because I do not know them to be true for some other person if I do not know whether or not that person is a brain in a vat, I do not know them for my own case. This seems wrong, for my own case is special: in it, I have a guarantee that object language and metalanguage coincide.

12. Wright 1992b considers the case of the name 'the Scarlet Pimpernel' and remarks that we say that "a thinker knows that 'the Scarlet Pimpernel' denotes the Scarlet Pimpernel . . . [even if the thinker . . . has no identifying knowledge of the Scarlet Pimpernel does not know who the Scarlet Pimpernel is" (p. 75). Perhaps this is what we would say in the ordinary case, where the thinker does not know whether the Scarlet Pimpernel is this or that person (though we would not want the existence of the Scarlet Pimpernel to follow from the disquotational premise alone). But it is much less clear that we would say the thinker knows that 'the Scarlet Pimpernel' denotes the Scarlet Pimpernel in the more relevant case where he does not know whether the name denotes a person, a constellation in the sky at night, or a mental image that is not necessarily *of* anything at all.

13. For a thoroughgoing extension of the notion of indexicality to natural-kind terms, see Almog 1981, which generalizes Putnam 1975. The possibility of an indexical reading of the argument is noted by Brueckner 1986a, p. 153, n. 10.

14. Though I diverge in places from his account, the influence of Evans 1982, pp. 151–70, is clear.

15. For Millianism, see Salmon 1986.

16. For "relevant alternative," see Goldman 1976.

17. Boghossian 1989, p. 14.

18. Keith DeRose suggested to me as an analogy to illustrate the point a case in which the subject is in a region filled with real but mobile barns which are switched around randomly at night. The subject's belief 'That's a barn' is knowledge because even in close possible situations where the externalist content of his belief is different because he is looking at a different barn, his belief is still true.

19. In addition to Boghossian 1989, this point holds against Brueckner's argument in Brueckner 1990: "I do *not* know that I am not thinking that some *twater* is dripping, since, according to externalism, if I were not Twin Earth thinking that some twater is dripping, things would seem exactly as they now seem . . . So I do not know that I am thinking that some water is dripping" (p. 448). But regardless of which alternative is the case, the thought I express with 'I am thinking that some water is dripping' is true. The point also holds against Stalnaker 1990: "nothing internal to Bert distinguishes . . . [Earth and Twin Earth] . . . so he doesn't know which one he is in. But then doesn't it follow that he doesn't know what the content of his belief is" (p. 144)? Stalnaker holds that it does not follow, but appeals to irrelevant relevant alternative considerations to explain why not.

20. For more on this issue, see McDowell 1992.

21. While this paper was being refereed, I read Falvey and Owens 1994. They argue, first, that semantic externalism does not engender skepticism about whether we understand our own words and thoughts, and, second, that semantic externalism cannot be uses as Putnam wants to use it to establish that we are not brains in vats. I agree with much that they say about why externalism does not engender skepticism. Though they establish the ineffectiveness of certain arguments that it does, however, they do not explain the mechanism that makes it possible to have special first-person access to externalist content. I think the indexicality model I have presented fills this lacuna. But the model also suggests that Falvey and Owen's subsequent argument against Putnam is unsuccessful. For example, they say that Putnam argues for 'If I am a BIV (and English is vat-English) then it is not the case that my utterances of "I am a BIV" are true iff I am a BIV', and then assert that this "borders on incoherence. How can it possibly be true if the truth conditions are being offered in a metalanguage that contains the object language . . ." Falvey and Owens, p. 132)? But even if the quoted conditional (their words, not Putnam's) is not well put, the intention that would be behind it is quite coherent. The antecedent of the conditional introduces a certain kind of context, one whose agent is a brain in a vat, and the (correct) thought underlying the consequent is that an utterance of 'I am a BIV' *in* such a context *by* its agent does not have the same truth value as a proposition, concerning the agent of the context, that it is a brain in a vat (that is, if Putnam *had* asserted this conditional, that is what he would have meant by it). Note that this defense of the conditional can also be given by a brain in a vat. On the construal of 'brain' as an indexical, metalanguage and object language still coincide here.

22. Wright puts the moral of his discussion of Putnam's proof this way: "the real spectre to be exorcised is the idea of a thought *standing behind* our thought that we are not brains-in-a-vat in just the way that our thought that they *are* mere brain-in-a-vat would stand behind the thought . . . of actual brains-in-a-vat that 'We are not brains-in-a-vat' " (Wright 1992b, p. 93).

23. Richard Grandy pointed out to me that, if certain psychological predicates are univocal between ordinarily embodied thinkers and brains in vats, then not merely are there truths the brains cannot express and so will never know, but there are falsehoods that they can express, would likely come to believe, and would never be able to detect their error for instance, "other people have feelings like me," in which 'other people' applies to image components.

CHAPTER 5

A Priori Knowledge of the World: Knowing the World by Knowing Our Minds

Ted A. Warfield

I believe, however, that there is no easy argument against skepticism from anti-individualism and authoritative self-knowledge.

(Burge 1988, p. 655)

I can achieve the anti-sceptical result DesCartes needed God to vouchsafe by exploiting considerations about what determines content. Ah the wonders of analytical philosophy!

It is an optimistic man who believes that Cartesian scepticism may be refuted in this way.

(McGinn 1989, p. 113)

I am an optimistic man. In this paper I will present and defend a case for optimism about semantic antiskeptical arguments. I will argue that my a priori knowledge of what I am thinking can be combined with my a priori knowledge of conditions necessary for my thinking what I am thinking to yield a type of a priori knowledge of my environment. This knowledge of my environment will allow me to rule out at least some skeptical hypotheses. In addition to presenting and defending this antiskeptical argument, I will dis-

I have learned much about skepticism and antiskepticism from conversations with Bruce Boyden, Keith DeRose, Chris Hill, Peter Klein, Barry Loewer, and Brian McLaughlin.

cuss several further issues. In the course of presenting and defending my argument, I will compare and contrast it with Hilary Putnam's most recent presentation of his famous antiskeptical argument.[1] After defending my argument, I will explain the difference between my argument and what I take to be the common understanding of the antiskepticism of G. E. Moore. After doing this, I will comment on the question of just what sorts of skepticism are and are not threatened by semantic antiskeptical arguments.

I think that I have lots of perceptual knowledge. For example, I claim to know that I am currently drinking water in part on the basis of my overall perceptual experience. One frequently discussed kind of skepticism denies that I know that I am currently drinking water and denies that anyone has any perceptual knowledge at all. I lack perceptual knowledge because, according to the skeptic, for all I know I am a brain in a vat in an otherwise "empty" world, where an otherwise empty world is a world containing only the brain in the vat and whatever is necessary to sustain the brain in the vat. And, the skeptic continues, because I know that the claim that I am a brain in a vat in an otherwise empty world implies the denial of the claim that I am currently drinking water, the fact that for all I know I am a brain in a vat in an otherwise empty world guarantees that I do not know that I am currently drinking water. Schematically, the argument (which I will call the Skeptical Argument) looks like this:

The Skeptical Argument

P1. I do not know that I am not a brain in a vat in an otherwise empty world.

P2. If I do not know that I am not a brain in a vat in an otherwise empty world then I do not know that I am currently drinking water.

C1. So, I do not know that I am currently drinking water.

This argument is valid and its premises seem at least initially plausible. One wishing to deny the soundness of this argument must, of course, deny the conjunction of its premises. One prominent strategy for responding to this argument objects to its second premise by challenging the epistemic closure principle which seems to support the premise. I know that the proposition that I am currently drinking water implies that I am not a brain in a vat in an otherwise empty world, so the second premise of the skeptical argument is well supported if (and for the *general* skeptical argument of which the above skeptical argument is an instance to be sound *only if*) it's true that where I know that p implies q, my not knowing that $\sim q$ implies that I don't know that $\sim p$. But many antiskeptical philosophers have argued that this closure principle is false and have therefore argued that the Skeptical Argument faces a serious difficulty.[2]

A second family of antiskeptical responses denies the first premise of the Skeptical Argument. Antiskeptical philosophers of this type claim, for a wide variety of reasons, that it is not true that I do not know that I am not a brain in a vat in an otherwise empty world. I am a member of this family.

The skeptic has claimed that my ordinary perceptual knowledge claims are false because for all I know I am a brain in a vat in an otherwise empty world. I disagree. I think that there is an a priori (in a sense to be explained) argument available to me that allows me to show that I am not such a brain in a vat. And further, the a priori nature of this antiskeptical argument allows me to evade the charge of "begging the question," which skeptical philosophers like to employ against their opponents. I will return to this charge of begging the question after presenting and defending my argument against the skeptic. First, let's look at the antiskeptical argument that I think allows me to know that I am not a brain in a vat in an otherwise empty world.

I think that I can infer that I am not a brain in a vat in an otherwise empty world from the conjunction of my (a priori) knowledge that I think that water is wet with my (a priori) knowledge that (it is necessarily true that) no brain in a vat in an otherwise empty world can think about water. Schematically, and suppressing for the moment the knowledge claims that would attach to each premise when arguing against the skeptic, my Antiskeptical Argument looks like this:

The Antiskeptical Argument

P1. I think that water is wet.

P2. No brain in a vat in an otherwise empty world can think that water is wet.

C1. So, I am not a brain in a vat in an otherwise empty world.

This argument is formally valid. I will now defend its premises and defend my claim to know the conclusion of the argument as a consequence of my knowledge of its premises. Furthermore, I will defend my claim that my knowledge of each premise is, in one important sense, a priori and that as a consequence my Antiskeptical Argument does not beg the question against the proponent of the Skeptical Argument.

I will begin with some discussion of premise 2 of the Antiskeptical Argument. I maintain that premise 2 is a necessary truth supported in large part by the familiar externalist thought experiments of Hilary Putnam, Tyler Burge and others.[3] The thought experiments are familiar and I will not repeat them here. The primary intuition being exploited in defense of premise 2 of the Antiskeptical Argument is the intuition that a brain in a vat "alone" in its otherwise empty world cannot think about something that it has had no causal contact with. Because there is no water in its world and because there aren't any other things in its world which would allow it to do so, a brain in a vat in an otherwise empty world cannot think that water is wet.

I am not, to be perfectly clear, claiming (or denying, though this would be my inclination) that one can think about Xs only if one has had causal contact with instances of X. Many philosophers would accept this strong claim. Putnam for example, in his most recent comments on his brain in a vat argument, seems to accept something like this strong claim when he says that one premise of his anti-skeptical argument is that reference to common objects like vats, and their physical properties (and also to the theoretical objects and properties of science, e.g., electrons, charge) is only possible if one has information carrying causal interactions with those objects and properties, or objects and properties in terms of which they can be described.

(Putnam 1992, p. 369)

Though I am not sure that I know exactly what Putnam is claiming in this passage, I am pretty sure that he is endorsing something quite similar to the strong claim I have identified above. If I understand Putnam's claim correctly, the claim is stronger than what is needed for my preferred version of semantic antiskepticism. Putnam's claim implies, but is not implied by, the corresponding premise (premise 2) of my argument.[4]

The apparent fact that we can think about unicorns and phlogiston, to give just two examples, raises at least prima facie difficulty for Putnam's claim in the quoted passage. Though perhaps there are ways to avoid this prima facie difficulty, we can at least apparently think about both of these things without causal contact with either. Let's briefly consider how this might be done, sticking with the example of water. Perhaps one can think about water in a world in which one has had no causal contact with water (and perhaps even in a world without water at all). There are at least two ways that this might happen. First, perhaps one can, armed with a respectable knowledge of theoretical chemistry, think about water in a world containing hydrogen and oxygen, but no water. And perhaps one can, via a complex chain of sociolinguistic deference to others in one's language community, think about water without personally having had causal contact with water.[5]

Even if one could, in both of these ways, think about water without having had causal contact with water, a brain in a vat in an otherwise empty world could not. A brain in a vat in an otherwise empty world has no causal contact with water. Furthermore, a brain in a vat in an otherwise empty world is in a world without hydrogen and oxygen and so cannot "theoretically construct" thoughts about water.[6] And, of course, the poor isolated brain in a vat has no language community to which it can defer for the simple reason that there is no such language community. The brain in a vat is alone. How then could the brain in a vat in an otherwise empty world think about water? I maintain that it could not.

Just as I did not claim that one can think about water only if one has had causal contact with water, I do not claim that "water" (the mental representation) in the mind of the brain in a vat refers to computer states or to phenomenal images or to anything at all. I remain neutral on this issue. Some antiskeptical philosophers have argued that I am not a brain in a vat because my "water" thoughts refer to water, while the "water" thoughts of a brain in a vat refer to, for example, the computer states that typically cause tokenings of "water" in the brain in the vat.[7] But I do not argue this way. I am not willing to argue that "water" in my language refers to water, while "water" in the language of a brain in a vat does not because, in the antiskeptical context, this would require me to offer a priori reasons for thinking that my "water" thoughts are referential, and I think the skeptic could plausibly insist that for all I know *a priori*, my "water" thoughts are like my "unicorn" thoughts (involving no reference at all).

Perhaps this objection can be overcome by philosophers who wish to argue in this way, but perhaps not. In any event, I am not arguing this way. I do not claim that the "water" thoughts of a brain in a vat are about computer states (or anything else). I claim only that they are not about water. And I claim this because no brain in a vat in an otherwise empty world can think about water. It follows that such a brain in a vat cannot think that water is wet. This is all that I claim in the second premise of my Antiskeptical Argument.

In arguing against the skeptic, however, I need to do more than just argue that premise 2 of my Antiskeptical Argument is true. I also need to *know* that premise 2 is true and, in order to not beg the question against the skeptic challenging my claims to ordinary perceptual knowledge, I need for my knowledge of the premises of my Antiskeptical Argument to be a priori at least in the fairly weak sense of nonperceptual. I do claim to know that premise 2 is true and I claim to know this on the basis of my "armchair" a priori reflections on the standard a priori externalist thought experiments. Were I pressed to do so I would be willing to claim that my knowledge of premise 2 is a fairly strong sort of a priori knowledge of a necessary truth. But for the purposes of my Antiskeptical Argument I need only for my knowledge of premise 2 to be knowledge that is independent of a perceptual investigation of my environment and this is what I claim it is. Because the thought experiments do provide overwhelming support for externalism I know that premise 2 is true.[8] And, as I will discuss in more detail later, because this knowledge is nonperceptual, my appeal to it does not beg the question against the proponent of the Skeptical Argument.

I know, without investigating my environment, that a brain in a vat in an otherwise empty world cannot think that water is wet. But, turning now to premise one of my Antiskeptical Argument, I know, without investigating my environment, that I do think that water is wet. I will now defend this premise of my Antiskeptical Argument.

I know the contents of at least a great many of my thoughts. It is very easy for me to know what I am thinking. For example: I have just introspectively "asked myself" what I think about water and my introspective faculty has "answered" by "telling me" that I think that water is wet.[9] I could of course be lying in reporting the content of this thought to you. Perhaps when I introspected I found myself thinking not that water is wet but that water is clear. Whatever the deliverance of my introspective faculty on this occasion and whatever your view of my honesty in reporting its deliverance, I think that we can agree that I am at least typically in a great position to truthfully report, and in fact *know*, the deliverances of my introspective faculty. We typically accept that one knows the contents of one's thoughts.

This is, it is important to note, a claim that even a skeptic who claims that I have no perceptual knowledge should be willing to grant and typically will grant. Most skeptics will grant my claim that I *think* that water is wet. The skeptic will protest only when I go on to make the further natural claim that I do not merely *think* that water is wet, I also *know* that water is wet. It is not at all hard to picture the skeptic responding to my claim to know that water is wet by remarking "well, you *think* that water is wet but your grounds for claiming to *know* that water is wet are defective" and then going on to articulate the standard skeptical challenge to such knowledge. Notice that this natural sort of skeptical reply would involve granting claims like premise 1 of my Antiskeptical Argument. Almost no philosopher would challenge my claim to know that I think that water is wet. We will look at one challenge to this sort of self-knowledge very soon. Before doing this, however, it is important to once again distinguish my premise (my claim to know that I am thinking that water is wet) from the corresponding premise of Hilary Putnam's antiskeptical argument.

To return to Putnam's most recent discussion of his famous brain-in-a-vat argument, Putnam says that, in addition to the premise about causal contact discussed above, the other premise of his argument is

> the disquotation scheme for reference (this assumes that the metalanguage contains the object language, which it does when the languages in question are my own):
>
> (D) "P" refers to Ps

(Putnam 1992, p. 369)

This premise may suffer from a difficulty that premise 1 of my Antiskeptical Argument does not. Consider the following substitution instance of Putnam's (D):

> (U) "Unicorn" refers to unicorns.

Depending on exactly what Putnam means by his schema (D), proposition (U) may show that Putnam's anti-skepticism faces a difficulty here.

Combining both premises of Putnam's argument and paraphrasing a bit, Putnam seems to think that he can unproblematically argue as follows:

Putnam's Antiskeptical Argument

P1. "Water" refers to water.

P2. Reference to water requires causal contact with water.

C1. So, I am in causal contact with water (and am not a brain in a vat in a world without water).

The problem for this type of argument, as should be apparent, is that substituting "unicorn" in appropriate places for "water" seems to yield an unsound argument because the conjunction of its premises would be false.[10] And yet Putnam does not say why this sort of objection does not cast significant doubt on his argument. Putnam is likely to want to modify his (D) in something like the following way:

(D′) "P" refers to Ps if there are any Ps

but if so he needs to explain just how he plans to reformulate his antiskeptical argument given this modification of his first premise. It would appear that his overall argument, with (D′) substituted for (D) will require a subargument for the antecedent of any substitution instance of (D′), which will be difficult to provide in the face of the skeptical challenge.

My argument, on the other hand, does not depend on the premise, plausible though it may be, that "water" in my language refers to water. This premise seems to carry with it an existential commitment that may not be appropriate in the context of providing an antiskeptical argument. I claim only to know that I can think that water is wet and do not claim (or deny, at least in presenting my Antiskeptical Argument) to know that "water" in my language refers to water. With this clarified, it is now time to discuss the primary objection to my claim to know that I think that water is wet.

In recent times, one significant objection to my claim to know what I think has taken center stage. Many philosophers have claimed that semantic externalism, the thesis that the contents of at least many of my thoughts depend at least in part on environmental factors, undercuts my knowledge of what I think.[11] It will not have escaped notice that I appealed to semantic externalism and my reflections on the thought experiments supporting it in defending premise 2 of my AntiSkeptical Argument. The present suggestion is that this appeal to externalism undercuts my knowledge of the contents of my thoughts, in particular undercutting my knowledge of premise 1 of my argument. Without knowledge of premise 1, of course, the antiskeptical force of my argument will be lost. This charge therefore, if it has merit, would bring an end to my semantic antiskeptical project and would indeed cripple every semantic antiskeptical argument of which I am aware. The charge, therefore, is a serious one.

Fortunately for proponents of semantic antiskepticism, however, the charge is not a well substantiated one. As far as I can tell, and as I have argued elsewhere, there is simply no reason to think that externalism about mental content undercuts my knowledge of the contents of my thoughts.[12] Rather than repeat much of that discussion, I will summarize what I take to be wrong with the most common reasons given for thinking that externalism is incompatible with this sort of self-knowledge and also offer a couple of additional reasons for doubting that my Antiskeptical Argument is vulnerable to this skepticism about self-knowledge.

From what I can tell there are three main reasons that philosophers have for thinking that externalism threatens one's knowledge of the contents of one's thoughts. The first of these worries is, thankfully, encountered more frequently in conversation than in print. Some philosophers seem to think that externalism literally puts contents and even minds themselves "out there in the world" and that as a consequence of this our knowledge of our minds and the contents of our thoughts is just as vulnerable to skeptical doubt as other claims we might make to knowledge of the world.

Leaving aside just how vulnerable that would make our knowledge of our thought contents, it should be clear that this objection need not be taken too seriously. Externalism is the thesis that the contents of at least some of our thoughts depend in part on environmental factors that do not supervene on our nervous systems. Externalism does not, and should not, say that our thoughts depend wholly on such factors nor does or should externalism literally identify thought contents with the environmental conditions on which they (partially) supervene. John Heil expresses what I take to be pretty much this same thought when he appropriately remarks that

> it is important to recognize that, although the "supervenience base" for intentional mental characteristics of agents may be broad, mental characteristics are not themselves "spread out".
>
> (Heil 1992, pp. 151–152)

Minds, thoughts, and thought contents are not literally out there in the environment to be looked at and played with by anyone who happens upon them.[13] To think otherwise is to simply misunderstand that implications of the externalist thought experiments.

Two other, more serious, reasons for thinking that externalism is incompatible with self-knowledge remain to be addressed. The first of these reasons was put forward originally by Paul Boghossian.[14] Boghossian showed how the assumption of externalism at least seems to allow cases to be constructed in which an individual does not know the contents of his thoughts. Kevin Falvey and Joseph Owens, though they ultimately reject the claim that externalism undercuts self-knowledge, share Boghossian's concern with cases in which it appears that externalism allows for cases to be constructed in which individuals fail to know the contents of their thoughts (Falvey and Owens 1994, p. 115).

This type of argument, however, is no cause for worry and certainly does not establish that externalism and self-knowledge are incompatible. The fact, if it is a fact, that we can construct stories in which externalism is true and an individual does not know the contents of his thoughts simply does not imply that externalism is incompatible with self-knowledge. Rather, such stories show at most that externalism is *consistent* with a lack of self-knowledge, which is a far cry from showing that externalism *implies* a lack of self-knowledge.

While this summary of the argument of Boghossian and others does not fully do justice to a fairly complex issue, I'm pretty sure that I have accurately summarized the main points of the debate and clarified my reasons for thinking that Boghossian's type of argument does not threaten to show that externalism undercuts self-knowledge. I turn now to the third main reason philosophers have offered for thinking that externalism is incompatible with self-knowledge.

This third reason has been pressed most forcefully by Michael McKinsey, though others have contributed to its recent defense.[15] In a nutshell, this third reason for claiming that externalism undercuts self-knowledge is that, in the opinion of proponents of this skeptical maneuver, the truth of both externalism and the type of self-knowledge in question would imply the availability of an implausibly strong antiskeptical argument, an argument that would allow agents to have a sort of a priori knowledge of their environments. Obviously *I'm* not going to be worried about this line of criticism! I find at least one antiskeptical argument made available by the conjunction of a priori self-knowledge and a priori knowledge of externalism to be extremely plausible.

Judgments of plausibility will differ and perhaps there is little more that can be said here than that this is just one more example of the overworked "one person's modus ponens is another's modus tollens." I would, however, like to stress that no one to my knowledge has said *why*, exactly, the sort of a priori knowledge of the world that I claim to have shown is available is supposed to be implausibly strong.

Instead of careful explanations of why this kind of a priori knowledge of the world is implausibly strong, we typically find comments such as these:

> Since you obviously *can't* know a priori that the external world exists . . .
>
> (McKinsey 1991, p. 16)

> Even if a subject can have a priori knowledge of such anti-sceptical propositions as the proposition that there is an external world, it is not plausible that a subject can have a priori knowledge of more specific facts about the world.
>
> (Brown 1995, p. 155)

We see in passages such as these, and the articles from which they are excerpted, no *arguments* for the view that the apparently available a priori knowledge of the environment is unacceptable. We find only assertions that this is the case.

Though I will not be able to settle this issue here, I would like to offer one reason for thinking that the apparent antiskeptical implications of a priori self-knowledge and a priori knowledge of externalism should not automatically be taken to warrant McKinsey's call for a reductio. Consider just how weak a notion of "a priori" is in play here. By "a priori" in my antiskeptical argument I have (following McKinsey's use of the term in discussions of self-knowledge) meant only "independent of a perceptual investigation of my environment." This weak understanding of "a priori" does not carry with it the baggage of a great number of stronger notions of the a priori. It is for this reason that even opponents of the antiskeptical strategy have labeled this understanding of "a priori" an "unhappy" one (Brown 1995, p. 149).[16] This weak understanding of "a priori" in my a priori Antiskeptical Argument should make the anti-skeptical conclusion somewhat more acceptable to fence sitters. The availability of an antiskeptical argument of any sort is bound to be found implausible by many. Such arguments are surprising and should attract a certain amount of critical reflection. What I hope to have convinced you of, however, is that such arguments should not lead you to conclude automatically that the conclusions are reductios of the premises.

This concludes my presentation of my reasons for rejecting the three main reasons philosophers have given for claiming that externalism is incompatible with introspective self-knowledge. I promised at least one additional point against this skeptical move and will now deliver on that promise.

If philosophers opposed to semantic antiskeptical arguments really do wish to claim that externalism is incompatible with knowledge of what I think, it should be made clear just how high the price of maintaining the skeptical stance has become. After all, the thought experiments of Burge and Putnam make an extremely compelling case for the truth of externalism and it would be amazing to give up on the thesis that on occasions on which I form beliefs about the contents of thoughts that are before my mind I have knowledge of what I think. When I do my best to truthfully report that I believe that water is wet, it would be amazing to think that I fail to report one of my beliefs, or that the reported belief is false, or that the reported belief is unwarranted. But one of these alternatives would have to be the case for my belief about the content of my thought to fail to be an instance of self-knowledge. So which will it be? Do we give up on self-knowledge or do we give up on externalism? And *how* do we give up on either? The skeptics typically do not say.[17]

A final reason for not being too quick to reject the semantic antiskeptical program is that the conclusion of such antiskeptical arguments (including my own) may not be as exciting as I have made it sound. As I will discuss at the end of this chapter, there is controversy over just how many and which kinds of skepticism are threatened by semantic antiskeptical arguments. The fewer types of skepticism threatened, the less reason one has to automatically reject the antiskeptical arguments.

But leaving that discussion aside for the moment, I find myself faced with an apparent choice between endorsing my preferred Antiskeptical Argument and the wildly implausible content skepticism of Boghossian, McKinsey, and others. Faced with this choice, I endorse semantic antiskepticism. Perhaps this move on my part is premature. Two issues remain before looking at the important question of just which skeptical hypotheses are threatened by semantic antiskepticism.

First, recall Tyler Burge's claim quoted at the beginning of this paper. Burge says that "there is no easy argument against skepticism from anti-individualism [externalism] and authoritative self-knowledge" (Burge 1988, p. 655). Burge, so that we are clear, is a compatibilist about externalism and what I have been calling (weak) a priori self-knowledge and is one primary architect of the a priori thought experiments supporting externalism. Indeed, the primary argument of the paper from which the above quote is taken is an argument for this compatibility thesis. Burge, however, also rejects semantic antiskeptical arguments. Unfortunately for those who would like to follow Burge in taking this seemingly moderate position, Burge does not tell us *how* and *why* he thinks one can, having accepted both externalism and self-knowledge, stop short in this way. He says, correctly but disappointingly, only that this "is a complicated matter best reserved for other occasions" (Burge 1988, p. 655).[18]

So Burge has not given us a reason for thinking that a priori self-knowledge and a priori knowledge of externalism are ineffective against the skeptic. One further and common reason for thinking that semantic antiskeptical arguments are ineffective against the skeptic is the claim that such arguments somehow "beg the question" against the skeptic. Let's consider this charge as it applies to my antiskeptical argument.

Charges of begging the question are quite common in philosophy and unfortunately there is no consensus on just what it takes to beg a question with an argument or against a position. Indeed, some philosophers think that there is no such thing as begging the question, though I believe that this position has been refuted.[19] Because of this uncertainty, it is no simple task to argue that my Antiskeptical Argument does not beg the question against the skeptic. I will do what I can in this direction by comparing my argument and its relation to the Skeptical Argument with another antiskeptical argument commonly agreed to beg the question against the skeptic, the antiskeptical argument of Moore.[20] My argument, I will show, is importantly different from Moore's at just the point at which Moore is typically charged with begging the question. While this will not *demonstrate* that my argument does not beg the question, it will at least be a positive step in that direction.

Recall the Skeptical Argument:

P1. I do not know that I am not a brain in a vat in an otherwise empty world.

P2. If I do not know that I am not a brain in a vat in an otherwise empty world then I do not know that I am currently drinking water.

C1. I do not know that I am currently drinking water.

Here is the common understanding of how Moore would respond to this argument. Moore rejects this argument by rejecting its first premise. Moore claims to know that he is not a brain in a vat of the sort mentioned in the premise by inference from his knowledge that he is currently drinking water. Moore thus "turns the skeptical argument around," inferring the falsity of its first premise by modus ponens from the negation of its conclusion and the contrapositive of its second premise. This antiskeptical move of Moore, bold and tempting though it is, is typically thought to beg the question against the skeptic. The skeptic has "called into question" our perceptual knowledge and Moore would have us refute the skeptic by appealing to this perceptual knowledge.

Contrast this with what I take to be the nonquestion begging move made by semantic antiskeptical arguments such as my argument. Like Moore, I deny the first premise of the Skeptical Argument. But I do so by offering an argument that appeals only to nonperceptual knowledge claims. I claim to show that the skeptic's first premise is false by inference from my (nonperceptual) knowledge of what I am thinking and my (nonperceptual) knowledge of conditions necessary for thinking what I am thinking. I thus do not appeal to knowledge that the perceptual knowledge skeptic has called into question in offering my reply to the skeptic. The sharp contrast with Moore is readily apparent. At the very least, the charge of begging the question does not stick as easily to my argument as it does to the argument of Moore.[21]

I turn finally to the question of just what sorts of skeptical hypotheses and positions are vulnerable to semantic antiskeptical arguments such as the one I have endorsed. Received wisdom has it that the answer to this question of how many kinds of skepticism are vulnerable to Putnam-style arguments is "not many." For more than a decade and a half, commentators on Putnam's brain in a vat argument have claimed that the argument is effective, if at all, only against a very narrowly specified kind of skeptical hypothesis. Just about every commentator on the brain in a vat argument has argued that Putnam refutes, at most, the skeptical hypothesis that he has not always been a brain in a vat. Similarly, these commentators would likely maintain that the particular version of Putnam's argument that I endorse seems to only rule out the skeptical hypothesis that I have not always been a brain in a vat in an otherwise empty world.

Both critics and supporters of Putnam have been quick to point out that there are many hypotheses worthy of the title "skeptical hypotheses" that are consistent with the falsity of the hypotheses that Putnam and I claim to rule out. Consider the following hypothesis. Up until one year (or one day, or one hour) ago I was a normal brain in a normal environment intimately connected to a normal body, at which time the evil scientist and his friends kidnapped me and "envatted" me. Call this hypothesis NSH for "new skeptical hypothesis" and ask how the Putnamian could hope to rule out NSH by means of a semantic antiskeptical argument.

NSH is incompatible with the hypothesis that I am currently drinking water and NSH seems to be resistant to semantic antiskeptical arguments. This is so because a brain in a vat of the sort specified in NSH seems, at least at first glance, to have had an intimate enough history of interaction with objects like water to think about them. This lifelong association of the NSH brain in a vat with water means that my favored Antiskeptical Argument would not, without a great deal of detailed supplementary argumentation, serve to refute NSH. While the fact that I think that water is wet is pretty clearly incompatible with the hypothesis that I am and always have been a brain in a vat in an otherwise empty world, this fact does not seem to be incompatible with NSH (and if it is incompatible with NSH, this must be for very different reasons than those employed in my Antiskeptical Argument). Semantic antiskepticism thus seems to be limited in scope. Some philosophers have even thought that it is hard to find a skeptical hypothesis other than the one Putnam constructed that is threatened by semantic antiskeptical arguments. The following remark from David Christensen nicely summarizes this common deflationary reaction to Putnamian antiskepticism:

> even if Putnam's anti-skeptical argument provides a convincing answer to one particular version of brain-in-vat skepticism, other versions of the same problem [e.g., those involving recent envatment] will remain untouched by his argument. Furthermore, it might well be argued that there is no significant loss of philosophical interest in the skeptic's move from a Putnamian brain-in-vat hypothesis to the recent envatment version sketched above, because the problem posed by the recent-envatment hypothesis is equivalent in power and plausibility to that posed by the Putnamian hypothesis.
>
> (Christenson 1993, pp. 314–315)

While I admit that there is a certain intuitive force to this objection to the scope of semantic antiskeptical arguments, I would like to suggest in closing that we should not be too quick to conclude that the range of applicability of semantic antiskeptical arguments is extremely narrow. After all, just which skeptical hypotheses are and are not vulnerable to such arguments is a function of the *details* of the externalist necessary conditions on thought and reference. We may have certain suspicions about what these details will look like. Probably externalism doesn't require *current* causal contact with Ps in order to think about Ps, but what about *recent* contact of a sort that would rule out many recent envatment cases? Many no doubt suspect that this condition is also too strong, but I do not think that we know enough about the semantics of thought and reference to be very confident in the truth of such suspicions.

The range of applicability of semantic antiskeptical arguments depends on how these sorts of issues are resolved and I see no way of resolving them without serious and detailed work on psychosemantic theories. The common deflationary view of Putnamian anti-skepticism is therefore at least a bit premature.

CONCLUSION

I have argued that, strange though it may seem, my a priori knowledge of what I am thinking can be combined with my a priori knowledge of conditions necessary for my thinking what I am thinking to yield a nonquestion begging refutation of one common skeptical argument directed at ordinary perceptual knowledge. I have also shown how my argument is different from and improves upon the famous antiskeptical argument defended by

Hilary Putnam and I have answered what I take to be the most pressing challenges to this sort of argument.

NOTES

1. I am referring to Putnam 1992, which so far as I am aware contains Putnam's most recent discussion of his famous argument.

2. Dretske (in this volume) contains one of the earliest contemporary denials of closure. Robert Audi (1988 and 1995) has offered the best of the recent attacks on closure. See also Brueckner 1985 and for a response to Audi's work, Feldman 1995. Klein (1995) offers an interesting argument for the conclusion that even if the closure principle is true it is useless to the skeptic.

3. Putnam 1975, Burge 1979, 1982, and 1986. See also McGinn 1989 (especially chapter 1) for sophisticated and important discussion of externalism.

4. If I am not understanding Putnam correctly here, then his claim is probably equivalent to my claim and my failure to understand his point merely a result of terminological differences.

5. Perhaps the first of these cases is covered by Putnam's remarks about relations to "objects or properties in terms of which they [the objects to which one refers] can be described" and perhaps the second is covered by some extended understanding of "causal interaction." If so, Putnam and I probably do not disagree about this point. Putnam may want to insist on a strict difference between reference to Ps and thoughts about Ps; if so he faces the difficulty I raise in note 10. There is much more that could be said about just what is and is not implied by the conjunction of externalism and an agent's thinking that water is wet. I have commented briefly on this issue elsewhere (Warfield 1994, note 5); see also, among others, Brown 1995, Brueckner 1992b and 1995, McKinsey 1991 and 1994, and Burge 1982.

6. It does not matter to my argument that my brain is partially composed of water. This is no more an objection to my discussion at this point than the similar point that my twin earth duplicate isn't *really* my molecule for molecule duplicate (my brain contains water molecules, but his doesn't) is an objection to the twin earth thought experiments.

7. Before his paper in this volume (see note 11 of that paper), Brueckner also typically formulated the anti-skeptical argument in this way, as have many others working on Putnam's argument.

8. I am, as should be apparent, less than overwhelmed by the recent wave of dissent about the force of the Putnam/Burge thought experiments, most of which is aimed at Burge. For some of this dissent see McKinsey 1993, Dretske 1993, Antony 1993, and Elugardo 1993.

9. Like everyone else, I have no idea how introspection works. I doubt very much that introspection is like ordinary visual perception, but do not know how to argue for this claim.

10. Putnam faces a dilemma. Either "unicorn" refers to unicorns or it doesn't. If it does not, then premise one of his argument is false. If it does, however, then reference to unicorns does not require causal contact with unicorns and premise two is false. If he were to provide an a priori method for distinguishing his referential and nonreferential thoughts, Putnam would avoid this dilemma, but Putnam has not done this and I doubt that he can.

11. Key references include Boghossian 1989, McKinsey 1991 and 1994, and Brown 1995. For additional references see the more extensive bibliographies of Warfield 1994 and 1995. Note that most of the literature is concerned with the question of whether externalism is compatible with some type of *privileged* self-knowledge and not with the simpler question of whether it is compatible with self-knowledge simpliciter (that is, independent of any considerations of privileged access).

12. I have defended this claim in Warfield 1992, 1994, and 1995. Others have also defended this point in somewhat different ways. See, for some examples, Ludwig 1992, Tymoczko 1990, Wright 1992b, and Forbes 1995.

13. I'm not saying that contents are in the head either (though I suppose that minds and mental states are in some sense in the head). I think that contents are abstract objects and so are neither in the head nor in the environment in just the way that the number two is neither in the head nor in the environment.

14. Boghossian argument appears in Boghossian 1989; I replied initially in Warfield 1992 and offered further thoughts in Warfield 1995.

15. See, among others, McKinsey 1991 and 1994, Brown 1995, and Noonan 1993.

16. To see why this understanding of "a priori" will bother many people, note that even a strongly perception like type of introspective knowledge in which an agent literally reads off the contents of her thoughts from the mentalese sentences which encode them would count as delivering "a priori" self-knowledge on this understanding of the a priori.

17. Boghossian, for instance, says that he in only presenting a paradox and says that he does not "seriously envisage that we do not know our own minds" (1989, p. 6). Nor does Boghossian think that rejecting exter-

nalism will solve the problem he thinks we face for he argues that any plausible internalism about content faces the same difficulty with self-knowledge that he thinks externalism faces.

18. Falvey and Owens 1994 also take this moderate position, but I am in at least broad agreement with Brueckner's 1994 critical discussion of that article, which seems to show that their overall position is unstable. I argued at length that the moderate position is unstable in Warfield 1994.

19. See Robinson 1971 and Sorensen 1996 for discussion.

20. I have no idea if the understanding of Moore that I work with, which is certainly a fairly common understanding, is faithful to the original.

21. There is an extremely complicated question lurking here of whether the skeptic can employ an argument formally identical to the Skeptical Argument against my claim to have knowledge of premise 1. If the skeptic's argument against perceptual knowledge extends unproblematically and naturally to knowledge of content as well, then the charge of begging the question may well justifiably resurface. But it is not easy to see why we should think that the scope of the Skeptical Argument is this broad.

PART TWO   Responses From
Epistemic
Externalism

CHAPTER 6

Philosophical Scepticism and Epistemic Circularity

Ernest Sosa

Epistemic circularity has dogged epistemology from the time of the Greek sceptics, through Descartes's circle and Hegel's serpent biting its tail, to serve finally as a source of today's relativism and scepticism—an important source, though of course only one of several. 'Since there is no way to justify one's overall practical or theoretical stance without circularity,' we are told, 'all justification must be ultimately relative to one's basic commitments, conceived perhaps as arbitrary creatures of the will. In comparing overall systems, anyhow, especially when these are equally coherent and self-support-ive, there is no way to privilege one's own except arbitrarily, irrationally or arationally, perhaps by adopting a frank and honest ethnocentrism.' That is today a wide- spread attitude. This paper aims to expose questionable assumptions on which it rests.

We shall consider the following thesis and its supporting argument.

Philosophical Scepticism. There is no way to attain full philosophical understanding of our knowledge. A fully general theory of knowledge is impossible.

The Radical Argument (RA)

A1. Any theory of knowledge must be internalist or externalist.

A2. A fully general internalist theory is impossible.

"Philosophical Scepticism and Epistemic Circularity" from *Aristotelian Society Supplementary Volume* 68 (1994, pp. 263–290). Reprinted by courtesy of the Editor of the Aristotelian Society.

A3. A fully general externalist theory is impossible.

C. From A1–A3, *philosophical scepticism* follows.

In discussing these, first it will be convenient to define some terminology. 'Formal internalism'—or 'internalism' for short—shall stand for the doctrine that a belief can be justified and amount to knowledge only through the backing of reasons or arguments. This is of course a special sense of the word, but internalism in this sense today enjoys substantial support. Here are some representative passages, drawn from the writings of Donald Davidson, Richard Rorty, Laurence Bonjour, and Michael Williams.

> [Nothing] . . . can count as a reason for holding a belief except another belief . . . [And it] . . . will promote matters at this point to review very hastily some of the reasons for abandoning the search for a basis for knowledge outside the scope of our beliefs. By 'basis' I mean here specifically an epistemological basis, a source of justification.[1]

> [It] . . . is absurd to look for . . . something outside [our beliefs] . . . which we can use to test or compare with our beliefs.[2]

> [Nothing] . . . counts as justification unless by reference to what we already accept, and there is no way to get outside our beliefs and our language so as to find some test other than coherence.[3]

> [We] can think of knowledge as a relation to propositions, and thus of justification as a relation between the propositions in question and other propositions from which the former may be inferred. Or we may think of both knowledge and justification as privileged relations to the objects those propositions are about. If we think in the first way, we will see no need to end the potentially infinite regress of propositions-brought-forward-in-defense-of-other-propositions. It would be foolish to keep conversation going on the subject once everyone, or the majority, or the wise, are satisfied, but of course we *can*. If we think of knowledge in the second way, we will want to get behind reasons to causes, beyond argument to compulsion from the object known, to a situation in which argument would be not just silly but impossible . . . To reach that point is to reach the foundations of knowledge.[4]

> To accept the claim that there is no standpoint outside the particular historically conditioned and temporary vocabulary we are presently using from which to judge this vocabulary is to give up on the idea that there can be reasons for using languages as well as reasons within languages for believing statements. This amounts to giving up the idea that intellectual or political progress is rational, in any sense of 'rational' which is neutral between vocabularies.[5]

> [The] notion of a [foundational] 'theory of knowledge' will not make sense unless we have confused causation and justification in the manner of Locke.[6]

> If we let ø represent the feature or characteristic, whatever it may be, which distinguishes basic empirical beliefs from other empirical beliefs, then in an acceptable foundationalist account a particular empirical belief B could qualify as basic only if the premises of the following justificatory argument were adequately justified:

(1) B has feature ø.

(2) Beliefs with feature ø are highly likely to be true.

Therefore, B is highly likely to be true.

> . . . But if all this is correct, we get the disturbing result that B is not basic after all, since its justification depends on that of at least one other empirical belief.[7]
>
> Only a legitimating account of our beliefs about the world will give an understanding of our knowledge of the world. This means that an account of our knowledge of the world must trace it to something that is *ours*, and that is *knowledge*, but that is not *knowledge of the world*.[8]

'Formal externalism' shall stand for the denial of formal internalism. And, again, for short we shall drop the qualifier, and speak simply of 'externalism'.

A very wide and powerful current of thinking would sweep away externalism root and branch. This torrent of thought in one way or another encompasses much of contemporary philosophy, both on the Continent and in the Anglophone sphere, as may be seen in the Continental rejection of presence to the mind as well as in the analytic rejection of the given. The Continentals have been led by Heidegger, Gadamer, Habermas, Foucault, and Derrida to a great variety of anti-foundationalisms, ranging from consensualism and hermeneutics to relativism and contextualism. The tide against the given on this side of the Channel is no less powerful and is illustrated by the passages already cited. Having also rejected the given and presence to the mind, others settle into an irresolvable frustration that recognizes the problems but denies the possibility of any satisfactory solution.[9] Many who now object to externalism in such terms offer little by way of support. Barry Stroud and William Alston are exceptional in spelling out the deep reasons why, in their view, externalism will leave us ultimately dissatisfied.[10] They have made as persuasive a case as can be made for the unacceptability in principle of any externalist circles in epistemology, and have done so on a very simple *a priori* basis grounded in what seem to be demands inherent in the traditional epistemological project itself. What follows will focus on their case against such externalism, but much of it applies *mutatis mutandis* to the reasoning, such as it is, offered by other thinkers as well.[11] Though the issue before us is phrased in the terms of analytic epistemology, it is a wellspring of main currents of thought that reach beyond analysis and epistemology. Yet the issue and its options, rarely faced directly, are very ill-understood.

One thing is already clear. Given our definition of externalism as simply the denial of internalism, premise A1 is trivially true and amounts to *p or not-p*.

Note further that an acceptable *internalist* epistemological account of all one's knowledge in some domain D would be, in the following sense, a 'legitimating' account of such knowledge.

A is a legitimating account of one's knowledge in domain D IFF D is a domain of one's beliefs that constitute knowledge and are hence justified (and more), and A specifies the sorts of inferences that justify one's beliefs in D, without circularity or endless regress.

But such an account cannot be attained for all one's knowledge:

The impossibility of general, legitimating, philosophical understanding of all one's *knowledge:* It is impossible to attain a legitimating account of absolutely all one's own knowledge; such an account admits only justification provided by inference or argument and, since it rules out circular or endlessly regressive inferences, such an account must stop with premises that it supposes or 'presupposes' that one is justified in accepting, without explaining how one is justified in accepting them in turn.

Accordingly, premise A2 of argument RA seems clearly right. And it all comes down to premise A3. If we are to resist philosophical scepticism we cannot accept that premise. What then are the prospects for a formal externalist epistemology?

The formal externalist has, it seems to me, three main choices today, concerning how a belief attains the status of knowledge, how it acquires the sort of epistemic justification (or aptness or warrant, or anyhow the positive epistemic status) required if it is to amount to knowledge. These three choices are:

E1. *Coherentism.* When a belief is epistemically justified, it is so in virtue of its being part of a coherent body of beliefs (or at least of one that is sufficiently coherent and appropriately comprehensive).

E2. *Foundationalism of the given.* When a belief is epistemically justified, it is so in virtue of being either the taking of the given, the mere recording of what is present to the mind of the believer, or else by being inferred appropriately from such foundations.

E3. *Reliabilism.* When a belief is epistemically justified, it is so in virtue of deriving from an epistemically, truth-conducively reliable process or faculty or intellectual virtue of belief acquisition.

E1. There is a lot to be said about coherentism, but I lack the space to say much of it here. Suffice it to say that the most comprehensive coherence accompanied by the truth of what one believes will not yet amount to knowledge. The New Evil Demon problem establishes this as follows. Consider the victim of Descartes's evil demon. In fact, suppose we are now such victims. Could that affect whether or not we are *epistemically justified* in believing what we believe? If we are justified as we are, we would *seem* equally justified, in some appropriate sense, so long as nothing changed within our whole framework of experiences and beliefs. However, if by sheer luck one happened to be right in the belief that one faces a fire, one's being *both* thus justified *and* right still would fall short of one's knowing about the fire.

So whatever is to be said for coherence, or even for comprehensive coherence, one thing seems clear: none of that will be enough just on its own to explain fully what a true belief needs in order to be knowledge. One's beliefs can be comprehensively coherent without amounting to knowledge, and the same goes for one's beliefs and experiences together. So the sense of 'epistemic justification' in play here is one that will not capture fully the epistemic status required in a true belief if it is to constitute knowledge.

E2. What of foundationalism of the given? *Cogito ergo sum* exclaimed Descartes, as he at last found a good apple off the tree of knowledge. By that time many other apples had already been judged defective, or at least not clearly enough undefective. Our perceptual beliefs had not qualified, since we could so easily be fooled into believing something false on the basis of sensory experience. For example, one could fall victim to illusion or hallucination, and, more dramatically, to an evil demon or a mad scientist who manipulated one's soul or one's brain directly, thus creating systematically the sorts of experiences that one would normally take to be indicative of a normal environment. None of this will affect the *cogito*, however, since even while hallucinating or while manipulated by evil demon or mad scientist, we must still exist and we must still be thinking, if we are to be fooled into thinking something incorrectly. One thought that could never be incorrect, is the thought that one exists, and another is the thought that one is thinking.

What is the feature of the *cogito* that explains its special assurance? Consider the proposition (a) that I am now standing. This proposition is true but only contingently so, since I might have been sitting now. In contrast, it is not only true but necessarily true (b) that either I am standing or I am not standing. Is it the necessity of (b) that accounts for its special certainty as compared with (a)? Not entirely. For much is necessary without being certain, and much is certain without being necessary. And, in any case, it cannot be the necessity of 'I think' or 'I exist' that gives such propositions their special epistemic status. For in itself the *cogito*, the proposition that I am thinking, is only true and not necessarily true: I might have been unconscious, or even dead, in which case I would not have been thinking. What is not just contingently true, what is necessarily true, is the fact that *if* I am thinking that I think, *then* I am right: no-one can think that they think without being right. Is it *this*, then, that distinguishes the *cogito* and makes it a legitimately known contingent truth, of which we can properly be assured?

No, that one must be right in believing something does not entail that one is justified in doing so. Take the proposition that there is no largest prime. Since that proposition is necessarily true, we could not possibly go wrong in believing it. Nevertheless, we are not justifiably assured in believing it if we are just guessing right and have seen no proof. That a belief could not be wrong is hence not enough to make it apt, nor is a belief necessarily apt just because even the Cartesian demon could not fool one into holding it incorrectly. A groundless belief is one that we hold in the absence of supporting reasons or arguments. Some such beliefs seem far superior to others: some amount to knowledge of the obvious, while others are no better than superstition or dogma. We are now after distinguishing properties or features that will help explain which groundless beliefs might qualify as knowledge and which could never do so, and for some account of why these properties or features can make such a difference.

A second main source of apt, groundless beliefs, according to the epistemological tradition, is presence to the mind, or what is given in sensory and other experience. What is involved in one's aptly believing something about the character of one's present sensory experience? It is required by the tradition that one be reporting simply how it is in one's experience itself. One must be reporting on the intrinsic, qualitative character of some experience.

But here again a similar problem arises. Suppose one eyes a well-lit surface with a medium-sized white triangle against a black background. In that case, assuming one is normally sighted, one would have visual experience of a certain distinctive sort, as if one saw a white triangle against a black background. Introspectively, then, one could easily come to know that one was then having experience of that sort: viz, that one was presented with a white triangular image, or the like. What now is the relevant feature of one's introspective belief, what is the feature that makes one's belief apt, makes it indeed a bit of knowledge? Is it simply that one is just reporting what is directly present to one's mind, what is given in one's experience?

No, that something is thus present to one's mind or given in one's experience is not enough to make it something of which one can be legitimately assured. Take that same situation and change the white image projected on the black surface from a triangle to a dodecagon. And suppose you believe yourself to be presented with a white dodecagon on a black surface, all other conditions remaining as before. Are you then properly assured about the character of your experience so that your introspective belief can then count as apt belief, and indeed as knowledge? What of someone poor at reporting dodecagons in visual experience, who often confuses them with decagons, but who now happens by luck to be right? Such a belief could hardly count as knowledge or even as apt belief.

What Descartes needs in order to explain the special status of the *cogito* is not just that one cannot incorrectly believe that one thinks, but rather that one could not possibly answer incorrectly the question whether one thinks (at least not sincerely and *in foro interno*). And how can one explain this special status enjoyed by that proposition? Descartes's explanation is of course that even a powerful evil demon could not fool one into thinking incorrectly that one thinks. For if the demon gets one to *think* that one thinks—and how else could he fool one into *thinking* incorrectly that one thinks?—then of course inevitably one *does* think and one is bound to be right.

However, that does only half the job. It explains only how one must be right if one thinks that one thinks. It does not explain why it is that one would never think that one does *not* think. Of course Descartes does *claim* that the proposition that one thinks is not only one with regard to which one is infallible, such that if one accepts it one must be right. He also thinks that it is an *indubitable* proposition. But whereas he explains incontestably why one must be right in thinking that one thinks, he does little or nothing to explain why it is that the *cogito* and other similarly simple, clear, distinct propositions are for us indubitable.

What of the doctrine of the given or of presence to the mind? Here the proposal would be that one aptly introspects P iff P describes a present state of one's own consciousness and while considering attentively and with a clear mind the question whether P is the case, one believes P. It is held to be very unlikely that one would ever opt wrong on such a proposition when in such circumstances.

By reflecting on how the doctrine of the given must be formulated in order to meet certain objections, we have arrived at a reliabilist version of foundationalism. What matters is not that one attend to the contents of one's mind, to one's experiences or beliefs or other states of mind, nor is what matters that one attend to simple necessary truths. For simplicity is a relative matter: what is simple for an experienced mathematician is far from it to the schoolchild learning arithmetic. It is important rather that the subject be reliable on the object of knowledge, and unlikely to go wrong on such subject matter.

E3. So we are down to the third and last of the options open to the formal externalist. But I view generic reliabilism as a *very* broad category indeed, one capacious enough to include thinkers as diverse as Descartes and Alvin Goldman. If we are to resist philosophical scepticism it would appear that here we must make a stand. For, remember, if A3 cannot be defeated, then philosophical scepticism seems the inevitable consequence. So let us consider some objections to generic reliabilism. Here we turn to the promised arguments by Barry Stroud and William Alston.

According to Stroud, 'we need some reason to accept a theory of knowledge if we are going to rely on that theory to understand how our knowledge is possible. That is what . . . no form of 'externalism' can give a satisfactory account of.'[12] Against Descartes, for example, and against the 'externalist' in general he objects on the basis of the following *metaepistemic requirement:*

> MR   In order to understand one's knowledge satisfactorily one must see oneself as having some reason to accept a theory that one can recognize would explain one's knowledge if it were true.

And how is MR to be defended? From the assumptions: (a) that understanding something is a matter of having good reason to accept something that would be an explanation if it were true, and (b) that, as generality-thirsty theorist of knowledge, one wants to understand how one knows the things one thinks one knows.[13] But MR does not follow from these assumptions.

From these assumptions it follows only that in order to understand one's knowledge one must in fact *have* good reason or at least justification to accept some appropriate explanation. Why must one also *see oneself as having* such reason?

Far from being just an isolated slip, MR represents rather a deeply held intuition that underlies a certain way of thinking about epistemology. We have seen already several passages that fit this intuition. According to such 'anti-externalism,' as Stroud might label it, what is important in epistemology is justification; and the justification of any given belief requires appeal to *other* beliefs that constitute one's reasons for holding the given belief. Of course, when one combines this with rejection of circularity, the case for scepticism is very strong, assuming that for limited humans an infinite regress of reasons or justifications is out of the question.

The 'externalist' therefore wants to allow some *other* way for a belief to acquire the epistemic status required for it to be knowledge, some way *other* than the belief's being based on some justification, argument, or reason. Note, moreover, how very broad this sense of 'externalism' is. Even arch-internalist Descartes is an 'externalist' in our present sense. We distinguish our present externalism as '*formal* externalism,' it will be recalled, which induces a corresponding type of internalism, 'formal internalism.' Formal internalism holds that there is only one way a belief can have the positive epistemic status required for knowledge, namely by having the backing of reasons or arguments. Note the connection with the requirement that a philosophically satisfactory account of how one knows must be a *legitimating* account, one that specifies the reasons favouring one's belief. Obviously, a formal internalist will believe that for *every* belief that amounts to knowledge there must be such a legitimating account, and that only once we have such an account can we understand what makes that belief knowledge.[14]

Consider now the naturalist, externalist epistemologist. Will he be able to understand how people know the things they do? He will only if he knows or has some reason to believe his scientific account of the world around him. According to Stroud, this dooms our epistemologist:

> If his goal was, among other things, to explain our scientific knowledge of the world around us, he will have an explanation of such knowledge only if he can see himself as possessing some knowledge in that domain. In studying other people, that presents no difficulty. It is precisely by knowing what he does about the world that he explains how others know what they do about the world. But if he had started out asking how anyone knows anything at all about the world, he would be no further along towards understanding how any of it is possible if he had not understood how he himself knows what he has to know about the world in order to have any explanation at all. He must understand himself as knowing or having some reason to believe that his theory is true.[15]

But it is again unclear why the epistemologist needs to *see himself as having* justification for his theory, or as knowing his theory, in order for it to give him understanding of how he and others know the things they know, either in general or in the domain in question. Why is it not enough that he in fact *have good reason to accept his theory* or perhaps even *know his theory to be true?* This is different from his knowing that he has good reason to believe his epistemologically explanatory theory, or even knowing that he knows his theory to be true. To this the response is as follows.

> [The externalist epistemologist] . . . is at best in the position of someone who has good reason to believe his theory if that theory is in fact true, but has no such reason to believe it if some other theory is true instead. He can see what he *would* have good reason to believe if the theory he believes were true, but he cannot see or understand himself as knowing or having good reason to believe what his theory says.[16]

> [Even] . . . if it is true that you can know something without knowing that you know it, the philosophical theorist of knowledge cannot simply insist on the point and expect to find acceptance of an 'externalist' account of knowledge fully satisfactory. If he could, he would be in the position of someone who says: 'I don't know whether I understand human knowledge or not. If what I believe about it is true and my beliefs about it are produced in what my theory says is the right way, I do know how human knowledge comes to be, so in that sense I do understand. But if my beliefs are not true, or not arrived at in that way, I do not. I wonder which it is. I wonder whether I understand human knowledge or not.' That is not a satisfactory position to arrive at in one's study of human knowledge—or of anything else.[17]

But again it is hard to see why the externalist theorist of knowledge must be in that position. Suppose that, as suggested earlier, he does *not* have to say or believe that he *does* know his theory of knowledge. Suppose he does not after all need to satisfy MR. Must he then say or believe that he *does not* know his theory of knowledge? Must he begin to wonder *whether* his theory of knowledge is true, or whether he does really understand human knowledge or not? Surely not.

Here the dialectic is given a further twist. It is replied that the sort of understanding of our knowledge of the external that we want in philosophy is not just understanding by dumb luck. What we want is rather *knowledgeable* understanding. And this we will never have until we are in a good position to accept our view of our own faculties (of perception or memory, for example), a view which properly underlies our trust in their reliability. But this view we will never be able to justify without relying in turn on already attained knowledge of the external. And this precludes our ever attaining a philosophically satisfactory understanding of all our knowledge in that domain.[18]

The demands introduced by this drive for *knowledgeable* philosophical understanding are different from those deriving from the twofold assumption that (a) epistemic justification is required for knowledge, and (b) reasons and arguments are universally required for epistemic justification. This twofold assumption—formal internalism—leads, as we have seen, to the impossibility of any fully general, legitimating, philosophical understanding of one's knowledge (and indeed to the impossibility of one's knowledge altogether). The new demands do not derive simply from such formal internalism. They derive rather from a distinctively epistemic circularity that came to philosophical consciousness long ago.

The dialectic of the diallelus is about as ancient as philosophy itself. Nor is Stroud the *only* philosopher today who argues extensively on the basis of epistemic circularity. Recent books by William Alston, for example, contain extensive discussion of these issues, and feature the following main theme:

> *if sense-perception is reliable,* a track-record argument will suffice to show that it is. Epistemic circularity does not in and of itself disqualify the argument. But even granting that point, the argument will not do its job unless we *are* justified in accepting its premises; and that is the case only if sense perception is in fact reliable. And this is to offer a stone instead of bread. We can say the same of any belief-forming practice whatever, no matter how disreputable. We can just as well say of crystal-ball gazing that if it *is* reliable, we can use a track record argument to show that it is reliable. But when we ask whether one or another source of belief is reliable, we are interested in *discriminating* those that can reasonably be trusted from those that cannot. Hence merely showing that *if* a given source is reliable it can be shown by its record to be reliable, does nothing to indicate that the source belongs with the sheep rather than with the goats. I have removed an allegedly crippling disability, but I have not given the argument a clean bill of health.[19]

Both in that book, and in more recent work,[20] Alston is forthright in his statement of the problem of circularity that he sees, and in his response to that perceived problem:

> Hence I shall disqualify epistemically circular arguments on the grounds that they do not serve to discriminate between reliable and unreliable doxastic practices.[21]

> Hence, when we reflect on our epistemic situation, we can hardly turn our backs *on our inability to give a satisfactory demonstration of SP and other doxastic practices . . .*[22]

In response to this, Alston argues instead that it is 'practically rational' for us to engage in our firmly rooted doxastic practices,[23] such as our 'sense perceptual practice,' SP, 'our customary ways of forming beliefs about the external environment on the basis of sense perception.'[24] And he believes that 'in showing it to be rational to engage in SP,' he has thereby, 'not shown SP to be reliable, but shown it to be rational to suppose SP to be reliable.'[25] This is so in the sense that it would be irrational for one to judge that SP is rational and deny that SP is reliable, or even to abstain from judging that SP is reliable if the question arises. So in accepting that SP is rational one 'pragmatically implies' and thereby 'commits oneself' to its being the case that SP is reliable.

Just how is it shown that it is 'rational' (or 'reasonable') to engage in SP? Here the argument begins by drawing from Thomas Reid the following claim:

1. The 'only (noncircular) basis we have for trusting rational intuition and introspection is that they are firmly established doxastic practices, so firmly established that we cannot help [doing so] . . .; and we have exactly the same basis for trusting sense perception, memory, nondeductive reasoning, and other sources of belief for which Descartes and Hume were demanding an external validation.'[26]

And it continues as follows:

2. '[Even if] we could adopt some basic way of forming beliefs about the physical environment other than SP, or some basic way of forming beliefs about the past other than memory, . . . why should we?'[27]

3. 'The same factors that prevent us from establishing the reliability of SP, memory, and so on without epistemic circularity would operate with the same force in these other cases.'[28]

4. 'These considerations seem to me to indicate that it is eminently *reasonable* for us to form beliefs in the ways we standardly do,'[29] such as SP.

This is presented as an argument for the practical rationality (or reasonableness) of using SP, one which avoids the 'epistemic circularity' that cripples track-record and other arguments for the *reliability* of SP. Where exactly is the circularity, and just how does it do its damage? The answer considers the use of a track-record argument, an argument that appeals to our past cognitive success through using SP:

> [If] I were to ask myself why I should accept the premises, I would, if I pushed the reflection far enough, have to make the claim that sense perception is reliable. For if I weren't prepared to make that claim on reflection, why should I, as a rational subject, countenance perceptual beliefs? Since this kind of circularity involves a commitment to the conclusion as a presupposition of our supposing ourselves to be *justified* in holding the premises, we can properly term it 'epistemic circularity'.[30]

However, consider again the earlier argument in favour of the conclusion that it is *rational* (or reasonable) to use SP, the argument presented above as 1–4. If we push reflection far enough with regard to why we should accept the premises of *this* argument, don't we find ourselves appealing precisely to *its* conclusion? And, if so, then is not this argument just as circular, and in a similar way, as the track-record argument in favour of the reliability of SP?

Epistemological reflection therefore leads to a situation that does seem 'fairly desperate' after all. We wonder whether we really know what we take ourselves to know. We wonder how we know whatever it is that we know. We hope that our way of forming beliefs—with its characteristic elements of memory, introspection, perception, and reason—does give us knowledge and explains how we know. But how can we be sure?

Suppose W is our total way of forming beliefs. If we believe that W is reliable, R(W), our belief B:R(W) is itself formed by W. And if a belief is justified iff formed in a reliable way, then our B:R(W) is justified iff W is reliable (given that it is formed by W). B:R(W) is justified, therefore, iff W *is* reliable.

Yet we must sympathize with the critics of 'externalism,' who argue that this is to 'give us a stone instead of bread,' and that the externalist 'is at best in the position of someone who ... can see what he *would* have good reason to believe if the theory he believes were true.' Let us consider carefully what they have to say.

Alston, in his recent books, argues as follows.

> Consider our sense-perceptual doxastic practice SP, (our total way of forming beliefs based on sense perception). The reliability of SP can be inferred, let us suppose, by relying on the deliverances of SP itself. Hence, assuming our reasoning is otherwise unobjectionable, belief B:R(SP) is justified if SP is reliable. But using the deliverances of SP to argue for B:R(SP) would be unacceptably circular.

Here, again, is how he puts it.

> [When] we ask whether one or another source of belief is reliable, we are interested in *discriminating* those that can reasonably be trusted from those that cannot. Hence merely showing that *if* a given source is reliable it can be shown by its record to be reliable, does nothing to indicate that the source belongs with the sheep rather than with the goats. I have removed an allegedly crippling disability, but I have not given the argument a clean bill of health. Hence I shall disqualify epistemically circular arguments on the grounds that they do not serve to discriminate between reliable and unreliable doxastic practices.[31]

But what exactly is the problem for the justification of B:R(SP)? And, even more generally, what exactly is the problem for the justification of B:R(W), where W is our total way of forming beliefs (of which SP would be only one among several components)?

Justification can be either a matter of one's internal rationality and coherence, or it can go beyond that to encompass some broader (or just different) state pertinent to whether one knows. Thus the victim of Descartes's evil demon may have internal justification for believing that there is a fire before him, but would still lack knowledge even if *by accident* he is right. Similarly, the hopelessly myopic Mr. Magoo may have internal justification for believing that it is safe to step ahead, but would still lack knowledge even if the board over the precipice does by accident still lie ahead.

For now let us focus just on internal justification or rational coherence. Are we bound to fall short of rational coherence if we form our belief that W is reliable—B:R(W)—through W itself? Alston suggests that we do fall short, in *some* way, since in asking whether one or another source of belief is reliable, we wish to *discriminate* sources that we can trust with good reason. Therefore, to show that *if* a given source is reliable it can be shown by its own use to be reliable does nothing to discriminate it from the many other possible sources equally able to pass that test.

We are thus offered the following view of the matter. We have before us a menu of sources, of ways of forming beliefs: W1, . . . , Wn. And we would like to discriminate the reliable from the unreliable. About Wi we discover that it has this much to be said for it: if one uses Wi to form beliefs, then by Wi one can form the belief B:R(Wi), the belief that Wi is reliable. And *if* Wi *is* reliable, then B:R(Wi) will itself of course be justified. When a way of forming beliefs, Wi, has this feature relative to a subject S in circumstances C, let us say that Wi is self-supportive for S in C: i.e., for S in C, Wi will deliver the belief on the part of S *that* Wi is itself reliable—B:R(Wi).

Here then is Alston's point about the feature of being self-supportive relative to oneself and one's circumstances: *several* (indefinitely many) ways of forming beliefs might well have this feature relative to oneself and one's circumstances, but many of these are palpably unacceptable. Indeed they might well be inconsistent in such a way that most by far are bound to be *unreliable*. Therefore, even once we reach the conclusion that Wi is self-supportive relative to us and our circumstances, that by itself does *not* enable us to conclude that it is acceptable, that it is a sheep, not a goat.

That much is surely right. But there is more. There is also the further proposal that if a way of forming beliefs W (a doxastic practice) is 'firmly established' for us, then we *can* conclude that it is *practically* acceptable, that we are practically rational in accepting it.[32] Presumably this feature of a doxastic practice of its being FE (firmly established) is thought to have an advantage over the feature of a doxastic practice of its being R (reliable), with regard to the dialectic above. But it is hard to see how it can possibly enjoy any such advantage. For in order to reach the belief that our total way of forming beliefs W is firmly established—B:FE(W)—we could hardly avoid using W itself. And it is not hard to see that indefinitely many crazy ways W* of forming beliefs might (conceivably) be equally effective, if used by one in one's circumstances, in leading to the belief—B:FE(W*)—that W* is firmly established for us, even though W* is still clearly unacceptable. What is more, it is also conceivable that there be a way W* that might *in fact* become firmly established, even though W* remained unacceptable (by our present lights, of course). Conclusion: It is hard to see the advantage in moving from reliability to firm establishment and practical reasonableness. True, even if using W to settle whether W is reliable would yield a positive verdict, that is not enough to lift W above its many competitors with an analogous feature. But, similarly, even if using W to settle whether W is firmly established would yield a positive verdict, that is not enough to lift W above its similar competitors *either*. It might be answered that we needn't *see* W *as firmly established* in order for its firm establishment to lend us practical justification for using it. But then why need we *see* W *as reliable* in order for its reliability to lend us epistemic justification for using it?

Again, suppose we use way W, and that the use of W assures us that W itself is reliable. Indeed, consider our situation in the very *best conceivable outcome.* Suppose:

a) W *is* reliable (and suppose even that, given our circumstances and fundamental nature, it is the *most* reliable overall way we could have).

b) We are *right* in our description of W: it *is* exactly W that we use in forming beliefs, and it is of course (therefore) W that we use in forming the belief that W is our way of forming beliefs.

c) We *believe* that W *is* reliable (correctly so, given *a* above), and this belief, too, is formed by means of W.

Now what? Are we still in a 'desperate situation'? What could possibly be missing? How could we possibly improve our epistemic situation?

It might be suggested that perhaps we could still search for some argument that would not be flawed by epistemic circularity. But is such circularity necessarily vicious? After all, what does an argument *ever* accomplish? Suppose you are given argument A with premises P and conclusion C and you correctly accept it as evidently valid. What this gives you in the first instance is the conviction that P entails C. And, unless you go back on this conviction, you are now *restricted* in the combinations of coherent attitudes that are open to you. But that is all that the argument by itself does: i.e., that is all you can derive from its validity. As far as the argument goes, its relevant deliverance is your belief that P entails C, and this justifies your believing C, given that you believe P, only by contrast with believing P and either disbelieving or consciously withholding on C. But it does not justify your believing C, given that you believe P, by contrast with many other optional attitudes: e.g., disbelieving C and disbelieving P.N.B.: it is a kind of intrinsic coherence that lifts the preferable attitudes over the lesser ones: once we have **(a) B:[P entails C]**, we need to avoid **(b) B:P and D:C,** and **(c) B:P and Wh:C**—where D:P means B: ~P, and Wh:P means consciously or deliberately withholding on whether P or ~P. Many other combinations of attitudes remain open options, of course, but so long as we retain (a), both (b) and (c) are to be avoided. Why so? Because they do not cohere well. There is some evident lack of fittingness or harmony in each of them. Here I won't try to spell out the exact nature of the incoherence that attaches not only to (a) & (b) but also to (a) & (c). I'll assume we can agree that it is there, whatever its nature. In fact, it is not really necessary to say anything that strong. A comparative judgment is enough. Consider: **(d) B:P and B:C.** All we need is the judgment that (a) & (d) is more coherent than either of (a) & (b) or (a) & (c). Given (a), which results from our supposed argument above, (d) is lifted over each of (b) and (c) in respect of coherence.

The upshot: all that (the validity of) an argument ever does is to raise some combinations of attitudes (to premises and conclusion respectively) above others in respect of coherence.

But now suppose that by using way W of forming beliefs (which may and probably will include the use of argument) we arrive at the conviction that W is our way of forming beliefs. Now, so long as we do not go back on that conviction, does that not restrict our coherent combinations of attitudes? Take: **(e) B:[W is my overall way of forming beliefs]**. And compare **(f) B:[W is reliable]**, **(g) D:[W is reliable]** and **(h) Wh:[W is reliable]**. Is it not evident that (e) & (f) would be more satisfyingly coherent than either of (e) & (g) or (e) & (h)?

If so, the question arises: Just how would any further argument provide a fundamentally different and superior source of justification or rationality for our accepting the reliability of our overall way W of forming beliefs, as compared with what we are provided already by our conviction that W is indeed that overall way of ours?

The answer might come back: 'But once we had an argument A for W being reliable from premises already accepted, we would embed our faith in W's reliability within a more comprehensively coherent whole that would include the premises of our argument A.' And it must be granted that such an argument *would* bring that benefit. However: we know that such an argument would *have* to be epistemically circular, since its premises can only qualify as beliefs of ours through the use of way W. That is to say, a correct and full response to rational pressure for disclosure of what justifies one in upholding the premises must circle back down to the truth of the conclusion. *Necessarily* such an argument must be epistemically circular—that much seems clear enough. To rue that fact at this stage is hence like pining for a patron saint of modesty (who blesses all and only those who do not bless themselves), once we have seen that there could not possibly be such a saint.

Perhaps the dissatisfaction emphasized by Alston and Stroud, and many others, has a different source than any we have considered. Perhaps it arises from the following reasoning:

> If we justify our belief in the reliability of our W—B:R(W)—by noting that W itself yields B:R(W), then anyone with a rival but self-supporting method W* would be able to attain an equal measure of justification through parallel reasoning. They would justify their belief B:R(W*) by noting that W* itself yields B:R(W*). So are we not forced to conclude that someone clever enough could attain a measure of rational justification equal to ours so long as their way of forming beliefs, W*, turned out to be, to the same extent, coherently and comprehensively self-supporting?

If *this* is the source of the discomfort, then it is discomfort we must learn to tolerate—though in time reason should be able to dispel it, just as it would dispel any desire to meet the saint who blesses all and only the nonself blessed. After all, discursive, inferential reason is not our only faculty; and logical brilliance does not even ensure sanity. In light of this, I see no sufficient argument why we must settle, at the end of the day, for any irresolvable theoretical frustration.

We need to distinguish the internal justification that amounts to rational coherence, or even to rational coherence plus rational intuition, from the broader intellectual virtue required for knowledge. In order to know that p, one's belief must not fail the test of rational, internal coherence. But it must be tested in other ways as well: it must be true, for one thing. And, more than that, it must be *apt*: it must be a belief that manifests overall intellectual virtue, and is not flawed essentially by vice. (Mr. Magoo can infer brilliantly and a belief of his can manifest *that* virtue, while it is still flawed by epistemic vice and fails to manifest overall virtue.) Finally, if it is to amount to knowledge a belief must be such that, in the circumstances, it *would* be held by that subject iff it were true, and this in virtue of its being apt in the way that it is apt, in virtue of deriving from the complex of virtues that form it and sustain it.

Suppose we are rationally justified in accepting the reliability of our way of forming beliefs W, and suppose our justification derives from the way that very belief coheres within our overall body of beliefs. Then we do of course commit ourselves to the consequence that anyone intelligent enough to secure an equal measure of coherence for their body of beliefs would attain thereby a comparable degree of rational justification for their belief in the reliability of their way of forming beliefs (a belief we may assume to be already part of their corpus). And this remains so even if their way amounts on the whole to madness! For in granting them logical coherence we need not grant thereby that there is *no* epistemically pertinent distinction between them and us. There are faculties other than reason, surely, and there is plenty of scope for madness and other vices beyond the ability to spin a coherent story.

To sum up: We can legitimately and with rational justification arrive at a belief that a certain set of faculties or doxastic practices are those that we employ *and* are reliable. That remains so, even though someone mad can weave a system of comparable internal coherence and can thereby attain a comparable degree of internal justification. But in granting this we must not grant that such coherently rational belief need only be true in order to be knowledge. A coherently rational belief can fail to be apt, surely, and can even be mad if formed by a mind that is brilliantly logical though deranged in its social and physical perception and perhaps also in its memory. (A rationally coherent belief *can* also be apt, of course, and can thereby amount to knowledge as well.) Anyhow, the point remains: there is no obstacle in principle to our conceivably attaining rationally coherent belief in some general account of our own epistemic faculties and their reliability. This would be bread, not a stone (or a sheep, not a goat). Why could we not conceivably attain thereby a general understanding of how we know whatever we do know?

We have also felt the attraction of Stroud's reasoning, however: his brief for a very general and fundamental doubt against our ever conceivably attaining any such general understanding.

Stroud's reasoning, and that of many others along the historical length and contemporary breadth of philosophy, may perhaps return us to an as-

sumption that seems questionable: the questionable assumption that a satisfyingly general philosophical account of human knowledge would have to
be a legitimating account that would reveal how all such knowledge can be
traced back to some epistemically prior knowledge from which it can be
shown to be derived (without logical or epistemic circularity).[33] There is no
good reason to make this assumption, especially when it is evident that no
such general account of all our knowledge could conceivably be obtained.

The desire for a fully general, legitimating, philosophical understanding
of all our knowledge is unfulfillable. It is unfulfillable for simple, demonstrable logical reasons. In this respect it is like the desire to find the saint who
blesses all and only the nonselfblessed. A trek through the Himalayas may
turn up likely prospects each of whom eventually is seen to fall short, until
someone in the expedition reflects that there could not possibly be such a
saint, and this for evident, logical reasons. How should they all respond to
this result? They may of course be very unhappy to have been taken in by a
project now clearly defective, and this may leave them frustrated and dissatisfied. But is it reasonable for them to insist that somehow the objective is
still worthy, even if unfortunately it turns out to be incoherent? Is this a sensible response? How would we respond if we found ourselves in that situation? Would it not be a requirement of good sense or even of sanity to put
that obviously incoherent project behind us, to just forget about it and to put
our time to better use? And is that not what we must do with regard to the
search for fully general, legitimating, philosophical accounts of our knowledge?

If it does not just return us to that questionable assumption, however,
then what can be the basis for the objection to a general theory of knowledge,
indeed to one so general that it encompasses not only all our knowledge of
the external but all of our knowledge in general? Suppose one's belief in
one's theory takes the following form:

T   A belief X amounts to knowledge if and only if it satisfies conditions
     C.

It would not be long before a philosopher would wonder in virtue of what T
itself is a piece of knowledge, and if T is held as an explanatory theory for all
of our knowledge, then the answer would not be far to seek: T is a piece of
knowledge because T itself meets conditions C. And how do we know that T
meets conditions C? Well, of course, *that* belief itself must meet conditions C
in turn. And so on, without end. Is there any unacceptability in principle
here, is there any unavoidable viciousness? Compare the following three
things.

E   A belief B in a general epistemological account of when beliefs are
     justified (or apt) that applies to B itself and explains in virtue of
     what it, too, is justified (apt).

G A statement S of a general account of when statements are grammatical (or a sentence S stating when sentences are grammatical) that applies to S itself and explains in virtue of what it, too, is grammatical.

P A belief B in a general psychological account of how one acquires the beliefs one holds, an account that applies to B itself and explains why it, too, is held.

Why should E be any more problematic than G or P? Why should there be any more of a problem for a general epistemology than there would be for a general grammar the grammaticality of whose statement is explained in turn by itself, or for a general psychology belief in which is explained by that very psychology?

It must be granted that what we want is a sort of explanation that would in principle enable us to understand how we have any knowledge at all. Question: 'Why are there chickens?' Answer: 'They come from eggs.' 'And why are there eggs?' 'They come from chickens.' This exchange could not provide a complete answer to a child's question, if the question is, more fully, that of why there are chickens *at all, ever*. To answer this question we need appeal to divine creation, or evolution, or anyhow to something entirely other than chickens. Consider now the analogous question about knowledge, about the sources of the epistemic status of our knowledgeable beliefs (and not now about the causal sources of their existence). A complete answer for this question must appeal to something other than beliefs claimed already to enjoy the status of knowledge. For we want an explanation of how beliefs *ever* attain that status *at all*.

It is important to avert a confusion. We shall never be able really to *have* an explanation of anything without our *having* some knowledge, the knowledge that constitutes our having the explanation, knowledge like

K X is the case in virtue of such and such.

Though we must have such knowledge if we are to understand why X is the case, however, there is no need to include any attribution of knowledge in the explanans of K, in the 'such and such.' The concept of knowledge need not be part of that explanans. Compare again our general theory of knowledge schema:

T A belief X amounts to knowledge if and only if it satisfies conditions C.

T is something we must *know* if it is to give us real understanding, and in offering it we are perhaps, in some sense, 'presupposing' that we know it. This does not mean that our theory must be less than fully general. Our theory T may still be fully general so long as no epistemic status—e.g., knowledge, or justification—plays any role in the 'conditions C' that constitute the explanans of T.

It is true that in epistemology we want *knowledgeable* understanding, and not just 'understanding by dumb luck' (which, in the relevant sense, is incoherent anyhow, and hence not to be had). But there is no apparent reason why we cannot have it with a theory such as T, without compromising the full generality of our account. Of course in explaining how we know theory T, whether to the sceptic or to ourselves, we have to appeal to theory T itself, given the assumptions of correctness and full generality that we are making concerning T. Given those assumptions there seems no way of correctly answering such a sceptic except by 'begging the question' and 'arguing circularly' against him. But, once we understand this, what option is left to us except to go ahead and 'beg' that question against *such* a sceptic (though 'begging the question' and 'arguing circularly' may now be misnomers for what we do, since it is surely no fallacy, not if it constitutes correct and legitimate intellectual procedure). Nor are we, in proceeding thus, by means of a self-supporting argument, assuming that *all self-supporting arguments are on a par.* This would be a serious mistake. It is not just *in virtue of being self-supporting* that our belief in T would acquire its epistemic status required for knowledge. Rather it would be in virtue of meeting conditions C.[34] And conditions C must not yield that a belief or a system of beliefs has the appropriate positive epistemic status provided simply that it is self-supporting. For this would obviously be inadequate. Therefore, our belief in T *would* be self-supporting, as had better be any successful and general theory of knowledge, but it would not amount to knowledge or even to a belief with the appropriate epistemic status, *simply in virtue of being self-supporting.*

In all our reflection and in all our discussion of objections to externalism we have found no good argument for the view that epistemically circular arguments must be disqualified globally as ineffectual in making discriminations between reliable and unreliable doxastic practices. Nor have we been able to find any good reason to yield to the sceptic or to reject externalist theories of knowledge globally and antecedently as theories that could not possibly give us the kind of understanding of human knowledge in general that is a goal of epistemology. And so we have found no good reason to accept *philosophical scepticism*, the main target thesis of this paper. As for any desperate retreat to relativism or ethnocentrism, finally, that now seems ill-conceived and imperceptive.[35] I mean the retreat into relativism that sees no way of adjudicating through reason among clashing, equally coherent systems. The recoil to ethnocentrism (or the like) betrays a rationalist *malgré lui* with no objective way to adjudicate except reason.[36] Who but a philosopher could expect so much from reason?[37] What privileges our position, if anything does, cannot be that it is self-supportive, as we have seen; *but nor can it possibly be just that it is ours.* Our position would be privileged rather by deriving from cognitive virtues, from the likes of perception and cogent thought, and not from derangement or superstition or their ilk.[38]

NOTES

1. Davidson 1983, p. 426.

2. Davidson 1983, p. 431.

3. Rorty 1979, p. 178.

4. Rorty 1979, p. 159.

5. Rorty 1989, p. 48. Note the ambiguity between 'reasons for using languages' that one *has* and adduces, versus reasons that there are whether or not one has them or adduces them. And note also the assumption that only what is based on reasonings from adduced reasons can be assessed as 'rational.' (One might of course yield the vocabulary of the 'rational' in the face of such uninhibited assumptions, for the sake of the conversation, so long as one could still distinguish among beliefs, and even among 'choices of vocabulary,' those that are 'apt,' in some apt sense, from those that are not.)

6. Rorty 1979, p. 152.

7. Bonjour 1985, p. 31.

8. Williams 1988, p. 246. (This paper sketches a view developed and defended in Williams 1991.) Here Williams is attributing a view to Stroud. But in his paper (and in his book) he evidently agrees that if there were a way of attaining a general philosophical understanding of our knowledge of the world, it would have to be in terms of a legitimating account; and he does not take seriously the possibility of a substantially externalist account.

9. Such overreaction against objective foundations may drive even someone brilliant to unfortunate excesses. Compare the writings of Paul Feyerabend. Moreover, the sort of internalism that enforces capitulation to 'circularity'-wielding relativists is not confined to the *avant-garde* we have already consulted. For just one example, earlier in the century, in an otherwise most illuminating paper, Alan Gewirth had this to say: 'Consequently, it is circular to say that the basic principles of science are themselves cognitive; for it is these principles or norms which determine whether anything else is to be called cognitive. Moreover, these principles are a selection from among other possible principles—possible, that is, in the sense that they are espoused by people who claim to have "science" or "knowledge" by methods which are in important respects different from those grounded in inductive and deductive logic. These other methods include those of Christian Science, astrology, phrenology, tribal medicine-men, and many others. Each of these other methods has its own way of defining what is to be meant by "fact," "knowledge," and so forth. Hence, if any of these latter is to be called "noncognitive," it will be by reference not to *its* norms or principles but to those of *some* other way of viewing "science" or "knowledge." To claim that any of those is "absolutely" non-cognitive is to ignore the relativity of all claims of cognitiveness to norms or principles which defined what is to be meant by "cognitive." . . . Hence, strictly speaking, the choice among different conceptions of "knowledge" or "science" cannot itself be said to be made by cognitive means.' (From Gewirth 1960; the passage quoted comes from the thirteenth paragraph.) Here again, we might well yield the vocabulary of 'choices made by cognitive means,' so long as we could keep a distinction between choices or commitments that are 'apt' and those that are not, where this is not just something 'relative' to raw or brute or 'arbitrary' commitments.

10. Alston is among those who settle into irresolvable frustration, insofar as he accepts externalism at the cost of a freely avowed dissatisfaction, which, as well shall see, he takes to be inherent in the human *theoretical* condition. Insofar as he tries to struggle against this, it is by conceding the theoretical frustration, and turning to a kind of practical reasonability, in a way we shall consider.

11. The position on these issues of my Sosa 1991, has repeatedly drawn an objection (as detailed in notes 19 and 33 below) that we shall consider in what follows.

12. Stroud 1989, p. 43.

13. Compare Stroud 1989, p. 44.: '[Descartes is] . . . a theorist of knowledge. He wants to understand how he knows the things he thinks he knows. And he cannot satisfy himself on that score unless he can see himself as having some reason to accept the theory that he (and all the rest of us) can recognize would explain his knowledge if it were true. That is not because knowing implies knowing that you know. It is because having an explanation of something in the sense of understanding it is a matter of having good reason to accept something that would be an explanation if it were true.'

14. Compare here again the passages from Davidson and Rorty cited earlier, and the consequences drawn by Rorty not only for theory but also for praxis.

15. Stroud 1989, p. 45.

16. Stroud 1989, p. 46.

17. Stroud 1989, p. 47.

18. Compare Stroud on this: 'We want witting, not unwitting, understanding. That requires knowing or having some reason to accept the scientific story you believe about how people know the things they know. And in the case of knowledge of the world around us, that would involve already knowing or having some reason to believe something in the domain in question. Not all the knowledge in that domain would thereby be explained.' (Stroud 1989, p. 48.) Also: 'The demand for completely general understanding of knowledge in a certain domain requires that we see ourselves at the outset as not knowing anything in that domain and then coming to have such knowledge on the basis of some independent and in that sense prior knowledge or experience . . . [When] we try to explain how we know . . . things [in a domain we are interested in] we find we can understand it only by assuming that we have got some knowledge in the domain in question. And that is not philosophically satisfying. We have lost the prospect of explaining and therefore understanding all of our knowledge with complete generality.' (Stroud 1989, pp. 48–9.)

19. Alston 1991, p. 148. In a review of my Sosa 1993, Alston adds that 'it is plausible to suppose that we cannot give an impressive argument for the reliability of sense perception without making use of what we have learned from sense perception. This problem affects Sosa's view as much as it does any other form of externalism that requires for justification or knowledge that the source of a belief be truth-conducive. To apply Sosa's view we would have to determine which belief forming habits are intellectual virtues, i.e., which can be depended on to yield mostly true beliefs. Doesn't epistemic circularity attach to these enterprises, by his own showing? What does he have to say about that?' (Alston, 1993b).

20. Alston 1993.

21. Alston 1993, p. 17. The problem is supposed to arise from the fact that the data on the basis of which a track-record argument reaches the conclusion that a certain doxastic practice DP is reliable, are data that derive (at some remove, if not immediately) from the use of that very practice DP.

22. Alston 1993a, p. 120. My emphasis.

23. Alston 1993a, p. 130.

24. Alston 1993a, p. 7.

25. Alston 1993a, p. 131.

26. Alston 1993a, p. 127.

27. Alston 1993a, p. 125.

28. Alston 1993a.

29. Alston 1993a, p. 126.

30. Alston 1993a, p. 15.

31. Alston 1993a, p. 17.

32. I will use 'firmly established' here as short for 'firmly established in the way described more fully by Alston and proposed by him as sufficient for practical reasonableness or rationality'.

33. See p. 96 above. And compare Paul Moser's statement of the difficulty as he sees it (Moser 1991): 'What . . . can effectively justify one's meta-belief in the virtue of memory? What can effectively justify the claim that "the products of such faculties are likely to be true"? These questions . . . ask what, if anything, can provide a cogent defense of the alleged reliability of memory against familiar sceptical queries . . . The . . . questions ask not for absolute proof, but for a non-questionbegging reason supporting the alleged reliability of memory, a reason that does not beg a key question against the sceptic. It is doubtful that we can deliver such a reason; coherence of mere beliefs will surely not do the job.' Wilkerson 1992 also joins the broad consensus against the supposed 'circularity' in externalism: 'How can I know that I am intellectually virtuous, that I have a settled ability or disposition to arrive at the truth? Indeed, how do I know that I have arrived at the truth? As Sosa points out, it is no good to answer that my beliefs are true in so far as they are justified by other beliefs: that way lies either old-fashioned foundationalism or coherentism. Nor presumably is it any good to say that they are justified because they have been acquired in an intellectually virtuous way: the circle seems swift and unbreakable.'

34. This seems the key to an answer for Alston's charge that epistemically circular arguments 'do not serve to discriminate between reliable and unreliable doxastic practices,' cited earlier. One can make such discriminations with epistemically circular arguments (ones with premises that are in fact true and justified, etc.) even if it is not the circular character of the reasoning that by itself effects the discrimination.

35. And a similar objection can be lodged, based on similar reflections, on the analogous retreat in moral and political philosophy.

36. About other views that are in some way 'relativist' I remain silent.

37. And, besides, the irrationalist cannot be answered nonquestionbeggingly anyhow, not if our answer presupposes the validity of reason. When thought through, the requirement of nonquestionbegging defensibility against all conceivable comers in ill-advised, and indeed incoherent. But once we see why that is so, we should see also that reason cannot plausibly be held above perception or memory as a proper source of epistemic status.

38. 'But that bare assertion is so empty! Which are these virtues? What means this cogency? What else is involved?' To this reaction the response would have to be a very long story, if told in full, one that turns now longer, now shorter, with every advance in our understanding of ourselves and our thought and our environment and our origins, and the relations among all these. One's epistemic perspective is joined indispensably to one's broader worldview.

CHAPTER 7   # Process Reliabilism and Cartesian Scepticism

Christopher S. Hill

SECTION I: INTRODUCTION

I will be concerned here with a theory of doxastic justification that was first proposed by Alvin Goldman in 1979.[1] This theory, which is generally known as *process reliabilism*, has in recent years gone through a number of changes, and each change has added significantly to its complexity and subtlety. However, for present purposes it suffices to consider a skeletal version of the theory that is similar to the version that was unveiled in Goldman's original advertisement. This version runs as follows: where S is any subject, and p is any proposition, S is epistemically justified in believing that p if and only if (i) S believes that p, (ii) S has this belief as the result of a cognitive process that is highly reliable, (iii) S is not in possession of any reliably formed beliefs that imply either that p is false or that the process mentioned in (ii) is unreliable, and (iv) S could not easily come into possession of any beliefs of the sorts mentioned in (iii).[2] As is usual, I am here using "epistemically justified" to stand for the form of justification that is most intimately bound up with knowledge. Further, as is also usual, I am assuming that "reliable" is to be understood in terms of probability of truth, where "probability" stands for some sort of *objective* likelihood. Thus, to say that a cognitive process is reli-

"Process Reliabilism and Cartesian Scepticism" from *Philosophy and Phenomenological Research* 56 (1996, pp. 567–581). Reprinted by permission of the publisher.

I have been helped enormously by Alvin Goldman's comments on three (!) ancestors of this paper, by Stewart Cohen's comments on the immediately preceding ancestor, and by conversations with Thomas Senor. I have also benefited from the comments of audiences at Central Michigan University, Indiana University, and the University of Pittsburgh. My research was supported by a N.E.H. Summer Stipend.

able is to say that beliefs produced by that process are, as a matter of objective, empirical fact, quite likely to be true.

Although process reliabilism enjoys considerable popularity at present, and is much discussed in the contemporary literature, very little has been written about the relationship between reliabilism and Cartesian scepticism. As a result, we have no real grasp of whether reliabilism has anything of importance to teach us about scepticism, nor of whether scepticism has anything of importance to teach us about process reliabilism. The present paper is my attempt to rectify this situation.

I will be concerned with several interrelated issues. After sketching a version of the Cartesian sceptic's argument in section II, I will consider an objection to process reliabilism that derives from certain properties of that argument. I will provide a detailed formulation of this objection in section III, and will attempt to answer the objection in section IV. Then, in sections V and VI, I will discuss the claim that considerations having to do with reliability are ultimately irrelevant to the sceptic's concerns. I will examine two arguments for this claim, and will endeavor to show that both of these arguments fail. If my replies to the arguments are successful, then, by the end of section VI, the way will be clear for the reliabilist to insist that the sceptic must address questions of reliability in conducting his investigations. In section VII I will conclude by arguing that the sceptic is unable to deal with questions of this sort in a satisfactory way. If the sceptic is obliged to confront such questions, then, I will maintain, the sceptical enterprise is bound to fail.

SECTION II: THE SCEPTIC'S ARGUMENT

Let McX be a normal human agent, and let the *Real World Hypothesis* (RWH) be the hypothesis that can be obtained by conjoining the following propositions: (i) McX has always had a normal human body; (ii) the sense experiences that McX has enjoyed in the past have been due to external phenomena of the sorts that McX has believed to be causally responsible for them (that is, they have been due to such common-sensical external causes as cats and dogs, and tables and chairs); and (iii) the pattern specified in (ii) continues to obtain in the present. Further, let SH be the sceptical hypothesis which claims (i) that unbeknownst to McX, McX's brain has been removed from his body and is being kept alive in a vat of fluids, (ii) that McX is connected to an extremely powerful computer that monitors all of McX's thoughts, (iii) that the sense experiences that McX has enjoyed in the past have been due to electrical pulses inside this computer, and (iv) that the pattern described in (iii) continues to obtain in the present.[3]

Having set the stage with these definitions, we can formulate an argument for Cartesian scepticism as follows:

First premise: Where S is any subject and H_1 and H_2 are any two empirical hypotheses, S is not justified in preferring H_1 to H_2 (i.e., in believing H_1 and rejecting H_2) unless S is in possession of evidence that supports H_1 more strongly than it supports H_2.

Second premise: In determining whether McX is justified in preferring RWH to SH, it is appropriate to set all non-sensory evidence aside, and to focus exclusively on facts involving McX's sense experiences and their purely sensory characteristics.

Third premise: Since RWH and SH differ only with respect to their claims about the causation of McX's sense experiences, and not at all with respect to their claims about the experiences themselves, the purely sensory evidence that is available to McX supports RWH and SH to the same degree.

Lemma: McX is not justified in preferring RWH to SH, and by the same token, McX is not justified in believing RWH.

Fourth premise: Where S is any subject and p is any proposition, S does not know that p unless S is justified in believing that p.

Conclusion: McX does not know that RWH is true.

This line of thought seems to capture the spirit of a number of standard formulations of scepticism. For example, it seems to capture most of the intuitions that are mobilized by the argument that appears in the *First Meditation.*

The first, third, and fourth premises of the argument all enjoy a considerable amount of intuitive plausibility, but the sceptic has often felt obliged to say something in support of the second premise. The standard defense of this premise is a line of thought that I will call the *evidence argument.* This line of thought runs as follows:

In order to count as evidence, extramental facts must be known to us. Now the senses are our only avenues of cognitive access to extramental facts. Accordingly, extramental facts can count as evidence only insofar as they are represented by the deliverances of the senses. It follows that all of our extramental evidence is in a sense included within our sensory evidence. Thus, if we are justified in holding a belief on the basis of extramental evidence, then we must also be justified in holding the belief on the basis of sensory evidence. And, by the same token, if we wish to determine whether a belief is justified by extramental facts, it suffices to consider the belief in relation to the available sensory evidence. It follows, of course, that in considering whether McX is justified in preferring RWH to SH, the sceptic is entitled to set all of McX's extramental evidence aside. It is entirely appropriate for the sceptic to focus on McX's sensory evidence.

This argument will play an important role in later sections.

The present version of the sceptic's reasoning is intended to do justice to the common core of a large family of arguments, and it is therefore silent on many issues that can arise in discussions of scepticism. Thus, for example, nothing is said about the possibility that McX is justified in preferring RWH to SH by considerations having to do with the supraempirical virtues (i.e., with such properties of hypotheses as simplicity and explanatory power).

The reader may feel that this omission limits the plausibility of the argument; but even so, it seems likely that he or she will at least grant that the argument makes a start, that it provides a foundation on which the sceptic might naturally hope to build. After all, the version of the argument that appears in the *First Meditation* says nothing of simplicity nor of any other supraempirical virtue; but it is usually thought to be philosophically challenging.

As is common, I have refrained from using the terms "epistemically justified" and "epistemic justification" in stating the argument. However, it is clear that epistemic justification is the form of justification that the sceptic has in mind. Thus, the fourth premise makes it explicit that the sceptic is concerned with a form of justification that is intimately bound up with knowledge. Given the standard definition of "epistemic justification," it follows immediately that epistemic justification is the target of the sceptic's argument.

SECTION III: AN OBJECTION TO PROCESS RELIABILISM

There are prima facie grounds for thinking that process reliabilism is called into question by the plausibility of the sceptic's argument—that is, by the fact that the sceptic's reasoning is extremely seductive. Reliabilism implies that questions of epistemic justification depend ultimately on contingent empirical facts having to do with the reliability ratings of cognitive processes. Hence, it implies that questions of epistemic justification are a posteriori. But the sceptic attempts to support a very general claim about epistemic justification—viz., the claim that common sense beliefs about the external world are unjustified—by an argument that seems to be entirely a priori. It appears, therefore, that if process reliabilism gives a correct account of epistemic justification, then the sceptic has made an absurd mistake—a mistake that should be apparent to anyone who has mastered the concept of epistemic justification. But we all know that scepticism is not absurd. As we all know, generations of philosophers and laymen have studied Cartesian scepticism, and it has won the grudging respect of almost all of these individuals. Usually, of course, they have found it impossible to accept the sceptic's conclusion, but for the most part they have been profoundly impressed by the reasoning that leads to that conclusion.

I have found that this objection to process reliabilism does not always seem persuasive when it is encountered for the first time, so I will repeat it here in somewhat different language: According to reliabilism, the question of whether one is epistemically justified in holding a belief is essentially an empirical question about the reliability ratings of the cognitive processes that are responsible for the belief. Hence, since the sceptic wishes to reject the claim that McX is epistemically justified in believing RWH, he is under an obligation to confront the question of whether McX's cognitive processes are reliable. In particular, he is under an obligation to assemble empirical data concerning actual degrees of reliability. However, as can be seen by examining the foregoing argument, the sceptic makes no attempt to discharge this obligation. Indeed, he says nothing whatsoever which suggests that he is aware that he is dealing with an empirical issue.

Thus, if process reliabilism gives a correct account of epistemic justification, the sceptic is guilty of an omission that is extremely damaging. Moreover, reliabilism seems to imply that it is an egregious omission—an omission that would be noticed by anyone who has grasped even the most basic facts about the nature of epistemic justification. However, philosophers and laymen have studied the argument for centuries without noticing the lacuna. Instead of complaining that the sceptic fails to address the issue of reliability ratings, they have come away profoundly troubled by the apparent strength of the argument. It appears, therefore, that process reliabilism has a consequence that is sharply at variance with the facts.[4]

SECTION IV: TWO REPLIES TO THE OBJECTION

Although this objection can seem to be quite telling, careful reflection shows that it can be answered. Indeed, there are two ways of answering it.

The first answer: This answer begins with an observation about the logical structure of the sceptic's argument—specifically, the observation that, contrary to what the objection maintains, the sceptic *does* address questions of reliability. To be sure, he does not address such questions explicitly. However, the argument implies that considerations of reliability can have no bearing on the points at issue, and that it is therefore entirely appropriate to set them aside. Thus, the first and second premises of the argument imply that McX's justification for preferring RWH to SH must derive *exclusively* from relations between beliefs and sense experience. Among other things, this rules out the possibility that McX's preference is justified by the reliability of certain of his belief-forming processes.

If all goes well for the sceptic, then, the first and second premises of the argument will neutralize the perception that considerations of reliability must somehow be relevant to the enterprise of assessing the justifactory status of McX's beliefs. But does it really seem likely that this could happen? After all, if the concept of epistemic justification really is fundamentally reliabilist in character, then we must have a fairly strong disposition to see questions of justification from a reliabilist perspective. Does it really seem that a disposition of this sort would be inhibited by the first and second premises? Our answer to this question must depend on the degree of plausibility that we suppose these premises to possess. Now as we saw, the first premise enjoys a considerable intuitive appeal.[5] However, as we also noticed, the second premise is at first sight somewhat problematic. If it is able to play a role in neutralizing a fairly deep-seated disposition, it must owe this ability to the evidence argument (that is, to the line of thought that we considered in the third paragraph of section II).

How about it? Does the evidence argument have an appropriate amount of plausibility? I am not of course in a position to speak for the reader, but I myself find the argument to be extremely persuasive. To my mind, it is quite capable of causing one to think that the sceptic has defined the area under dispute, and the resources available to the contending parties, in a fair and accurate way, and that it would therefore be a mistake to attempt to introduce new considerations into the discussion. The argument is capable of causing one to think that the sceptic's game must be played by the sceptic's rules.

The second answer: This answer consists in citing a line of thought which can reasonably be supposed to play a role in shaping the form of debates about scepticism. This line of thought, which I will call *the circularity argument*, runs as follows:

> SH implies that McX's beliefs about extramental facts are false, and it purports to explain their plausibility away. In view of these considerations, it is clear that McX's beliefs about extramental facts must be regarded as controversial in any context in which SH is up for assessment. Because of this, if McX were to attempt to defend his preference for RWH over SH by appealing to any propositions about extramental facts, he would beg the question. But a defense that begs the question is not a real defense. Hence, propositions about extramental facts cannot provide a justification for McX's preference.

Of course, since propositions about reliability fall within the category of propositions about extramental reality, the conclusion of this argument implies that propositions about reliability can have no bearing on the question of whether McX's preference is justified. In effect, the conclusion tells us that the sceptic has every right to set considerations having to do with reliability aside.

Like the evidence argument, I find the circularity argument to be highly persuasive. Moreover, while I do not know of any published version of the sceptic's reasoning in which the argument figures explicitly, I have found that it has a strong tendence to surface, sooner or later, in conversations about scepticism. My guess is that both the sceptic and his audience have versions of the circularity argument implicitly in mind, and that these implicit versions are partly responsible for the fact that there is a tendency to ignore considerations of reliability in discussions of scepticism.

To summarize: According to the objection stated in section III, the sceptic completely overlooks the relevance of considerations of reliability to the question of whether McX is justified in preferring RWH to SH. Reflection shows that this claim is highly questionable. The sceptic may not make explicit mention of reliability; but there are two plausible lines of thought which suggest that he is entitled to set considerations of reliability aside, and it is reasonable to suppose that he is counting on these lines of thought to neutralize the reliabilist perceptions of his audience.

SECTION V: WHY THE EVIDENCE ARGUMENT FAILS

We must now turn to consider whether the evidence argument and the circularity argument are ultimately successful. Do they show that considerations of reliability are irrelevant to the sceptic's main concerns, or do they fall short of establishing this claim? I will discuss the evidence argument in the present section and the circularity argument in section VI.

Now as I see it, the evidence argument is free from internal flaws; as far as it goes, it is a successful argument. Reflection shows, however, that it fails to serve the sceptic's purpose. Its conclusion is unable to bear the logical weight that the sceptic assigns to it.

The conclusion of the evidence argument can be represented by the following proposition:

> *Proposition A:* If one wishes to determine whether McX is justified in preferring RWH to SH, it is permissible to set all of McX's extramental evidence aside, and to focus exclusively on McX's sensory evidence.

What the sceptic needs, however, is a proposition which implies the second premise of the main sceptical argument. As the reader may remember, this premise runs as follows:

> *Proposition B:* In determining whether McX is justified in preferring RWH to SH, it is appropriate to set all non-sensory evidence aside, and to focus exclusively on facts involving McX's sense experiences and their purely sensory characteristics.

Prima facie, it appears that Proposition B follows easily from Proposition A; but closer inspection reveals that there is a substantial logical gap between the two propositions. Proposition A tells us that we may focus on *a certain set of evidentiary phenomena*, namely, McX's sense experiences. On the other hand, Proposition B tells us that we may focus on *a certain set of facts involving those phenomena*. Specifically, it tells us that we may focus on facts whose only constituents are McX's sense experiences and purely sensory characteristics of such experiences. Thus, while Proposition A leaves it open which facts involving McX's sense experiences are relevant to the task at hand (i.e., the task of determining whether McX's perceptual beliefs are justified), Proposition B makes a definite claim about which facts are relevant to this task. In short, Proposition B is more restrictive than Proposition A. It follows that Proposition B has more content than Proposition A, and by the same token, it follows that Proposition B is not implied by Proposition A.

Perhaps it would be useful to characterize the gap between A and B in terms of an example. Suppose that C is the characteristic *being an experience of a sensory type T such that experiences of type T are usually produced in normal human beings by visual interactions with crows.* Further, suppose that F is the fact that C is exemplified by a certain one of McX's sense experiences. Now Proposition A leaves it open whether we are entitled to consider facts like F in determining whether McX is justified in holding his perceptual beliefs. But Proposition B tells us that we may ignore such facts. For Proposition B authorizes us to ignore all facts involving McX's sense experiences other than purely sensory facts, that is, facts that involve only purely sensory characteristics. (C is a characteristic of sense experiences, but it is not a purely sensory characteristic, because it is a characteristic that sense experiences have in virtue of certain of their relations to extramental particulars. It is an *informational* characteristic of sense experiences.)

But is the logical gap between A and B of any importance for our present concerns? Is it connected in any way with the sceptics's dialectical responsibilities? Does the sceptic make life any easier for himself by obtaining an (invalid) authorization to set aside all facts other than purely sensory facts? It is clear that the answer is "yes." As the example in the previous paragraph shows, Proposition B gives the sceptic leave to ignore facts involving the *informational characteristics* of McX's sense experiences, that is, the characteristics that McX's experiences possess in virtue of their causal and probabilistic relations to extramental objects and events. It also gives the sceptic leave to ignore facts involving the *truth-generating propensities* of sense experiences, that is, facts involving characteristics that sense experiences have in virtue of their tendencies to trigger reliable cognitive processes. In general, Proposition B gives the sceptic leave to ignore all of the sorts of facts that externalists believe to be constitutive of the evidentiary status of sense experiences. It appears, then, that by fallaciously passing from Proposition A to Proposition B, the sceptic is in effect sidestepping the question of whether an externalist theory of evidentiary status might be correct. But clearly, this question is of fundamental importance for the sceptic's project. If an externalist theory of evidentiary status is correct, then the sceptic cannot hope to establish a sceptical conclusion by an a priori argument. If an externalist theory of evidentiary status is correct, then, instead of proceeding along an a priori path, the sceptic should set about amassing empirical data concerning the informational characteristics and/or the truth-generating propensities of McX's sense experiences.[6]

It appears, then, that the sceptic's reasoning is badly flawed. It involves a logical error, namely, the error of thinking that Proposition B is a consequence of Proposition A. Moreover, this error makes a difference. Because of the error, the sceptic is able to sidestep a set of ideas that threaten to call his entire *modus operandi* into question.

But now we must ask: Why is the error so seductive? This question can be partly answered by appealing to the superficial linguistic similarities between Proposition A and Proposition B. I think, however, that if we are to do full justice to the seductiveness of the error, we must find an additional explanation. I will briefly sketch a view that provides one.

According to the view that I have in mind, we are in possession of two concepts of evidential support, one externalist and the other internalist, and we have a tendency to confuse them. Very roughly speaking, the externalist conception can be explained as follows: Where T is a sense experience and B is a belief, T can provide evidentiary support for B if and only if there is a cognitive process P and a set S of experiences such that (i) S includes T, (ii) S would cause P to produce B if its members were given to P as inputs, (iii) the set that results from S by deleting T does not have this causal power, and (iv) the outputs of P have a fairly high objective probability of truth.[7] The internalist conception is like this externalist conception in that it invokes a form of probability, but it is different in that the form it invokes is "personal" or "subjective" in character. According to this second concept, sense experiences (or propositions about sense experiences) are capable of influencing subjective probabilities, and since they are, it is appropriate to think of them as being capable of providing evidence for beliefs. Now the capacities of sense experiences to influence the subjective probabilities of beliefs are independent of relations between sense experiences and extramental objects and events. (Thus, the subjective probabilities of McX's beliefs would be affected by his sense experiences in the same way in a world in which McX was a brain in a vat as they are in the actual world, provided only that the experiences themselves were the same in intrinsic nature and in order of occurrence.) Accordingly, the second conception represents the evidentiary statuses of sense experiences as independent of their informational characteristics and their truth-generating propensities.

Let us assume that we really are in possession of two concepts of evidential support, and that these concepts roughly fit the foregoing characterizations. Now these concepts are similar in a fundamental respect: They both represent evidential support as depending on the abilities of sense experiences to probabilify beliefs. To be sure, the notions of probability to which they appeal are markedly different. However, as is shown by the history of theories of probability, the human mind finds it extremely difficult to distinguish between different ways in which beliefs can be probabilified by experience. (It is arguable that the tools that are necessary for drawing the appropriate distinctions in a fully adequate way did not become available until 1931, when Ramsey's "Truth and Probability" appeared.)[8] Hence, it is reasonable to suppose that there is a tendency to confuse the externalist conception of evidential support with the internalist conception. But if we are disposed to confuse the externalist conception with the internalist conception, then, surely, we are also disposed to make logical errors in contexts in which the differences between these two conceptions are relevant. Accordingly, since the context of appraising the justificational status of McX's empirical beliefs is a context of precisely this sort, it is reasonable to suppose that we have a disposition that would cause us to fall readily into the logical trap that is created by the superficial linguistic similarities between Proposition A and Proposition B. In other words, on the view I am presently sketching, it is reasonable to see the sceptic's logical error as entirely natural.[9,10]

SECTION VI: WHY THE CIRCULARITY ARGUMENT FAILS

Let us turn now to consider the circularity argument. Is there any reason to think that, despite initial appearances to the contrary, this second argument is flawed?

Yes. The circularity argument depends crucially on a premise that can be stated as follows: If S is obliged to beg the question in defending a belief, then the belief is unjustified. After reflection, it becomes clear that this premise is false. Thus, according to the standard definition of "begging the question," one begs the question in defending a belief if, in the course of stating one's defense, one assumes the very point that is to be established. This definition allows that it is possible to be justified in holding a belief even though one would perforce beg the question in attempting to defend it. To appreciate this, suppose that McV has a terrible headache, but that McV's employer, who has grounds for thinking that McV is a malingerer, doubts this. Here it is natural to suppose that McV is fully justified in believing that he is in pain; but, assuming that no machine for scanning McV's brain is available, and that he has no fever nor any other overt symptom whose force is uncontroversial, he is incapable of getting his employer to share his belief. All he can do is assert that he is in pain. Since any such assertion "assumes the very point that is to be established," McV has no choice but to beg the question in defending his belief.

Reflection shows that the notion of begging the question serves a rather different set of interests than the notion of being unjustified. The former notion is an essentially pragmatic concept: it is designed to help us with the task of evaluating the persuasive force of arguments. Thus, when we deploy this notion, we do so because we wish to criticize someone for defending a claim in a way that is bound to be unpersuasive. We think it is bad to beg the question in defending a claim because a defense that begs the question is inevitably as controversial as the point that the defense is designed to support. On the other hand, questions of epistemic justification are logically independent of questions of persuasive force. To be epistemically justified in holding a belief is to be *entitled* to hold it. The question of whether one is entitled to hold a belief is logically independent of whether one is in a position to convince others that one is so entitled, and, a fortiori, logically independent of the question of whether one is in a position to convince others to adopt the belief themselves.

Any decent theory of epistemic justification will sustain this point, but it is made especially vivid by process reliabilism. According to reliabilism, if a belief is produced by a reliable process, then, normally, one is justified in holding this belief. But it is clear that the question of whether a belief is reliably formed is independent of whether one is able to persuade others that it is reliably formed, and, a fortiori, independent of whether one is able to persuade others that the belief is true.

But is it genuinely plausible to say that the sceptic has in effect confused a question of justificatory force with a question of persuasive force? I think so. After all, the question of whether one is justified in holding a belief tends to arise only in situations in which the belief is at least somewhat controversial. Because of this, it is reasonable to suppose that one's sense of whether a belief is justified is largely determined by one's sense of whether one is in a position to dispel controversy about the belief. Moreover, one knows from experience that one's ability to dispel controversy depends entirely on the persuasive force of the considerations that one is able to adduce in defending the belief. In view of these facts, it seems that human subjects would find it hard *not* to confuse questions of justificatory force with questions of persuasive force.

SECTION VII: ADDITIONAL PROBLEMS FOR THE SCEPTIC

I urged in section IV that the sceptic has two reasons for thinking it appropriate to set considerations having to do with reliability aside—the evidence argument and the circularity argument. We have found that neither of these reasons is ultimately valid. Accordingly, it may well be the case that the sceptic is obliged to consider the question of whether McX's empirical beliefs are formed by reliable processes.

Let us suppose that process reliabilism is true,[11] and that the sceptic *does* have an obligation to consider this question. Does it seem at all likely that he could succeed in showing that McX's cognitive processes are not reliable? In particular, does it seem at all likely that he could succeed in showing that McX's *perceptual* processes are not reliable? Well, since questions of reliability are empirical questions, the sceptic would be under an obligation to appeal to empirical data. An appeal of this sort would of course be something of an embarrassment to the sceptic, holding as he does that no empirical beliefs are epistemically justified. But, what is worse, it seems that it would be impossible for him to come up with empirical data of the required sort. Thus, pace Sextus Empiricus, it seems that it would be impossible to find empirical data which establish that perceptual processes are globally unreliable—or, at least, impossible to find empirical data which establish that the perceptual processes of an average individual like McX are globally unreliable. To be sure, there are occasional conflicts between the deliverances of the senses; and science occasionally calls a prima facie robust perceptual datum into question. But facts of this sort are hardly numerous enough to establish the sweeping generalization that the sceptic needs. It seems that, on the whole, the available evidence indicates that the perceptual processes of normal individuals like McX are quite reliable.

It seems appropriate to conclude that reliabilism, so far from being refuted by scepticism, as we initially feared, may actually help us to understand why skepticism is ultimately unsatisfactory.

NOTES

1. Goldman 1979.

2. As any reasonable theory of epistemic justification recognizes, it can happen that a belief seems prima facie to be justified, but that the belief falls short of being fully or ultimately justified because its possessor has other beliefs that call either the truth or the justification of the first belief into question. In short, a prima facie justification can be annulled or "defeated" by other considerations. Clauses (iii) and (iv) in the present formulation of process reliabilism are intended to accommodate this intuition about the defeasibility of justification.

Now, according to (iii) and (iv), if the prima facie justification that is possessed by one belief is defeated by another belief, then it must be the case that the second belief is produced by a reliable process. There are philosophers, I think, who would prefer to weaken (iii) and (iv) so as to block this implication. That is to say, they would prefer to replace (iii) and (iv) with weaker conditions that run as follows: (iii′) S is not in possession of any beliefs (whether reliably formed or not) that imply either that p is false or that the process mentioned in (ii) is unreliable, and (iv′) S could not easily come into possession of any beliefs of the sorts mentioned in (iii′).

This alternative view of defeasibility seems wrong to me, but I will not attempt to criticize it here. Suffice it to say that nothing of substance in the present paper turns on the claim that (iii) and (iv) are correct: if they were replaced by (iii′) and (iv′), it would be necessary to change the details of several of the arguments, but the conclusions of the arguments would remain fundamentally the same.

3. As is well known, Hilary Putnam has developed an engaging and provocative objection to sceptical hypotheses like SH. (See, for example, Putnam, in this volume.) Putnam's objection lies outside the scope of the present paper; but since I attempt in the present paper to construct a quite different objection, I would like to sketch very briefly my reason for being dissatisfied with Putnam's objection.

It seems to me that Putnam's objection commits a fallacy of relevance. As I understand his argument, one of Putnam's main premises is the causal theory of reference (which, very roughly speaking, asserts that the reference of terms depends on their causal relations to extralinguistic phenomena), and the other main premise is the disquotational theory of reference (which, again very roughly speaking, asserts that all instances of the schema "'T' refers to x if and only if x is (a) T" are analytic). (Here I am following Brueckner and Wright. See Brueckner [in this volume]. See also Wright 1992b.) As I see it, the claims that these theories make about reference are radically different—so different that they could not possibly both be true unless they involved different concepts of reference, different senses of "refer." (As my colleague Edward Minar puts it, while the causal theory implies that facts involving reference are *deep* facts, the disquotational theory implies that such facts are *superficial* or *trivial* facts.) If this is right, then the argument contains an ineliminable equivocation.

4. Here I am developing an argument that I presented earlier in Hill 1991, pp. 135–37 and 139–40.

As I have already indicated, I wind up retracting this objection to reliabilism in the present paper. Fortunately, this retraction does not seriously impair any of the main arguments of Hill 1991. Thus, contrary to what I believed at the time of writing that earlier work, I was not there obliged to reject reliabilism; the issues with which I was concerned turn out to be independent, to a very large extent, of the controversy between internalists and externalists.

I hope to discuss this topic at greater length elsewhere.

5. Actually, a contemporary philosopher might have deep reservations about the first premise. It implies that all questions of epistemic justification are decided by considerations having to do with evidence. In responding to this claim, a contemporary philosopher might maintain that questions of justification often depend crucially on considerations having to do with the supraempirical virtues (i.e., on considerations having to do with plausibility, simplicity, and explanatory power).

As against such philosophers, I hold that the connection between the supraempirical virtues and scepticism is problematic. Thus, as I see it, if we were to expand the area of our present concern so a to include considerations having to do with the supraempirical virtues, the sceptic could legitimately respond by questioning the relevance of such considerations to matters having to do with *epistemic* justification. Consider the two virtues that sceptical hypotheses most conspicuously lack plausibility and explanatory power. (Both Descartes's evil genius hypothesis and the contemporary brain-in-a-vat hypothesis are inferior to the real world hypothesis in point of explanatory power. Neither of the former can be said to explain our sense experiences. At most, they are mere gestures in the direction of explanations.) The sceptic might allow that considerations having to do with either or both of these virtues are germane to questions of *practical* or *pragmatic* justification. But he would maintain that there is no reason for saying that beliefs with greater plausibility and/or explanatory power are thereby in a better position to count as instances of *knowledge*. In my view, this response is sufficient to shift the burden of proof back onto the shoulders of the sceptic's opponents.

6. Can the evidence argument be strengthened in such a way as to make its conclusion more useful to the sceptic? I think not not without strengthening the key premise in a way that would make it unacceptable to externalists.

As it stands, the evidence argument contains a number of inessential (and possibly misleading) embellishments. When these embellishments are stripped away, it becomes clear that the argument has a purely empirical character. It begins with the claim that our information about extramental phenomena comes to us by way of the senses, and it goes on to conclude that any information about extramental phenomena that is available to the part of the mind that is responsible for perceptual judgments must somehow be represented at the sensory level that is, at the level of sense experience. These are both empirical claims (or, if you like, metaphysical claims), and as such, they are silent on the question that is of primary concern in discussions of scepticism. They carry no implications concerning the epistemological question of whether it is the purely sensory characteristics of such experiences or their informational characteristics and truth-generating propensities that determine whether perceptual beliefs are justified. Now, if we were to change the argument in such a way that it did have a bearing on this question, and in particular, in such a way that it resolved the question in the way the sceptic requires, then the argument would in effect put forward an internalistic theory of epistemic justification. Any such argument would fail to serve the sceptic's purpose.

The sceptic wishes to give an argument that *establishes* the second premise of the main sceptical argument. This means that he wishes to give an argument that has two characteristics: first, it should be transparently valid; and second, it should be epistemologically neutral, in the sense of having premises that would be found plausible when assessed from *any* sane epistemological perspective. This second characteristic is essential. If the sceptic offered a line of thought that depended at any point upon a claim that is rejected by a particular epistemological school, then, since the sceptic's ultimate conclusion is extremely counterintuitive, the line of thought would be seen, not as presenting a paradox, but rather as a reductio of the given claim, and by the same token, as a defense of the given epistemological school.

Needless to say, it is not the sceptic's intention to provide a defense of externalism.

7. This definition is only a first approximation to an adequate characterization of the externalist concept of evidence. The main difficulty with the definition may be expressed as follows: While it explains what it means to say that a sense experience *provides evidential support* for a belief, it does not explain what it means to speak of *degrees of evidential support*. (By the same token, it does not explain what it means to say that a sense experience *increases the support* for a belief, nor what it means to say that a belief *receives more support* from a set of sense experiences than does another belief.) I believe that it is possible to characterize a more serviceable notion of evidential support in externalist terms (and indeed in more or less reliabilist terms), but the task of providing such a characterization lies outside the scope of the present paper.

8. Ramsey's paper first appeared in a collection of his papers edited by R. B. Braithwaite. See Ramsey 1931.

9. Since the idea of subjective probability is internalist in character, it might be thought that it is at variance with the spirit of reliabilism. Moved by this perception, the reader might come to feel that the line of thought of the last two paragraphs actually has some tendency to undermine the reliabilist line that I am defending in this paper. Process reliabilism claims that our central concepts of epistemic appraisal can be explained in reliabilist terms. How can this be true, it might be asked, if it is necessary to introduce concepts that are at variance with the spirit of reliabilism in discussing the issues that are raised by the sceptic's argument?

In response to this worry, I will stress that I have claimed only that we have a concept of evidential support that is grounded in the concept of subjective probability, and that we have a tendency to confuse this concept with an objective, externalist concept of evidential support. Neither of these claims implies that there is a connection between the concept of subjective probability and the concept of *epistemic* justification. By the same token, neither claim poses any threat to process reliabilism. (Process reliabilism offers objective, externalist analyses of the concept of epistemic justification and a handful of closely related concepts of epistemic appraisal. Period. It is entirely possible to embrace these analyses while holding that we are in possession of a concept of doxastic appraisal that is not objective and externalist, provided only that it is not claimed that this concept has a logical connection with the practice of *epistemic* appraisal.)

10. It might be useful to restate the point of the last two paragraphs in somewhat different language.

It appears that the following proposition is conceptually true: Where E is any possible sense experience and p is any proposition, E counts as *evidence for* p if and only if E is capable of contributing to the probability of p. Further, it appears to be true that there are two concepts of probability: First, as Bayesians have urged, there is a concept that stands for degrees of rational belief; and second, as objectivists have claimed, there is a concept that stands for tendencies of stochastic processes to display reliable frequencies. These observations suggest that there may well be two concepts of evidence one having to do with degrees of rational belief, and the other having to do with objective probabilities of truth.

I will hereafter assume that there really are two such concepts. I will call them the "subjective conception" and the "objective conception," respectively.

We must recognize, I believe, that human beings have a tendency to confuse these concepts. My suggestion is that the plausibility of the sceptic's reasoning is partly due to this tendency. If we could fully appreciate the relevance of the objective conception of evidence to the sceptic's claims, we would find those claims to be quite unpersuasive. However, partly because of subtle linguistic traps, and partly because of the forementioned tendency, our reaction to the sceptic's reasoning is to a large extent determined by the subjective conception of evidence. This is unfortunate, because the sceptic's reasoning is much more attractive when it is viewed from the perspective defined by the subjective conception.

Of course, in addition to claiming that we are in possession of two conceptions of evidence, and that the plausibility of scepticism depends in part on a tendency to confuse these conceptions, I am also making a third claim the claim that it is the objective conception that is intimately bound up with the concept of knowledge.

11. I offer some arguments in support of this assumption in Hill 1994, pp. 12–28.

PART THREE

Relevant Alternatives and Denying Closure

CHAPTER 8   # Epistemic Operators

Fred Dretske

Suppose Q is a necessary consequence of P. Given only this much, it is, of course, quite trivial that if it is true that P, then it must also be true that Q. If it is a fact that P, then it must also be a fact that Q. If it is necessary that P, then it is necessary that Q; and if it is possible that P, then it must also be possible that Q.

I have just mentioned four prefixes: 'it is true that', 'it is a fact that', 'it is necessary that', and 'it is possible that'. In this paper I shall refer to such affixes as *sentential operators* or simply *operators;* when affixed to a sentence or statement, they operate on it to generate another sentence or statement. The distinctive thing about the four operators I have just mentioned is that, if Q is a necessary consequence of P, then the statement we get by operating on Q with one of these four operators is a necessary consequence of the statement we get by operating on P with the same operator. This may be put more succinctly if we let 'O' stand for the operator in question and 'O(P)' for the statement we get by affixing the operator 'O' to the statement 'P'. We can now say that the above four operators share the following property: if P entails Q, then O(P) entails O(Q). I shall call any operator having this property a *penetrating operator* (or, when emphasis is required, a *fully penetrating operator*). In operating on P these operators penetrate to every necessary consequence of P.

We are now in a position to ask ourselves a preliminary question. The answer to this question is easy enough, but it will set the stage for more dif-

"Epistemic Operators" from the *Journal of Philosophy* 67 (1970, pp. 1007–1023). Reprinted by permission of the publisher.

Versions of this paper were read to the philosophy departments of several universities in the United States and Canada during the year 1969/70. I profited greatly from these discussions. I wish especially to thank Paul Dietl who helped me to see a number of points more clearly (perhaps still not clearly enough in his opinion). Finally, my exchanges with Mr. Don Affeldt were extremely useful; I am much indebted to him in connection with some of the points made in the latter portions of the paper.

ficult questions. Are all sentential operators fully penetrating operators? Are all operators such that if P entails Q, then $O(P)$ entails $O(Q)$? If *all* operators are penetrating operators, then each of the following statements must be true (when P entails Q):

(1) You cannot have a reason to believe that P unless you have a reason to believe that Q.

(2) You cannot know that P unless you know that Q.

(3) You cannot explain why P is the case unless you can explain why Q is the case.

(4) If you assert that P, then you assert that Q.

(5) If you hope that P, then you hope that Q.

(6) If it is strange (or accidental) that P, then it must be strange (or accidental) that Q.

(7) If it was a mistake that P, then it was a mistake that Q.

This list begins with two epistemic operators, 'reason to believe that' and 'know that'. Since I shall be concerned with these later in the paper, let me skip over them now and look at those appearing near the end of the list. They will suffice to answer our opening question, and their status is much less problematic than that of some of the other operators.

'She lost' entails 'Someone lost'. Yet, it may be strange that she lost, not at all strange that someone lost. 'Bill and Susan married each other' entails that Susan got married; yet, it may be quite odd that (strange that, incredible that) Bill and Susan married each other but quite unremarkable, not at all odd that, Susan got married. It may have been a mistake that they married each other, not a mistake that Susan got married. Or finally, 'I hit the bull's-eye' entails that I either hit the bull's-eye or the side of the barn; and though I admit that it was lucky that (accidental that) I hit the bull's-eye, I will deny that it was lucky, an accident, that I hit either the bull's-eye or the side of the barn.

Such examples show that not all operators are fully penetrating. Indeed, such operators as 'it is strange that', 'it is accidental that' and 'it is a mistake that' fail to penetrate to some of the most elementary logical consequences of a proposition. Consider the entailment between '$P \cdot Q$' and 'Q'. Clearly, it may be strange that P and Q, not at all strange that P, and not at all strange that Q. A concatenation of factors, no one of which is strange or accidental, may itself be strange or accidental. Taken by itself, there is nothing odd or suspicious about Frank's holding a winning ticket in the first race. The same could be said about any of the other races: there is nothing odd or suspicious about Frank's holding a winning ticket in the nth race. Nonetheless, there is something very odd, very suspicious, in Frank's having a winning ticket in n races.

Therefore, not only are these operators *not* fully penetrating, they lie, as it were, on the other end of the spectrum. They fail to penetrate to some of the most elementary consequences of a proposition. I shall refer to this class of operators as *nonpenetrating* operators. I do not wish to suggest by this label that such operators are totally impotent in this respect (or that they are all uniform in their degree of penetration). I mean it, rather, in a rough, comparative, sense: their *degree of penetration* is less than that of any of the other operators I shall have occasion to discuss.

We have, then, two ends of the spectrum with examples from both ends. Anything that falls between these two extremes I shall call a *semi-penetrating operator*. And with this definition I am, finally, in a position to express my main point, the point I wish to defend in the rest of this paper. It is, simply, that all epistemic operators are semi-penetrating operators. There is both a trivial and a significant side to this claim. Let me first deal briefly with the trivial aspect.

The epistemic operators I mean to be speaking about when I say that all epistemic operators are semi-penetrating include the following:

- (a) *S* knows that . . .
- (b) *S* sees (or can see) that . . .
- (c) *S* has reason (or a reason) to believe that . . .
- (d) There is evidence to suggest that . . .
- (e) *S* can prove that . . .
- (f) *S* learned (discovered, found out) that . . .
- (g) In relation to our evidence it is probable that . . .

Part of what needs to be established in showing that these are all semi-penetrating operators is that they all possess a degree of penetration greater than that of the nonpenetrating operators. This is the trivial side of my thesis. I say it is trivial because it seems to me fairly obvious that if someone knows that *P* and *Q*, has a reason to believe that *P* and *Q*, or can prove that *P* and *Q*, he thereby knows that *Q*, has a reason to believe that *Q*, or can prove (in the appropriate epistemic sense of this term) that *Q*. Similarly, if *S* knows that Bill and Susan married each other, he (must) know that Susan got married (married someone). If he knows that *P* is the case, he knows that *P* or *Q* is the case (where the 'or' is understood in a sense which makes '*P* or *Q*' a necessary consequence of '*P*'). This is not a claim about what it would be appropriate to say, what the person himself thinks he knows or would say he knows. It is a question, simply, of what he knows. It may not be appropriate to *say* to Jim's wife that you know it was either her husband, Jim, or Harold who sent the neighbor lady an expensive gift *when you know it was Harold*. For, although you do know this, it is misleading to say you know it—especially to Jim's wife.

Let me accept, therefore, without further argument that the epistemic operators are not, unlike 'lucky that', 'strange that', 'a mistake that', and 'accidental that', nonpenetrating operators. I would like to turn, then, to the more significant side of my thesis. Before I do, however, I must make one point clear lest it convert my entire thesis into something as trivial as the first half of it. When we are dealing with the epistemic operators, it becomes crucial to specify whether the agent in question knows that P entails Q. That is to say, P may entil Q, and S may know that P, but he may not know that Q *because*, and perhaps *only* because, he fails to appreciate the fact that P entails Q. When Q is a simple logical consequence of P we do not expect this to happen, but when the propositions become very complex, or the relationship between them very complex, this might easily occur. Let P be a set of axioms, Q a theorem. S's knowing P does not entail S's knowing Q just because P entails Q; for, of course, S may not know that P entails Q, may not know that Q is a *theorem*. Hence, our epistemic operators will turn out *not* to be penetrating because, and perhaps *only* because, the agents in question are not fully cognizant of all the implications of what they know to be the case, can see to be the case, have a reason to believe is the case, and so on. Were we all ideally astute logicians, were we all fully apprised of all the necessary consequences (supposing this to be a well defined class) of every proposition, perhaps then the epistemic operators would turn into fully penetrating operators. That is, assuming that if P entails Q, we *know* that P entails Q, then every epistemic operator is a penetrating operator: the epistemic operators penetrate to all the *known* consequences of a proposition.

It is this latter, slightly modified, claim that I mean to reject. Therefore, I shall assume throughout the discussion that when Q is a necessary consequence of P, every relevant agent *knows that it is*. I shall be dealing with only the *known consequences* (in most cases because they are immediate and obvious consequences). What I wish to show is that, even under this special restriction, the epistemic operators are *only* semi-penetrating.

I think many philosophers would disagree with this contention. The conviction is that the epistemic worth of a proposition is hereditary under entailment, that whatever the epistemic worth of P, *at least* the same value must be accorded the known consequences of P. This conviction finds expression in a variety of ways. Epistemic logic: if S knows that P, and knows that P entails Q, then S knows that Q. Probability theory: if A is probable, and B is a logical consequence of A, then B is probable (relative to the same evidence, of course). Confirmation theory: if evidence e tends to confirm hypothesis h, then e indirectly confirms all the logical consequences of h. But perhaps the best evidence in favor of supposing that most philosophers have taken the epistemic operators to be fully penetrating is the way they have argued and the obvious assumptions that structure their arguments. Anyone who has argued in the following way seems to me to be assuming the thesis of penetrability (as I shall call it): if you do not know whether Q is true or not, and P cannot be true unless Q is true, then you (obviously) do not know whether P is true or not. A slightly more elaborate form of the same argument goes like this: If S does not know whether or not Q is true, then for all he knows it might be false. If Q is false, however, then P must also be false. Hence, for all S knows, P may be false. Therefore, S does not know that P is true. This pattern of argument is sprinkled throughout the epistemological literature. Almost all skeptical objections trade on it. *S* claims to know that this is a tomato. A necessary consequence of its being a tomato is that it is not a clever imitation which only looks and feels (and, if you will, tastes) like a tomato. But *S* does not know that it is *not* a clever imitation that only looks and feels (and tastes) lke a tomato. (I assume here that no one is prepared to argue that anything that looks, feels, and tastes like a tomato to *S must be* a tomato.) Therefore, *S* does not know that this is a tomato. We can, of course, reply with G. E. Moore that we certainly do know it is a tomato (after such an examination) and since tomatoes are not imitations we know that this is not an imitation. It is interesting to note that this reply presupposes the same principle as does the skeptical objection: they both assume that if *S* knows that this is a *P*, and knows that every *P* is a *Q*, then *S* knows that this is a *Q*. The only difference is that the skeptic performs a modus tollens, Moore a modus ponens. Neither questions the principle itself.

Whether it be a question of dreams or demons, illusions or fakes, the same pattern of argument emerges. If you know this is a chair, you must know that you are not dreaming (or being deceived by a cunning demon), since its being a (real) chair entails that it is not simply a figment of your own imagination. Such arguments assume that the epistemic operators, and in particular the operator 'to know', penetrate to all the known consequences of a proposition. If these operators were not penetrating, many of these objections might be irrelevant. Consider the following exchange:

> S: How strange! There are tomatoes growing in my apple tree.
>
> K: That isn't strange at all. Tomatoes, after all, are physical objects and what is so strange about physical objects growing in your apple tree?

What makes K's reply so silly is that he is treating the operator 'strange that' as a fully penetrating operator: it cannot be strange that there are tomatoes growing in the apple tree unless the consequences of this (e.g., there are objects growing in your apple tree) are also strange. Similarly, it *may not* be at all relevant to object to someone who claims to know that there are tomatoes in the apple tree that he does not know, cannot be absolutely sure, that there are really any material objects. Whether or not this is a relevant objection will depend on whether or not this particular consequence of there being tomatoes in the apple tree is one of the consequences to which the epistemic operators penetrate. What I wish to argue in the remainder of this paper is that the traditional skeptical arguments exploit precisely those consequences of a proposition to which the epistemic operators do not penetrate, precisely those consequences which distinguish the epistemic operators from the fully penetrating operators.

In support of this claim let me begin with some examples which are, I think, fairly intuitive and then turn to some more problematic cases. I shall begin with the operator 'reason to believe that' although what have to say could be said as well with any of them. This particular operator has the added advantage that if it can be shown to be only semi-penetrating, then many accounts of knowledge, those which interpret it as a form of justified true belief, would also be committed to treating 'knowing that' as a semi-penetrating operator. For, presumably, 'knowing that' would not penetrate any deeper than one's 'reasons for believing that'.

Suppose you have a reason to believe that the church is empty. *Must* you have a reason to believe that it is a church? I am not asking whether you generally have such a reason. I am asking whether one can have a reason to believe the church empty without having a reason to believe that it is a church which is empty. Certainly your reason for believing that the church is empty is not *itself* a reason to believe it is a church; or it *need not* be. Your reason for believing the church to be empty may be that you just made a thorough inspection of it without finding anyone. That is a good reason to believe the church empty. Just as clearly, however, it is not a reason, much less a good reason, to believe that what is empty is a church. The fact is, or so it seems to me, I do not have to have *any* reason to believe it is a church. Of course, I would never *say* the church was empty, or that I had a reason to believe that the church was empty, unless I believed, and presumably had a reason for so believing, that *it was* a church which was empty, but this is a presumed condition of my *saying* something, not of my having a reason to believe something. Suppose I had simply assumed (correctly as it turns out) that the building was a church. Would this show that I had no reason to believe that the church was empty?

Suppose I am describing to you the "adventures" of my brother Harold. Harold is visiting New York for the first time, and he decides to take a bus tour. He boards a crowded bus and immediately takes the last remaining seat. The little old lady he shouldered aside in reaching his seat stands over him glowering. Minutes pass. Finally, realizing that my brother is not going to move, she sighs and moves resignedly to the back of the bus. Not much of an adventure, but enough, I hope, to make my point. I said that the little old lady realized that my brother would not move. Does this imply that she realized that, or knew that, *it was my brother* who refused to move? Clearly not. We can say that S knows that X is Y without implying that S knows that *it is X* which is Y. We do not *have* to describe our little old lady as knowing that *the man* or *the person* would not move. We can say that she realized that, or knew that, *my brother* would not move (minus, of course, this pattern of emphasis), and we can say this because saying this does not entail that the little old lady knew that, or realized that, it was my brother who refused to move. She knew that my brother would not move, and she knew this despite the fact that she did not know something that was necessarily implied by what she did know—viz., that the person who refused to move was my brother.

I have argued elsewhere that to see that A is B, that the roses are wilted for example, is not to see, not even to be able to see, that they are roses which are wilted.[1] To see that the widow is limping is not to see that it is a widow who is limping. I am now arguing that this same feature holds for all epistemic operators. I can know that the roses are wilting without knowing that they are roses, know that the water is boiling without knowing that it is water, and prove that the square root of 2 is smaller than the square root of 3 and, yet, be unable to prove what is entailed by this—viz., that the number 2 *has* a square root.

The general point may be put this way: there are certain presuppositions associated with a statement. These presuppositions, although their truth is entailed by the truth of the statement, are not part of what is *operated on* when we operate on the statement with one of our epistemic operators. The epistemic operators do not *penetrate to* these presuppositions. For example, in saying that the coffee is boiling I assert that the coffee is boiling, but in asserting this I do not assert that *it is* coffee which is boiling. Rather, this is taken for granted, assumed, presupposed, or what have you. Hence, when I say that I have a reason to believe that the coffee is boiling, I am not saying that this reason applies to the fact that it is coffee which is boiling. This is *still* presupposed. I may have such a reason, of course, and chances are good that I do have such a reason or I would not have referred to what I believe to be boiling *as coffee*, but to have a reason to believe the coffee is boiling is not, thereby, to have a reason to believe it is coffee which is boiling.

One would expect that if this is true of the semi-penetrating operators, then it should also be true of the nonpenetrating operators. They also should fail to reach the presuppositions. This is exactly what we find. It may be accidental that the two trucks collided, but not at all accidental that it was two trucks that collided. Trucks were the only vehicles allowed on the road that day, and so it was not at all accidental or a matter of chance that the accident took place between two trucks. Still, it was an accident that the two trucks collided. Or suppose Mrs. Murphy mistakenly gives her cat some dog food. It need not be a mistake that she gave the food to *her* cat, or *some* food to *a* cat. This was intentional. What was a mistake was that it was dog food that she gave to her cat.

Hence, the first class of consequences that differentiate the epistemic operators from the fully penetrating operators is the class of consequences associated with the presuppositions of a proposition. The fact that the epistemic operators do not penetrate to these presuppositions is what helps to make them semi-penetrating. And this is an extremely important fact. For it would appear that if this is true, then to know that the flowers are wilted I do not have to know that they are flowers (which are wilted) and, therefore, do not have to know all those consequences which follow from the fact that they are flowers, real flowers, which I know to be wilted.

Rather than pursue this line, however, I would like to turn to what I consider to be a more significant set of consequences—"more significant" because they are the consequences that are directly involved in most skeptical arguments. Suppose we assert that x is A. Consider some predicate, 'B', which is incompatible with A, such that nothing can be both A and B. It then follows from the fact that x is A that x is not B. Furthermore, if we conjoin B with any other predicate, Q, it follows from the fact that x is A that x is not-(B

and Q). I shall call this type of consequence a *contrast consequence*, and I am interested in a particular subset of these; for I believe the most telling skeptical objections to our ordinary knowledge claims exploit a particular set of these contrast consequences. The exploitation proceeds as follows: someone purports to know that x is A, that the wall is red, say. The skeptic now finds a predicate 'B' that is incompatible with 'A'. In this particular example we may let 'B' stand for the predicate 'is white'. Since 'x is red' entails 'x is not white' it also entails that x is not-(white and Q) where 'Q' is any predicate we care to select. Therefore, the skeptic selects a 'Q' that gives expression to a condition or circumstance under which a white wall would appear exactly the same as a red wall. For simplicity we may let 'Q' stand for: 'cleverly illuminated to look red'. We now have this chain of implications: 'x is red' entails 'x is not white' entails 'x is not white cleverly illuminated to look red'. If 'knowing that' is a penetrating operator, then if anyone knows that the wall is red he must know that it is not white cleverly illuminated to look red. (I assume here that the relevant parties know that if x is red, it cannot be white made to look red.) He must know that this particuar contrast consequence is true. The question is: do we, generally speaking, know anything of the sort? Normally we never take the trouble to check the lighting. We seldom acquire any *special* reasons for believing the lighting normal although we can talk vaguely about there being no reason to think it unusual. The fact is that we habitually take such matters for granted, and although we normally have *good* reasons for making such routine assumptions, I do not think these reasons are sufficiently good, not without special precautionary checks in the particular case, to say of the particular situation we are in that we *know* conditions are normal. To illustrate, let me give you another example—a silly one, but no more silly than a great number of skeptical arguments with which we are all familiar. You take your son to the zoo, see several zebras, and, when questioned by your son, tell him they are zebras. Do you know they are zebras? Well, most of us would have little hesitation in saying that we did know this. We know what zebras look like, and, besides, this is the city zoo and the animals are in a pen clearly marked "Zebras." Yet, something's being a zebra implies that it is not a mule and, in particular, not a mule cleverly disguised by the zoo authorities to look like a zebra. Do you know that these animals are not mules cleverly disguised by the zoo authorities to look like zebras? If you are tempted to say "Yes" to this question, think a moment about what reasons you have, what evidence you can produce in favor of this claim. The evidence you *had* for thinking them zebras has been effectively neutralized, since it does not count toward their *not* being mules cleverly disguised to look like zebras. Have you checked with the zoo authorities? Did you examine the animals closely enough to detect such a fraud? You might do this, of course, but in most cases you do nothing of the kind. You have some general uniformities on which you rely, regularities to which you give expression bysuch remarks as, "That isn't very likely" or "Why should the zoo authorities do that?" Granted, the hypothesis (if we may call it that) is not very plausible, given what we know about people and zoos. But the question here is not whether this alternative is plausible, not whether it is more or less plausible than that there are real zebras in the pen, but whether *you know* that this alternative hypothesis is false. I don't think you do. In this I agree with the skeptic. I part company with the skeptic only when he concludes from this that, therefore, you do not know that the animals in the pen are zebras. I part with him because I reject the principle he uses in reaching this conclusion—the principle that if you do not know that Q is true, when it is known that P entails Q, then you do not know that P is true.

What I am suggesting is that we simply admit that we do *not* know that some of these contrasting "skeptical alternatives" are *not* the case, but refuse to admit that we do not know what we originally said we knew. My knowing that the wall is red certainly entails that the wall is red; it also entails that the wall is not white and, in particular, it entails that the wall is not white cleverly illuminated to look red. But it does not follow from the fact that I know that the wall is red that I *know* that it is not white cleverly illuminated to look red. Nor does it follow from the fact that I know that those animals are zebras that I know that they are not mules cleverly disguised to look like zebras. These are some of the contrast consequences to which the epistemic operators do not penetrate.

Aside from asserting this, what arguments can be produced to support it? I could proceed by multiplying examples, but I do not think that examples alone will support the full weight of this view. The thesis itself is sufficiently counterintuitive to render controversial most of the crucial examples. Anyone who is already convinced that skepticism is wrong and who is yet troubled by the sorts of skeptical arguments I have mentioned will, no doubt, take this itself as an argument in favor of my claim that the epistemic operators are only semi-penetrating. This, however, hardly constitutes an argument against skepticism. For this we need *independent* grounds for thinking that the epistemic operators do not penetrate to the contrast consequences. So I shall proceed in a more systematic manner. I shall offer an analogy with three other operators and conclude by making some general remarks about what I think can be learned from this analogy. The first operator is 'explains why' or, more suggestively (for the purposes of this analogy):

(A) *R* is the reason (explanatory reason) that (or why) . . .

For example, the reason why *S* quit smoking was that he was afraid of getting cancer. The second operator has to do with reasons again, but in this case it is a reason which tends to *justify* one in doing something:

(B) *R* is a reason for . . . (*S* to do *Y*).[2]

For example, the fact that they are selling the very same (type of) car here much more cheaply than elsewhere is a reason to buy it here rather than elsewhere. The status of this as a reason will, of course, depend on a variety of circumstances, but situations can easily be imagined in which this would be a reason for someone to buy the car here. Finally, there is a particular modal relationship which may be construed as a sentential operator:

(C) R would not be the case unless . . .

For example, he would not have bid seven no-trump unless he had all four aces. I shall abbreviate this operator as '$R \rightarrow$ . . . '; hence our example could be written 'he bid seven no-trump $\rightarrow$ he had all four aces'.

Each of these operators has features similar to those of our epistemic operators. If one retraces the ground we have already covered, one will find, I think, that these operators all penetrate deeper than the typical nonpenetrating operator. If R explains why (or is the reason that) P and Q are the case, then it explains why (is the reason that) Q is the case.[3] If I can explain why Bill and Harold are always invited to every party, I can explain why Harold is always invited to every party. From the fact that it was a mistake for me to quite my job it does not follow that it was a mistake for me to do something, but if I had a reason to quit my job, it does follow that I had a reason to do something. And if the grass would not be green unless it had plenty of sunshine and water, it follows that it would not be green unless it had water.

Furthermore, the similarities persist when one considers the presuppositional consequences. I argued that the epistemic operators fail to penetrate to the presuppositions; the above three operators display the same feature. In explaining why he takes his lunch to work, I do not (or need not) explain why he goes to work or why he works at all. The explanation may be obvious in some cases, of course, but the fact is I need not be able to explain why he works (he is *so* wealthy) to explain why he takes his lunch to work (the cafeteria food is *so* bad). The reason why the elms on Main Street are dying is *not* the reason there are elms on Main Street. I have a reason to feed my cat, no reason (not, at least, the same reason) to have a cat. And although it is quite true that he would not have known about our plans if the secretary had not told him, it does not follow that he would not have known about our plans if *someone other than the secretary* had told him. That is, (He knew about our plans) $\rightarrow$ (The secretary told him) even though it is *not* true that (He knew about our plans) $\rightarrow$ (It was the secretary who told him). Yet, the fact that *it was the secretary who* told him is (I take it) a presuppositional consequence of the fact that *the secretary* told him. Similarly, if George is out to set fire to the first empty building he finds, it may be true to say that George would not have set fire to the church unless it (the church) was empty, yet false to say that George would not have set fire to the church unless *it was a church*.

I now wish to argue that these three operators do not penetrate to a certain set of contrast consequences. To the extent that the epistemic operators are similar to these operators, we may then infer, by analogy, that they also fail to penetrate to certain contrast consequences. This is, admittedly, a weak form of argument, depending as it does on the grounds there are for thinking that the above three operators and the epistemic operators share the same logic in this respect. Nonetheless, the analogy is revealing. Some may even find it persuasive.

(A) The pink walls in my living room clash with my old green couch. Recognizing this, I proceed to paint the walls a compatible shade of green. This is the reason I have, and give, for painting the walls green. Now, in having this explanation for why I painted the walls green, I do not think I have an explanation for two other things, both of which are entailed by what I do have an explanation for. I have not explained why I did not, *instead* of painting the walls green, buy a new couch or cover the old one with a suitable slip cover. Nor have I explained why, instead of painting the walls green, I did not paint them white and illuminate them with green light. The same effect would have been achieved, the same purpose would have been served, albeit at much greater expense.

I expect someone to object as follows: although the explanation given for painting the walls green does not, by itself, explain why the couch was not changed instead, it nonetheless succeeds as an explanation for why the walls were painted green only in so far as there is an explanation for why the couch was not changed instead. If there is no explanation for why I did not change the couch instead, there has been no real, no complete, examination for why the walls were painted green.

I think this objection wrong. I may, of course, have an explanation for why I did not buy a new couch: I love the old one or it has sentimental value. But then again I may not. It just never occurred to me to change the couch; or (if someone thinks that its not occurring to me *is* an explanation of why I did not change the couch) I may have thought of it but decided, for what reasons (if any) I cannot remember, to keep the couch and paint the walls. That is to say, I cannot explain why I did not change the couch. I thought of it but I did not do it. I do not know why. Still, I *can* tell you why I painted the walls green. They clashed with the couch.

(B) The fact that they are selling Xs so much more cheaply here than elsewhere may be a reason to buy your Xs here, but it certainly need not be a reason to do what is a necessary consequence of *buying* your Xs here—viz., not *stealing* your Xs here.

(C) Let us suppose that S is operating in perfectly normal circumstances, a set of circumstances in which it is true to say that the wall he sees would not (now) look green to him unless it was green (if it were any other color it would look different to him). Although we can easily imagine situations in which this is true, it does not follow that the wall would not (now) look green to S if it were white cleverly illuminated to look green. That is,

(i)   The wall looks green (to S) → the wall is green.

(ii) The wall is green *entails* the wall is not white cleverly illuminated to look green (to S).

are both true; yet, it is *not true* that

(iii) The wall looks green (to S) → the wall is not white cleverly illuminated to look green (to S).

There are dozens of examples that illustrate the relative impenetrability of
this operator. We can truly say that A and B would not have collided if B had
not swerved at the last moment and yet concede that they would have collided without any swrve on the part of B *if* the direction in which A was
moving had been suitably altered in the beginning.[5]

The structure of these cases is virtually identical with that which appeared in the case of the epistemic operators, and I think by looking just a little more closely at this structure we can learn something very fundamental
about our class of epistemic operators and, in particular, about what it means
to know something. If I may put it this way, within the context of these operators no fact is an island. If we are simply rehearsing the facts, then we can
say that it is a fact that Brenda did not take any dessert (though it was included in the meal). We can say this without a thought about what sort of
person Brenda is or what she might have done had she ordered dessert.
However, if we put this fact into, say, an explanatory context, if we try to explain this fact, it suddenly appears within a network of related facts, a network of possible alternatives which serve to define *what it is that is being explained*. What is being explained is a function of two things—not only the fact
(Brenda did not order any dessert), but also the range of relevant alternatives. A relevant alternative is an alternative that might have been realized in
the existing circumstances if the actual state of affairs had not materialized.[6]
When I explain why Brenda did not order any dessert by saying that she was
full (was on a diet, did not like anything on the dessert menu), I explain why
she did not order any dessert *rather than, as opposed to, or instead of* ordering
some dessert and *eating it*. It is this competing possibility which helps to define what it is that I am explaining when I explain why Brenda did not order
any dessert. Change this contrast, introduce a different set of relevant alternatives, and you change what it is that is being explained and, therefore,
what counts as an explanation, even though (as it were) the same fact is being explained. Consider the following contrasts: ordering some dessert and
throwing it at the waiter; ordering some dessert and taking it home to a sick
friend. With these contrasts none of the above explanations are any longer
explanations of why Brenda did not order dessert. Anyone who really wants
to know why Brenda did not order dessert and throw it at the waiter will not
be helped by being told that she was full or on a diet. This is only to say that,
within the context of explanation and within the context of our other operators, the proposition on which we operate must be understood as embedded
within a matrix of relevant alternatives. We explain why P, but we do so
within a framework of competing alternatives A, B, and C. Moreover, if the
possibility D is not within this contrasting set, not within this network of relevant alternatives, then even though not-D follows necessarily from the fact,
P, which we do explain, we do not explain why not-D. Though the fact that
Brenda did not order dessert and throw it at the waiter follows necessarily

from the fact that she did not order dessert (the fact that is explained), this necessary consequence is not explained by the explanation given. The only contrast consequences to which this operator penetrates are those which figured in the original explanation as relevant alternatives.

So it is with our epistemic operators. To know that x is A is to know that x is A within a framework of relevant alternatives, B, C, and D. This set of contrasts, together with the fact that x is A, serve to define what it is that is known when one knows that x is A. One cannot change this set of contrasts without changing what a person is said to know when he is said to know that x is A. We have subtle ways of shifting these contrasts and, hence, changing what a person is said to know *without changing the sentence that we use to express what he knows*. Take the fact that Lefty killed Otto. By changing the emphasis pattern we can invoke a different set of contrasts and, hence, alter what it is that S is said to know when he is said to know that Lefty killed Otto. We can say, for instance, that S knows that *Lefty* killed Otto. In this case (and I think this is the way we usually hear the sentence when there is no *special* emphasis) we are being told that S knows the identity of Otto's killer, that *it was Lefty* who killed Otto. Hence, we expect S's reasons for believing that Lefty killed Otto to consist in facts that single out Lefty as the assailant *rather than* George, Mike, or someone else. On the other hand, we can say that S knows that Lefty *killed* Otto. In this case we are being told that S knows *what Lefty did to Otto*; he killed him *rather than* merely injuring him, killed him *rather than* merely threatening him, etc. A good reason for believing that Lefty *killed* Otto (rather than merely injuring him) is that Otto is dead, but this is not much of a reason, if it is a reason at all, for believing that *Lefty* killed Otto. Changing the set of contrasts (from 'Lefty rather than George or Mike' to 'killed rather than injured or threatened') by shifting the emphasis pattern changes what it is that one is alleged to know when one is said to know that Lefty killed Otto.[7] The same point can be made here as we made in the case of explanation: the operator will penetrate *only* to those contrast consequences which form part of the network of relevant alternatives structuring the original context in which a knowledge claim was advanced. Just as we have not explained why Brenda did not order some dessert and throw it at the waiter when we explained why she did not order some dessert (although what we have explained—her not ordering any dessert—entails this), so also in knowing that Lefty *killed* Otto (knowing that what Lefty did to Otto was kill him) we do not *necessarily* (although we may) know that *Lefty* killed Otto (know that *it was Lefty* who killed Otto). Recall the example of the little old lady who knew that my brother would not move without knowing that it was my brother who would not move.

The conclusions to be drawn are the same as those in the case of explanation. Just as we can say that within the original setting, within the original framework of alternatives that defined what we were trying to explain, we *did explain* why Brenda did not order any dessert, so also within the original setting, within the set of contrasts that defined what it was we were claiming to know, we *did know* that the wall was red and *did know* that it was a zebra in the pen.

To introduce a novel and enlarged set of alternatives, as the skeptic is inclined to do with our epistemic claims, is to exhibit consequences of what we know, or have reason to believe, which we may not know, may not have a reason to believe; but it does not show that we did not know, did not have a reason to believe, whatever it is that has these consequences. To argue in this way is, I submit, as much a mistake as arguing that we have not explained why Brenda did not order dessert (within the original, normal, setting) because we did not explain why she did not order some and throw it at the waiter.

NOTES

1. Dretske 1969, pp. 93–112, and also Dretske 1968.

2 Unlike our other operators, this one does not have a propositional operand. Despite the rather obvious differences between this case and the others, I still think it useful to call attention to its analogous features.

3. One must be careful not to confuse sentential conjunction with similar-sounding expressions involving a relationship between two things. For example, to say Bill and Susan got married (if it is intended to mean that they married *each other*), although it entails that Susan got married, does not do so by *simplification*. 'Reason why' penetrates through logical simplification, *not* through the type of entailment represented by these two propositions. That is, the reason they got married is that they loved each other; that they loved each other is not the reason Susan got married.

4. I think that those who are inclined to give a causal account of knowledge should be particularly interested in the operator 'R . . .' since, presumably, it will be involved in many instances of knowledge ("many" not "all," since one might wish to except some form of immediate knowledge knowledge of one's own psychological state from the causal account). If this operator is only semi-penetrating, then any account of knowledge that relies on the relationship expressed by this operator (as I believe causal accounts must) will be very close to giving a "semi-penetrating" account of 'knowing that'.

5. The explanation for why the modal relationship between R and P ($R \rightarrow P$) fails to carry over (penetrate) to the logical consequences of P (i.e., $R \rightarrow Q$ where Q is a logical consequence of P) is to be found in the set of circumstances that are taken as *given*, or *held fixed*, in subjunctive conditionals. There are certain logical consequences of P which, by bringing in a reference to circumstances tacitly held fixed in the original subjunctive ($R \rightarrow P$), introduce a possible variation in these circumstances and, hence, lead to a *different framework* of fixed conditions under which to assess the truth of $R \rightarrow Q$. For instance, in the last example in the text, when it is said that A and B would not have collided if B had not swerved at the last moment, the truth of this conditional clearly takes it *as given* that A and B possessed the prior trajectories they in fact had on the occasion in question. *Given* certain facts, including the fact that they were traveling in the direction they were, they would not have collided if B had not swerved. Some of the logical consequences of the statement that B swerved do not, however, leave these conditions unaltered—e.g., B did not move in a perfectly straight line in a direction $2°$ counterclockwise to the direction it actually moved. This consequence "tinkers" with the circumstances originally taken *as given* (held fixed), and a failure of penetration will usually arise when this occurs. It *need not be true* that A and B would not have collided if B had moved in a perfectly straight line in a direction $2°$ counterclockwise to the direction it actually moved.

6. I am aware that this characterization of "a relevant alternative" is not, as it stands, very illuminating. I am not sure I can make it more precise. What I am after can be expressed this way: if Brenda *had* ordered dessert, she *would not* have thrown it at the waiter, stuffed it in her shoes, or taken it home to a sick friend (she has no sick friend). These are not alternatives that *might* have been realized in the existing circumstances if the actual state of affairs had not materialized. Hence, they are not relevant alternatives. In other words, the 'might have been' in my characterization of a relevant alternative will have to be unpacked in terms of counterfactuals.

7. The same example works nicely with the operator '$R \rightarrow$ . . .'. It may be true to say that Otto would not be dead unless Lefty *killed* him (unless what Lefty did to him was kill him) without its being true that Otto would not be dead unless *Lefty* killed him (unless it was Lefty who killed him).

CHAPTER 9   # Skepticism, Relevant Alternatives, and Deductive Closure

Gail Stine

Discussions of skepticism, defined with varying degrees of precision, are of course perennial in philosophy. Some recent discussions of the issue[1] give prominence to the notion of 'relevant alternatives', according to which a claim to know that p is properly made in the context of a limited number of competing alternatives to p; to be justified in claiming to know p (or simply to know p) it is sufficient to be able to rule out alternatives relevant to that context. This seems to me to be a correct and heartening development. Recent epistemological discussions have also brought up a relatively new subject, which is the validity of the general form of argument:

(A) a knows that p

$\underline{a \text{ knows that } p \text{ entails } q}$

$\therefore a$ knows that q

I shall call this the principle of epistemic deductive closure, or simply, in this paper, deductive closure.[2] What is interesting about recent comments on this principle is that it is perceived to have something to do with skepticism - in fact to lead to it - and hence is currently of very bad repute. And 'relevant alternatives' views of knowledge vis-à-vis skepticism are supposed to show us the falsity of the principle.

In this paper I propose to do three things. First, to give a qualified argu-

"Skepticism, Relevant Alternatives, and Deductive Closure" from *Philosophical Studies* 29 (1976, pp. 249–261). © 1976 by D. Reidel Publishing Company, Dordrecht-Holland. Reprinted with kind permission from Kluwer Academic Publishers.

ment for deductive closure. Second, to give a qualified argument against skepticism which will make use of the relevant alternatives idea. It will be similar to others in leaving rather indeterminate the way in which the context determines what is taken to be a relevant alternative, although I shall distinguish different sources of this indeterminateness and draw some further conclusions. Third, I shall give an unqualified argument to the effect that the questions of the validity of the principle of epistemic deductive closure and skepticism are completely *irrelevant* to one another, and that in fact proper attention to the idea of relevant alternatives tends to confirm the principle. This, of coure, puts me in direct conflict with the recent trend I have mentioned.

1. EPISTEMIC DEDUCTIVE CLOSURE

I am in principle suspicious of all principles of epistemic logic on the general grounds that while the logic of a knower who is in some way simplified and idealized may be useful for limited purposes, what we are ultimately interested in are actual knowers who can be pretty obtuse and idiosyncratic, yet still lay claim to knowledge. For this, among other reasons, I have elsewhere been concerned with epistemic logic which eschews possible worlds semantics imposing strong constraints on knowers.[3] Certainly, I would reject the pattern which goes:

(B) a knows that p

p entails q
_____
$\therefore a$ knows that q

However, the pattern which I have labeled epistemic deductive closure does seem to represent a certain bare minimum. One looks naturally for counterinstances involving failure of belief where p and q are very complicated, but any such case I can imagine turns out to be apparent only because it invariably raises doubts about the truth of the second premise which are as strong as the doubts about the truth of the conclusion. The principle seems to be on a par with epistemic conjunction, to wit:

(C) a knows p

a knows q
_____
$\therefore a$ knows p and q

There have, of course, been problems in reconciling this principle with commitments to rational belief in terms of degrees of confirmation and knowledge in terms of rational belief,[4] but one feels strongly inclined to the view that the adjustment must be made in the area of these commitments and not in the principle of conjunction.

In addition to failure of belief, one may look for counter-examples to the principle of epistemic deductive closure in the area of failure of evidence or warrant. One's initial reaction to this idea is that if one's evidence is not sufficient for knowing q, it is not sufficient for knowing p, either, where p is known to entail q. I shall be returning to this subject later, for some philosophers to whom I have referred deny this point which seems, initially, fairly obvious and I shall argue that their reasons are mistaken.

Actually, if instead of (A) we adopt the stronger epistemic deductive closure principle:

(D) a knows p

a knows q

a knows ($p \cdot q$ entails r)

∴ a knows r

(A) and (C) may be seen as instances of a common principle, provided we allow 'a knows ($p \cdot q$ entails $p \cdot q$)' as an uncontroversial instance of the third premise.[5] (D) is, ultimately, what we need, anyway to capture the idea of knowing the known logical consequences of what one knows, for (A) covers only the known consequences of the things one knows taken individually, not the known consequences of one's whole body of knowledge. And although (D) is stronger than (A), the arguments for (A) work just as strongly for (D), and, so far as I can see, there are no arguments that anyone might seriously offer against (D) which do not also apply to (A). However, for the sake of simplicity and conformity to other discussions in the literature, I shall continue to discuss deductive closure in the form of (A).

In summary, I am not absolutely convinced of the validity of the principle of epistemic deductive closure, as I am not absolutely convinced of the validity of the principle of epistemic conjunction, but in neither case can I think of an objection, and in both cases, apparent problems they lead to (skepticism, inconsistency) are either apparent only or are better handled by giving up other less obvious principles.

2. SKEPTICISM

In *Belief, Truth and Knowledge*, D. M. Armstrong argues:

> It is not a conclusive objection to a thermometer that it is only reliable in a certain sort of environment. In the same way, reliability of belief, but only within a certain sort of environment, would seem to be sufficient for the believer to earn the accolade of knowledge if that sort of environment is part of his boundary-conditions.[6]

For example, I know that the striped animal I see in the zoo is a zebra.[7] I know this despite the fact that I have no particular evidence that it is not a mule painted to look like a zebra (I have not looked for a paint can, tried paint remover on the animal, etc.). In this context—under normal circumstances, in zoos of integrity, etc.—that an animal on display has been deliberately disguised to fool trusting zoo-goers is just not a relevant hypothesis, one that I need trouble myself about rejecting. If the skeptic tries to persuade me to his position by stressing my lack of evidence against such an hypothesis, my proper response is to turn a deaf ear. He has ensnared me by improper means and is more than halfway to (illegitimately) winning his point if he gets me to agree that I must argue with him, go look for further evidence, etc.

This view, which I call the relevant alternative view, seems to me fundamentally correct. It does leave a lot of things unsaid. What are normal circumstances? What makes an alternative relevant in one context and not in another? However, in ordinary life, we do exhibit rather strong agreement about what is relevant and what is not. But there are grey areas. Alvin Goldman makes this point nicely with the following example which he attributes to Carl Ginet: if on the basis of visual appearances obtained under optimum conditions while driving through the countryside. Henry identifies an object as a barn, normally we say that Henry knows that it is a barn. Let us suppose, however, that unknown to Henry, the region is full of expertly made papier-mâché facsimiles of barns. In this case, we would not say Henry knows that the object is a barn, unless he has evidence against it being a papier-mâché facsimile, which is now a relevant alternative. So much is clear, but what if no such facsimiles exist in Henry's surroundings, although they do in Sweden? What if they do not now exist in Sweden, but they once did? Are either of these circumstances sufficient to make the hypothesis relevant? Probably not, but the situation is not so clear.

Another area of obscurity resides not in the nature of the case but in the formulation of the view in question. Goldman seems to hold what I regard as the correct version of it, which is that:

(1) an alternative is relevant only if there is some reason to think that it is true.

But there is also the view that:

(2) an alternative is relevant only if there is some reason to think it *could* be true.

Clearly, the force of the 'could' cannot be mere logical possibility, or the relevant alternative view would lose its distinguishing feature. However, if the 'could' is read in some stronger way, we could still have a version of the relevant alternative view. Dretske's 'Conclusive Reasons'[8] paper, espousing a view according to which if one knows, then given one's evidence, one could not be wrong (he reads 'could' as 'physically possible') suggests that we should consider an hypothesis a live one unless it *could not* be true, given one's evidence. Hence any alternative would be relevant, in the sense of blocking knowledge, if one has not the evidence to rule it out, so long as it is physically possible, given one's evidence. Also, the passage in 'Epistemic Operators' where Dretske says: "A relevant alternative is an alternative that *might* have been realized in the existing circumstances if the actual state of affairs had not materialized,"[9] is more akin to (2) than (1), although so taking it depends on the force of his 'might'. This, I think, is the wrong way to take the relevant alternative view. First of all, however unclear it may be as to when there is some reason to think an alternative is true, it is much more unclear as to when there is reason to think it could be true. Certainly, if there is a difference between (1) and (2), (2) is weaker, allows more to count as a relative alternative. So possibly Descartes thought there was some reason to think that there *could*, in some sense stronger than logical possibility, be an evil genius. But it seems safe to say he was wrong if he thought that there was some reason to think that there *was* an evil genius. That is, the evil genius hypothesis is not a relevant alternative according to (1) but may be according to (2) (although I shall qualify this). But the whole thrust of the relevant alternative position, as I conceive it, is that such an hypothesis is not relevant. To allow it as relevant seems to me to preclude the kind of answer to the skeptic which I sketched in the opening paragraph of this section.

In truth, Dretske does combine a relevant alternative view with an answer to skepticism. But his account is tied in with a view of knowledge, which, although it does defeat skepticism, does so in a way which gives small comfort. On his account, we do know many things, i.e., there are many things about which given our evidence, we could not be wrong. However, he does not merely reject the view that knowing entails knowing that one knows.[10] He also seems committed to the view that one rarely, if ever, knows that one knows, for it is well high impossible on his account to defend the claim that one *knows*, given one's evidence, that one *could not* be wrong, in his sense of 'could'. Perhaps this is preferable to skepticism, but at best it is going from the fire into the frying pan.

Here some qualifications of this position that the relevant alternative view provides an answer to the skeptic are in order. In truth, *in some sense* skepticism is unanswerable. This rather supports the relevant alternative view, for the uncertainty which infects (1) as to when there is some reason to think an alternative true explains why this is so. The relevant alternative view does provide a kind of answer to the skeptic—the only kind of answer which can be given. But the skeptic has an entering wedge, and rightly so. It is an essential characteristic of our concept of knowledge that tighter criteria are appropriate in different contexts.[11] It is one thing in a street encounter, another in a classroom, another in a law court—and who is to say it cannot be another in a philosophical discussion? And this is directly mirrored by the fact we have different standards for judging that there is some reason to think an alternative is true, i.e., relevant. We can point out that some philosophers are very perverse in their standards (by *some* extreme standard, there is some reason to think there is an evil genius, after all)—but we cannot legitimately go so far as to say that their perversity has stretched the concept of knowledge out of all recognition—in fact they have played on an essential feature of the concept. On the other hand, a skeptical philosopher is wrong if he holds that *others* are wrong in any way—i.e., are sloppy, speaking only loosely, or whatever—when they say we know a great deal. And the relevant alternative view gives the correct account of why a skeptic is wrong if he makes such accusations.

3. DEDUCTIVE CLOSURE AND SKEPTICISM

Proponents of the relevant alternative view have tended to think that it provides grounds for rejecting deductive closure. Although many philosophers have recently taken this position, Dretske has provided the fullest published argument to this effect. He writes:

> To know that X is A is to know that X is A within a fraework of relevant alternatives, B, C, and D. This set of contrasts together with the fact X is A, serve to define what it is that is known when one knows that X is A. One cannot change this set of contrasts without changing what a person is said to know when he is said to know that X is A. We have subtle ways of shifting these contrasts and, hence, changing what a person is said to know *without changing the sentence that we use to express what he knows.*[12]

Consider the following instance of (A):

(E) John knows that the animal is a zebra

John knows that [*the animal is a zebra* entails *the animal is not a mule painted to look like a zebra*]

∴John knows that the animal is not a mule painted to look like a zebra

In Dretske's zoo example, the animal's being a mule painted to look like a zebra is not a relevant alternative. So what one means when one says that John knows the animal is a zebra, is that he knows it is a zebra, as opposed to a gazelle, an antelope, or other animals one would normally expect to find in a zoo. If, however, being a mule painted to look like a zebra became a relevant alternative, then one would literally mean something different in saying that John knows that the animal is a zebra from what one meant originally and that something else may well be false. Now, normally, in saying that one knows that p, one presupposes (in some sense) that not-p is a relevant alternative; hence one does not know p unless one has evidence to rule out not-p. This is in fact Dretske's view, for he holds that one does *not* know that the animal is not a mule painted to look like a zebra because one has no evidence to rule out the possibility that it is. However, according to Dretske, so long as the animal's being a mule painted to look like a zebra is not a relevant alternative, the fact that John does not know that it is not does not count against John's knowing that it is a zebra. Hence, deductive closure fails (we are assuming that John's knowing an animal's being a zebra entails his knowing that it is not a mule); i.e., (E) and hence (A), are invalid.

I submit that there is another account of this example on the relevant alternative view which does not entail giving up deductive closure. On this account, to say that John knows that p does normally presuppose that not-p is a relevant alternative. This is, however, a pragmatic, not a semantic presupposition.[13] That is, it is the speaker, not the sentence (or proposition) itself, who does the presupposing. Thus, the presupposition falls in the category of those which Grice labels 'cancellable'.[14] It is possible for 'John knows that p' to be true even though a pragmatic presupposition, that not-p is a relevant alternative, is false. I would say that we may create some sort of special circumstance which cancels the normal presupposition when we utter the sentence in the course of making a deductive closure argument. After all, the utterance has got to be an odd case where we are given that not-p is not a relevant alternative to begin with—we can expect something unusual to happen, other than being forced to admit that it is a relevant alternative, after all. For even if we would not normally *affirm* 'John knows that p' in such a situation, we would not normally *say* that John does *not* know that p, either. Or it may happen that stating a deductive closure argument affects normal presuppositions in another way. If we hesitate to say "John knows that the animal is not a mule painted to look like a zebra," we *may* well hesitate to affirm "John knows the animal is a zebra." If this is so, not being a mule painted to look like a zebra will have become a relevant alternative—we will have decided there is some reason to think it true—with respect to the latter sentence as well. Perhaps the mere utterance of the former sentence is enough to make us loosen up our notion of what counts as a relevant aternative.

Either way, my account holds the set of relevant alternatives constant from beginning to end of the deductive closure argument. This is as it should be; to do otherwise would be to commit some logical sin akin to equivocation. If the relevant alternatives, which have after all to do with the truth or falsity of the premises and conclusion, cannot be held fixed, it is hard so see on what basis one can decide whether the argument form is valid or not. And if the set of relevant alternatives is one thing for the first premise and another for the conclusion, how do we determine what it is for the second premise, and how does this affect the truth of the second premise? There is no reason for my account of the matter to make skeptics of us all. The skeptical argument goes: If you know it is a zebra, and you know its being a zebra entails its not being a painted mule, then you know it is not a mule painted to look like a zebra. But you do not know the last, so you do not know the first—i.e., you do not know it is a zebra. With our account in hand, let us see how the skeptic is to be treated. There are two possibilities. First, the skeptic may be up to something legitimate. He is beginning by suggesting that being a mule painted to look like a zebra is a relevant alternative—i.e., that there is some reason to think it is true. We point out to the skeptic that under normal circumstances, given what we know of people and zoos, etc., this is not the case. The skeptic may, however, persevere, playing on the looseness of 'some reason to think true'. At this point, while we cannot argue the skeptic out of his position, we are perfectly within our rights in refusing to adopt the skeptic's standards and can comfort ourselves by feeling that the skeptic, if not flatly wrong, is at least very peculiar. On the other hand, the skeptic may be up to something illegitimate. He may be trying to get us to doubt that we know it is a zebra without going through the hard work of convincing us that being a mule painted to look like a zera is a relevant alternative. The skeptic seeks to persuade us of his conclusion by getting us to admit that we do not know it is not a mule painted to look like a zebra because we do not have evidence to rule out the possibility that it is. This is what Dretske believes and this is why he believes we must give up deductive closure to defeat the skeptic. I think this a wrong move. We do know it is not a mule painted to look like a zebra. Let us grant temporarily for the sake of this argument we do not have evidence. But Dretske is deluded by the fact that many knowledge claims require evidence on the part of the knower into thinking that all knowledge claims require evidence. Normally, as I have admitted, saying 'a knows that p' presupposes that not-p is a relevant alternative. And it does sound odd to say that we know it is not a mule painted to look like a zebra when its being one is not a relevant alternative. But the fact that it sounds odd—is indeed perhaps misleading or even improper to say— does not mean as we have seen that the presupposition is not cancellable, and that the proposition in question is not true. We often get results which sound odd to *say* when we draw valid conclusions from true premises the utterance of which does not sound odd. 'John knows that it is raining' may be true and quite in order to say to convey its literal meaning. But on the assumption of minimal logical competence on John's part and deductive closure, it entails 'John knows that it is either raining or not raining'. But this sentence, if uttered at all, is most likely to be used to suggest the negation of the first sentence. We might, in fact, say that the speaker presupposes it. Given knowledge of the first sentence, the latter is too obviously true to bother uttering at all, except for purposes of sarcasm, ironic effect, or some purpose other than conveying the information expressed by the literal meaning of the words. Yet, for all that, it is literally true. Or take a case with perhaps more analgies to our example. This is an example from Grice.[15] 'My wife is in the kitchen' implies 'My wife is in the kitchen or in the bedroom'. Yet, the utterance of the latter, in normal circumstances, presupposes the speaker's ignorance of the former and is thus an improper or at best misleading thing for him to say if he knows the former. But for all that, the latter is true if the former is, and the presupposition is cancellable.

The logical consequences of knowledge claims which the skeptic draws by deductive closure of the sort Dretske discusses, are the sorts of propositions which, in normal circumstances, are such that their negations are not relevant alternatives. Thus they sound odd to say and often have the effect of suggesting that the circumstances are abnormal. It is indeed improper to utter them in normal circumstances unless one explicitly cancels the relevant alternative presupposition which they carry, because one misleads. Nevertheless, they are literally true in normal circumstances. I endorse here a view which I believe to be Austin's.[16] This view is adumbrated in the following passage:

> If, for instance, someone remarks in casual conversation, 'As a matter of fact I live in Oxford', the other party to the conversation may, if he finds it worth doing, verify this assertion; but the *speaker,* of course, has no need to do this— he knows it to be true (or, if he is lying, false). . . . Nor need it be true that he is in this position by virtue of having verified his assertion at some previous stage; for of how many people really, who know quite well where they live, could it be said that they have at any time *verified* that they live there? When could they be supposed to have done this? In what way? And why? What we have here, in fact, is an erroneous doctrine . . . about evidence.[17]

The point is that one does know what one takes for granted in normal circumstances. I do know that it is not a mule painted to look like a zebra. I do not need evidence for such a proposition. The evidence picture of knowledge has been carried too far. I would say that I do not have evidence that it is a zebra, either. I simply *see* that it is one. But that is perhaps another matter. The point I want to make here is simply that if the negation of a proposition is not a relevant alternative, then I know it—obviously, without needing to provide evidence—and so obviously that it is odd, misleading even, to give utterance to my knowledge. And it is a virtue of the relevant alternative view that it helps explain why it is odd.

There is another way in which (E) could be defended. This line could be to claim that John does, after all, in his general knowledge of the ways of zoos and people, etc., have evidence that the animal is not a mule painted to look like a zebra. The same would hold for other consequences of knowledge claims which the skeptic draws by deductive closure. This would involve a notion of evidence according to which having evidence is not just limited to cases in which one has a specific datum to which to point. Malcolm expresses this point of view when he says:

> . . . The reason is obvious for saying that my copy of James's book does not have the characteristic that its print undergoes spontaneous changes. I have read millions of printed words on many thousands of printed pages. I have not encountered a single instance of a printed word vanishing from a page or being replaced by another printed word, suddenly and without external cause. Nor have I heard of any other person who had such an encounter. There is *overwhelming evidence* that printed words do not behave in that way. It is just as conclusive as the evidence that houses do not turn into flowers. That is to say, *absolutely conclusive evidence*[18] (underscore mine).

It is true that in the last sentence of this passage Malcolm talks about evidence for a universal proposition to the effect that printed words do not behave in a certain way, but the thrust of his argument is such that he commits himself to the view that he also (thereby) has evidence that the printed words on his particular copy of James's book will not behave that way. I am not inclined towards such a view of what it is to have adequate evidence for the proposition that the print of my own particular copy of James's book did not undergo a spontaneous change. I am inclined to reject Malcolm's view, and others akin, in favor of the Austinian sort of one previously discussed—that is, that in such a case, evidence is not required to support a knowledge claim. I mention the view only as a possible alternative view of defending epistemic deductive closure in a way consonant with the relevant alternative view.

4. SUMMARY

My view is that the relevant alternative position should be conceived of as in two parts:

(1) With respect to many propositions, to establish a knowledge claim is to be able to support it as opposed to a limited number of alternatives—i.e., only those which are relevant in the context.

(2) With respect to many propositions—in particular those which are such that their negations are not relevant alternatives in the context in question—we simply know them to be true and do not need evidence, in the normal sense, that they, rather than their negations, are true.

So conceived, the relevant alternative view neither supports the abandomnent of deductive closure, nor is such abandonment in any way needed to provide the relevant alternative view with an answer to the skeptic, insofar as he can be answered.[19]

NOTES

1. I am partial to Austin's approach in Austin 1961 and 1962, Chap. X. Other more recent and more explicitly developed accounts include those of Fred Dretske, most importantly in Dretske (in this volume), but also in Dretske 1972; Armstrong 1973; Goldman 1976; Cargile 1973; Malcolm 1963 is more concerned with certainty than knowledge but his discussion of when a proposition is 'possible' is very much in accord with considerations which go towards making a proposition a 'relevant alternative'.

2. Dretske (in this volume); Cargile 1973; Goldman 1976.

3. Cf. Stine 1973 and 1974.

4. Cf. discussions of the place of a principle of conjunction in an account of rational belief in, for example, Levi 1967; Swain 1970; Kyburg 1970; Lehrer 1970. This case for conjunction holding for rational belief is, of course, more problematic than the case for knowledge.

5. I owe this point to David Kaplan.

6. Armstrong, 1973, p. 174.

7. The example is in Dretske (in this volume).

8. Dretske 1971.

9. Dretske, in this volume, p. 142.

10. This view has been criticized, for example, in DeSousa 1970, against defenders of it such as Hintikka 1962 and Lehrer 1968. The view is also rejected by Armstrong 1973, p. 146, and at least implicitly rejected on such accounts of knowledge as, for example, those of Goldman 1967; Skyrms 1967; and Unger 1968.

11. Here I take a view directly opposed to that of Unger 1971, according to which knowledge is an 'absolute' concept, like the flatness of geometers.

12. Dretske, in this volume, p. 143.

13. Here I distinguish pragmatic from semantic presuppositions in the manner of Stalnaker 1972. Attributing the notion of a semantic presupposition to van Fraassen 1966 and 1968, Stalnaker says (p. 387):

> According to the *semantic* concept, a proposition P presupposes a proposition Q if and only if Q is necessitated both by P and by *not*-P. That is, in every model in which P is either true or false, Q is true. According to the *pragmatic* conception, presupposition is a propositional attitude, not a semantic relation. People, rather than sentences or propositions are said to have, or make, presuppositions in this sense.
>
> . . . In general, any semantic presupposition of a proposition expressed in a given context will be a pragmatic presupposition of the people in that context, but the converse clearly does not hold. To presupposes a proposition in the pragmatic sense is to take its truth for granted, and to assume that others involved in the context do the same.

14. Grice 1961.

15. Grice 1961.

16. In Austin 1961 and 1962.

17. Austin 1962, pp. 117–118.

18. Malcolm 1963, p. 38.

19. A slightly different and shorter version of this paper was read at the Eastern Division meetings of the American Philosophical Association, December 1974.

CHAPTER 10

Philosophical Explanations

Robert Nozick

You think you are seeing these words, but could you not be hallucinating or dreaming or having your brain stimulated to give you the experience of seeing these marks on paper although no such thing is before you? More extremely, could you not be floating in a tank while super-psychologists stimulate your brain electrochemically to produce exactly the same experiences as you are now having, or even to produce the whole sequence of experiences you have had in your lifetime thus far? If one of these other things was happening, your experience would be exactly the same as it now is. So how can you know none of them is happening? Yet if you do not know these possibilities don't hold, how can you know you are reading this book now? If you do not know you haven't always been floating in the tank at the mercy of the psychologists, how can you know anything—what your name is, who your parents were, where you come from?

The skeptic argues that we do not know what we think we do. Even when he leaves us unconverted, he leaves us confused. Granting that we do know, how *can* we? Given these other possibilities he poses, how is knowledge possible?[1] In answering this question, we do not seek to convince the skeptic, but rather to formulate hypotheses about knowledge and our connection to facts that show how knowledge can exist even given the skeptic's possibilities. These hypotheses must reconcile our belief that we know things with our belief that the skeptical possibilities are logical possibilities.

The skeptical possibilities, and the threats they pose to our knowledge, depend upon our knowing things (if we do) mediately, through or by way of something else. Our thinking or believing that some fact p holds is connected somehow to the fact that p, but is not itself identical with that fact. Intermediate links establish the connection. This leaves room for the possibility of these intermediate stages holding and producing our belief that p, without the fact that p being at the other end. The intermediate stages arise in a completely different manner, one not involving the fact that p although giving rise to the appearance that p holds true.[2]

Are the skeptic's possibilities indeed logically possible? Imagine reading a science fiction story in which someone is raised from birth floating in a tank with psychologists stimulating his brain. The story could go on to tell of the person's reactions when he is brought out of the tank, of how the psychologists convince him of what had been happening to him, or how they fail to do so. This story is coherent, there is nothing self-contradictory or otherwise impossible about it. Nor is there anything incoherent in imagining that you are now in this situation, at a time before being taken out of the tank. To ease the transition out, to prepare the way, perhaps the psychologists will give the person in the tank thoughts of whether floating in the tank is possible, or the experience of reading a book that discusses this possibility, even one that discusses their easing his transition. (Free will presents no insuperable problem for this possibility. Perhaps the psychologists caused all your experiences of choice, including the feeling of freely choosing; or perhaps you do freely choose to act while they, cutting the effector circuit, continue the scenario from there.)

Some philosophers have attempted to demonstrate there is no such coherent possibility of this sort.[3] However, for any reasoning that purports to show this skeptical possibility cannot occur, we can imagine the psychologists of our science fiction story feeding *it* to their tank-subject, along with the (inaccurate) feeling that the reasoning is cogent. So how much trust can be placed in the apparent cogency of an argument to show the skeptical possibility isn't coherent?

The skeptic's possibility is a logically coherent one, in tension with the existence of (almost all) knowledge; so we seek a hypothesis to explain how, even given the skeptic's possibilities, knowledge is possible. We may worry that such explanatory hypotheses are ad hoc, but this worry will lessen if they yield other facts as well, fit in with other things we believe, and so forth. Indeed, the theory of knowledge that follows was not developed in order to explain how knowledge is possible. Rather, the motivation was external to epistemology; only after the account of knowledge was developed for another purpose did I notice its consequences for skepticism, for understanding how knowledge is possible. So whatever other defects the explanation might have, it can hardly be called ad hoc.

My original aim was to make progress on the topic of free will. Early in the flurry of journal articles presenting counterexamples to increasingly complicated accounts of knowledge, stimulated by Edward Gettier's counterexample to the traditional account of knowledge as justified true belief,[4] I despaired of anyone's getting it exactly right. So messy did it all seem that I just stopped reading that literature. I was led back to the task of formulating conditions for knowledge, by the following line of reasoning.

In knowledge, a belief is linked somehow to the fact believed; without this linkage there may be true belief but there will not be knowledge. Plato first made the point that knowledge is not simply a belief that is true; if someone knowing nothing about the matter separately tells you and me contradictory things, getting one of us to believe p while the other believes not-p, although one of us will have a belief that happens to be true, neither of us will have knowledge. Something more is needed for a person S to know that p, to go alongside

    (1) p is true

    (2) S believes that p.

This something more, I think, is not simply an additional fact, but a way that 1 and 2 are linked. Thus, consider the traditional third condition stemming from Plato's account: S is justified in believing that p, or S has adequate evidence that p. Here, a two-part linkage connects S's belief that p with the fact that p: the link between the fact that p and the evidence, and the link between the evidence and the belief that p.

Recently it has been urged, with some plausibility, that the requisite linkage of belief to facts is a causal one, that the third condition is something like: the fact that p (partially) causes S to believe that p, that is, 2 because 1.[5] A drunk who hallucinates a pink elephant in a bar where, behind a screen, there is a pink elephant does not know there is a pink elephant there. The elephant's being there is not a cause of his believing it there. Whereas, in tracing back through the causes of your believing there now is a book before you, we eventually reach the fact that there *is* a book before you. The causal account of knowledge thus has a certain plausibility. Since, on this view, the causation (in a certain way) of our beliefs is necessary for us to have knowledge, such causation therefore is desirable. To be sure, there are difficulties with the causal account of knowledge, most noticeably with mathematical knowlege and ethical knowledge but elsewhere as well.[6] In these cases, the appropriate kind of causal connection fails to hold. Yet where it does hold, when a belief is caused appropriately by the fact, that connection appears desirable and plausibly is held to constitute knowledge.

In contrast, we strongly feel that the causal determination of action threatens responsibility and is undesirable. It is puzzling that what is desirable for belief, perhaps even necessary for knowledge, is threatening for action. Might not there be a way for action to parallel belief, to be so connected to the world, even causally, in a way that is desirable? At the least, it would be instructive to see where and why the parallel fails. If it did not fail, causality of action would be rendered harmless—determinism would be defanged.

The idea is to investigate how action is to be connected to the world, to parallel the connection of belief to fact when there is knowledge. This need not assume a causal account of knowledge. The causal linkage which appears to be a constituent in knowledge may be merely one way of realizing a more general linkage that constitutes knowledge. This would leave some room for ethical and mathematical knowledge, and perhaps even for a non-causal connection of action to the world that is not undercut by causality, just as mathematical knowledge, presumably, is not undercut by belief's being caused. To see if our actions desirably can be like knowledge, the first task is to see precisely what connection of belief to fact knowledge involves—then we shall know what it is that action must parallel.

It was this line of thought, this project of paralleling, that led me to investigate the details of the knowledge-link in the hope that it could be put to use later. What started as a means to another topic provided, along the way, an explanation of how knowledge is possible. This side result is especially fortunate in view of the free will problem's intractability.

I. KNOWLEDGE

Conditions for Knowledge

Our task is to formulate further conditions to go alongside

(1) p is true

(2) S believes that p.

We would like each condition to be necessary for knowledge, so any case that fails to satisfy it will not be an instance of knowledge. Furthermore, we would like the conditions to be jointly sufficient for knowledge, so any case that satisfies all of them will be an instance of knowledge. We first shall formulate conditions that seem to handle ordinary cases correctly, classifying as knowledge cases which are knowledge, and as nonknowledge cases which are not; then we shall check to see how these conditions handle some difficult cases discussed in the literature.[7]

The causal condition on knowledge, previously mentioned, provides an inhospitable environment for mathematical and ethical knowledge; also there are well-known difficulties in specifying the type of causal connection. If someone floating in a tank oblivious to everything around him is given (by direct electrical and chemical stimulation of the brain) the belief that he is floating in a tank with his brain being stimulated, then even though that fact is part of the cause of his belief, still he does not know that it is true.

Let us consider a different third condition:

(3) If p weren't true, S wouldn't believe that p.

Throughout this work, let us write the subjunctive 'if-then' by an arrow, and the negation of a sentence by prefacing "not-" to it. The above condition thus is rewritten as:

(3) not-$p \rightarrow$ not-(S believes that p).

This subjunctive condition is not unrelated to the causal condition. Often when the fact that p (partially) causes someone to believe that p, the fact also will be causally necessary for his having the belief—without the cause, the effect would not occur. In that case, the subjunctive condition 3 also will be satisfied. Yet this condition is not equivalent to the causal condition. For the causal condition will be satisfied in cases of causal overdetermination, where either two sufficient causes of the effect actually operate, or a back-up cause (of the same effect) would operate if the first one didn't; whereas the subjunctive condition need not hold for these cases.[8] When the two conditions do agree, causality indicates knowledge because it acts in a manner that makes the subjunctive 3 true.

The subjunctive condition 3 serves to exclude cases of the sort first described by Edward Gettier, such as the following. Two other people are in my office and I am justified on the basis of much evidence in believing the first owns a Ford car; though he (now) does not, the second person (a stranger to me) owns one. I believe truly and justifiably that someone (or other) in my office owns a Ford car, but I do not know someone does. Concluded Gettier, knowledge is not simply justified true belief.

The following subjunctive, which specifies condition 3 for this Gettier case, is not satisfied: if no one in my office owned a Ford car, I wouldn't believe that someone did. The situation that would obtain if no one in my office owned a Ford is one where the stranger does not (or where he is not in the office); and in that situation I still would believe, as before, that someone in my office does own a Ford, namely, the first person. So the subjunctive condition 3 excludes this Gettier case as a case of knowledge.

The subjunctive condition is powerful and intuitive, not so easy to satisfy, yet not so powerful as to rule out everything as an instance of knowledge. A subjunctive conditional "if p were true, q would be true," $p \rightarrow q$, does not say that p entails q or that it is logically impossible that p yet not-q. It says that in the situation that would obtain if p were true, q also would be true. This point is brought out especially clearly in recent 'possible-worlds' accounts of subjunctives: the subjunctive is true when (roughly) in all those worlds in which p holds true that are closest to the actual world, q also is true. (Examine those worlds in which p holds true closest to the actual world, and see if q holds true in all these.) Whether or not q is true in p worlds that are still farther away from the actual world is irrelevant to the truth of the subjunctive. I do not mean to endorse any particular possible-worlds account of subjunctives, nor am I committed to this type of account.[9] I sometimes shall use it, though, when it illustrates points in an especially clear way.[10]

The subjunctive condition 3 also handles nicely cases that cause difficulties for the view that you know that p when you can rule out the relevant alternatives to p in the context. For, as Gail Stine writes, "what makes an alternative relevant in one context and not another? ... if on the basis of visual appearances obtained under optimum conditions while driving through the countryside Henry identifies an object as a barn, normally we say that Henry knows that it is a barn. Let us suppose, however, that unknown to Henry, the region is full of expertly made papier-mâché facsimiles of barns. In that case, we would not say that Henry knows that the object is a barn, unless he has evidence against it being a papier-mâché facsimile, which is now a relevant alternative. So much is clear, but what if no such facsimiles exist in Henry's surroundings, although they once did? Are either of these circumstances sufficient to make the hypothesis (that it's a papier-mâché object) relevant? Probably not, but the situation is not so clear."[11] Let p be the statement that the object in the field is a (real) barn, and q the one that the object in the field is a papier-mâché barn. When papier-mâché barns are scattered through the area, if p were false, q would be true or might be. Since in this case (we are supposing) the person still would believe p, the subjunctive

(3) not-$p \rightarrow$ not-(S believes that p)

is not satisfied, and so he doesn't know that p. However, when papier-mâché barns are or were scattered around another country, even if p were false q wouldn't be true, and so (for all we have been told) the person may well know that p. A hypothesis q contrary to p clearly is relevant when if p weren't true, q would be true; when not-$p \rightarrow q$. It clearly is irrelevant when if p weren't true, q also would not be true; when not-$p \rightarrow$ not-q. The remaining pssibility is that neither of these opposed subjunctives holds; q might (or might not) be true if p weren't true. In this case, q also will be relevant, according to an account of knowledge incorporating condition 3 and treating subjunctives along the lines sketched above. Thus, condition 3 handles cases that befuddle the "relevant alternatives" account; though that account can adopt the above subjunctive criterion for when an alternative is relevant, it then becomes merely an alternate and longer way of stating condition 3.[12]

Despite the power and intuitive force of the condition that if p weren't true the person would not believe it, this condition does not (in conjunction with the first two conditions) rule out every problem case. There remains, for example, the case of the person in the tank who is brought to believe, by direct electrical and chemical stimulation of his brain, that he is in the tank and is being brought to believe things in this way; he does not know this is true. However, the subjunctive condition is satisfied: if he weren't floating in the tank, he wouldn't believe he was.

The person in the tank does not know he is there, because his belief is not sensitive to the truth. Although it is caused by the fact that is its content, it is not sensitive to that fact. The operators of the tank could have produced any belief, including the false belief that he wasn't in the tank; if they had, he would have believed that. Perfect sensitivity would involve beliefs and facts varying together. We already have one portion of that variation, subjunctively at least: if p were false he wouldn't believe it. This sensitivity as specified by a subjunctive does not have the belief vary with the truth or falsity of p in all possible situations, merely in the ones that would or might obtain if p were false.

The subjunctive condition

(3) not-$p \rightarrow$ not-(S believes that p)

tells us only half the story about how his belief is sensitive to the truth-value of p. It tells us how his belief state is sensitive to p's falsity, but not how it is sensitive to p's truth; it tells us what his belief state would be if p were false, but not what it would be if p were true.

To be sure, conditions 1 and 2 tell us that p is true and he does believe it, but it does not follow that his believing p is sensitive to p's being true. This additional sensitivity is given to us by a further subjunctive: if p were true, he would believe it.

(4) $p \rightarrow$ S believes that p.

Not only is p true and S believes it, but if it were true he would believe it. Compare: not only was the photon emitted and did it go to the left, but (it was then true that): if it were emitted it would go to the left. The truth of antecedent and consequent is not alone sufficient for the truth of a subjunctive; 4 says more than 1 and 2.[13] Thus, we presuppose some (or another) suitable account of subjunctives. According to the suggestion tentatively made above, 4 holds true if not only does he actually truly believe p, but in the "close" worlds where p is true, he also believes it. He believes that p for some distance out in the p neighborhood of the actual world; similarly, condition 3 speaks not of the whole not-p neighborhood of the actual world, but only of the first portion of it. (If, as is likely, these explanations do not help, please use your own intuitive understanding of the subjunctives 3 and 4.)

The person in the tank does not satisfy the subjunctive condition 4. Imagine as actual a world in which he is in the tank and is stimulated to believe he is, and consider what subjunctives are true in that world. It is not true of him there that if he were in the tank he would believe it; for in the close world (or situation) to his own where e is in the tank but they don't give him the belief that he is (much less instill the belief that he isn't) he doesn't believe he is in the tank. Of the person actually in the tank and believing it, it is not true to make the further statement that if he were in the tank he would believe it—so he does not know he is in the tank.[14]

The subjunctive condition 4 also handles a case presented by Gilbert Harman.[15] The dictator of a country is killed; in their first edition, newspapers print the story, but later all the country's newspapers and other media deny the story, falsely. Everyone who encounters the denial believes it (or does not know what to believe and so suspends judgment). Only one person in the country fails to hear any denial and he continues to believe the truth. He satisfies conditions 1 through 3 (and the causal condition about belief) yet we are reluctant to say he knows the truth. The reason is that if he had heard the denials, he too would have believed them, just like everyone else. His belief is not sensitively tuned to the truth, he doesn't satisfy the condition that if it were true he would believe it. Condition 4 is not satisfied.[16]

There is a pleasing symmetry about how this account of knowledge relates conditions 3 and 4, and connects them to the first two conditions. The account has the following form.

> (1)
>
> (2)
>
> (3) not-1 → not-2
>
> (4) 1 → 2

I am not inclined, however, to make too much of this symmetry, for I found also that with other conditions experimented with as a possible fourth condition there was some way to construe the resulting third and fourth conditions as symmetrical answers to some symmetrical looking questions, so that they appeared to arise in parallel fashion from similar questions about the components of true belief.

Symmetry, it seems, is a feature of a mode of presentation, not of the contents presented. A uniform transformation of symmetrical statements can leave the results nonsymmetrical. But if symmetry attaches to mode of presentation, how can it possibly be a deep feature of, for instance, laws of nature that they exhibit symmetry? (One of my favorite examples of symmetry is due to Groucho Marx. On his radio program he spoofed a commercial, and ended, "And if you are not completely satisfied, return the unused portion of our product and we will return the unused portion of your money.") Still, to present our subject symmetrically makes the connection of knowledge to true belief especially perspicuous. It seems to me that a symmetrical formulation is a sign of our understanding, rather than a mark of truth. If we cannot understand an asymmetry as arising from an underlying symmetry through the operation of a particular factor, we will not understand why that asymmetry exists in that direction. (But do we also need to understand why the underlying asymmetrical factor holds instead of its opposite?)

A person knows that p when he not only does truly believe it, but also would truly believe it and wouldn't falsely believe it. He not only actually has a true belief, he subjunctively has one. It is true that p and he believes it; if it weren't true he wouldn't believe it, and if it were true he would believe it. To know that p is to be someone who would believe it if it were true, and who wouldn't believe it if it were false.

It will be useful to have a term for this situation when a person's belief is thus subjunctively connected to the fact. Let us say of a person who believes that p, which is true, that when 3 and 4 hold, his belief *tracks* the truth that p. To know is to have a belief that tracks the truth. Knowledge is a particular way of being connected to the world, having a specific real factual connection to the world: tracking it.

One refinement is needed in condition 4. It may be possible for someone to have contradictory beliefs, to believe p and also believe not-p. We do not mean such a person to easily satisfy 4, and in any case we want his belief-state, sensitive to the truth of p, to focus upon p. So let us rewrite our fourth condition as:

(4) $p \rightarrow$ S believes that p and not-(S believes that not-p).[17]

As you might have expected, this account of knowledge as tracking requires some refinements and epicycles. Readers who find themselves (or me) bogged down in these refinements should move on directly to this essay's second part, on skepticism, where the pace picks up.

II. SKEPTICISM

The skeptic about knowledge argues that we know very little or nothing of what we think we know, or at any rate that this position is no less reasonable than the belief in knowledge. The history of philosophy exhibits a number of different attempts to refute the skeptic: to prove him wrong or show that in arguing against knowledge he presupposes there is some and so refutes himself. Others attempt to show that accepting skepticism is unreasonable, since it is more likely that the skeptic's extreme conclusion is false than that all of his premises are true, or simply because reasonableness of belief just means proceeding in an anti-skeptical way. Even when these counterarguments satisfy their inventors, they fail to satisfy others, as is shown by the persistent attempts against skepticism.[18] The continuing felt need to refute skepticism, and the difficulty in doing so, attests to the power of the skeptic's position, the depth of his worries.

An account of knowledge should illuminate skeptical arguments and show wherein lies their force. If the account leads us to reject these arguments, this had better not happen too easily or too glibly. To think the skeptic overlooks something obvious, to attribute to him a simple mistake or confusion or fallacy, is to refuse to acknowledge the power of his position and the grip it can have upon us. We thereby cheat ourselves of the opportunity to reap his insights and to gain self-knowledge in understanding why his arguments lure us so. Moreover, in fact, we cannot lay the specter of skepticism to rest without first hearing what it shall unfold.

Our goal is not, however, to refute skepticism, to prove it is wrong or even to argue that it is wrong. In the Introduction [to Nozick 1981] we distinguished between philosophy that attempts to prove, and philosophy that attempts to explain how something is possible. Our task here is to explain how knowledge is possible, given what the skeptic says that we do accept (for example, that it is logically possible that we are dreaming or are floating in the tank). In doing this, we need not convince the skeptic, and we may introduce explanatory hypotheses that he would reject. What is important for our task of explanation and understanding is that *we* find those hypotheses acceptable or plausible, and that they show us how the existence of knowledge fits together with the logical possibilities the skeptic points to, so that these are reconciled within our own belief system. These hypotheses are to explain to ourselves how knowledge is possible, not to prove to someone else that knowledge *is* possible.[19]

Skeptical Possibilities

The skeptic often refers to possibilities in which a person would believe something even though it was false: really, the person is cleverly deceived by others, perhaps by an evil demon, or the person is dreaming or he is floating in a tank near Alpha Centauri with his brain being stimulated. In each case, the *p* he believes is false, and he believes it even though it is false.

How do these possibilities adduced by the skeptic show that someone does not know that *p*? Suppose that someone is you; how do these possibilities count against your knowing that *p*? One way might be the following. (I shall consider other ways later.) If there is a possible situation where *p* is false yet you believe that *p*, then in that situation you believe that *p* even though it is false. So it appears you do not satisfy condition 3 for knowledge.

(3) If *p* were false, S wouldn't believe that *p*.

For a situation has been described in which you do believe that *p* even thugh *p* is false. How then can it also be true that if *p* were false, you wouldn't believe it? If the skeptic's possible situation shows that 3 is false, and if 3 is a necessary condition for knowledge, then the skeptic's possible situation shows that there isn't knowledge.

So construed, the skeptic's argument plays on condition 3; it aims to show that condition 3 is not satisfied. The skeptic may seem to be putting forth

R: Even if *p* were false, S still would believe *p*.[20]

This conditional, with the same antecedent as 3 and the contradictory consequent, is incompatible with the truth of 3. If 3 is true, then R is not. However, R is stronger than the skeptic needs in order to show 3 is false. For 3 is false when if *p* were false, S might believe that *p*. This last conditional is weaker than R, and is merely 3's denial:

T: not-[not-*p* → not-(S believes that *p*)].

Whereas R does not simply deny 3, it asserts an opposing subjunctive of its own. Perhaps the possibility the skeptic adduces is not enough to show that R is true, but it appears at least to establish the weaker T; since this T denies 3, the skeptic's possibility appears to show that 3 is false.[21]

However, the truth of 3 is not incompatible with the existence of a possible situation where the person believes p though it is false. The subjunctive

(3) not-$p \rightarrow$ not-(S believes p)

does not talk of all possible situations in which p is false (in which not-p is true). It does not say that in all possible situations where not-p holds, S doesn't believe p. To say there is no possible situation in which not-p yet S believes p, would be to say that not-p entails not-(S believes p), or logically implies it. But subjunctive conditionals differ from entailments; the subjunctive 3 is not a statement of entailment. So the existence of a possible situation in which p is false yet S believes p does not show that 3 is false;[22] 3 can be true even though there is a possible situation where not-p and S believes that p.

What the subjunctive 3 speaks of is the situation that would hold if p were false. Not every possible situation in which p is false is the situation that would hold if p were false. To fall into possible worlds talk, the subjunctive 3 speaks of the not-p world that is closest to the actual world, or of those not-p worlds that are closest to the actual world, or more strongly (according to my suggestion) of the not-p neighborhood of the actual world. And it is of this or these not-p worlds that it says (in them) S does not believe that p. What happens in yet other more distant not-p worlds is no concern of the subjunctive 3.

The skeptic's possibilities (let us refer to them as SK), of the person's being deceived by a demon or dreaming or floating in a tank, count against the subjunctive

(3) if p were false then S wouldn't believe that p

only if (one of) these possibilities would or might obtain if p were false; only if one of these possibilities is in the not-p neighborhood of the actual world. Condition 3 says: if p were false, S still would not believe p. And this can hold even though there is some situation SK described by the skeptic in which p is false and S believes p. If p were false S still would not believe p, even though there is a situation SK in which p is false and S does believe p, provided that this situation SK wouldn't obtain if p were false. If the skeptic describes a situation SK which would not hold even if p were false then this situation SK doesn't show that 3 is false and so does not (in this way at least) undercut knowledge. Condition C acts to rule out skeptical hypotheses.

C: not-$p \rightarrow$ SK does not obtain.

Any skeptical situation SK which satisfies condition C is ruled out. For a skeptical situation SK to show that we don't know that p, it must fail to satisfy C which excludes it; instead it must be a situation that might obtain if p did not, and so satisfy C's denial:

not-(not-$p \rightarrow$ SK doesn't obtain).

Although the skeptic's imagined situations appear to show that 3 is false, they do not; they satisfy condition C and so are excluded.

The skeptic might go on to ask whether we know that his imagined situations SK are excluded by condition C, whether we know that if *p* were false SK would not obtain. However, typically he asks something stronger: do we know that his imagined situation SK does not actually obtain? Do we know that we are not being deceived by a demon, dreaming, or floating in a tank? And if we do not know this, how can we know that *p*? Thus we are led to the second way his imagined situations might show that we do not know that *p*.

Skeptical Results

According to our account of knowledge, S knows that the skeptic's situation SK doesn't hold if and only if

(1) SK doesn't hold

(2) S believes that SK doesn't hold

(3) If SK were to hold, S would not believe that SK doesn't hold

(4) If SK were not to hold, S would believe it does not.

Let us focus on the third of these conditions. The skeptic has carefully chosen his situations SK so that if they held we (still) would believe they did not. We would believe we weren't dreaming, weren't being deceived, and so on, even if we were. He has chosen situations SK such that if SK were to hold, S would (still) believe that SK doesn't hold—and this is incompatible with the truth of 3.[23]

Since condition 3 is a necessary condition for knowledge, it follows that we do not know that SK doesn't hold. If it were true that an evil demon was deceiving us, if we were having a particular dream, if we were floating in a tank with our brains stimulated in a specified way, we would still believe we were not. So, we do not know we're not being deceived by an evil demon, we do not know we're not in that tank, and we do not know we're not having that dream. So says the skeptic, and so says our account. And also so we say—don't we? For how could we know we are not being deceived that way, dreaming that dream? If those things *were* happening to us, everything would seem the same to us. There is no way we can know it is not happening for there is no way we could tell if it were happening; and if it were happening we would believe exactly what we do now—in particular, we still would believe that it was not. For this reason, we feel, and correctly, that we don't know—how could we?—that it is not happening to us. It is a virtue of our account that it yields, and explains, this result.

The skeptic asserts we do not know his possibilities don't obtain, and he is right. Attempts to avoid skepticism by claiming we do know these things are bound to fail. The skeptic's possibilities make us uneasy because, as we deeply realize, we do not know they don't obtain; it is not surprising that attempts to show we do know these things leave us suspicious, strike us even as bad faith.[24] Nor has the skeptic merely pointed out something obvious and trivial. It comes as a surprise to realize that we do not know his possibilities don't obtain. It is startling, shocking. For we would have thought, before the skeptic got us to focus on it, that we did know those things, that we did know we were not being deceived by a demon, or dreaming that dream, or stimulated that way in that tank. The skeptic has pointed out that we do not know things we would have confidently said we knew. And if we don't know these things, what can we know? So much for the supposed obviousness of what the skeptic tells us.

Let us say that a situation (or world) is doxically identical for S to the actual situation when if S were in that situation, he would have exactly the beliefs (*doxa*) he actually does have. More generally, two situations are doxically identical for S if and only if he would have exactly the same beliefs in them. It might be merely a curiosity to be told there are nonactual situations doxically identical to the actual one. The skeptic, however, describes worlds doxically identical to the actual world in which almost everything believed is false.[25]

Such worlds are possible because we know mediately, not directly. This leaves room for a divergence between our beliefs and the truth. It is as though we possessed only two-dimensional plane projections of three-dimensional objects. Different three-dimensional objects, oriented appropriately, have the same two-dimensional plane projection. Similarly, different situations or worlds will lead to our having the very same beliefs. What is surprising is how very different the doxically identical world can be—different enough for almost everything believed in it to be false. Whether or not the mere fact that knowledge is mediated always makes room for such a very different doxically identical world, it does so in our case, as the skeptic's possibilities show. To be shown this is nontrivial, especially when we recall that we do not know the skeptic's possibility doesn't obtain: we do not know that we are not living in a doxically identical world wherein almost everything we believe is false.[26]

What more could the skeptic ask for or hope to show? Even readers who sympathized with my desire not to dismiss the skeptic too quickly may feel this has gone too far, that we have not merely acknowledged the force of the skeptic's position but have succumbed to it.

The skeptic maintains that we know almost none of what we think we know. He has shown, much to our initial surprise, that we do not know his (nontrivial) possibility SK doesn't obtain. Thus, he has shown of one thing we thought we knew, that we didn't and don't. To the conclusion that we know almost nothing, it appears but a short step. For if we do not know we are not dreaming or being deceived by a demon or floating in a tank, then how can I know, for example, that I am sitting before a page writing with a pen, and how can you know that you are reading a page of a book?

However, although our account of knowledge agrees with the skeptic in saying that we do not know that not-SK, it places no formidable barriers before my knowing that I am writing on a page with a pen. It is true that I am, I believe I am, if I weren't I wouldn't believe I was, and if I were, I would believe it. (I leave out the reference to method.) Also, it is true that you are reading a page (please, don't stop now!), you believe you are, if you weren't reading a page you wouldn't believe you were, and if you were reading a page you would believe you were. So according to the account, I do know that I am writing on a page with a pen, and you do know that you are reading a page. The account does not lead to any general skepticism.

Yet we must grant that it appears that if the skeptic is right that we don't know we are not dreaming or being deceived or floating in the tank, then it cannot be that I know I am writing with a pen or that you know you are reading a page. So we must scrutinize with special care the skeptic's "short step" to the conclusion that we don't know these things, for either this step cannot be taken or our account of knowledge is incoherent.

Nonclosure

In taking the "short step," the skeptic assumes that if S knows that *p* and he knows that '*p* entails *q*' then he also knows that *q*. In the terminology of the logicians, the skeptic assumes that knowledge is closed under known logical implication; that the operation of moving from something known to something else known to be entailed by it does not take us outside of the (closed) area of knowledge. He intends, of course, to work things backwards, arguing that since the person does not know that *q*, assuming (at least for the purposes of argument) that he does know that *p* entails *q*, it follows that he does not know that *p*. For if he did know that *p*, he would also know that *q*, which he doesn't.

The details of different skeptical arguments vary in their structure, but each one will assume some variant of the principle that knowledge is closed under known logical implication. If we abbreviate "knowledge that *p*" by "Kp" and abbreviate "entails" by the fishhook sign " ⊰," we can write this principle of closure as the subjunctive principle

P: K(p ⊰ q) & Kp → Kq.

If a person were to know that *p* entails *q* and he were to know that *p* then he would know that *q*. The statement that *q* follows by modus ponens from the other two stated as known in the antecedent of the subjunctive principle P; this principle counts on the person to draw the inference to *q*.

You know that your being in a tank on Alpha Centauri entails your not being in place X where you are. (I assume here a limited readership.) And you know also the contrapositive, that your being at place X entails that you are not then in a tank on Alpha Centauri. If you knew you were at X you would know you're not in a tank (of a specified sort) at Alpha Centauri. But you do not know this last fact (the skeptic has argued and we have agreed) and so (he argues) you don't know the first. Another intuitive way of putting the skeptic's argument is as follows. If you know that two statements are incompatible and you know the first is true then you know the denial of the second. You know that your being at X and your being in a tank on Alpha Centauri are incompatible; so if you knew you were at X you would know you were not in the (specified) tank on Alpha Centauri. Since you do not know the second, you don't know the first.[27]

No doubt, it is possible to argue over the details of principle P, to point out it is incorrect as it stands. Perhaps, though Kp, the person does not know that he knows that p (that is, not-KKp) and so does not draw the inference to q. Or perhaps he doesn't draw the inference because not-KK(p ⌐ q). Other similar principles face their own difficulties: for example, the principle that K(p → q) → (Kp → Kq) fails if Kp stops $p → q$ from being true, that is, if Kp → not-(p → q); the principle that K(p ⌐ q) → K(Kp → Kq) faces difficulties if Kp makes the person forget that (p ⌐ q) and so he fails to draw the inference to q. We seem forced to pile K upon K until we reach something like KK(p ⌐ q) & KKp → Kq; this involves strengthening considerably the antecedent of P and so is not useful for the skeptic's argument that p is not known. (From a principle altered thus, it would follow at best that it is not known that p is known.)

We would be ill-advised, however, to quibble over the details of P. Although these details are difficult to get straight, it will continue to appear that something like P is correct. If S knows that 'p entails q' and he knows that p and knows that '(p and p entails q) entails q' (shades of the Lewis Carroll puzzle we discuss below [in Nozick 1981]!) and he does draw the inference to q from all this and believes q via the process of drawing this inference, then will he not know that q? And what is wrong with simplifying this mass of detail by writing merely principle P, provided we apply it only to cases where the mass of detail holds, as it surely does in the skeptical cases under consideration? For example, I do realize that my being in the Van Leer Foundation Building in Jerusalem entails that I am not in a tank on Alpha Centauri; I am capable of drawing inferences now; I do believe I am not in a tank on Alpha Centauri (though not solely via this inference, surely); and so forth. Won't this satisfy the correctly detailed principle, and shouldn't it follow that I know I am not (in that tank) on Alpha Centauri? The skeptic agrees it should follow; so he concludes from the fact that I don't know I am not floating in the tank on Alpha Centauri that I don't know I am in Jerusalem. Uncovering difficulties in the details of particular formulations of P will not weaken the principle's intuitive appeal; such quibbling will seem at best like a wasp attacking a steamroller, at worst like an effort in bad faith to avoid being pulled along by the skeptic's argument.

Principle P is wrong, however, and not merely in detail. Knowledge is not closed under known logical implication.[28] S knows that p when S has a true belief that p, and S wouldn't have a false belief that p (condition 3) and S would have a true belief that p (condition 4). Neither of these latter two conditions is closed under known logical implication.

Let us begin with condition

(3) if p were false, S wouldn't believe that p.

When S knows that p, his belief that p is contingent on the truth of p, contingent in the way the subjunctive condition 3 describes. Now it might be that p entails q (and S knows this), that S's belief that p is subjunctively contingent on the truth of p, that S believes q, yet his belief that q is not subjunctively dependent on the truth of q, in that it (or he) does not satisfy:

(3') if q were false, S wouldn't believe that q.

For 3' talks of what S would believe if q were false, and this may be a very different situation than the one that would hold if p were false, even though p entails q. That you were born in a certain city entails that you were born on earth.[29] Yet contemplating what (actually) would be the situation if you were not born in that city is very different from contemplating what situation would hold if you weren't born on earth. Just as those possibilities are very different, so what is believed in them may be very different. When p entails q (and not the other way around) p will be a stronger statement than q, and so not-q (which is the antecedent of 3') will be a stronger statement than not-p (which is the antecedent of 3). There is no reason to assume you will have the same beliefs in these two cases, under these suppositions of differing strengths.

There is no reason to assume the (closest) not-p world and the (closest) not-q world are doxically identical for you, and no reason to assume, even though p entails q, that your beliefs in one of these worlds would be a (proper) subset of your beliefs in the other.

Consider now the two statements:

p = I am awake and sitting on a chair in Jerusalem;

q = I am not floating in a tank on Alpha Centauri being stimulated by electrochemical means to believe that p.

The first one entails the second: p entails q. Also, I know that p entails q; and I know that p. If p were false, I would be standing or lying down in the same city, or perhaps sleeping there, or perhaps in a neighboring city or town. If q were false, I would be floating in a tank on Alpha Centauri. Clearly these are very different situations, leading to great differences in what I then would believe. If p were false, if I weren't awake and sitting on a chair in Jerusalem, I would not believe that p. Yet if q were false, if I was floating in a tank on Alpha Centauri, I would believe that q, that I was not in the tank, and indeed, in that case, I would still believe that p. According to our account of knowledge, I know that p yet I do not know that q, even though (I know) p entails q.

This failure of knowledge to be closed under known logical implication stems from the fact that condition 3 is not closed under known logical implication; condition 3 can hold of one statement believed while not of another known to be entailed by the first.[30] It is clear that any account that includes as a necessary condition for knowledge the subjunctive condition 3, not-p →

not-(S believes that p), will have the consequence that knowledge is not closed under known logical implication.[31]

When p entails q and you believe each of them, if you do not have a false belief that p (since p is true) then you do not have a false belief that q. However, if you are to know something not only don't you have a false belief about it, but also you wouldn't have a false belief about it. Yet, we have seen how it may be that p entails q and you believe each and you wouldn't have a false belief that p yet you might have a false belief that q (that is, it is not the case that you wouldn't have one). Knowledge is not closed under the known logical implication because "wouldn't have a false belief that" is not closed under known logical implication.

If knowledge were the same as (simply) true belief then it would be closed under known logical implication (provided the implied statements were believed). Knowledge is not simply true belief, however; additional conditions are needed. These further conditions will make knowledge open under known logical implication, even when the entailed statement is believed, when at least one of the further conditions itself is open. Knowledge stays closed (only) if all of the additional conditions are closed. I lack a general nontrivial characterization of those conditions that are closed under known logical implication; possessing such an illuminating characterization, one might attempt to prove that no additional conditions of that sort could provide an adequate analysis of knowledge.

Still, we can say the following. A belief that p is knowledge that p only if it somehow varies with the truth of p. The causal condition for knowledge specified that the belief was "produced by" the fact, but that condition did not provide the right sort of varying with the fact. The subjunctive conditions 3 and 4 are our attempt to specify that varying. But however an account spells this out, it will hold that whether a belief that p is knowledge partly depends on what goes on with the belief in some situations when p is false. An account that says nothing about what is believed in any situation when p is false cannot give us any mode of varying with the fact.

Because what is preserved under logical implication is truth, any condition that is preserved under known logical implication is most likely to speak only of what happens when p, and q, are true, without speaking at all of what happens when either one is false. Such a condition is incapable of providing "varies with"; so adding only such conditions to true belief cannot yield an adequate account of knowledge.[32]

A belief's somehow varying with the truth of what is believed is not closed under known logical implication. Since knowledge that p involves such variation, knowledge also is not closed under known logical implication. The skeptic cannot easily deny that knowledge involves such variation, for his argument that we don't know that we're not floating in that tank, for example, uses the fact that knowledge does involve variation. ("If you were floating in the tank you would still think you weren't, so you don't know that you're not.") Yet, though one part of his argument uses that fact that knowledge involves such variation, another part of his argument presupposes that knowledge does not involve any such variation. This latter is the part that depends upon knowledge being closed under known logical implication, as when the skeptic argues that since you don't know that not-SK, you don't know you are not floating in the tank, then you also don't know, for example, that you are now reading a book. That closure can hold only if the variation does not. The skeptic cannot be right both times. According to our view he is right when he holds that knowledge involves such variation and so concludes that we don't know, for example, that we are not floating in that tank; but he is wrong when he assumes knowledge is closed under known logical implication and concludes that we know hardly anything.[33]

Knowledge is a real factual relation, subjunctively specifiable, whose structure admits our standing in this relation, tracking, to p without standing in it to some q which we know p to entail. Any relation embodying some variation of belief with the fact, with the truth (value), will exhibit this structural feature. The skeptic is right that we don't track some particular truths—the ones stating that his skeptical possibilities SK don't hold—but wrong that we don't stand in the real knowledge-relation of tracking to many other truths, including ones that entail these first mentioned truths we believe but don't know.

The literature on skepticism contains writers who endorse these skeptical arguments (or similar narrower ones), but confess their inability to maintain their skeptical beliefs at times when they are not focusing explicitly on the reasoning that led them to skeptical conclusions. The most notable example of this is Hume:

> I am ready to reject all belief and reasoning, and can look upon no opinion even as more probable or likely than another ... Most fortunately it happens that since reason is incapable of dispelling these clouds, nature herself suffices to that purpose, and cures me of this philosophical melancholy and delirium, either by relaxing this bent of mind, or by some avocation, and lively impression of my senses, which obliterate all these chimeras. I dine, I play a game of backgammon, I converse, and am merry with my friends; and when after three or four hours' amusement, I would return to these speculations, they appear so cold, and strained, and ridiculous, that I cannot find in my heart to enter into them any farther.
> (*A Treatise of Human Nature*, Book I, Part IV, section VII)

> The great subverter of Pyrrhonism or the excessive principles of skepticism is action, and employment, and the occupations of common life. These principles may flourish and triumph in the schools; where it is, indeed, difficult, if not impossible, to refute them. But as soon as they leave the shade, and by the presence of the real objects, which actuate our passions and sentiments, are put in opposition to the more powerful principles of our nature, they vanish like smoke, and leave the most determined skeptic in the same condition as other mortals ... And though a Pyrrhonian may throw himself or others into a momentary amazement and confusion by his profound reasonings; the first and most trivial event in life will put to flight all his doubts and scruples, and leave him the same, in every point of action and

speculation, with the philosophers of every other sect, or with those who never concerned themselves inany philosophical researches. When he awakes from his dream, he will be the first to join in the laugh against himself, and to confess that all his objections are mere amusement.

(*An Enquiry Concerning Human Understanding*, Section XII, Part II)

The theory of knowledge we have presented explains why skeptics of various sorts have had such difficulties in sticking to their far-reaching skeptical conclusions "outside the study", or even inside it when they are not thinking specifically about skeptical arguments and possibilities SK.

The skeptic's arguments do show (but show only) that we don't know the skeptic's possibilities SK do not hold; and he is right that we don't track the fact that SK does not hold. (If it were to hold, we would still think it didn't.) However, the skeptic's arguments don't show we do not know other facts (including facts that entail not-SK) for we do track these other facts (and knowledge is not closed under known logical entailment.) Since we do track these other facts—you, for example, the fact that you are reading a book; I, the fact that I am writing on a page—and the skeptic tracks such facts too, it is not surprising that when he focuses on them, on his relationship to such facts, the skeptic finds it hard to remember or maintain his view that he does not know those facts. Only by shifting his attention back to his relationship to the (different) fact that not-SK, which relationship is not tracking, can he revive his skeptical belief and make it salient. However, this skeptical triumph is evanescent, it vanishes when his attention turns to other facts. Only by fixating on the skeptical possibilities SK can he maintain his skeptical virtue; otherwise, unsurprisingly, he is forced to confess to sins of credulity.

NOTES

1. This chapter's focus upon the existence (and possibility) of bits of knowledge that *p*. Knowledge is diverse. We know particular current facts about ourselves and our immediate environments, facts about our pasts, our parents, our pans, facts we were taught or read about history, other societies, current affairs, things science has found out, parts of mathematics, even perhaps whole subjects; also, there are people and places we know, and things we know how to do.

Moreover, our knowledge is not simply a bunch of separate items; it forms an interconnected network. It is not quite a system—more a fabric: some parts more tightly woven than others, with holes and rents, some patches, worn spots and many threads dangling. (Think of it as a child's security blanket.) There are also many interesting questions about the overall structure and shape of this fabric, and how its parts interconnect, the overall pattern, if any, the differently colored threads exhibit. (In representing a current state of knowledge we would want to include not only the current state and interconnections of what is known—the fabric—but also the problems known of, ongoing attempts at solution, and so forth.) Such questions will receive more attention with the decline of the view, predominant for centuries, of knowledge as a structure with foundations.

2. There also is the possibility wherein there is no intermediate route; the experiences arise uncaused, at random. Unlike the skeptical possibilities, however, this one would not explain why the experiences are had.

3. Most recently, my colleague Hilary Putnam has used considerations from the theory of reference in an attempt toward formulating a transcendental argument that would undercut the skeptical possibility: if we can successfully describe the possibility, using constituent terms that refer, then it cannot hold true. (See Putnam 1977; he extends the argument in this volume). Recall another earlier attempt. The "paradigm case argument" held that since some situations were the very type of situation wherein was taught the application of a term, "free will" for example, the term must refer to that type of situation. This argument is now rightly discredit-

ed; one would expect Putnam's more sophisticated use of a theory of reference to fall before correspondingly more sophisticated versions of the earlier objections.

First, at best, Putnam's arguments shows the terms have something they refer to, not that we are in any sort of direct contact with the referents. For all the arguments shows, we could be floating in the tank using terms whose reference is parasitic on the terms of the psychologists, who are not. Second, we cannot tell from Putnam's argument which terms will have a referent that fits them; for the meaning of some can be built up out of the other terms (for subatomic particles, say) which, while they do refer, are not explicitly mentioned in the skeptic's science fiction story. Third, though the "tank" is a salient device to pose the problem, the story need not assume you are materially ensconced; then the mode of influence exerted by the other conscious-nesses will not be mediated materially.

4. Gettier 1963.

5. See Goldman 1967.

6. Paul Benacerraf wrestles with the problems a causal account causes for mathematical knowledge in Benac-erref 1973. For an attempt to defend the causal account in application to mathematics, see Steiner 1975.

7. Despite some demurrals in the literature, there is general agreement that conditions 1 and 2 are necessary for knowledge. (For some recent discussions, see Armstrong 1973, chap. 10; Lehrer 1974, chaps. 2,3.) I shall take for granted that this is so, without wishing to put much weight on its being belief that is the precise cog-nitive attitude (as opposed to thinking it so, accepting the statement, and so on) or on the need to introduce truth as opposed to formulating the first condition simply as: p.

I should note that our procedure here does not stem from thinking that every illuminating discussion of an important philosophical notion must present (individually) necessary and (jointly) sufficient conditions.

8. Below, we discuss further the case where though the fact that p causes the person's belief that p, he would believe it anyway, even if it were not true. I should note here that I assume bivalence throughout this chapter, and consider only statements that are true if and only if their negations are false.

9. See Stalnaker 1968; Lewis 1973; and Bennett 1974.

Our purposes require, for the most part, no more than an intuitive understanding of subjunctives. How-ever, it is most convenient to examine here some further issues, which will be used once or twice later. Lewis's account has the consequence that p $\rightarrow$ q whenever p and q are both true; for the possible world where p is true that is the closest to the actual world is the actual world itself, and in that world q is true. We might try to rem-edy this by saying that when p is true, p $\rightarrow$ q is true if and only if q is true in all p worlds closer (by the metric) to the actual world than is any not-p world. When p is false, the usual accounts hold that p $\rightarrow$ q is true when q holds merely in the closest p worlds to the actual world. This is too weak, but how far out must one go among the p worlds? A suggestion parallel to the previous one is: out until one reaches another not-p world (still fur-ther out). So if q holds in the closest p world w1 but not in the p world w2, even though no not-p world lies be-tween w_1 and w_2, then, (under the suggestion we are considering) the subjunctive is false. A unified account can be offered for subjunctives, whatever the truth value of their antecedents. The p neighborhood of the ac-tual world A is the closest p band to it; that is, w is in the p neighborhood of the actual world if and only if p is true in w and there are no worlds w_1 and w_2 such that not-p is true in w_1 and p is true in w_2 and w_1 is closer to A than w_2 is to A, and w_2 is at least as close to A as w1 is to A. A subjunctive p $\rightarrow$ q is true if and only if q is true throughout the p neighborhood of the actual world.

If it is truly a random matter which slit a photon goes through, then its going through (say) the right slit does not establish the subjunctive: if a photon were fired at that time from that source it would go through the right hand slit. For when p equals A photon is fired at that time from that source, and q equals the photon goes through the right hand slit, q is not true everywhere in the p neighborhood of the actual world.

This view of subjunctives with a possible-worlds framework is inadequate if there is no discrete p band of the actual world, as when for each positive distance from the actual world A, there are both p and not-p worlds so distant. Even if this last is not generally so, many p worlds that interest us may have their distances from A matched by non-p worlds. Therefore, let us redefine the relevant p band as the closes spread of p worlds such that there is no not-p world intermediate in distance from A to two p worlds in the spread unless there is also another p world in the spread the very same distance from A. By definition it is only p worlds in the p band, but some not-p worlds may be equidistant from A.

Though this emendation allows us to speak of the closest spread of p worlds, it no longer is so clear which worlds in this p band subjunctives (are to) encompass. We have said it is not sufficient for the truth of p $\rightarrow$ q that q hold in that one world in the p band closest to the actual world. Is it necessary, as our first sugges-tion has it, that q hold in all the p worlds in the closest p band to the actual world? Going up until the first "pure" stretch of not-p worlds is no longer as natural a line to draw as when we imagined "pure" p neighbor-hoods. Since there are already some not-p worlds the same distance from A as some members of the p band, what is the special significance of the first unsullied not-p stretch? There seems to be no natural line, though, coming before this stretch yet past the first p world. Perhaps nothing stronger can be said than this: p $\rightarrow$ q when q holds for some distance out in the closest p band to the actual world, that is, when all the worlds in this first part of that closest p band are q. The distance need not be fixed as the same for all subjunctives, al-though various general formulas might be imagined, for example, that the distance is a fixed percentage of the width of the p band.

I put forth this semantics for subjunctives in a possible-worlds framework with some diffidence, having little inclination to pursue the details. Let me emphasize, though, that this semantics does not presuppose any realist view that all possible worlds obtain. (Such a view was discussed in the previous chapter.) I would hope that into this chapter's subjunctively formulated theoretical structure can be plugged (without too many modifications) whatever theory of subjunctives turns out to be adequate, so that the theory of knowledge we formulate is not sensitive to variations in the analysis of subjunctives. In addition to Lewis and Stalnaker cited above, see Adams 1976; J.H. Sobel, "Probability, Chance and Choice" (unpublished book manuscript); and a book by Igal Kvart.

10. If the possible-worlds formalism is used to represent counterfactuals and subjunctives, the relevant worlds are not those p worlds that are closest or most similar to the actual world, unless the measure of closeness or similarity is: what would obtain if p were true. Clearly, this cannot be used to explain when subjunctives hold true, but it can be used to represent them. Compare utility theory which represents preferences but does not explain them. Still, it is not a trivial fact that preferences are so structured that they can be represented by a real-valued function, unique up to a positive linear transformation, even though the representation (by itself) does not explain these preferences. Similarly, it would be of interest to know what properties hold of distance metrics which serve to represent subjunctives, and to know how subjunctives must be structured and interrelated so that they can be given a possible worlds representation. (With the same one space serving all subjunctives?)

    One further word on this point. Imagine a library where a cataloguer assigns call numbers based on facts of sort F. Someone, perhaps the cataloguer, then places each book on the shelf by looking at its call number, and inserting it between the two books whose call numbers are most nearly adjacent to its own. The call number is derivative from facts of type F, yet it plays some explanatory role, not merely a representational one. "Why is this book located precisely there? Because of its number." Imagine next another library where the person who places books on the shelves directly considers facts of type F, using them to order the books and to interweave new ones. Someone else might notice that this ordering can be represented by an assignment of numbers, numbers from which other information can be derived as well, for example, the first letter of the last name of the principal author. But such an assigned number is no explanation of why a book in this library is located between two others (or why its author's last name begins with a certain letter). I have assumed that utility numbers stand to preferences, and closeness or similarity measures stand to subjunctives, as the call numbers do to the books, and to the facts of type F they exhibit, in the second library.

11. G.C. Stine (reprinted in this volume) who attributes the example to Carl Ginet.

12. This last remark is a bit too brisk, for that account might use a subjunctive criterion for when an alternative q to p is relevant (namely, when if p were not to hold, q would or might), and utilize some further notion of what it is to rule out relevant alternatives (for example, here evidence against them), so that it did not turn out to be equivalent to the account we offer.

13. More accurately, since the truth of the antecedent and consequent is not necessary for the truth of the subjunctive either, 4 says something different from 1 and 2.

14. I experimented with some other conditions which adequately handled this as well as some other problem cases, but they succumbed to further difficulties. Though much can be learned from applying these conditions, presenting all the details would engage only the most masochistic readers. So I simply will list them, each at one time a candidate to stand alone in place of condition 4.

    (a) S believes that not-p → not-p.

    (b) S believes that not-p → not-p or it is through some other method that S believes not-p. (Methods are discussed on pp. 179–187 of Nozick 1981.)

    (c) (S-believes p or S believes not-p) → not-(S believes p, and not-p holds) and not-(S believes not-p, and p holds).

    (d) not-(S believes that p) → not-(p and S believes that not-p).

    (e) not-(p and S believes that p) → not-(not-p and S believes that p or p and S believes that not-p).

15. Harman 1973, chap. 9, pp. 142–154.

16. What if the situation or world where he too hears the later false denials is not so close, so easily occurring? Should we say that everything that prevents his hearing the denial easily would not have happened, and does not in some close world?

17. This reformulation introduces an apparent asymmetry between the consequents of conditions 3 and 4. Since we have rewritten 4 as

    p → S believes that p and not-(S believes that not-p),

why is 3 not similarly rewritten as

    not-p → not-(S believes that p) and S believes that not-p?

It is knowledge that p we are analyzing, rather than knowledge that not-p. Knowledge of p involves a stronger relation to p than to not-p. Thus, we did not first write the third condition for knowledge of p as: not-p → S believes that not-p; also the following is not true: S knows that p → (not-p → S knows that not-p). Imagine that someone S knows whether or not p, but it is not yet clear to us which he knows, whether he knows that p or knows that not-p. Still, merely given that S knows that ———, we can say:

    not-p → not-(S believes that p)

    p → not-(S believes that not-p)

Now when the blank is filled in, either with p or with not-p, we have to add S's believing it to the consequent of the subjunctive that begins with it. That indicates which one he knows. Thus, when it is p that he knows, we have to add to the consequent of the second subjunctive (the subjunctive that begins with p): S believes that p. We thereby transform the second subjunctive into:

$p \rightarrow$ not-(S believes that not-p) and S believes that p.

Except for a rearrangement of which is written first in the consequent, this is condition 4. Knowledge that p especially tracks p, and this special focus on p (rather than not-p) gets expressed in the subjunctive, not merely in the second condition.

There is another apparent asymmetry in the antecedents of the two subjunctives 3 and 4, not due to the reformulation. When actually p is true and S believes that p, condition 4 looks some distance out in the p neighborhood of the actual world, while condition 3 looks some distance out in the not-p neighborhood, which itself is farther away from the actual world than the p neighborhood. Why not have both conditions look equally far, revising conditions 3 to require merely that the closest world in which p is false yet S believes that p be some distance from the actual world? It then would parallel condition 4, which says that the closest world in which p yet p is not believed is some distance away from the actual world. Why should condition 3 look farther from the actual world than condition 4 does? However, despite appearances, both conditions look at distance symmetrically. The asymmetry is caused by the fact that the actual world, being a p world, is not symmetrical between p and not-p. Condition 3 says that in the closest not-p world, not-(S believes that p), and that this 'not-(S believes that p)' goes out through the first part of the not-p neighborhood of the actual world. Condition 4 says that in the closest p world, S believes that p, and that this 'S believes that p' goes out through the first part of the p neighborhood of the actual world. Thus the two conditions are symmetrical; the different distances to which they extend stems not from an asymmetry in the conditions but from one in the actual world—it being (asymmetrically) p.

18. There is an immense amount of literature concerning skepticism. See, for example, Empiricus; Popkin 1964; Naess 1968; Descartes 1960; "Proof of an External World," "A Defense of Common Sense," "Certainty," and "Four Forms of Skepticism" in Moore 1959; Austin 1961; Wittgenstein 1969; Lehrer 1978; Unger 1975; Slote 1970; Firth 1967; Clarke 1972; and Cavell 1979.

19. From the perspective of explanation rather than proof, the extensive philosophical discussion, deriving form Charles S. Peirce, of whether the skeptic's doubts are real is beside the point. The problem of explaining how knowledge is possible would remain the same, even if no one ever claimed to doubt there was knowledge.

20. Subjunctive with actually false antecedents and actually true consequents have been termed by Goodman *semifactuals*. R is the semi-factual: not-$p \rightarrow$ S believes p.

21. Should one weaken condition 3, so that the account of knowledge merely denies the opposed subjunctive R? That would give us: not-(not-$p \rightarrow$ S believes p). This holds when 3 does not, in situations where if p were false, S might believe p, and also might not believe it. The extra strength of 3 is needed to exclude these as situations of knowledge.

22. Though it does show the falsity of the corresponding entailment, "not-p entails not-(S believes that p)."

23. If a person is to know that SK doesn't hold, then condition 3 for knowledge must be satisfied (with "SK doesn't hold" substituted for p). Thus, we get

(3) not-(SK doesn't hold) $\rightarrow$ not-(S believes that SK doesn't hold).

Simplifying the Antecedent, we have.

(3) SK holds $\rightarrow$ not-(S believes that SK doesn't hold).

The skeptic has chosen a situation SK such that the following is true of it:

SK holds $\rightarrow$ S believes that SK doesn't hold.

Having the same antecedent as 3 and a contradictory consequent, this is incompatible with 3. Thus, condition 3 is not satisfied by the person's belief that SK does not hold.

24. Descartes would presumably would refute the tank hypothesis as he did the demon hypothesis, through a proof of the existence of a good God who would not allow anyone, demon or psychologist, permanently to deceive us. The philosophical literature has concentrated on the question of whether Descartes can prove this (without begging the question against the demon hypothesis). The literature has not discussed whether even a successful proof of the existence of a good God can help Descartes to conclude he is not almost always mistaken. Might not a good God have his own reasons foe deceiving us; might he not deceive us temporarily—a period which includes all of our life thus far (but not in the afterlife)? To the question of why God did not create us so that we never would make errors, Descartes answers that the motives of God are inscrutable to us. Do we know that such an inscrutable God could not be motivated to deceive us?

Alternatively, could not such a good God be motivated to deceive itself temporarily, even if not another? (Compare various Indian doctrines designed to explain our ignorance of our own true nature, that is, Atman-Brahman's or, on another theory, the purusha's nature.) Whether from playfulness or whatever motive, such a good God would temporarily deceive itself, perhaps even thinking it is a human being living in a material realm. Can we know, via Descartes' argument, that this is not our situation? And so forth.

These possibilities, and others similar, are so obvious that some other explanation, I mean the single-minded desire to refute skepticism, must be given for why they are not noticed and discussed.

Similarly, one could rescrutinize the *cogito* argument. Can "I think" only be produced by something that exists? Suppose Shakespeare had written for Hamlet the line, "I think, therefore I am," or a fiction is written in which a character named Descartes says this, or suppose a character in a dream of mine says this; does it follow that they exist? Can someone use the cogito argument to prove he himself is not a fictional or dream character? Descartes asked how he could know he wasn't dreaming; he should have asked how he could know he wasn't dreamed. See further Nozick 1980.

25. I say almost everything, because there still could be some true beliefs such as "I exist." More limited skeptical possibilities present worlds doxically identical to the actual world in which almost every belief of a certain sort is false, for example, about the past, or about other people's mental states. See the discussion below in the section on narrower skepticisms.

26. Let $w_1, \ldots, w_n$ be worlds doxically identical to the actual world for S. He doesn't know he is not in w_1, he doesn't know he is not in $w_2, \ldots$; does it follow that he doesn't know he is in the actual world w_A or in one very much like it (in its truths)? Not if the situation he would be in if the actual world w_A did not obtain wasn't one of the doxically identical worlds; if the world that then would obtain would show its difference form the actual one w_A, he would then not believe he was in w_A.

However, probably there are some worlds not very different from the actual world (in that they have mostly the same truths) and even doxically identical to it, which might obtain if w_A did not. In that case, S would not know he was in w_A specified in all its glory. But if we take the disjunction of these harmless worlds (insofar as drastic skeptical conclusions go) doxically identical with w_A, then S will know that this disjunction holds. For if it didn't, he would notice that.

27. This argument proceeds from the fact that floating in the tank is incompatible with being at X. Another form of the skeptic's argument, one which we shall consider later, proceeds from the fact that floating in the tank is incompatible with knowing that you are at X (or almost anything else).

28. Note that I am not denying that Kp & K(p $\rightarrow$ q) $\rightarrow$ Believes q.

29. Here again I assume a limited readership. And ignore possibilities such as those described in Blish, *Cities in Flight*.

30. Thus, the following is not a deductively valid form of inference.

$p \rightarrow q$ (and S knows this)

not-p $\rightarrow$ not-(S believes that p)

Therefore, not-q $\rightarrow$ not-(S believes that p).

Furthermore, the example in the text shows that even the following is not a deductively valid form of inference.

$p \rightarrow q$ (and S knows this)

not-$p \rightarrow$ not-(S-believes that p)

Therefore, not-$q \rightarrow$ not-(S believes that p).

Nor is this one deductively valid:

$p \rightarrow q$

not-$q \rightarrow r$

Therefore, not-$p \rightarrow r$.

31. Does this same consequence of nonclosure under known logical implication follow as well from condition 4: $p \rightarrow$ S believes that p? When p is not actually true, condition 4 can hold of p yet not of a q known to be entailed by p. For example, let p be the (false) statement that I am in Antarctica, and let q be the disjunction of p with some other appropriate statement; for example, let q be the statement that I am in Antarctica or I lost some object yesterday though I have not yet realized it. If p were true I would know it, p entails q, yet if q were true I wouldn't know it, for the way it would be true would be my losing some object without realizing it, and if that happened I would not know it.

This example to show that condition 4 is not closed under known logical implication depends on the (actual) falsity of p. I do not think there is any suitable example to show this in the case where p is true, leaving aside the trivial situation when the person simply does not infer the entailment statement q.

32. Suppose some component of the condition, call it C', also speaks of some cases when p is false, and when q is false; might it then provide "varies with", even though C' is preserved under known logical implication, and is transmitted form p to q when p entails q and is known to entail q? If this condition C' speaks of some cases where not-p and of some cases where not-q, then C' will be preserved under known logical implication if, when those cases of not-p satisfy it, and p entails q, then also those cases of not-q satisfy it. Thus, C' seems to speak of something as preserved from some cases of not-p to some cases of not-q, which is preservation in the reverse direction to the entailment involving these, from not-q to not-p. Thus, a condition that is preserved under known logical implication and that also provides some measure of "varies with" must contain a component condition saying that something interesting (other than falsity) is preserved in the direction opposite to the logical implication (for some cases); and moreover, that component itself must be preserved in the direction of the logical implication because the condition including it is. It would be interesting to see such a condition set out.

33. Reading an earlier draft of this chapter, friends pointed out to me that Fred Dretske already had defended the view that knowledge (as one among many epistemic concepts) is not closed under logical implication (See Dretske, in this volume). Furthermore, Dretske presented a subjunctive condition for knowledge (Dretske

1971), holding that S knows that p on the basis R only if: R would not be the case unless p were the case. Here Dretske ties the evidence subjunctively to the fact, and the belief based on the evidence subjunctively to the fact through the evidence. (Our account of knowledge has not yet introduced or discussed evidence or reasons at all. While this condition corresponds to our condition 3, he has nothing corresponding to 4.) So Dretske has hold of both pieces of our account, subjunctive and nonclosure, and he even connects them in a passing footnote (Dretske, in this volume, n. 4), noticing that any account of knowledge that relies on a subjunctive conditional will not be closed under known logical implication. Dretske also has the notion of a relevant alternative as "one that might have been realized in the existing circumstances if the actual state of affairs had not materialized" (p. 142), holding that the skeptic is right about some things but not about others.

It grieves me somewhat to discover that Dretske also had all this, and was there first. It raises the question, also, of why these views have not yet had the proper impact. Dretske makes his points in the midst of much other material, some of it less insightful. The independent statement and delineation of the position here, without the background noise, I hope will make clear its many merits.

After Goldman's paper on a causal theory of knowledge (Goldman 1967), an idea then already "in the air," it required no great leap to consider subjunctive conditions. Some two months after the first version of this chapter was written, Goldman himself published a paper on knowledge utilizing counterfactuals (Goldman 1976), also talking of relevant possibilities (without using the counterfactuals to identify which possibilities are relevant); and an unpublished survey article by Robert Shope has called my attention to a paper of Carrier 1971 that also used subjunctive conditions including our condition 3. Armstrong's reliability view of knowledge (Armstrong 1973, pp. 166, 169) involving a lawlike connection between the belief that p and the state of affairs that makes it true. Clearly, the idea is one whose time has come.

PART FOUR

Contextualist Responses

CHAPTER 11

Solving the Skeptical Problem

Keith DeRose

1. THE PUZZLE OF SKEPTICAL HYPOTHESES

Many of the most celebrated, intriguing, and powerful skeptical arguments proceed by means of skeptical hypotheses. Brutally pared to their barest essentials, they are roughly of the following form, where 'O' is a proposition about the external world one would ordinarily think one knows (e.g., I have hands[1]) and 'H' is a suitably chosen skeptical *hypothesis* (e.g., I am a bodiless brain in a vat who has been electrochemically stimulated to have precisely those sensory experiences I've had, henceforth a 'BIV'[2]):

The Argument from Ignorance (AI)[3]

1. I don't know that not-H.
2. If I don't know that not-H, then I don't know that O.

So,

C. I don't know that O.[4]

Setting aside the distracting side issues that immediately threaten from all directions, and keeping AI in this stark, uncomplicated form, I will, in what follows, present and defend, at least in broad outline, the correct solution to the puzzle AI confronts us with. And AI does present us with a puzzle, because, for reasons we'll investigate in later sections, each of its premises is initially plausible, when H is well chosen. For however improbable or even bizarre it may seem to suppose that I am a BIV, it also seems that I don't know that I'm not one. How *could* I know such a thing? And it also seems that if, for all I know, I am a BIV, then I don't know that I have hands. How could I know that I have hands if, for all I know, I'm bodiless (and therefore handless)? But, at the same time, it initially seems that I do know that I have hands. So two plausible premises yield a conclusion whose negation we also find plausible. So something plausible has to go. But what? And equally importantly, how?

To be sure, the premises are only plausible, not compelling. Thus, we will always have recourse to the Moorean reaction to this argument: Declare that it is more certain that one knows that one has hands than it is that either of the premises of the argument is true (much less that their conunction is true), and therefore reject one of those premises, rather than accept the conclusion. But also available is the skeptical reaction, which is to accept the conclusion.

But we should hope for a better treatment of the argument than simply choosing which of the three individually plausible propositions—the two premises and the negation of the conclusion—seems least certain and rejecting it on the grounds that the other two are true. In seeking a solution to this puzzle, we should seek an explanation of how we fell into this skeptical trap in the first place, and not settle for making a simple choice among three distasteful ways out of the trap. We must explain how two premises that together yield a conclusion we find so incredible can themselves seem so plausible to us. Only with such an explanation in place can we proceed with confidence and with understanding to free ourselves from the trap.

Many of those working on AI in recent years seem to have understood this.[5] And I have good news to report: Substantial progress towards finally solving this skeptical puzzle has been made along two quite different fronts. The bad news is that, as I shall argue, neither approach has solved the puzzle. But the culminating good news is that, as I will also argue, the new solution I present here, which incorporates important aspects of each of the two approaches, *can* finally solve this perennially thorny philosophical problem. While more details and precision will be called for in the resulting solution than I will provide, there will be enough meat on the bones to make it plausible that the fully articulated solution lies in the direction I point to here.

In section 2–4 of this paper, I explore the contextualist approach to the problem of skepticism, and show why it has thus far fallen short of solving the puzzle. In sections 5–9, I turn to Robert Nozick's attempt to solve our puzzle. Since the shortcomings of Nozick's treatment of knowledge and skepticism have been, at least to my satisfaction, duly demonstrated by others, it will not be my purpose here to rehearse those shortcomings, but rather to explore and expand upon the substantial insight that remains intact in Nozick's account. In sections 10–17, I present and defend my own contextualist solution, which I argue is the best solution to our puzzle. Since, as I argue in sections 15–17, the skeptic's own solution, according to which we accept AI's conclusion, is among the solutions inferior to the one I present, AI does not successfully support that conclusion.

2. CONTEXTUALIST SOLUTIONS: THE BASIC STRATEGY

Suppose a speaker A (for "attributor") says, "S knows that P," of a subject S's true belief that P. According to contextualist theories of knowledge attributions, how strong an epistemic position S must be in with respect to P for A's assertion to be true can vary according to features of A's conversational context.[6]

Contextualist theories of knowledge attributions have almost invariably been developed with an eye toward providing some kind of answer to philosophical skepticism. For skeptical arguments like AI threaten to show, not only that we fail to meet very high requirements for knowledge of interest only to misguided philosophers seeking absolute certainty, but that we don't meet even the truth conditions of ordinary, out-on-the-street knowledge attributions. They thus threaten to establish the startling result that we never, or almost never, truthfully ascribe knowledge to ourselves or to other mere mortals.

But, according to contextualists, the skeptic, in presenting her argument, manipulates the semantic standards for knowledge, thereby creating a context in which she can *truthfully* say that we know nothing or very little.[7] Once the standards have been so raised, we *correctly* sense that we only could falsely claim to know such things as that we have hands. Why then are we puzzled? Why don't we simply accept the skeptic's conclusion and henceforth refrain from ascribing such knowledge to ourselves or others? Because, the contextualist continues, we also sense this: As soon as we find ourselves in more ordinary conversational contexts, it will not only be true for us to claim to know the very things that the skeptic now denies we know, but it will also be wrong for us to deny that we know these things. But then, isn't the skeptic's present denial equally false? And wouldn't it be equally true for us now, in the skeptic's presence, to claim to know?

What we fail to realize, according to the contextualist solution, is that the skeptic's present denials that we know various things are perfectly compatible with our ordinary claims to know those very propositions. Once we realize this, we can see how both the skeptic's denials of knowledge and our ordinary attributions of knowledge can be correct.

Thus, it is hoped, our ordinary claims to know can be safeguarded from the apparently powerful attack of the skeptic, while, at the same time, the persuasiveness of the skeptical argument is explained. For the fact that the skeptic can invoke very high standards that we don't live up to has no tendency to show that we don't satisfy the more relaxed standards that are in place in more ordinary conversations and debates.

Three important points about contextualist strategies as described above should be made before I move on. First, this type of strategy will leave untouched the timid skeptic who purports by AI merely to be establishing the weak claim that in some (perhaps "high" or "philosophical") sense (perhaps induced by the presentation of AI) we don't know the relevant O, while not even purporting to establish the bold thesis that our ordinary claims to know that same proposition are false. Whether such a timid skeptical stance is of any interest is a topic for another paper. The contextualist strategy is important because AI initially seems to threaten the truth of our ordinary claims—it threatens to boldly show that we've been wrong all along in thinking and saying that we know this and that. For it doesn't seem as if it's just in some "high" or "philosophical" sense that AI's premises are true: They seem true in the ordinary sense of 'know'. In fact, one is initially tempted to say that there's *no* good sense in which I know that I'm not a BIV or in which I can know I have hands if I don't know that I'm not a BIV. How (and whether) to avoid the bold skeptical result is puzzle enough.

Second, in presenting the contextualist strategy, I have above assumed a skeptic-friendly version of contextualism—one according to which the philosophical skeptic can (fairly easily), and does, succeed in raising the standards for knowledge in such a way as to make her denials of knowledge true. Some contextualists may think that it's not so easy to so raise the standards for knowledge, and that a determined opponent of the skeptic can, by not letting the skeptic get away with raising them, keep the standards low. But the important point is to identify the mechanism by which the skeptic at least threatens to raise the standards for knowledge. Whether the skeptic actually succeeds against a determined opponent in so raising the standards is of little importance. To safeguard ordinary claims to know while at the same time explaining the persuasiveness of the skeptical arguments (which is the goal of his strategy), the contextualist can provisionally *assume* a skeptic-friendly version of contextualism, leaving it as an open question whether and under which conditions the skeptic actually succeeds at raising the standards. The contextualist's ultimate point will then be this: To the extent that the skeptic *does* succeed, she does so only by raising the standards for knowledge, and so the success of her argument has no tendency to show that our ordinary claims to know are in any way defective.

Third, AI can be puzzling even when one is not in the presence of a skeptic who is presenting it. The argument has about the same degree of intuitive appeal when one is just considering it by oneself, without anybody's *saying* anything. But the contextualist explanation, as described above, involves the standards for knowledge being changed by what's being said in a conversation.[8] For the most part, I will frame the contextualist explanation in terms of such conversational rules, largely because that's what been done by my contextualist predecessors, with whom I want to make contact. But we must realize that the resulting solution will have to be generalized to explain why the argument can be so appealing even when one is considering it in solitude, with nothing being said. The basic idea of the generalization will take either or both of the following two forms. First, it can be maintained that there is a rule for the changing of the standards for knowledge that governs the truth conditions of our *thoughts* regarding what is and is not known that mirrors the rule for the truth conditions of what is *said* regarding knowledge. In that case, an analogue of the contextualist solution can be given for thought, according to which the premises and conclusion of AI are truly thought, but my true thought that, say, I don't know that I have hands, had when in the grip of AI, will be compatible with my thought, made in another context, that I do know that very thing. Second, our judgment regarding whether something can or cannot be truly asserted (under appropriate conditions) might be held to affect our judgment regarding whether it's true or false, even when we make this judgment in solitude, with nothing being said at all. That the premises of AI could be truly asserted, then, makes them (at least) seem true even when they're just being thought.

My own solution will employ the basic contextualist strategy explained in this section. But, as should be apparent already, we haven't explained the persuasiveness of AI, and thus haven't solved our puzzle, if we haven't located and explained the conversational rule or mechanism by which the skeptic raises (or threatens to raise) the standards for knowledge. And here contextualists have had little to offer. The two main proposals that have been put forward are discussed in the following two sections.

3. SOME OLD CONTEXTUALIST SOLUTIONS: LEWIS'S "RULE OF ACCOMMODATION"

Though substantial papers have been largely devoted to contextualism and its ability to explain the workings of skeptical arguments like AI, one of the best attempts to explain how (by what rule or conversational mechanism) skeptics raise the standards for knowledge is to be found in David Lewis's "Scorekeeping in a Language Game" (1979b), a paper that, while not primarily about knowledge attributions, does treat them in passing.[9]

According to Lewis, "rules of accommodation" operate in many spheres of discourse that contain context-sensitive terms.[10] Such rules specify that when a statement is made containing such a term, then—ceteris paribus and within certain limits—the "conversational score" tends to change, if need be, so as to make that statement true. For example, 'flat', according to Lewis, is a context-sensitive term: how flat a surface must be in order for a sentence describing it as "flat" to be true is a variable matter that is determined by conversational context. And one way to change the conversational score with respect to the standards in place for flatness is to say something that would require for its truth such a change in standards. Suppose, for example, that in a certain conversation the standards for flatness are relaxed enough that my desktop counts as being flat. If I were then to say, "My desktop is not flat," what I say would be false if it were evaluated according to the standards for flatness in place imediately before this is said. But the Rule of Accommodation specifies that in such a situation—at least under the right circumstances, where the ceteris paribus clause is met—the standards for flatness are raised so as to make my statement true.

Lewis suggests that skeptics manipulate a similar rule to change the standards for what is to count as knowledge. According to Lewis's explanation of the plausibility of skepticism, then, the skeptic's statements change the conversational score—here, raise the standards for knowledge[11]—so as to make the skeptic's statements true. Once the standards for knowledge have been so raised, then

> the commonsensical epistemologist must concede defeat. And yet he was in no way wrong when he laid claim to infallible knowledge. What he said was true with respect to the score as it then was.[12]

Here Lewis displays the basic contextualist strategy: He protects the truth of what we ordinarily say, or say before the skeptic gets a hold of us, from the skeptic's attack by explaining the success of that attack in terms of the skeptic's changing what counts as knowledge, or, here, "infallible knowledge." Thus, the persuasiveness of the skeptic's attack is explained in such a way as to make it unthreatening to our ordinary claims of knowledge.

And this explanation initially appears to be tailor-made for AI, for AI's first premise is a denial of knowledge—precisely the type of assertion that a rise in the standards for knowledge can help to make true. Such a denial, then, is just the sort of thing that can raise the standards for knowledge via a Rule of Accommodation. Perhaps when the skeptic asserts this first premise, the standards for knowledge are raised, via the Rule of Accommodation, to a level at which we count as knowing neither that we're not BIVs, nor that we have hands.[13]

But a Rule of Accommodation cannot really explain the persuasiveness of AI, or, more generally, of any argument by skeptical hypothesis. To vividly illustrate why this is so, let us imagine and compare two skeptics who are trying to convince you that you don't know that you have hands. The "AI skeptic," true to her name, relies on AI, which, as I noted in section 1, is pretty powerful. The "simple skeptic," on the other hand, simply insists that you don't know that you have hands, offering no reasoning at all for this skeptical assertion.

In seeking a solution to the puzzle generated by AI, we should hope for a solution that, at the very least, explains why the AI skeptic is more convincing than the simple skeptic. If our explanation does not do this much, then we haven't explained how the skeptical argument works on us in any way sufficient to differentiate it from a bald (and dogmatic!) skeptical assertion.

But the Rule of Accommodation, as it stands, appears to be equally accommodating to both of our imagined skeptics. When the simple skeptic claims that I don't know that I have hands, the supposed Rule of Accommodation should raise the standards for knowledge to such a point as to make her claim true. Of course, the ceteris paribus clause may block this result, depending on how it is fleshed out. But there is nothing to this Rule, at least as it has so far been articulated, that would favor the AI skeptic over the simple skeptic. Thus, the explanation based on this Rule does not differentiate between these two skeptics. But if it doesn't do that, it doesn't solve our puzzle.

To avoid possible misunderstanding, let me clearly state that my objection is not to the proposed solution's lack of precision—that we're not given a very clear idea of when the Rule of Accommodation takes effect, that the Rule says merely that the standards *tend* to change in a certain way provided that the (highly unarticulated) ceteris paribus clause is met. My own solution will be likewise imprecise. No, the problem isn't that the Rule isn't completely filled in, but rather that, for the reasons given above, since the explanatory work needed to solve the puzzle isn't done by the aspects of the Rule that have been provided, it will have to be done by just those aspects of the Rule that haven't been provided. And, as we've little idea what these aspects are, we've little idea of what it is that may solve the puzzle.[14]

Perhaps, when it's more fully articulated, the operative Rule of Accommodation can be seen to contain a feature that favors the AI skeptic over the simple skeptic. In that case, the solution to our puzzle, which has so far eluded us, may (at least in part) be found in a fuller articulation of that Rule.

But I doubt that the solution even lies in that direction. One (secondary) reason for my doubt is that positive claims to know that skeptical hypotheses don't obtain seem to raise the standards for knowledge as well as do denials of such knowledge.

To illustrate this I'll use Fred Dretske's familiar example of mules cleverly painted to look like zebras (in this volume, 138–139). If I saw what looked to be zebras in the zebra cage at a zoo, I would ordinarily claim to know that the animals in the cage are zebras. (Suppose, for instance, that my son asked me, "Do you know what those animals are?" I would respond positively.) A skeptic might challenge this supposed knowledge with an instance of AI where O is *Those animals are zebras* and H is *Those animals are mules cleverly painted to look like zebras.* The resulting premises are individually plausible, since I couldn't tell a cleverly painted mule from a zebra. A contextualist treatment of this instance of AI will claim that in asserting the first premise, the skeptic raises the standards for knowledge to a level at which I count as knowing neither that the animals are not cleverly painted mules nor that they're zebras.

And it indeed does seem that once this skeptical hypothesis is brought into play, I cannot happily claim to know what I so happily claimed to know before. To be in a good enough position to claim to know that the animals are zebras according to the standards brought into play by the skeptic, one must be in a good enough position that one can rule out[15] the hypothesis that they are cleverly painted mules. Since I'm not in that kind of epistemic position, I don't count as knowing, although perhaps someone more familiar with mules and zebras would still count as knowing, even at these higher standards—someone, for instance, who was in a position to say, "No, they can't be mules: no mule's head is shaped like that."

But these same higher standards seem to be induced when the skeptical hypothesis is brought into play by a positive claim to know that it doesn't obtain. Suppose, to vary Dretske's example, that I am confronted, not by a skeptic, but by a boastful zoologist. He brags, "Due to my vast knowledge of zebra and mule anatomy, I know that those animals are not mules cleverly painted to look like zebras; so I know that they're really zebras." This zoologist, as much as the skeptic, seems to invoke higher standards for knowledge at which he, but not I, will count as knowing that the animals are zebras. He certainly seems to be claiming more than the mundane knowledge that even I possess—and claim to possess—in an ordinary zoo setting, where there's no such zoologist telling me what's what.

But a Rule of Accommodation cannot account for *this* rise in standards, for the zoologist doesn't deny any supposed knowledge. To the contrary, what he does is make positive claims to know, and a rise in standards for knowledge can never help to make true a positive claim to know. So, as I said, a Rule of Accommodation can't do anything to explain this notable rise in epistemic standards.[16]

My primary reason for doubting that our solution is to be found in a fuller articulation of the Rule of Accommodation in this: To explain the persuasiveness of AI (and, in particular, of its first premise) in such a way as to differentiate the AI skeptic from the simple skeptic, we must identify the feature of skeptical hypotheses that makes it particularly hard to claim or to think that one knows that *they* are false. Far from being found in a Rule of Accommodation, then, a solution to our puzzle, if it's to be found at all, is to be found in an explanation of what it is about skeptical hypotheses that makes these propositions, as opposed to ever so many other propositions, such effective skeptical weapons. So, to solve the puzzle, we must locate or articulate this peculiarly potent feature of just these propositions (the skeptical hypotheses). And, once we see what this feature is and how it works, the Rule of Accommodation is destined to play only a rather subsidiary role (see note 14) in explaining the effectiveness of the skeptic's attack.

My secondary reason for doubting that the Rule of Accommodation might solve our puzzle was worth bringing up both because it seems to me to have some force, and because it vividly illustrates this important fact: The upward pressure on the standards for knowledge that bringing skeptical hypotheses into play exerts is exerted whether the hypotheses are raised in denials of knowledge or in positive claims to know.

4. SOME OLD CONTEXTUALIST SOLUTIONS: THE "RELEVANT ALTERNATIVES" APPROACH AND THE RULE OF RELEVANCE[17]

Perhaps the most popular solution to our puzzle has been put forward by advocates of the "Relevant Alternatives" theory of knowledge (RA). Again suppose a speaker A says, "S knows that P." According to RA, such an assertion is made within and must be evaluated against a certain framework of *relevant alternatives* to P. To know that P is to have a true belief that P and to be able to rule out these relevant alternatives. But not every contrary of or alternative to P is a *relevant* alternative.[18] In an ordinary case of claiming to know that some animals in the zoo are zebras, to again use Dretske's example, the alternative that they're cleverly painted mules is not relevant. Thus,

I can truthfully claim to know they're zebras despite my inability to rule out this fanciful alternative.

But in various *extraordinary* cases, the painted mules hypothesis *is* a relevant alternative. It might be made relevant by some extraordinary feature of S (the putative subject of knowledge) or her surroundings.[19] But most RA theorists are contextualists, and allow that features of the conversational context in which A (the ascriber of knowledge) finds himself, in addition to features of S and her surroundings, can influence which alternatives are relevant.[20] Alvin Goldman, for instance, suggests that "if the speaker is in a class in which Descartes's evil demon has just been discussed," then certain alternatives may be relevant that ordinarily are not (1976, 776).

It is this contextualist aspect of (most versions of) RA that facilitates the most commonly proposed solution to our puzzle, the Relevant Alternatives Solution (henceforth, 'RAS'). With some slight variations in detail in different presentations of it, the basic idea of RAS is this: The AI skeptic's *mentioning* of the BIV hypothesis in presenting the first premise of AI *makes* that hypothesis relevant. Once the skeptical hypothesis has been made relevant, we correctly sense that we cannot truthfully claim to know anything contrary to it unless we can rule it out. Since we are unable to rule it out, and since it is an alternative to both *I am not a BIV* and to *I have hands*, we correctly sense that we could only falsely claim to know these things. So the skeptic truthfully asserts that we don't know that the hypothesis doesn't obtain, and then truthfully concludes that we don't know that we have hands.[21]

Why then are we puzzled? Because we at the same time sense that the BIV hypothesis is not ordinarily relevant. We realize that in most of the conversational circumstances in which we find ourselves, our inability to rule out the skeptic's far-fetched hypothesis is no bar to our truthfully claiming to know such things as that we have hands. Thus, even as we find the skeptic's denials of knowledge persuasive, we realize that when we again find ourselves in more ordinary contexts, it will not only be correct for us to claim to know such things, it would be wrong to deny that we know them merely because we can't rule out the BIV hypothesis. What we fail to realize, according to RAS, is that our ordinary claims to know such things as that we have hands are compatible with the skeptic's present denial that we know those very things.

RAS, then, is an instance of the general contextualist strategy—one according to which the raising of the standards consists in enlarging the range of alternatives that are relevant and that one must therefore be in a position to rule out in order to count as knowing. The conversational rule or mechanism that RAS posits for enlarging that range (raising the standards for knowledge), then, is that *mentioning* a proposition Q—ceteris paribus and within certain limits, no doubt—tends to make Q a contextually relevant alternative to any P that is contrary to Q. Call this the *Rule of Relevance*.[22]

Note that this Rule of Relevance, as opposed to the Rule of Accommodation, can handle cases like that of the boastful zoologist, in which a positive claim to know that a skeptical hypothesis doesn't obtain seems to have the same effect on the meaning of sentences containing 'know' as would a denial of such knowledge. This is to be expected on the present Rule of Relevance, on which both the denial and the claim to know will, by including a mention of the skeptical hypothesis, expand the range of relevant alternatives so that it will include that hard-to-rule-out hypothesis.

But to explain the persuasiveness of AI (particularly of its first premise), and to thereby solve our puzzle, a treatment of AI must tell us what it is about skeptical hypotheses that makes it difficult to claim to know that they don't obtain. The key feature of skeptical hypotheses that RAS seizes on is clearly this: we can't rule them out.

And isn't there something to this explanation? For it seems that we indeed can't rule out (effective) skeptical hypotheses, and it further seems that it is precisely this fact that makes them such effective skeptical weapons.

But though it is plausible to suppose we can't rule out skeptical hypotheses, and also plausible to say that we don't know that they don't obtain, it is futile to try to explain the plausibility of the latter by that of the former.

Indeed, there are plenty of other phrases that can be used plausibly to describe our apparently limited epistemic position with regard to effective skeptical hypotheses. All of the following descriptions about my position vis-à-vis the BIV hypothesis have some initial plausibility: I cannot rule it out, I don't know that it doesn't obtain (and don't know whether it obtains), I can't tell that it doesn't obtain (and can't tell whether it obtains), I can't discern that it doesn't obtain (and can't discern whether it obtains), and I can't distinguish its obtaining from its not obtaining, and so on, and so forth. But citing one of these to explain the plausibility of another doesn't occasion even the slightest advance in our understanding.

What accounts for the plausibility of saying that I don't know that I'm not a BIV? The fact that I can't discern that I'm not one? This is no explanation. It seems just as good (in fact, to me, better) to reverse things and claim that the fact that I don't know that I'm not a BIV accounts for the plausibility of saying that I can't discern that I'm not one.

Likewise for ruling out. It is indeed plausible to suppose that we can't rule out skeptical hypotheses. And it's plausible that we don't know that they don't obtain. But it doesn't seem to advance our understanding much to explain the plausibility of either by that of the other.

(An exercise for the reader: Randomly pick two of the above negative assessments of our epistemic position vis-à-vis effective skeptical hypotheses. Then consider whether the plausibility of the first can be explained by reference to the second. Then reverse things and consider whether the plausibility of the second can be explained by reference to the first. Try the same procedure on another pair of descriptions. (If you're running low on such negative assessments, you'll find it's easy, following my lead, to come up with many more on your own.) *Then* evaluate the success of explaining the plausibility of AI's first premise by reference to the fact that we can't rule out effective skeptical hypotheses.)

To explain why we feel some pull towards describing our epistemic position with regard to skeptical hypotheses in any of the above less than flattering ways—as well as very many other ways that I didn't bother to mention—we need an explanation that reaches outside this circle of all-too-closely related terms of epistemic appraisal.[23] Indeed, as will emerge in the following sections (especially section 8), the best explanation for the plausibility of AI's first premise also seems to provide a good account of why it seems that we can't rule out skeptical hypotheses, as well as an explanation of the plausibility of the various other pessimistic evaluations. Once this explanation is in place, it becomes even clearer that none of the things it's used to explain can be properly used to explain each other.

5. THE SUBJUNCTIVE CONDITIONALS ACCOUNT (SCA) OF THE PLAUSIBILITY OF AI'S FIRST PREMISE

The main stumbling block of the contextualist solutions we've discussed has been a failure to explain what it is about skeptical hypotheses that makes it so plausible to suppose that we don't know that they're false. This point of weakness in the contextualist solutions is the particular point of strength of Nozick's treatment of AI in his *Philosophical Explanations* (1981). In this and the following three sections I'll present and defend the *Subjunctive Conditionals Account* (SCA) of the plausibility of AI's first premise, which I've abstracted from Nozick's account of knowledge and skepticism.

According to SCA, the problem with my belief that I'm not a BIV—and I do have such a belief, as do most of us—is that I would have this belief (that I'm not a BIV) even if it were false (even if I were one). It is this that makes it hard to claim to *know* that I'm not a BIV. For, according to SCA, we have a very strong general, though not exceptionless, inclination to think that we don't know that P when we think that our belief that P is a belief we would hold even if P were false. Let's say that S's belief that P is *insensitive* if S would believe that P if P were false. SCA's generalization can then be restated as follows: We tend to judge that S doesn't know that P when we think S's belief that P is insensitive.

As is well worth noting, this general inclination explains the operation of nonphilosophical skeptical hypotheses that are far less radical than the BIV hypothesis or even the painted mule hypothesis. Just so, it serves to explain why, even though I feel inclined to say that I know the Bulls won their game last night because I read the result in a single newspaper, I still feel strongly pulled toward admitting the (mildly) skeptical claim that I don't know that the paper isn't mistaken about which team won: I realize that my belief that the paper isn't mistaken is a belief I would hold even if it were false (even if the paper were mistaken).

Indeed, after encountering a couple of instances of AI with different skeptical hypotheses plugged into the 'H' slot (for example, the BIV, the painted mules, and the mistaken paper hypotheses), one develops a sense of what makes for an effective skeptical hypothesis and, thus, an ability to construct convincing instances of AI oneself. To make AI's second premise convincing, it is usually sufficient (though not necessary) that H be incompatible with O. But what about the first premise? To make *it* convincing, we instinctively look for a hypothesis that elicits in the listener both the belief that the hypothesis doesn't obtain and an acknowledgement that this belief is one she would hold even if the hypothesis *did* obtain.

Upon hearing the hypothesis, typically one can't help but projecting oneself into it. How would things seem to me if that situation obtained? Well, pretty much (or sometimes exactly) as they actually seem to me. And, so, what would I believe if such a "strange" situation obtained? Pretty much (or exactly) what I actually believe. For example, and in particular, if I *were* a BIV, I would believe every bit as firmly as I actually do that I *wasn't* one. But if this belief is one I would hold even if it were false, how can I be in a position to tell that, or discern that, or *know* that, it's true?

As I've just hinted, a similar explanation, in terms of subjunctive conditionals, can explain the plausibility of the other ways we feel inclined to describe our seemingly limited epistemic position vis-à-vis effective skeptical hypotheses. Consider especially the description involving 'ruling out'. In a normal zoo setting, most of us would take ourselves to know that the animals in the zebra cage are zebras. From this, it seems, we should be able to infer that they're not cleverly painted mules, since zebras aren't mules. So why are we reluctant to count our seeing the zebras and performing this inference as a case of ruling out the painted mule hypothesis? Because, the explanation goes, even after performing the inference, it still seems we would believe the observed animals weren't painted mules if they were precisely that. Why does it seem we can't tell that they're not painted mules? Because we would believe they weren't even if they were. Ditto for why we seemingly can't discern that they're not and why it seems we can't distinguish their being cleverly painted mules from their not being such, etc.

Also worth noting is the usefulness of SCA in explaining our reluctance to ascribe knowledge in certain lottery situations. Even where the odds of your being a loser are astronomically high (there are 20 million tickets, only one of which is a winner, and you have but one ticket), it can seem that you don't know that you're a loser of a fair lottery if the winner hasn't yet been announced. SCA accounts for this seeming: Your belief that you're a loser is one you would hold even if you were the winner.

SCA is a powerful explanation. But there are problems. As I suggested above, there are exceptions to the general inclination to which SCA appeals: There are cases in which it seems to us that some S does know that P even though we judge that S would believe that P even if P were false. Some of these exceptions will be quickly discussed in sections 6 and 7 below. The first and main point to make regarding such exceptions, of course, is that this very general inclination needn't be exceptionless to perform the explanatory role SCA assigns it. In section 8 we will see strong grounds for endorsing SCA as being at least on the right track despite the exceptions to the generalization to which it appeals. But these exceptions are still worth examining, for they will indicate certain important directions in which SCA can be improved, even though we won't be in a position to make SCA ideally precise here.

6. SCA, GRANDMOTHERS, AND METHODS

First, then, consider a case discussed by Nozick:

> A grandmother sees her grandson is well when he comes to visit; but if he were sick or dead, others would tell her he was well to spare her upset. Yet this does not mean she doesn't know he is well (or at least ambulatory) when she sees him. (1981, 179)

Here, it seems, the grandmother knows her grandson is well, though it can seem that she doesn't satisfy the third condition of a preliminary form of Nozick's analysis of S knows that P, which is:

(3) If p weren't true, S wouldn't believe that p.

Nozick's response is to relativize this third condition to the method by which S has come to believe that p, yielding:

(3) If p weren't true and S were to use M to arrive at a belief whether (or not) p, then S wouldn't believe, via M, that p (1981, 179),

where 'M' is the method by which S has come to believe that p.[24]

Unlike Nozick, I'm not presenting an analysis of propositional knowledge. But his grandmother case also seems to be an exception to the general inclination SCA appeals to: Here we're not at all incined to think the grandmother doesn't know her grandson is well, even though it can seem that if he weren't well, she would still believe he was. The generalization SCA utilizes says that we tend to judge that S doesn't know where S does not satisfy Nozick's third condition for knowledge. One possibility here is to follow Nozick *very* closely by modifying that generalization so that it refers to Nozick's modified, rather than his original, third condition, and thus, like Nozick, explicitly relativizing our account to the method by which S believes that P.

Often, though, context takes care of this for us. Even to one aware of the likelihood that the grandmother's family would have kept her in the dark about her grandson's condition were he not well, it *can* seem that even Nozick's initial formulation of the third condition for knowledge is met by the grandmother. On one way of evaluating that simple conditional, it seems that if the grandson were not well, the grandmother would *not* believe he was well. After all, she's looking right at him! The standard possible-worlds semantics for counterfactual conditionals can illuminate what's going on here. When one searches for the possible worlds most similar to the actual world in which the grandson is not well, the respects in which the possible worlds are to resemble the actual world is a highly context-sensitive matter. Especially where the context focuses one's attention on the grandmother and her cognitive and recognitional abilities, one *can* place heavy weight upon similarity with respect to the method she is using to arrive at her belief, and then it can seem that in the closest world in which the grandson is not well, she's looking right at him and seeing that he's not well, and so does *not* believe he is well. On this way of evaluating the conditional, the grandmother *does* satisfy even the initial formulation of Nozick's third condition, and she's no counter-example to the generalization utilized by SCA. But, in evaluating that simple conditional, one can also stress other similarities, particularly ones involving the propensities and plans of the various family members (or whatever facts ground the judgment that if her grandson weren't well, the grandmother would be effectively lied to), to reach the verdict that if he were not well, she *would* believe that he was well.

We can sharpen SCA by specifying that we tend to judge that S doesn't know when she fails to satisfy Nozick's initial formulation of (3), where (3) is evaluated in such a way that heavy emphasis is put upon similarity with respect to the method of belief formation utilized by S, or, following Nozick, we can insert a specification of the method into the antecedent of (3).[25] But in neither case is this to make a very precise modification; rather, it merely indicates the direction in which a more precise account might lie, for any such use of the notion of *methods* of belief formation in our account invites a host of questions (many of which Nozick wrestles with) involving how such methods are to be specified and individuated.

7. SCA AND SOME SKEPTICAL HYPOTHESES THAT DON'T WORK

Certain instances of AI aren't very persuasive. The first premise of the argument can be quite unconvincing despite the fact that SCA predicts that we'd find it plausible. Suppose, for instance, that in an attempt to show by AI that I don't know I have hands, a skeptic utilizes, instead of the BIV hypothesis, the following simple H: I falsely believe that I have hands. The resulting instance of AI seems to pack little or no more punch than a simple skeptic's unsupported claim that I don't know I have hands. It's at the first premise that this ill-fated instance of AI fizzles. But my belief that I don't falsely believe that I have hands is insensitive: If this belief were false (if I did falsely believe that I have hands) I would still believe it was true (I'd still believe that I don't falsely believe that I have hands). Likewise insensitive is my belief that the following hypothesis is false: I'm an intelligent dog who's always incorrectly thinking that I have hands. If this belief of mine were false (if I were such a deluded intelligent dog) I'd still believe it was true (I'd still believe that I wasn't such a creature). So SCA, as it has so far been formulated, predicts that it will seem to us that the above beliefs don't amount to knowledge and that we'll find plausible the first premise of AI that results when the above hypotheses are used. But in fact these instances of AI's first premise are far from convincing. As opposed to the BIV hypothesis, it seems that one *does* know that the deluded dog hypothesis and the simple false belief hypothesis are false.

Again, the main point to make here is that SCA's generalization needn't be exceptionless to be explanatory. While a more precisely Chisholmed refinement of SCA might not have the negations of these ineffective H's as instances of those propositions it says we tend to judge we don't know, I'll here just make a preliminary observation as to what might be going wrong. Part of the problem with these "hypotheses" is that they don't give us much of an idea of *how* I come to have the false belief they assign to me. Hypotheses are supposed to explain; skeptical hypotheses should explain how we might come to believe something despite its being false. The first of these hypotheses simply stipulates that I'm wrong about my having hands, without indicating how I came to be so sadly mistaken. The second adds to the first that I'm a dog, which adds little to our understanding of how my mistake about having hands came about. By contrast, when we encounter effective skeptical hypotheses, we have some understanding of how (if H is true) we have come to falsely believe that O. If either of our ineffective hypotheses is filled in so as to make it clear to us how I came to falsely believe I have hands, it becomes effective.

SCA's generalization was this: We tend to judge that S doesn't know that P when we think that S's belief that P is insensitive (when we think that S would believe P even if P were false). The limitation of SCA's generalization that's suggested by these cases is this: We *don't* so judge ourselves ignorant of P where not-P implies something we take ourselves to know to be false, without providing an explanation of how we came to falsely believe this thing we think we know. Thus, *I falsely believe that I have hands* implies that I don't have hands. Since I do take myself to know that I have hands (*this* belief isn't insensitive), and since the above italicized proposition doesn't explain how I went wrong with respect to my having hands, I'll judge that I do know that proposition to be false. But this again is just a preliminary statement, and there's room for a lot more refinement here. What we need now is some assurance that we're headed in the right direction.

8. SCA CONFIRMED

Such assurance is to be found by considering what it would take to make it seem to us that we *do* know skeptical hypotheses to be false.

But let's first reconsider the lottery case. As noted above in section 5, we are puzzlingly reluctant to claim knowledge in certain lottery situations. The explanation provided by SCA for this phenomenon is intuitively appealing: It does seem that the fact that we would believe that we were losers even if we were winners is largely what's behind our judgment that we don't know we're losers. SCA receives further powerful support when we consider the grounds that *do* seem to us sufficient for knowledge of one's being a loser. In the lottery situation, even a very minute chance of being wrong seems to deprive one of knowledge. But if we're going to worry about even such minute chances of error, then why does it seem that you do know you're a loser after the winning number has been announced on the radio and you've compared the numbers on your ticket with the sadly different numbers announced? After all, radio announcements *can* be in error; what you're hearing *may* not be a real radio announcement but the voice of a friend who's rigged up a practical joke; you *might* be suffering from some weird momentary visual illusion and misreading the numbers on your ticket; and so forth. All very remote possibilities, to be sure. But, since we're already countenancing even the most minute chances of error, why don't these possibilities rob us of knowledge even after the announcement has been made and heard?

SCA's explanation of why we don't think we know *before* the announcement is made is that we at that time judge that if we weren't losers, we'd still believe that we were. Note that once you've heard the announcement of the winning numbers and compared them with the numbers on your ticket, it *no longer* seems that if you had been the winner, you'd believe you were a loser. Rather, we judge that in that case you'd now believe you were the winner or would at least be suspending judgment as you frantically double-checked the match. It's very impressive that the very occurrence that would suffice to make it seem to us that you do know you're a loser (the radio announcement) also reverses our judgment regarding the truth of the conditional appealed to in SCA to explain why it seems to us that you don't know before the announcement is made. The occurrence which gets us to judge that we know here also removes what SCA posits as the block to our judging that we know. This is an indication that SCA has correctly identified the block.

SCA similarly provides a very intuitively appealing explanation for why it seems to us that we don't know that skeptical hypotheses are false, as was also noted in section 5. It again receives powerful further confirmation as we look to cases in which one seemingly does know that a skeptical hypothesis doesn't obtain (cases in which skeptical hypotheses that are ordinarily effective fail to be effective). The boastful zoologist I introduced toward the end of section 3, it seems, knows that the animals in the zebra cage are not cleverly painted mules, while I, it seems, do not. But the very anatomical knowledge that seemingly enables him to know they're not painted mules also has the consequence that if the animals *were* cleverly painted mules, the zoologist, unlike me, would *not* believe that they weren't. And although I don't seem to know they're not painted mules simply by looking at them, I could, it seems, get to know this if I undertook some special investigation—perhaps, as has been suggested in the literature (Stine, in this volume, p. 148), one involving paint remover. *Which* special investigations would do the trick (and under which circumstances would they)? A survey of various scenarios yields an impressive correlation: The investigations that would seemingly allow me to know that the animals aren't painted mules would also affect our judgment as to the truth value of the subjunctive conditional so critical to SCA. Once I have completed the investigation, it seems that I, like the zoologist, would *not* believe that the animals weren't painted mules if in fact they were. Likewise, by checking appropriately independent sources, I could get myself into a position in which I seemingly *would* know that the newspaper isn't mistaken about whether the Bulls won last night. But the checks that would seemingly allow this knowledge would also make it seem that if the paper were mistaken, I would *not* believe it wasn't. Again and again, SCA posits a certain block to our judging tht we know, and the changes that would clear the way for our judging that we know also remove this block. This makes it difficult not to believe that SCA is at least roughly correct.

In the case of the BIV hypothesis, it's hard to test SCA in this way, for it's difficult to imagine a situation in which it seems a subject does know that she's not a BIV. But this only confirms SCA: While it's difficult to imagine a situation in which one seems to know that one's not a BIV, it's likewise difficult to imagine circumstances in which the block SCA posits is removed. It's difficult, that is, to imagine a situation in which someone believes they're not a BIV but in which the conditional *If S were a BIV, then S would believe she wasn't a BIV* isn't true. For, as the BIV hypothesis is formulated, one's brain is electrochemically stimulated so that one has precisely those sensory experiences one actually has had. But wouldn't one then have formed precisely those beliefs that one actually has formed, including the belief that one's not a BIV?

Unlike that involved in the Relevant Alternatives Solution, the present explanation for the plausibility of AI's first premise can't be happily reversed: Trying to account for the plausibility of the subjunctive conditional *If H were true, I would believe it was false,* by reference to the (presumed) fact that I don't know that H is false certainly seems to get things backwards. Much better to follow the proposed Nozickean route in explaining the plausibility of denying knowledge by reference to the conditional.

Further, as was the case with not knowing, the investigations that would reverse our other pessimistic judgments regarding your standing vis-à-vis a skeptical hypothesis would also put you in a position to say that you wouldn't believe the hypothesis is false if it were true. Thus, for instance, to make it seem that you can tell that those animals aren't painted mules, you must put yourself in such a position that you wouldn't believe they weren't if they were. And, as was the case with not knowing, none of these explanations by subjunctive conditionals seems happily reversible.

It seems that this explanation, SCA, for the plausibility of AI's first premise must be (at least roughly) correct and, therefore, that it points to part of the solution to our puzzle.

Indeed, some readers will wonder why I have claimed only that our general tendency not to count insensitive beliefs as instances of knowledge explains that premise's plausibility and have stopped short of accepting sensitivity as a necessary condition for knowledge[26] and therefore simply endorsing that first premise as true. But while we've just seen strong grounds for simply accepting AI's first premise, there are also strong grounds for accepting AI's second premise and for accepting the denial of its conclusion. We have to stop short somewhere; we can't simply accept all three members of this triad as true. To solve this puzzle, I'll claim that AI's first premise, while not *simply* true, is true according to unusually high standards for knowledge. But, I'll argue, my solution explains why that premise seems true and, more generally, why sensitivity seems necessary for knowledge. If my solution provides the best explanation for how all three members of our puzzling triad seem true, that will be good reason for stopping short where my solution tells us to, rather than where one of its inferior rivals—bold skepticism, for example—tells us to.

9. NOZICK'S OWN SOLUTION AND THE ABOMINABLE CONJUNCTION

Nozick's own treatment of AI, from which SCA was abstracted, fails. This treatment is based on Nozick's account of knowledge as true, *sensitive* belief, where, very roughly, one's true belief that p is sensitive to the truth value of p if one would not have believed that p if p had been false.[27] Thus, Nozick's treatment of AI involves accepting the skeptic's first premise. But, at the same time, and much more unfortunately, it also involves denying the second. You *don't* know that you're not a BIV, Nozick claims, because any belief you might have to this effect is insensitive: You would have held this belief even if it were false (even if you were a BIV). By contrast, Nozick claims, your belief that you have hands *is* a sensitive belief: If *it* were false—if you didn't have hands—you wold not hold it. So you do know you have hands even though you don't know that you're not a BIV. The skeptic's mistake—the second premise—is supposing that you can know you have hands only if you also know that you're not a BIV.

Or so Nozick claims. This is not the place for a general evaluation of Nozick's analysis of propositional knowledge, so let us confine ourselves to the results of this analysis as applied to the beliefs in question in AI. Here Nozick's account does very well in issuing the intuitively correct verdict for the relevant particular judgments regarding what is known and what is not. Most of us would judge that we do know such things as that we have hands, and this is Nozick's verdict. And, when a skeptical hypothesis is well chosen, it does seem quite plausible to most of us that we don't know that it doesn't obtain. But there are three relevant issues to our puzzle: Is the first premise of AI true? Is the second premise true? Is the conclusion true? And it's easy to endorse the intuitively correct answer to two out of the three questions if you're willing to take the implausible stand on the remaining one.

Nozick takes his implausible stand on the issue of the second premise, denying it in the face of its evident intuitive appeal.[28] Accepting his treatment involves embracing the abominable conjunction that while you don't know you're not a bodiless (and handless!) BIV, still, you know you have hands. Thus, while his account does quite well on the relevant particular intuitions regarding what is and isn't known, it yields an intuitively bizarre result on the comparative judgment the second premise embodies.[29]

As promised, I won't here rehearse the powerful objections to Nozick's analysis of propositional knowledge that have been put forward,[30] but, assuming that this analysis isn't independently convincing before we turn to the problem of skeptical hypotheses,[31] we're left with little reason to follow Nozick in choosing to take an implausible stand precisely where he has rather than someplace else.

This leaves us in a bind. For, as we saw in sections 5 and 8 above, SCA is quite powerful. That explanation is that we realize that any belief we might have to the effect that an (effective) skeptical hypothesis doesn't obtain is insensitive, and we're inclined to think that insensitive beliefs don't constitute knowledge. How can we appropriate that explanation without following Nozick in having to implausibly deny the second premise of AI and embrace the abominable conjunction?

10. STRENGTH OF EPISTEMIC POSITION AND AI'S SECOND PREMISE

Here's how: by incorporating SCA into a contextualist solution to our puzzle that avoids such a fumbling of AI's second premise. Indeed, I propose *a very strong endorsement* of that second premise.

Recall that according to contextualist theories of knowledge attributions, how strong a subject's epistemic position must be to make true a speaker's attribution of knowledge to that subject is a flexible matter that can vary according to features of the speaker's conversational context. Central to contextualism, then, is the notion of *(relative) strength of epistemic position*. In presenting and defending contextualism, I've found that most listeners feel that they understand pretty well what's meant when I claim, for instance, that sometimes the standards for knowledge are higher than usual, or that in some conversational situations one's epistemic position must be stronger than in others to count as knowing. But it would be good to clarify this important notion of strength of epistemic position as best we can by, for instance, supplying an intuitive test for when one epistemic position is stronger than another. The best such device is that of *comparative conditionals*. One can have a variety of grounds for assenting to conditionals like *If Mugsy is tall, then Wilt is tall,* and *If Wilt is not tall, then Mugsy is not tall.* But one very good basis for assenting to these conditionals is the comparative knowledge that Wilt is at least as tall as Mugsy. Likewise, where S is a putative subject of knowledge, P is a true proposition that S believes, and A and B are situations in which S is found, we can have similarly comparative grounds for assenting to conditionals of the form *If S knows that P in A, then S knows that P in B.* In such a case, the comparative grounds for our assent is our realization that S is in *at least as strong* an epistemic position with respect to P in situation B as he is in with respect to that same proposition in situation A, and this comparative conditional serves as a good intuitive test for that comparative fact: It brings that fact to light.

So, for instance, to borrow some examples from Alvin Goldman (1976), let Henry be our subject, and let *What Henry is seeing is a barn* be the thing Henry putatively knows. Both in situation F (for "fakes") and in situation N ("no fakes"), Henry is driving through the countryside and, having no reason to think there's anything unusual going on, very firmly believes, and takes himself to know, that the object he's seeing is a barn. And indeed, in both cases, it is a barn. But in F, unbeknownst to him, Henry is in an area that is filled with very convincing fake barns—papier-mâché barn facades. In fact, we may suppose that Henry has just been fooled more than twenty times by such fakes, although he's now looking at the only actual barn for miles around, and so this time truly believes that what he's seeing is a barn. N is exactly like F, except that there are no fakes in the area—the things Henry has taken to be barns have all actually been barns. With regard to these examples, the conditional *If Henry knows in F, then he knows in N* seems to get the comparison right, indicating that Henry's in at least as strong an epistemic position in situation N as he is in situation F. The evident failure of *If Henry knows in N, then he knows in F* to get the comparison right shows that Henry's not in as strong a position to know in F as in N. Together, these results indicate that Henry's in a stronger epistemic position in N than in F.

As is important to our discussion of AI's second premise, comparative conditionals can similarly be used to test the relative strength of epistemic position of a single subject with respect to *different propositions* that subject believes in the same situation: Thus, the intuitive correctness of *If S knows that P, then S knows that Q* and *If S doesn't know that Q, then S doesn't know that P* can indicate that S is in at least as strong an epistemic position with respect to Q as she's in with respect to P.[32]

Sometimes no clear verdict results when we attempt to evaluate a conditional in this comparative way, for the good reason that it's unclear how the two epistemic positions we're evaluating compare with one another. Thus, if we compare a situation in which Henry has a good look at the barn but in which there are a couple of fake barns several miles away that Henry hasn't encountered with a situation in which there are no fakes at all in Henry's vicinity but in which he doesn't have quite as good a look at the barn, the relevant conditionals can be difficult to evaluate. But, in many instances, some of the relevant conditionals *are* clearly true on comparative grounds.

Such is the case with instances of AI's second premise, where the skeptical hypothesis is well chosen. They seem true and *are* true, I suggest, for just this comparative reason: As we realize, we *are* in at least as good a position to know that the hypothesis is false as we're in to know the targeted piece of presumed ordinary knowledge.[33] Let's look briefly at some instances. Recall the following epistemologically perplexing pairs of propositions:

not-H	*O*
I'm not a BIV.	I have hands.
Those animals aren't just cleverly painted mules.	Those animals are zebras.
The paper isn't mistaken about whether the Bulls won last night.	The Bulls won last night.

Given natural background assumptions, we can sense that the following comparative fact holds for each of the above pairs: I am in no better a position to know that O than I am in to know that not-H. This comparative fact is revealed in each case by the highly plausible conditional that is AI's second premise: If I don't know that not-H, then I don't know that O. Closely tied to that comparative fact in each case is the related and intuitively compelling realization that it would be no wiser to bet one's immortal soul on O's being true than to bet it on not-H's being true.

I propose then to accept the relevant conditional with respect to each of the above pairs, and to accept other convincing instances of AI's second premise. Indeed, these conditionals are true *regardless of how high or low the standards for knowledge are set.* Just as the comparative fact that Wilt is at least as tall as Mugsy has the result that the conditional *If Wilt is not tall, then Mugsy is not tall* will be true regardless of how high or low the standards for tallness are set, so the comparative fact that I'm in at least as strong an epistemic position with respect to not-H as I'm in with respect to O will result in *If I don't know that not-H, then I don't know that O* being true regardless of how high or low the standards for knowledge are set. Thus, we will never have to follow Nozick in accepting the abominable conjunction: that conjunction is false at any epistemic standard.

With that ringing endorsement of AI's second premise anchored firmly in place, we can return to the first premise, hoping to incorporate SCA into a contextualist account of that premise's plausibility.

11. STRENGTH AND SENSITIVITY

As has become very apparent, two notions that are central to my attempt to solve our puzzle are, on the one hand, the Nozickean notion of the sensitivity of beliefs and, on the other, the notion of strength of epistemic position. While both notions stand in need of a good deal of sharpening and explanation (only some of which they'll receive here), we've already obtained interesting results applying them to the epistemologically perplexing pairs of propositions displayed above. In each case, one's belief in O is sensitive, while one's belief in not-H is insensitive. Yet, at the same time, one is in at least as strong an epistemic position with respect to not-H as one is in with respect to O.

For each of the second and third pairs of propositions, one could gather further evidence, strengthen one's epistemic position with respect to both not-H and O, and *make* even one's belief that not-H sensitive. But even before this further evidence is gathered, one's belief that O is *already* sensitive, despite the fact that one is in no stronger an epistemic position with respect to this O than one is in with respect to not-H. (With respect to the first pair of propositions, it is difficult to imagine a situation in which one is in such a strong position with respect to one's not being a BIV that this belief is sensitive.)

This leads us to an important insight regarding skeptical hypotheses: One's epistemic position with respect to propositions to the effect that skeptical hypotheses don't hold must be stronger than it is with respect to other, more ordinary propositions (e.g., our above Os) if belief in such propositions is to be sensitive.

An explanation of our two central notions in terms of possible worlds will provide a partial and quite rough-and-ready, but still somewhat enlightening, picture of how this situation can arise. An important component of being in a strong epistemic position with respect to P is to have one's belief as to whether P is true match the fact of the matter as to whether P is true, not only in the actual world, but also at the worlds sufficiently close to the actual world. That is, one's belief should not only be true, but should be non-accidentally true, where this requires one's belief as to whether P is true to match the fact of the matter at nearby worlds. The further away one can get from the actual world, while still having it be the case that one's belief matches the fact at worlds that far away and closer, the stronger a position one is in with respect to P. (Recalling the results of section 6, we should remember either to restrict our attention solely to those worlds in which the subject uses the same method of belief-formation she uses in the actual world, or to weigh similarity with respect to the subject's method very heavily in determining the closeness of possible worlds to the actual world.) If the truth-tracking of one's belief as to whether P extends far enough from actuality to reach the closest not-P worlds, then one doesn't believe that P in those closest not-P worlds, and one's belief that P is sensitive. But how far from actuality must truth-tracking reach—how strong an epistemic position must one be in—to make one's belief that P sensitive? That, of course, depends on how distant from actuality the closest not-P worlds are.

Consider my belief that I have hands. I believe this at the actual world, and it's true. What's more, in the other nearby worlds in which I have hands, I believe that I do. There are also, at least in my own case, some alarmingly close worlds in which I don't have hands. These include worlds in which I lost my hands years ago while working on my uncle's garbage truck. In the closest of these not-P worlds, I'm now fully aware of the fact that I'm hand-less, and my belief as to whether I have hands matches the fact of the matter. My belief as to whether I have hands doesn't match the fact in various worlds in which I'm a BIV, of course, but these are *very* distant. While there are closer worlds in which the match fails, it seems that in a fairly wide range of worlds surrounding the actual world, my belief as to whether I have hands does a good job of matching the fact of the matter. Thus, I'm in a pretty strong epistemic position with respect to that matter.

Now let P be *I'm not a BIV.* Where not-P (here, *I am a BIV*) is quite remote, one can be in a quite strong epistemic position with respect to P merely by believing that P in all the nearby worlds. As I do believe this P in such nearby worlds, I'm in a pretty strong epistemic position with respect to this P. This can occur, and in my case, does occur, even though one's belief as to whether P doesn't match the fact of the matter in the closest not-P worlds: Since even the closest of the not-P worlds are quite distant, one's belief as to whether P needn't match the fact of the matter that far from the actual world for one to be in a quite strong position with respect to P.

But for one's belief that P to be sensitive, one must *not* believe that P in the closest not-P worlds. Since skeptical hypotheses tend to fasten on somewhat remote (and sometimes very remote) possibilities, then, one can be in a relatively (and sometimes a very) strong position with respect to beliefs to the effect that they don't obtain (since one's belief as to whether they obtain matches the fact of the matter over a wide range of worlds closest to the actual world), while these beliefs remain insensitive (since one would still believe that the hypotheses didn't obtain in the closest worlds in which they do obtain). By contrast, where P is such that there are both P and not-P worlds very close to the actual world, one's belief that P must be sensitive (one must not believe that P in the closest not-P worlds) in order for one to be in even a minimally strong epistemic position with respect to P, and, conversely, one needn't be in a very strong position for one's belief to be sensitive.

12. THE RULE OF SENSITIVITY AND THE BEGINNINGS OF A NEW CONTEXTUALIST SOLUTION

The important insight regarding skeptical hypotheses—that one's epistemic position with respect to propositions to the effect that skeptical hypotheses don't hold must be stronger than it is with respect to other propositions before beliefs in such propositions can be sensitive—suggests a new contextualist account of how, in presenting AI, the skeptic raises the standards for knowledge. Let's call the conversational rule this new account posits as the mechanism by which the skeptic raises the standards for knowledge the "Rule of Sensitivity." Although a more general formulation of this rule is desirable, I will here state it in such a way that it applies only to attributions (and denials) of knowledge, since such applications are what's needed to address the present puzzle.[34] So limited, our rule is simply this: When it is asserted that some subject S knows (or does not know) some proposition P, the standards for knowledge (the standards or how good an epistemic position one must be in to count as knowing) tend to be raised, if need be, to such a level as to require S's belief in that particular P to be sensitive for it to count as knowledge. Where the P involved is to the effect that a skeptical hypothesis does not obtain, then this rule dictates that the standards will be raised to a quite high level, for, as we've seen, one must be in a stronger epistemic position with respect to a proposition stating that a skeptical hypothesis is false—relative to other, more ordinary, propositions—before a belief in such a proposition can be sensitive.

A story in terms of possible worlds again provides a rough-and-ready, but still perhaps enlightening, picture of how the Rule of Sensitivity operates. Context, I've said, determines how strong an epistemic position one must be in to count as knowing. Picture this requirement as a contextually determined sphere of possible worlds, centered on the actual world, within which a subject's belief as to whether P is true must match the fact of the matter in order for the subject to count as knowing. (Given the results of section 6, we must again remember either to restrict our attention solely to those worlds in which the subject uses the same method of belief formation she uses in the actual world, or to weigh similarity with respect to the subject's method very heavily in determining the closeness of possible worlds to the actual world.) Call this sphere the sphere of epistemically relevant worlds. As the standards for knowledge go up, the sphere of epistemically relevant worlds becomes larger—the truth-tracking of one's belief must extend further from actuality for one to count as knowing. Given this picture, the Rule of Sensitivity can be formulated as follows: When it's asserted that S knows (or doesn't know) that P, then, if necessary, enlarge the sphere of epistemically relevant worlds so that it at least includes the closest worlds in which P is false.

A powerful solution to our puzzle results when we follow the basic contextualist strategy (see section 2) and utilize this Rule of Sensitivity to explain how the standards for knowledge are raised by the skeptic's presentation of AI. While many noteworthy features and virtues of this solution are best explained by comparing it with the other proposed solutions to our puzzle, as I'll do in following sections, the basic idea of the present solution is this. In utilizing AI to attack our putative knowledge of O, the skeptic instinctively chooses her skeptical hypothesis, H, so that it will have these two features: (1) We will be in at least as strong a position to know that not-H as we're in to know that O, but (2) Any belief we might have to the effect that not-H will be an insensitive belief (a belief we would hold even if not-H were false—that is, even if H were true). Given feature (2), the skeptic's assertion that we don't know that not-H, by the Rule of Sensitivity, drives the standards for knowledge up to such a point as to make that assertion true. By the Rule of Sensitivity, recall, the standards for knowledge are raised to such a level as to require our belief that not-H to be sensitive before it can count as knowledge. Since our belief that not-H isn't sensitive (feature (2)), the standards are driven up to such a level that we don't count as knowing that not-H. And since we're in no stronger an epistemic position with respect to O than we're in with respect to not-H (feature (1)), then, at the high standards put in place by the skeptic's assertion of AI's first premise, we also fail to know that O. At these high standards, the skeptic truthfully asserts her second premise (which, recall, is also true at lower standards), and then truthfully asserts AI's conclusion that we don't know that O.[35] This accounts for the persuasiveness of AI. But since, on this account, the skeptic gets to truthfully state her conclusion only by raising the standards for knowledge, AI doesn't threaten the truth of our odinary claims to know the very Os our knowledge of which the skeptic attacks. For the fact that the skeptic can install very high standards that we don't live up to has no tendency to show that we don't satisfy the more relaxed standards that are in place in more ordinary conversations and debates.

13. THE RULE OF SENSITIVITY AND SCA: A COMPARISON OF OUR NEW SOLUTION WITH THE OTHER CONTEXTUALIST SOLUTIONS AND WITH NOZICK'S SOLUTION

Recall that the problem with the other contextualist solutions we've seen is that they fail to adequately explain why AI's first premise has the intuitive pull it has (when the skeptical hypothesis employed is well chosen). Our new contextualist solution gains an important advantage over its contextualist rivals by incorporating SCA. We explain the plausibility of AI's first premise by reference to the following two facts. First, any belief we might have to the effect that a skeptical hypothesis doesn't obtain (where that hypothesis is well chosen) is insensitive: as we realize, we would hold this belief even if it were false (even if the hypothesis did obtain). And, second, we have a very general inclination to think that we don't know that P when we realize that our belief that P is insensitive—when we realize that we would believe that P even if P were false.

We follow Nozick in employing SCA. But we diverge from Nozick's treatment in our account of why the second fact above holds. On Nozick's account, we have the general inclination asserted there because our concept of knowledge just is, roughly, that of true, sensitive belief. This would account for our inclination to deny the status of knowledge to insensitive beliefs alright, but it would also have us happily asserting abominable conjunctions, which, in fact, we're loathe to do.

Our new solution avoids this unhappiness by not building a sensitivity requirement into the very concept of knowledge. The notion of sensitivity, rather, finds its happier home in our contextualist account of how the standards for knowledge are raised, and the second fact above is accounted for as follows. Where S's belief that P is not sensitive, S is not in a good enough epistemic position to count as knowing that P by the standards that, according to the Rule of Sensitivity, would be put in place by the very claim that S knows (or doesn't know) that P. Thus, an assertion that S doesn't know that P, where S's belief that P is insensitive, will raise the standards for knowledge to a level high enough to make that denial of knowledge true. A positive claim that S *does* know such a P, on the other hand, is doomed to failure: The making of the claim will raise the standards for knowledge to a level high enough to make that claim false. So, whenever S's belief that P is insensitive, we can *truthfully* assert that S *doesn't* know that P, and can only *falsely* say that S *does* know that P. No wonder, then, that the second fact holds!

Thus, we successfully incorporate SCA, explaining the plausibility of AI's first premise, without following Nozick in licensing abominable conjunctions.

14. OUR NEW CONTEXTUALIST SOLUTION CLARIFIED AND COMPARED WITH THE STRAIGHTFORWARD SOLUTIONS

The puzzle of skeptical hypotheses, recall, concerns the premises of AI together with the negation of its conclusion:

1. I don't know that not-H.
2. If I don't that not-H, then I don't know that O.

not-C   I do know that O.

A solution to the puzzle must, of course, issue a verdict as to the truth of each of these three, but it must also explain why we find all of them plausible.

Let's be clear about what our present contextualist solution has to say about each of these. Our verdict regarding (2) is that it's true regardless of what epistemic standard it's evaluated at, so its plausibility is easily accounted for. But this, combined with a similarly enthusiastic endorsement of (1), would land us in bold skepticism. We avoid that fate by endorsing (1) as true, not at all standards, but only at the unusually inflated standards conducive to skepticism. Thus, on our solution, we do know, for instance, that we're not BIVs, according to ordinary low standards for knowledge. But, though (1) is false when evaluated according to those ordinary low standards, we're able to explain its plausibility, as we've seen, by means of the fact that the high standards at which (1) is true are precisely the standards that an assertion or denial of it put into play. Since attempts to assert (1) are bound to result in truth, and attempts to deny it are destined to produce falsehood,[36] it's no surprise that we find it so plausible.

But what of (not-C)? On the present solution, claims to know ordinary propositions are true according to ordinary low standards but false according to the highly inflated standards that, by the Rule of Sensitivity, are put in place by the assertion of (1). (Not-C) seems plausible because it's true when evaluated at the standards most normally applied to it. But, it will be asked, why do we find these claims to know plausible even when we're in a context in which the skeptic has raised the standards to such a level that these claims are false? A little caution is in order here. It's controversial just how intuitively correct (not-C) does seem to us in such a context. Most of us feel some ambivalence. Such ambivalence is to be expected whenever we're dealing with a puzzle consisting of mutually inconsistent propositions, all of which are individually plausible. For when the propositions are considered together, one will have this good reason for doubting each of them: that the others seem true. And it's difficult to distinguish the doubt of (not-C) that arises from this very general source (that its falsehood follows from other things one finds plausible) from that which arises from the fact that the standards are high. At any rate, the very strong pull that (not-C) continues to exert on (at least most of) us even when the standards are high is explained in the manner out-lined in section 2: Even while we're in a context governed by high standards at which we don't count as knowing that O, we at the same time sense that as soon as we find ourselves in more ordinary conversational contexts, it will not only be true for us to claim to know these very Os that the skeptic now denies we know, but it will also be wrong for us to deny that we know these things. It's easy, then, to think that the skeptic's present denial must be equally false and that it would be equally true for us now, in the skeptic's presence, to claim to know that O.

The verdicts the present solution issues regarding the truth values of the members of the triad are complicated by the fact that ours is a contextualist solution. Only (2) receives the same verdict regardless of what the epistemic standards are; the truth values of (1) and (not-C) vary with context. It's just this variance that our solution so essentially relies on in explaining how we fall into our puzzling conflict of intuitions. Noncontextualist (henceforth, "straightforward") solutions, on the other hand, must choose one of the members of this triad to deny, claiming this loser to be false according to the invariant epistemic standards that govern all attributions and denials of knowledge: The "Moorean" solution in this way denies (1),[37] the "Nozickean" (2), and the "Bold Skeptical" solution thus denies (not-C), accepting that we speak falsely whenever, even in ordinary, nonphilosophical discussions, we claim to know the O in question.

From the perspective of our present contextualist solution, each of these straightforward solutions results in part, of course, from a failure to see the truth of contextualism. But which straightforward solution an invariantist confusedly adopts will depend on the standards that dominate her evaluation of our beliefs in O and in not-H. If her evaluation is dominated by the relatively low standards that govern our ordinary, out-on-the-street talk of knowledge, she will end up a Moorean. If she evaluates the beliefs in question according to the high standards that are put into place by the skeptic's presentation of AI, bold skepticism is the result. The Nozickean solution ensues from evaluating each belief according to the standards that would most often be used in evaluating that belief. For reasons we've seen, a claim to know (or an admission that one doesn't know) that a skeptical hypothesis is false will, by the Rule of Sensitivity, tend to invite a very high reading, at which the admission is true and the claim is false. But a claim to know that O doesn't so demand a high reading. From the present perspective, the Nozickean is reacting to the fact that one can usually truthfully claim that one does know that O and can usually truthfully claim not to know that not-H. What the Nozickean misses is how difficult it is to make these two claims together: once you have admitted that you don't know that not-H, it seems the reverse of intuitively correct to claim to know that O, at least until the conversational air is cleared.

To succeed, a straightforward solution must explain what leads our intuitions astray with respect to the unlucky member of the triad which that solution denies. Otherwise, we'll have little reason for denying just that member of the triad. Nozick himself provides no such explanation with respect to (2), parenthetically leaving this vital task to "further exploration,"[38] and other Nozickeans, if any there be, have not, to the best of my knowledge, progressed any farther along this front. Mooreans, to the best of my knowledge, have fared no better in explaining why we're so reluctant to claim the status of knowledge for our insensitive beliefs. It's the defenders of bold skepticism who've made the most progress here. In the remaining sections, I'll explain why our contextualist solution is superior to that of the bold skeptic.

15. BOLD SKEPTICISM AND THE WARRANTED ASSERTABILITY MANEUVER

Almost all of the time, it seems to almost all of us that we do know the Os that the skeptic claims we don't know. According to the bold skeptic, whenever we say or think that we know these things, we say or think something false. The bold skeptic thus implicates us, speakers of English, in systematic and widespread falsehood in our use, in speech and in thought, of our very common word 'know'. Equally paradoxically, the bold skeptic holds that we're speaking the truth whenever we say that someone doesn't know these Os, even though it seems to most of us that we'd then be saying something quite false. What leads us astray? Peter Unger and Barry Stroud have suggested on behalf of bold skepticism that although we don't know these O's, it's often useful for us to claim that we do know them, and we are therefore often warranted or justified in making such claims. What then leads us astray is this: We mistake this useful/justified/warranted assertability of knowledge ascriptions for truth.[39] On the other side of the coin, presumably, we're mistaking the useless/unwarranted/unjustified assertability of denials of knowledge for falsehood.

Two serious problems emerge for the bold skeptic at this point. The first is that such "warranted assertability maneuvers" could be attempted by advocates of the other solutions as well. Warranted assertability indeed can be mistaken for truth, and unwarranted assertability for falsehood, but this by itself does not favor the bold skeptic's solution over the other straightforward approaches. Each of the straightforward approaches denies a member of the triad constituting our puzzle, and each it seems could claim that the reason this loser they've chosen seems true, though it's in fact false, is that we're often warranted in asserting it, and we mistake this warranted assertability for truth. Thus, the Moorean, for instance, could claim that although we do indeed know that H is false, we're not warranted in claiming that we know this (though this claim would be true), but are rather warranted in saying that we don't know (though this latter is false). Simply attributing apparent truth to warranted assertability is a game almost any party to this dispute can fairly easily play.[40] That this line of thought would eventually work out any better for the bold skeptic than for his opponents would take some showing.[41]

It's at (1) that the skeptic has his best hope of gaining an advantage over my solution, for that premise indeed does seem true, and, unlike the skeptic, I've stopped short of fully endorsing it, making do with an explanation of its plausibility. But the skeptic's other problem lurks here. Usually, while solving a philosophical puzzle consisting of a set of individually plausible but mutually inconsistent claims, one only has to explain (away) the plausibility of those members of the set one denies, and one is relieved of the burden of explaining the plausibility of those members that one endorses, their truth and our ability to recognize that truth being explanation enough of their apparent truth. But truth does not suffice to explain apparent truth where one makes us out to be absolutely horrible judges of truths of the kind in question. Thus, the skeptic's second big problem is that, because he holds that we're subject to constant and radical error as to the scope of our knowledge, consistently thinking we know things when we don't, the skeptic, although he thinks (1) is true, owes us an explanation for its plausibility. Given that our habit of mistaking our ignorance for knowledge is so pervasive, why doesn't it seem to us *here* that we know what, in fact, we don't—that these skeptical hypotheses are false? Why does our lack of knowledge, which we're so pervasively blind to, shine through so clearly to us just where the issue is whether we know a skeptical hypothesis to be false?

The skeptic's initial answer will certainly be that we're *not* warranted in claiming to know that skeptical hypotheses don't obtain, and thus can't mistake warranted assertability for truth here. But then, to see why skeptical hypotheses are effective, we must be told why we're not warranted in claiming to know that skeptical hypotheses are false, given that, according to the skeptic, we are warranted in claiming to know all manner of other things that in fact we don't know. And here skeptics have little to offer. But if the results of sections 5 and 8 above are correct, the answer must involve the lack of sensitivity enjoyed by our beliefs that skeptical hypotheses don't obtain. The skeptic's use of SCA will take this form: Although we know nothing (or very little), it's when our beliefs are insensitive that we're not even warranted in asserting that we know and we therefore recognize our lack of knowledge. But the skeptic must now also address AI's second premise, making sure his endorsement of SCA is made in such a way as to account for our intuitions here. Indeed, whether or not he buys into SCA, the skeptic faces this question: If, as he claims, we're usually under the delusion that we know that O, but we customarily recognize that we don't know that not-H, why aren't we happy to conjoin this error with that insight and embrace the abominable conjunction?

This may look like a difficult question, but the skeptic has a ready answer. His problem is that the warranted assertability maneuver by itself didn't really solve our puzzle, but rather re-introduced it in a new form. And the only way I've seen to incorporate SCA into a treatment of AI that also handles the other pieces of our puzzle is to employ the idea that contextually sensitive epistemic standards govern our use of 'know', and to posit the Rule of Sensitivity as the mechanism by which the AI skeptic drives those standards up, as I've advocated here. But wise invariantists typically accept that contextually varying standards govern our use of ascriptions and denials of knowledge. The sensible invariantist will admit that, of course, what passes for knowledge in some contexts won't so pass in others. Being an invariantist, he'll deny that the truth conditions of knowledge attributions vary in the way the contextualist claims they do. But the clever invariantist will maintain that the varying epistemic standards that the contextualist supposes govern the truth conditions of these sentences in fact govern their conditions of warranted assertability.[42]

This allows the bold skeptic to mimic any contextualist solution, and in particular the solution I'm advocating here, by means of a simple twist. With respect to my solution, the bold skeptic can maintain that the Rule of Sensitivity is a rule for the raising of the epistemic standards governing our use of sentences ascribing knowledge to subjects, alright, but insist that it governs the warranted assertability conditions of these sentences, rather than their truth conditions, which, he'll maintain, remain constant at a level beyond the reach of mere mortals to satisfy. The warranted assertability maneuver can then be employed: We mistake warranted assertability for truth (and unwarranted assertability for falsehood). Thus, since we're never warranted in claiming to know that skeptical hypotheses don't obtain (due to the operation of the twisted Rule of Sensitivity), we're led to judge (correctly) that such claims to knowledge would be false. And since AI's second premise is always warranted, we judge (again correctly) that this premise is true. But since a claim to know some O is usually warranted, due to the low standards for warranted assertability that would ordinarily be applied to such a claim, we judge (incorrectly) that we know this O. Thus, my solution, like other contextualist solutions, can be easily adapted to suit the purposes of the bold skeptic. The result is a theory parallel to my own contextualist solution, which differs in its semantics of 'know': According to this parallel invariantist theory, the context-sensitive varying epistemic standards we've discovered govern the warranted assertability conditions of attributions and denials of knowledge, rather than their truth conditions, which are held to be invariant.[43] How shall we rationally decide between a contextualist solution, and in particular the one I'm here defending, and the bold skeptic's analogue of it?[44]

16. BOLD SKEPTICISM AND SYSTEMATIC FALSEHOOD

Like its contextualist relatives, our new solution is designed largely with the goal i mind of crediting most of our attributions of knowledge with truth. And no wonder. We in general take it as a strike against a theory of a common term of a natural language that it involves the speakers of that language in systematic and widespread falsehood in their use of that term. Let's borrow an example and suppose, for instance, that a crazed philosopher claimed that there are no physicians, because, in addition to holding a medical degree, a necessary condition for being a physician is that one be able to cure any conceivable illness.[45] On what grounds should we reject this bizarre conjecture in favor of a more traditional and less demanding account of what it is to be a physician? Our language certainly could have been such that S's having the ability to cure any conceivable illness was a truth condition of 'S is a physician' (although the word 'physician' would not have been very useful in that case). In virtue of what is our language in fact such that the strange theory is not true of it? I'm of course not in a position to give a complete answer to this question, but it's eminently reasonable to suppose that such facts as these, regarding our use, in thought and in speech, of the term 'physician' are involved: that we take to be physicians many licensed practitioners of medicine who don't satisfy the demanding requirement alleged; that we seriously describe these people as being physicians; that we *don't deny* that these people are physicians; etc. It's no doubt largely in virtue of such facts as these that the traditional view, rather than the conjecture of our crazed philosopher, is true of our language. (The correctness of the traditional view largely *consists* in such facts.) And these facts also provide us with our best reasons or evidence for accepting the traditional, rather than the strange, hypothesis regarding the semantics of 'physician'. In this case, that the peculiar theory implicates us in systematic and widespread falsehood in our speech and thought involving 'physicians' is a (constitutive and evidential) strike against the theory that proves quite decisive.

If our crazed philosopher tried to account for the above facts regarding our use of the term 'physician' via the quick and easy conjecture that the less demanding requirements that are more traditionally assigned to 'physician', while they don't accurately specify the truth conditions of sentences involving that term, do articulate these sentences' warranted assertability conditions, we should not, on the basis of this maneuver, suspend our judgment against his contention. That his theory involves us in systematic falsehood continues to constitute a strike against it, and in the absence of quite weighty counterbalancing considerations that favor the strange theory over the traditional one, this strike remains decisive.

Of course, the problem with this hopeless nonstarter of a theory is that there don't seem to be any such counterbalancing considerations in its favor. By contrast, bold skepticism can appear to be supported by skeptical arguments like AI. Though the bold skeptic's resolution of our puzzle involves us in systematic falsehood because of its unwavering acceptance of AI's conclusion, it at the same time can seem to make sense of *other* pieces of the puzzle (that we're inclined to say that we don't know that skeptical hypotheses are false and to say that we don't know various ordinary things if we don't know these hypotheses to be false), making the warranted assertability maneuver seem more motivated here than it is in the hands of our imagined crazed philosopher. But, as we saw in the previous section, this appearance is deceptive. Bold skepticism, by itself, does not explain the plausibility of AI's premises. To help the skeptic solve the puzzle, I've had to ascribe to him an analogue of our new solution.[46] But once we see that the skeptical puzzle can be solved just as well without the bold skeptic's systematic falsehood, we're left with no reason for paying that high price for a solution.[47] Indeed, since the bold skeptical solution and our new contextualist solution under consideration closely parallel each other, there's not much difference in how they solve the puzzle. That the bold skeptical resolution involves us in systematic falsehood is one of the few differences to be found here, and it's a weighty consideration against that resolution. And, with there being little room for weighty compensating advantages for this resolution over the contextualist's (given how similar they are in other respects), this consideration proves decisive. So, as with the crazed philosopher's theory of 'physician', the bold skeptic's resolution of AI should be rejected because it involves us in systematic and wide-spread falsehood in our use of a common term of our language.

17. BEGGING THE QUESTION AGAINST THE SKEPTIC?

If skeptics are allowed to play King of the Mountain—they start off on top (never mind how they got there) and it's the anti-skeptics' job to knock them off—displacing them can be a very difficult task. How difficult depends on several factors, one of which is what premises the anti-skeptic is allowed to appeal to in an argument designed to dethrone the skeptic. If the skeptic won't allow any premises to be available, then, as Thomas Reid noted, "It would be impossible by argument to beat him out of this stronghold; and he must even be left to enjoy his scepticism" (1895, 447).[48] If, to make the game a bit more interesting, a slim range of claims is allowed to pass inspection and be available for use in the anti-skeptical campaign, then (as Reid again recognized) it's often difficult to say what, if anything, of importance would follow from the fact that the skeptic can or cannot be knocked from his perch by arguments from premises of that particular type.

I have little interest in playing King of the Mountain. But skeptical arguments like AI threaten to show that the skeptic needn't just play this game, but can *gain* the top of the mountain—that starting from our own beliefs and intuitions, he can give us better reasons for accepting his skepticism than we have for rejecting it. I've here argued that the bold skeptic cannot win *this* battle—that of providing the best resolution of our puzzling conflict of intuitions. Although AI's premises are initially plausible, the best resolution for the conflict of intuitions generated by AI is not that of the bold skeptic.

Along the way, I've been assuming certain things that we believe but that the skeptic claims we can't know, thereby perhaps raising the concern that I'm begging the question against the skeptic. For instance, in claiming that my belief that I have hands is sensitive, I betray my conviction that I'm not a BIV, either in the actual world or in any nearby worlds. Indeed, I'm ready to admit to the skeptic that if I am a BIV, then I don't know I have hands, according to any standards for knowledge. But, of course, as I firmly believe, I'm not a BIV.

Is it legitimate for me to use this conviction in a debate against the skeptic? Not if we're playing King of the Mountain. But if the skeptic is marshalling deeply felt intuitions of ours in an attempt to give us good reasons for accepting his skepticism, it's legitimate to point out that other of our beliefs militate against his position, and ask why we should give credence to just those that favor him. And if we can further show that those beliefs that seem to favor his solution can be accommodated in our solution better than he can accommodate those of our beliefs that are hostile to him, the best conclusion we can draw is that we're *not* ordinarily mistaken when we claim or ascribe knowledge, despite the bold skeptic's attempt to show that we are. Instead, the main insights to be drawn from a study of AI involve the context-sensitivity of attributions of knowledge, and the role that the Rule of Sensitivity plays in changing the epistemic standards that govern these attributions.[49]

NOTES

1. I choose this O partly for its historical connections to Descartes' First Meditation, and also because I think it *is* an exemplary case of something we ordinarily think we know. But while we would ordinarily think we know this O, we'd seldom have occasion to *say* that we know it, because cases in which such a claim to knowledge would be conversationally in order are quite rare. (Exception: A teacher begins an epistemology lecture by matter-of-factly listing various things she knows, and that any plausible theory of knowledge should make her come out to know. In the course of this listing, she says, "And I know that I have hands.") For this and various related reasons, some might not like my choice of O. Such readers are invited to supply their own favorite exemplary cases of things we know as the skeptic's target.

2. Those who think that Hilary Putnam may have already disarmed BIV-inspired skepticism should understand the BIV hypothesis to be the hypothesis that one's brain has been *recently* envatted after many years of normal embodiment. For even if Putnam is right in claiming that the content of the beliefs of the BIV's of his scenario is such that these BIVs aren't massively deceived, it seems that recently envatted BIVs are so deceived.

3. AI takes its name primarily from its first premise. But since one of AI's best formulations (to which I hereby refer readers seeking a good version of AI that has not been so brutally pared) is in Unger 1975, chap. 1, it is in more than one sense that it is an argument "from ignorance."

4. I actually haven't pared AI to its *barest* essentials. It could be further pared to a one-premise argument: I don't know that not-H; so, I don't know that O. The second, "bridge" premise has been added to facilitate my treatment of the argument, nicely dividing those issues that impact on the acceptability of the first premise from those germane to the second.

Contextualist Responses

AI is the first and great argument by skeptical hypothesis. And the second, like unto it, is *The Argument from Possibility* (AP), which, like AI, takes its name from it first premise, and which has this form:

1.   It is possible that H_{ind}.
2.   If it is possible that H_{ind}, then it is possible that not-O_{ind}.
So, 3.   If is possible that not-O_{ind}.
4.   If it is possible that not-O_{ind}, then I don't know that O.
So, C.   I don't know that O.

(The subscript 'ind' indicates that what occurs in the scope of 'It is possible that' is to be kept in the indicative mood, so that the possibility expressed will be an epistemic one. The "bridge" premises, 2 and 4, can be omitted.) In this paper I address only AI, but let me quickly indicate how AP should be handled. Premise 4, which initially strikes many as AP's weakest link, is actually correct (DeRose 1991, section G). Thus, the AP skeptic must be stopped *before* she reaches step 3. Fortunately, the treatment of AI that I present in this paper can be generalized to handle the initial phase (steps 1–3) of AP as well. This treatment of AP is left here as an exercise for the reader, but is explained in chapter 3, especially section K, of my 1990.

5. This is especially true of Stewart Cohen, to whom I'm indebted for his general setup of the puzzle as a conflict of intuitions, a satisfactory solution of which requires an explanation of why the puzzle arises. See Cohen 1988, 93-94.

6. For a bit more on the nature of contextualist theories, see my 1992. The notion of (comparative) strength of epistemic position, central to my characterization of contextualism, will be explicated below in sections 10 and 11.

7. This is at least so according to *skeptic-friendly* versions of contextualist solutions, as will be explained later in this section.

8. Thanks to Richard Grandy and to Peter Unger for pressing this point.

9. I am here distinguishing among contextualist solutions according to the mechanism or rule that they allege raises the standards for knowledge. Although there are suggestions of the Relevant Alternatives (RA) approach in "Scorekeeping," Lewis's Rule of Accommodation is quite different from the mechanism most RA theories posit—thus the separate treatment of Lewis. To the extent that Lewis *is* a relevant alternativist, the RA aspects of his treatment are addressed below in section 4.

10. See especially 346–47.

11. For Lewis, as for Relevant Alternatives theorists (see section 4, below), this raising of epistemic standards consists in expanding the range of relevant alternatives to what one believes, that is, the range of alternatives that one must be in a position to eliminate in order to count as knowing.

12. Why can't the commonsensical epistemologist simply declare again that he knows, and rely on a Rule of Accommodation to lower the standards back down so as to make *his* claim true? To this Lewis responds that, for some admittedly unknown reason, the standards are more easily raised than lowered (355).

13. To be fair, Lewis, as I've pointed out, treats knowledge only in passing. Although the skeptic he imagines does utilize a skeptical hypothesis (that one is the victim of a deceiving demon (355)), *suggesting* that the treatment Lewis offers should be helpful in solving the puzzle of skeptical hypotheses, he never explicitly attempts a solution to our puzzle. Still, since the solution at least suggested by Lewis is one of the best on offer, it's worth establishing that it can't really solve the puzzle.

14. None of this is to deny that there is some Rule of Accommodation according to which the standards for knowledge tend to be raised to "accommodate" denials of knowledge. Nor is it even to deny that such Rules of Accommodation help the AI skeptic. In fact, I find it plausible to suppose that many denials of knowledge, including those of AI skeptics, often do exert an upward pressure on the standards for knowledge via some such rule. Likewise, certain settings (in addition to courts of law, certain philosophy classes are good examples), it seems to me, tend to militate in favor of high epistemic standards. AI skeptics may take advantages of these factors, the influence of which may explain some of the persuasiveness of their skeptical performances. But to solve our puzzle, we want primarily to explain what the nature of the skeptical argument itself adds to the effectiveness of the skeptic's performance that goes beyond what is contributed by the skeptic's setting and the fact that she asserts her conclusion.

15. For some comments on this notion of "ruling out" see sections 4 and 5, below.

16. It's been proposed to me, on behalf of the Rule of Accommodation and the solution to AI that can be based on it, that the boastful zoologist, while he does not say that I don't know, does strongly suggest or imply that I don't, and the Rule of Accommodation operates here on his suggestion: the standards go up so as to make the suggestion true. I am skeptical of this attempt to salvage the solution for two reasons. First, I suspect that the rule becomes far too powerful if it's allowed to work on what we suggest as well as on what we say. Second, the standards for knowledge seem likewise raised even if the boastful zoologist thinks I am also an expert, and thinks he is informing me that he too knows what's what. Here he's not even suggesting that I don't know.

17. Fred Dretske (see his 1970, 1971, 1981a, 1981b), although he does advocate a Relevant Alternatives theory

of knowledge, proposes a treatment of AI quite different from that described below. I'm not certain whether Dretske's is even a contextualist version of RA. (As I note in part 2 of my 1992, one can be an RA theorist without being a contextualist.) One thing is clear about Dretske's treatment of AI: He denies premise (2). Given this, his treatment runs into the same difficulties as does Nozick's; see especially section 9 below.

18. See, for example, Dretske, in this volume, p. 143; Goldman 1976, p. 772; and Stine, in this volume, p. 145.

19. Thus, if S is at a zoo that fairly consistently uses painted mules in an attempt to fool the zoo-going public, then the painted mule hypothesis is relevant. So, even though S is lucky enough to be at this zoo on one of the rare days when actual zebras are being used, S cannot truthfully be said to know that they're zebras unless she is able to rule out the painted mule hypothesis, which she can't do unless she knows more than I do about zebras and mules.

20. As I explain in part 2 of my 1992, an RA theorist can be an invariantist if he allows only factors about the putative subject of knowledge and her surroundings, and not conversational factors pertaining to the speaker (the ascriber of knowledge), to affect which alternatives are relevant. Matters get tricky with first-person knowledge claims, where S and A are identical. Here, in addition to allowing features that affect how good an epistemic position our subject actually is in, and that thereby attach to her qua putative subject of knowledge, contextualist RA theorists will also allow features of her conversational context, which affect how good a position she must be in to count as knowing, and which thereby attach to her qua attributor of knowledge, to influence what the range of relevant alternatives is.

21. Again, here I'm only giving the skeptic-friendly version of this contextualist solution. An RA theorist might be less friendly to the skeptic by holding, for example, that mentioning an alternative makes that alternative relevant only if one's conversational partner lets one get away with making it relevant.

22. Of course, it shouldn't be held that just any mention of a proposition makes that proposition a relevant alternative. In order to be made relevant, the proposition must, no doubt, be inserted into a conversation in the right way. But the advocate of RAS can plausibly claim to have explained the persuasiveness of AI even if he hasn't given an exact specification of the conditions under which a mentioning of a proposition makes that proposition a relevant alternative. Plausibly holding that in presenting AI the skeptic *does* insert her skeptical hypothesis into the conversation in the right way, the advocate of RAS can leave it as a future project to specify more exactly just which ways are the right ways. Although this by itself will be neither necessary nor sufficient for the mentioning of a proposition to be of the right kind to enlarge the range of relevant alternatives so as to include it, it nonetheless may be relevant that in the skeptic's presentation of AI's first premise, the mentioning of the hypothesis occurs within the scope of an epistemic operator "S does not know that. . . ."

23. Goldman 1976 cashes out "discriminating" what one believes from a relevant alternative to it in terms of what one would believe if the alternative obtained. This, combined with the Rule of Relevance, could yield an approach to skepticism close to the one I'll here defend. Goldman himself does not propose a solution to the skeptical problem; he strives to remain neutral on the issue. But I'll be working in the general direction I think Goldman points to.

24. Precisely, what Nozick does is this: He analyzes the technical locution 'S knows, via method M, that p', and then in turn analyzes the relation of S's knowing that p in terms of this technical locution. The revised third condition I've displayed is part of Nozick's attempt to analyze the technical locution.

25. These are not identical modifications. On the first option, similarity with respect to method is weighted heavily, but can be outweighed by other factors. Thus, even so evaluated, the most similar world(s) in which the antecedent of the original (3) are true may be worlds that diverge from the actual world with respect to the method by which S came to believe that P. By contrast, on the second option, since the method by which S believes that P becomes part of the antecedent of the conditional we're evaluating (the modified (3)), the closest possible world(s) in which that antecedent is true cannot be worlds that diverge from the actual world with respect to method.

26. Or, given the exceptions to the general tendency that we've discussed in sections 6 and 7, why I haven't accepted that some properly Chisholmed refinement of the sensitivity requirement (which has as instances of it convincing instances of AI's first premise) is necessary for knowledge?

27. Though this statement of Nozick's account of knowledge is rough, that will not affect my treatment, which would apply equally well to Nozick's full account. I've skipped entirely Nozick's fourth condition for knowledge, but I believe this fourth condition to be redundant, anyway: It automatically holds whenever true belief is present. Also, as I've already noted, Nozick takes account of the method of belief formation in his final version of the third condition. The same thing happens with the fourth.

28. In this volume, p. 170, Nozick admits this appeal, and later he writes, "Thus, if our notion of knowledge was as strong as we naturally tend to think (namely, closed under known logical implication) then the skeptic would be right. (But why do we naturally think this? Further exploration and explanation is needed of the intuitive roots of the natural assumption that knowledge is closed under known logical implication)" (1981, p. 242).

Nozick is quite hard on anti-skeptics who choose rather to deny the first premise; he writes: "The skeptic asserts we do not know his possibilities don't obtain, and he is right. Attempts to avoid skepticism by claiming we do know these things are bound to fail. The skeptic's possibilities make us uneasy because, as we deeply realize, we do not know they don't obtain; it is not surprising that attempts to show we do know these things leave us suspicious, strike us even as bad faith" (in this volume, 167–168). But similar remarks could be made about Nozick. As Nozick himself admits, the second premise has its own intuitive appeal. So why not say that what we "deeply realize" is that if you don't know that you're not a BIV, then you don't know you have hands, and that the skeptic is right about *this*? Nozick's denial of the second premise leaves me about as "suspicious" as does a denial of the first, and though Nozick's denial doesn't strike me as an instance of bad faith, denials of the first premise seem no better candidates for that charge.

29. What are Nozick's grounds for rejecting the second premise? Nozick notes that the premise is an instance of a very general principle to the effect the knowledge is closed under known implication (see note 33), After admitting that the closure principle *seems* true (in this volume, p. 170), Nozick claims that it's wrong, and his reasons for this claim are made entirely from within his analysis of knowledge: Given his analysis, knowledge won't be closed (see especially 170–173). So Nozick is relying on his analysis to show us that the second premise is fale despite its intuitive appeal. And indeed, Nozick has developed and defended his analysis of knowledge (in part 1 of his essay in this volume) before he applies it to the issue of skepticism (in part 2).

30. Unfortunately, what is perhaps the most powerful attack on Nozick's theory of knowledge, made by Saul Kripke in lectures, circa 1985, has not, to the best of my knowledge, found its way into print. For those interested in critical literature on Nozick, a good place to start is with Forbes 1984 and several of the essays in Luper-Foy 1987. For still further reading, Luper-Foy 1987 contains an excellent bibliography.

31. As remarked in note 29, Nozick depends heavily on the independent plausibility of this analysis to provide the momentum for his treatment of AI.

32. And, of course, such conditionals can be used to make all manner of other comparisons: comparative strength of the epistemic positions of two *different subjects* with respect to the same proposition or with respect to different propositions, the strength of the epistemic position of a subject with respect to one proposition in one situation as compared with that same subject's epistemic position with respect to a different proposition in a different situation, etc.

33. As is well known, instances of AI's second premise are often instances of the principle that knowledge is closed under known logical implication: Kp & K(p entails q) → Kq. (In the next paragraph I explain why this is not always the case, at least when the closure principle isn't strengthened as there described.) As is also well known, there are exceptions to the principle so formulated, and it might take a lot of tinkering to get it exactly right. But, as Nozick, the arch denier of closure, puts it, "We would be ill-advised, however, to quibble over the details of P [the principle that knowledge is closed under known logical implication]. Although these details are difficult to get straight, it will continue to appear that something like P is correct" (in this volume, p. 170). Nozick goes on to claim that this appearance is deceiving. I believe that something like P is correct, but that doesn't compete with my present account of AI's second premise: When a conditional is an instance of the properly formulated closure principle, the relevant comparative fact involving strength of epistemic position holds. See Brueckner 1985 for arguments that the denial of knowledge closure principles "is not a fruitful anti-skeptical project" (112).

While restrictions will have to be put on the closure principle that will weaken it in certain respects, there may be other respects in which it can be strengthened. Some instances of AI's second premise are convincing even though H is compatible with O. For instance, the BIV hypothesis seems to undermine my putative knowledge of *I'm in Houston* as well as of *I have hands*, but, of course, that I'm a bodiless BIV is compatible with my being in Houston. Perhaps if S is to know that P, then S must know that not-Q for any Q (but here restrictions must be added) such that if Q were true, S would not know that P. Thus, the range of Qs that must be known not to obtain may be broadened so as to include not only propositions that are incompatible with P, but also others such that if they were the case, then S wouldn't know that P. Those Qs that *are* incompatible with P itself will then be seen as special cases of those that are at odds with S's knowing that P. Barry Stroud discusses a stronger closure principle such as this in his 1984, pp. 25–30.

34. Introducing a skeptical hypothesis into a conversation in any number of ways other than in attributions and denials of knowledge can seem to raise the standards for knowledge. For instance, instead of arguing, "You don't know that the paper isn't mistaken about the result of last night's game; therefore, you don't know that the Bulls won," a skeptic may urge, "Consider this proposition: The newspaper is mistaken about who won the game. Now, keeping that proposition clearly in mind, answer me this: Do you *really* know that the Bulls won?" Of course, as with the Rule of Relevance (see note 22), not just *any* mention of a skeptical hypothesis seems to trigger the mechanism for raising the standards of knowledge I'm about to articulate.

35. Again, I'm here assuming a skeptic-friendly version of contextualism. See the second important point made at the end of section 2.

36. But for cases in which it seems one can truthfully say "S knows that not-H," despite the fact that S's belief that not-H is insensitive, see chapter 3, section J ("Low-Strength Claims to Know that Skeptical Hypotheses Do Not Obtain") of my 1990. In such cases, given certain features of the conversational situation, the Rule of Sensitivity does not operate. These constitute exceptions to the rule that one cannot truthfully call an insensitive belief knowledge. As I explain there, I welcome these exceptions, and would actually be a bit worried if there weren't such exceptions. For it's a feature of my treatment of AI that we do know skeptical hypotheses to be false according to low epistemic standards. I would find it a bit embarrassing if we could never *claim* to have such knowledge by means of simple knowledge attributions, and I'm reassured by the result that in special conversational circumstances, it seems we *can* truthfully claim to know that not-H, despite the fact that our belief that not-H is insensitive.

37. This is called the "Moorean" solution because Moore responded in this way to the dream argument. It's

far from certain that Moore would have so responded to other instances of AI that utilize different skeptical hypotheses.

38. See the first paragraph of note 28, above.

39. This is the basic line Unger takes in his defense of bold skepticism in his 1975; see especially pages 50–54. Stroud, though not himself advocating bold skepticism, does seek to defend the bold skeptic along these lines in chapter 2 of his 1984; see especially pages 55–82.

40. By contrast, our new contextualist solution attributes the apparent truth of (1) to (1)'s *truth* (and not just its warranted assertability) at the very standards its assertion invokes.

41. For my own part, for reasons I can't go into here, I think the resulting Moorean position would be slightly more defensible; thus, if I had to reject contextualism and adopt a straightforward solution, I'd be a Moorean.

42. Stroud thus claims that on the skeptic's conception of our practices, we operate under certain "practical constraints" (1984, p. 75) in our everyday uses of 'know', and asserts that our standards for saying we know vary from case to case (pp. 65–66). Thus, on the skeptic's conception, the standards for ascribing knowledge that we employ in everyday use depend upon our "aims and interests at the moment" (p. 65). According to contextualism, these varying standards reflect a corresponding variation in the truth conditions for attributions of knowledge. But on Stroud's skeptic's conception, when we ascribe knowledge in everyday situations, we are typically saying something literally false, although "the exigencies of action" justify these false attributions. The best exploration of this type of idea is provided by Unger 1984.

43. Going back to the bold skeptic's first problem, note that all this maneuvering can be mimicked by the Moorean, who can also hold that a Rule of Sensitivity governs the warranted assertability conditions of knowledge ascriptions. Like the bold skeptic, the Moorean can hold that the truth conditions of such attributions of knowledge remain invariant, but in the Moorean's hands, these constant epistemic standards will be meetably low.

44. Readers of Unger's 1984 will see the strong influence of that excellent book on my procedure here, though I come to very different conclusions than he does in that work. (But see his more recent 1986.)

45. See Stroud 1984, p. 40, who in turn borrowed the example from elsewhere.

46. Of course, skeptics are free to refuse this help and propose other solutions. Like practically any claim to have provided the best explanation of something, my claim here is hostage to the possible future development of a better explanation coming along.

47. Well, little reason. In his 1984, as part of his case for his relativist conclusion that there's no fact of the matter as to whether contextualism or skeptical invariantism is correct, Unger tries to balance this relative disadvantage of skeptical invariantism against contextualism's relative disadvantage that it does not make the truth conditions of knowledge attributions appropriately independent from the current intents and interests of those who happen to be speaking on a given occasion (in this volume, pp. 258–261). In part 3 of my 1992, I argue that contextualism can handle the most serious consequences one might suspect would follow from this lack of independence. Whatever independence concerns might remain with contextualism seem quite swamped by the cost of the bold skeptic's solution, which, as I've here argued, is quite high indeed.

In his review of Unger 1984, Brueckner, relating the advantages of invariantism, writes, "In particular, speakers' intuitions concerning the correct use of 'know' seem to conform to the closure principle for knowledge asserted by the invariantist yet denied by the contextualist" (1986c, p. 512). If invariantism, but not contextualism, upheld closure, I would take this to be a very important advantage for invariantism—perhaps even weighty enough to make the contest between the two theories interesting. But, as I've argued, contextualism need not, and, properly developed, does not, take an implausible stand on the issue of closure. (See section 10 and especially note 33, above.)

48. I discuss this in section II.B of my 1989.

49. This paper is dedicated to the memory of Ken Konyndyk, my first philosophy teacher. Thanks to Anthony Brueckner, John Carroll, Graeme Forbes, Richard Grandy, Mark Heller, Edward Stein, Holly Thomas, an anonymous reader for the *Philosophical Review*, and to audiences at Rice University and at the University of Virginia, Charlottesville for helpful comments on earlier drafts of this paper. Special thanks are due to Peter Unger for his important writings on this topic, from which I've learned much; for three years of almost daily philosophical discussions, many of which were on the topic of knowledge and skepticism and almost all of which were enjoyable and enlightening; and for his many comments on various drafts of this paper and its ancestors.

CHAPTER 12   # Elusive Knowledge

David Lewis

We know a lot. I know what food penguins eat. I know that phones used to ring, but nowadays squeal, when someone calls up. I know that Essendon won the 1993 Grand Final. I know that here is a hand, and here is another.

We have all sorts of everyday knowledge, and we have it in abundance. To doubt that would be absurd. At any rate, to doubt it in any serious and lasting way would be absurd; and even philosophical and temporary doubt, under the influence of argument, is more than a little peculiar. It is a Moorean fact that we know a lot. It is one of those things that we know better than we know the premises of any philosophical argument to the contrary.

Besides knowing a lot that is everyday and trite, I myself think that we know a lot that is interesting and esoteric and controversial. We know a lot about things unseen: tiny particles and pervasive fields, not to mention one another's underwear. Sometimes we even know what an author meant by his writings. But on these questions, let us agree to disagree peacefully with the champions of 'post-knowledgeism'. The most trite and ordinary parts of our knowledge will be problem enough.

For no sooner do we engage in epistemology—the systematic philosophical examination of knowledge—than we meet a compelling argument that we know next to nothing. The sceptical argument is nothing new or fancy. It is just this: it seems as if knowledge must be by definition infallible. If you claim that *S* knows that *P*, and yet you grant that *S* cannot eliminate a certain

"Elusive Knowledge" from the *Australasian Journal of Philosophy* 74 (1996, pp. 549–567). Reprinted by permission of the publisher.

Thanks to many for valuable discussions of this material. Thanks above all to Peter Unger; and to Stewart Cohen, Michael Devitt, Alan Hajek, Stephen Hetherington, Denis Robinson, Ernest Sosa, Robert Stalnaker, Jonathan Vogel, and a referee for this Journal. Thanks also to the Boyce Gibson Memorial Library and to Ormond College.

possibility in which not-P, it certainly seems as if you have granted that S does not after all know that P. To speak of fallible knowledge, of knowledge despite uneliminated possibilities of error, just *sounds* contradictory.

Blind Freddy can see where this will lead. Let your paranoid fantasies rip—CIA plots, hallucinogens in the tap water, conspiracies to deceive, old Nick himself—and soon you find that uneliminated possibilities of error are everywhere. Those possibilities of error are far-fetched, of course, but possibilities all the same. They bite into even our most everyday knowledge. We never have infallible knowledge.

Never—well, hardly ever. Some say we have infallible knowledge of a few simple, axiomatic necessary truths; and of our own present experience. They say that I simply cannot be wrong that a part of a part of something is itself a part of that thing; or that it seems to me now (as I sit here at the keyboard) exactly as if I am hearing clicking noises on top of a steady whirring. Some say so. Others deny it. No matter; let it be granted, at least for the sake of the argument. It is not nearly enough. If we have only that much infallible knowledge, yet knowledge is by definition infallible, then we have very little knowledge indeed—not the abundant everyday knowledge we thought we had. That is still absurd.

So we know a lot; knowledge must be infallible; yet we have fallible knowledge or none (or next to none). We are caught between the rock of fallibilism and the whirlpool of scepticism. Both are mad!

Yet fallibilism is the less intrusive madness. It demands less frequent corrections of what we want to say. So, if forced to choose, I choose fallibilism. (And so say all of us.) We can get used to it, and some of us have done. No joy there—we know that people can get used to the most crazy philosophical sayings imaginable. If you are a contented fallibilist, I implore you to be honest, be naive, hear it afresh. 'He knows, yet he has not eliminated all possibilities of error.' Even if you've numbed your ears, doesn't this overt, explicit fallibilism *still* sound wrong?

Better fallibilism than scepticism; but it would be better still to dodge the choice. I think we can. We will be alarmingly close to the rock, and also alarmingly close to the whirlpool, but if we steer with care, we can—just barely—escape them both.

Maybe epistemology is the culprit. Maybe this extraordinary pastime robs us of our knowledge. Maybe we do know a lot in daily life; but maybe when we look hard at our knowledge, it goes away. But only when we look at it harder than the sane ever do in daily life; only when we let our paranoid fantasies rip. That is when we are forced to admit that there always are uneliminated possibilities of error, so that we have fallible knowledge or none.

Much that we say is context-dependent, in simple ways or subtle ways. Simple: 'it's evening' is truly said when, and only when, it is said in the evening. Subtle: it could well be true, and not just by luck, that Essendon played rottenly, the Easybeats played brilliantly, yet Essendon won. Different contexts evoke different standards of evaluation. Talking about the Easybeats we apply lax standards, else we could scarcely distinguish their better days from their worse ones. In talking about Essendon, no such laxity is required. Essendon won because play that is rotten by demanding standards suffices to beat play that is brilliant by lax standards.

Maybe ascriptions of knowledge are subtly context-dependent, and maybe epistemology is a context that makes them go false. Then epistemology would be an investigation that destroys its own subject matter. If so, the sceptical argument might be flawless, when we engage in epistemology—and only then![1]

If you start from the ancient idea that justification is the mark that distinguishes knowledge from mere opinion (even true opinion), then you well might conclude that ascriptions of knowledge are context-dependent because standards for adequate justification are context-dependent. As follows: opinion, even if true, deserves the name of knowledge only if it is adequately supported by reasons; to deserve that name in the especially demanding context of epistemology, the arguments from supporting reasons must be especially watertight; but the special standards of justification that this special context demands never can be met (well, hardly ever). In the strict context of epistemology we know nothing, yet in laxer contexts we know a lot.

But I myself cannot subscribe to this account of the context-dependence of knowledge, because I question its starting point. I don't agree that the mark of knowledge is justification.[2] First, because justification is not sufficient: your true opinion that you will lose the lottery isn't knowledge, whatever the odds. Suppose you know that it is a fair lottery with one winning ticket and many losing tickets, and you know how many losing tickets there are. The greater the number of losing tickets, the better is your justification for believing you will lose. Yet there is no number great enough to transform your fallible opinion into knowledge—after all, you just might win. No justification is good enough—or none short of a watertight deductive argument, and all but the sceptics will agree that this is too much to demand.[3]

Second, because justification is not always necessary. What (non-circular) argument supports our reliance on perception, on memory, and on testimony?[4] And yet we do gain knowledge by these means. And sometimes, far from having supporting arguments, we don't even know how we know. We once had evidence, drew conclusions, and thereby gained knowledge; now we have forgotten our reasons, yet still we retain our knowledge. Or we know the name that goes with the face, or the sex of the chicken, by relying on subtle visual cues, without knowing what those cues may be.

The link between knowledge and justification must be broken. But if we break that link, then it is not—or not entirely, or not exactly—by raising the standards of justification that epistemology destroys knowledge. I need some different story.

To that end, I propose to take the infallibility of knowledge as my starting point.[5] Must infallibilist epistemology end in scepticism? Not quite. Wait and see. Anyway, here is the definition. Subject S *knows* proposition P iff P holds in every possibility left uneliminated by S's evidence; equivalently, iff S's evidence eliminates every possibility in which not-P.

The definition is short, the commentary upon it is longer. In the first place, there is the proposition, P. What I choose to call 'propositions' are individuated coarsely, by necessary equivalence. For instance, there is only one necessary proposition. It holds in every possibility; hence in every possibility left uneliminated by S's evidence, no matter who S may be and no matter what his evidence may be. So the necessary proposition is known always and everywhere. Yet this known proposition may go unrecognised when presented in impenetrable linguistic disguise, say as the proposition that every even number is the sum of two primes. Likewise, the known proposition that I have two hands may go unrecognised when presented as the proposition that the number of my hands is the least number n such that every even number is the sum of n primes. (Or if you doubt the necessary existence of numbers, switch to an example involving equivalence by logic alone.) These problems of disguise shall not concern us here. Our topic is modal, not hyperintensional, epistemology.[6]

Next, there are the possibilities. We needn't enter here into the question whether these are concreta, abstract constructions, or abstract simples. Further, we needn't decide whether they must always be maximally specific possibilities, or whether they need only be specific enough for the purpose at hand. A possibility will be specific enough if it cannot be split into subcases in such a way that anything we have said about possibilities, or anything we are going to say before we are done, applies to some subcases and not to others. For instance, it should never happen that proposition P holds in some but not all sub-cases; or that some but not all sub-cases are eliminated by S's evidence.

But we do need to stipulate that they are not just possibilities as to how the whole world is; they also include possibilities as to which part of the world is oneself, and as to when it now is. We need these possibilities *de se et nunc* because the propositions that may be known include propositions *de se et nunc.*[7] Not only do I know that there are hands in this world somewhere and somewhen. I know that *I* have hands, or anyway I have them *now.* Such propositions aren't just made true or made false by the whole world once and for all. They are true for some of us and not for others, or true at some times and not others, or both.

Further, we cannot limit ourselves to 'real' possibilities that conform to the actual laws of nature, and maybe also to actual past history. For propositions about laws and history are contingent, and may or may not be known.

Neither can we limit ourselves to 'epistemic' possibilities for S—possibilities that S does not know not to obtain. That would drain our definition of content. Assume only that knowledge is closed under strict implication. (We shall consider the merits of this assumption later.) Remember that we are not distinguishing between equivalent propositions. Then knowledge of a conjunction is equivalent to knowledge of every conjunct. P is the conjunction of all propositions not-W, where W is a possibility in which not-P. That suffices to yield an equivalence: S knows that P iff, for every possibility W in which not-P, S knows that not-W. Contraposing and cancelling a double negation: iff every possibility which S does not know not to obtain is one in which P. For short: iff P holds throughout S's epistemic possibilities. Yet to get this far, we need no substantive definition of knowledge at all! To turn this into a substantive definition, in fact the very definition we gave before, we need to say one more thing: S's epistemic possibilities are just those possibilities that are uneliminated by S's evidence.

So, next, we need to say what it means for a possibility to be eliminated or not. Here I say that the uneliminated possibilities are those in which the subject's entire perceptual experience and memory are just as they actually are. There is one possibility that actually obtains (for the subject and at the time in question); call it *actuality*. Then a possibility W is *uneliminated* iff the subject's perceptual experience and memory in W exactly match his perceptual experience and memory in actuality. (If you want to include other alleged forms of basic evidence, such as the evidence of our extrasensory faculties, or an innate disposition to believe in God, be my guest. If they exist, they should be included. If not, no harm done if we have included them conditionally.)

Note well that we do not need the 'pure sense-datum language' and the 'incorrigible protocol statements' that for so long bedevilled foundationalist epistemology. It matters not at all whether there are words to capture the subject's perceptual and memory evidence, nothing more and nothing less. If there are such words, it matters not at all whether the subject can hit upon them. The given does not consist of basic axioms to serve as premises in subsequent arguments. Rather, it consists of a match between possibilities.

When perceptual experience E (or memory) eliminates a possibility W, that is not because the propositional content of the experience conflicts with W. (Not even if it is the narrow content.) The propositional content of our experience could, after all, be false. Rather, it is the existence of the experience that conflicts with W: W is a possibility in which the subject is not having experience E. Else we would need to tell some fishy story of how the experience has some sort of infallible, ineffable, purely phenomenal propositional content . . . Who needs that? Let E have propositional content P. Suppose even—something I take to be an open question—that E is, in some sense, fully characterized by P. Then I say that E eliminates W iff W is a possibility in which the subject's experience or memory has content different from P. I do *not* say that E eliminates W iff W is a possibility in which P is false.

Maybe not every kind of sense perception yields experience; maybe, for instance, the kinaesthetic sense yields not its own distinctive sort of sense-experience but only spontaneous judgements about the position of one's limbs. If this is true, then the thing to say is that kinaesthetic evidence eliminates all possibilities except those that exactly resemble actuality with respect to the subject's spontaneous kinaesthetic judgements. In saying this, we would treat kinaesthetic evidence more on the model of memory than on the model of more typical senses.

Finally, we must attend to the word 'every'. What does it mean to say that every possibility in which not-*P* is eliminated? An idiom of quantification, like 'every', is normally restricted to some limited domain. If I say that every glass is empty, so it's time for another round, doubtless I and my audience are ignoring most of all the glasses there are in the whole wide world throughout all of time. They are outside the domain. They are irrelevant to the truth of what was said.

Likewise, if I say that every uneliminated possibility is one in which *P*, or words to that effect, I am doubtless ignoring some of all the uneliminated alternative possibilities that there are. They are outside the domain, they are irrelevant to the truth of what was said.

But, of course, I am not entitled to ignore just any possibility I please. Else true ascriptions of knowledge, whether to myself or to others, would be cheap indeed. I may properly ignore some uneliminated possibilities; I may not properly ignore others. Our definition of knowledge requires a *sotto voce* proviso. *S knows* that *P* iff *S*'s evidence eliminates every possibility in which not-*P*—Psst!—except for those possibilities that we are properly ignoring.

Unger suggests an instructive parallel.[8] Just as *P* is known iff there are no uneliminated possibilities of error, so likewise a surface is flat iff there are no bumps on it. We must add the proviso: Psst!—except for those bumps that we are properly ignoring. Else we will conclude, absurdly, that nothing is flat. (Simplify by ignoring departures from flatness that consist of gentle curvature.)

We can restate the definition. Say that we *presuppose* proposition *Q* iff we ignore all possibilities in which not-*Q*. To close the circle: we *ignore* just those possibilities that falsify our presuppositions. *Proper* presupposition corresponds, of course, to proper ignoring. Then *S* knows that *P* iff *S*'s evidence eliminates every possibility in which not-*P*—Psst!—except for those possibilities that conflict with our proper presuppositions.[9]

The rest of (modal) epistemology examines the *sotto voce* proviso. It asks: what may we properly presuppose in our ascriptions of knowledge? Which of all the uneliminated alternative possibilities may not properly be ignored? Which ones are the 'relevant alternatives'?—relevant, that is, to what the subject does and doesn't know?[10] In reply, we can list several rules.[11] We begin with three prohibitions: rules to tell us what possibilities we may not properly ignore.

First, there is the *Rule of Actuality.* The possibility that actually obtains is never properly ignored; actuality is always a relevant alternative; nothing false may properly be presupposed. It follows that only what is true is known, wherefore we did not have to include truth in our definition of knowledge. The rule is 'externalist'—the subject himself may not be able to tell what is properly ignored. In judging which of his ignorings are proper, hence what he knows, we judge his success in knowing—not how well he tried.

When the Rule of Actuality tells us that actuality may never be properly ignored, we can ask: *whose* actuality? Ours, when we ascribe knowledge or ignorance to others? Or the subject's? In simple cases, the question is silly. (In fact, it sounds like the sort of pernicious nonsense we would expect from someone who mixes up what is true with what is believed.) There is just one actual world, we the ascribers live in that world, the subject lives there too, so the subject's actuality is the same as ours.

But there are other cases, less simple, in which the question makes perfect sense and needs an answer. Someone may or may not know who he is; someone may or may not know what time it is. Therefore I insisted that the propositions that may be known must include propositions *de se et nunc*; and likewise that the possibilities that may be eliminated or ignored must include possibilities *de se et nunc*. Now we have a good sense in which the subject's actuality may be different from ours. I ask today what Fred knew yesterday. In particular, did he then know who he was? Did he know what day it was? Fred's actuality is the possibility *de se et nunc* of being Fred on September 19th at such-and-such possible world; whereas my actuality is the possibility *de se et nunc* of being David on September 20th at such-and-such world. So far as the world goes, there is no difference: Fred and I are worldmates, his actual world is the same as mine. But when we build subject and time into the possibilities *de se et nunc*, then his actuality yesterday does indeed differ from mine today.

What is more, we sometimes have occasion to ascribe knowledge to those who are off at other possible worlds. I didn't read the newspaper yesterday. What would I have known if I had read it? More than I do in fact know. (More and less: I do in fact know that I left the newspaper unread, but if I had read it, I would not have known that I had left it unread.) I-who-did-not-read-the-newspaper am here at this world, ascribing knowledge and ignorance. The subject to whom I am ascribing that knowledge and ignorance, namely I-as-I-would-have-been-if-I-had-read-the-newspaper, is at a different world. The worlds differ in respect at least of a reading of the newspaper. Thus the ascriber's actual world is not the same as the subject's. (I myself think that the ascriber and the subject are two different people: the subject is the ascriber's otherworldly counterpart. But even if you think the subject and the ascriber are the same identical person, you must still grant that this person's actuality *qua* subject differs from his actuality *qua* ascriber.)

Or suppose we ask modal questions about the subject: what must he have known, what might he have known? Again we are considering the subject as he is not here, but off at other possible worlds. Likewise if we ask questions about knowledge of knowledge: what does he (or what do we) know that he knows?

So the question 'whose actuality?' is not a silly question after all. And when the question matters, as it does in the cases just considered, the right answer is that it is the subject's actuality, not the ascriber's, that never can be properly ignored.

Next, there is the *Rule of Belief.* A possibility that the subject believes to obtain is not properly ignored, whether or not he is right to so believe. Neither is one that he ought to believe to obtain—one that evidence and arguments justify him in believing—whether or not he does so believe.

That is rough. Since belief admits of degree, and since some possibilities are more specific than others, we ought to reformulate the rule in terms of degree of belief, compared to a standard set by the unspecificity of the possibility in question. A possibility may not be properly ignored if the subject gives it, or ought to give it, a degree of belief that is sufficiently high, and high not just because the possibility in question is unspecific.

How high is 'sufficiently high'? That may depend on how much is at stake. When error would be especially disastrous, few possibilities may be properly ignored. Then even quite a low degree of belief may be 'sufficiently high' to bring the Rule of Belief into play. The jurors know that the accused is guilty only if his guilt has been proved beyond reasonable doubt.[12]

Yet even when the stakes are high, some possibilities still may be properly ignored. Disastrous though it would be to convict an innocent man, still the jurors may properly ignore the possibility that it was the dog, marvellously well-trained, that fired the fatal shot. And, unless they are ignoring other alternatives more relevant than that, they may rightly be said to know that the accused is guilty as charged. Yet if there had been reason to give the dog hypothesis a slightly less negligible degree of belief—if the world's greatest dog-trainer had been the victim's mortal enemy—then the alternative would be relevant after all.

This is the only place where belief and justification enter my story. As already noted, I allow justified true belief without knowledge, as in the case of your belief that you will lose the lottery. I allow knowledge without justification, in the cases of face recognition and chicken sexing. I even allow knowledge without belief, as in the case of the timid student who knows the answer but has no confidence that he has it right, and so does not believe what he knows.[13] Therefore any proposed converse to the Rule of Belief should be rejected. A possibility that the subject does not believe to a sufficient degree, and ought not to believe to a sufficient degree, may nevertheless be a relevant alternative and not properly ignored.

Next, there is the *Rule of Resemblance*. Suppose one possibility saliently resembles another. Then if one of them may not be properly ignored, neither may the other. (Or rather, we should say that if one of them may not properly be ignored *in virtue of rules other than this rule*, then neither may the other. Else nothing could be properly ignored; because enough little steps of resemblance can take us from anywhere to anywhere.) Or suppose one possibility saliently resembles two or more others, one in one respect and another in another, and suppose that each of these may not properly be ignored (in virtue of rules other than this rule). Then these resemblances may have an additive effect, doing more together than any one of them would separately.

We must apply the Rule of Resemblance with care. Actuality is a possibility uneliminated by the subject's evidence. Any other possibility W that is likewise uneliminated by the subject's evidence thereby resembles actuality in one salient respect: namely, in respect of the subject's evidence. That will be so even if W is in other respects very dissimilar to actuality—even if, for instance, it is a possibility in which the subject is radically deceived by a demon. Plainly, we dare not apply the Rules of Actuality and Reemblance to conclude that any such W is a relevant alternative—that would be capitulation to scepticism. The Rule of Resemblance was never meant to apply to *this* resemblance! We seem to have an *ad hoc* exception to the Rule, though one that makes good sense in view of the function of attributions of knowledge. What would be better, though, would be to find a way to reformulate the Rule so as to get the needed exception without *ad hocery*. I do not know how to do this.

It is the Rule of Resemblance that explains why you do not know that you will lose the lottery, no matter what the odds are against you and no matter how sure you should therefore be that you will lose. For every ticket, there is the possibility that it will win. These possibilities are saliently similar to one another: so either every one of them may be properly ignored, or else none may. But one of them may not properly be ignored: the one that actually obtains.

The Rule of Resemblance also is the rule that solves the Gettier problems: other cases of justified true belief that are not knowledge.[14]

(1) I think that Nogot owns a Ford, because I have seen him driving one; but unbeknownst to me he does not own the Ford he drives, or any other Ford. Unbeknownst to me, Havit does own a Ford, though I have no reason to think so because he never drives it, and in fact I have often seen him taking the tram. My justified true belief is that one of the two owns a Ford. But I do not know it; I am right by accident. Diagnosis: I do not know, because I have not eliminated the possibility that Nogot drives a Ford he does not own whereas Havit neither drives nor owns a car. This possibility may not properly be ignored. Because, first, actuality may not properly be ignored; and, second, this possibility saliently resembles actuality. It resembles actuality perfectly so far as Nogot is concerned; and it resembles actuality well so far as Havit is concerned, since it matches actuality both with respect to Havit's carless habits and with respect to the general correlation between carless habits and carlessness. In addition, this possibility saliently resembles a third possibility: one in which Nogot drives a Ford he owns while Havit neither drives nor owns a car. This third possibility may not properly be ignored, because of the degree to which it is believed. This time, the resemblance is perfect so far as Havit is concerned, rather good so far as Nogot is concerned.

(2) The stopped clock is right twice a day. It says 4:39, as it has done for weeks. I look at it at 4:39; by luck I pick up a true belief. I have ignored the uneliminated possibility that I looked at it at 4:22 while it was stopped saying 4:39. That possibility was not properly ignored. It resembles actuality perfectly so far as the stopped clock goes.

(3) Unbeknownst to me, I am travelling in the land of the bogus barns; but my eye falls on one of the few real ones. I don't know that I am seeing a barn, because I may not properly ignore the possibility that I am seeing yet another of the abundant bogus barns. This possibility saliently resembles actuality in respect of the abundance of bogus barns, and the scarcity of real ones, hereabouts.

(4) Donald is in San Francisco, just as I have every reason to think he is. But, bent on deception, he is writing me letters and having them posted to me by his accomplice in Italy. If I had seen the phoney letters, with their Italian stamps and postmarks, I would have concluded that Donald was in Italy. Luckily, I have not yet seen any of them. I ignore the uneliminated possibility that Donald has gone to Italy and is sending me letters from there. But this possibility is not properly ignored, because it resembles actuality both with respect to the fact that the letters are coming to me from Italy and with respect to the fact that those letters come, ultimately, from Donald. So I don't know that Donald is in San Francisco.

Next, there is the *Rule of Reliability.* This time, we have a presumptive rule about what *may* be properly ignored; and it is by means of this rule that we capture what is right about causal or reliabilist theories of knowing. Consider processes whereby information is transmitted to us: perception, memory, and testimony. These processes are fairly reliable.[15] Within limits, we are entitled to take them for granted. We may properly presuppose that they work without a glitch in the case under consideration. Defeasibly—*very* defeasibly!—a possibility in which they fail may properly be ignored.

My visual experience, for instance, depends causally on the scene before my eyes, and what I believe about the scene before my eyes depends in turn on my visual experience. Each dependence covers a wide and varied range of alternatives.[16] Of course, it is possible to hallucinate—even to hallucinate in such a way that all my perceptual experience and memory would be just as they actually are. That possibility never can be eliminated. But it can be ignored. And if it is properly ignored—as it mostly is—then vision gives me knowledge. Sometimes, though, the possibility of hallucination is not properly ignored; for sometimes we really do hallucinate. The Rule of Reliability may be defeated by the Rule of Actuality. Or it may be defeated by the Rules of Actuality and of Resemblance working together, in a Gettier problem: if I am not hallucinating, but unbeknownst to me I live in a world where people mostly do hallucinate and I myself have only narrowly escaped, then the uneliminated possibility of hallucination is too close to actuality to be properly ignored.

We do not, of course, presuppose that nowhere ever is there a failure of, say, vision. The general presupposition that vision is reliable consists, rather, of a standing disposition to presuppose, concerning whatever particular case may be under consideration, that we have no failure in that case.

In similar fashion, we have two permissive *Rules of Method.* We are entitled to presuppose—again, very defeasibly—that a sample is representative; and that the best explanation of our evidence is the true explanation. That is, we are entitled properly to ignore possible failures in these two standard methods of non-deductive inference. Again, the general rule consists of a standing disposition to presuppose reliability in whatever particular case may come before us.

Yet another permissive rule is the *Rule of Conservatism*. Suppose that those around us normally do ignore certain possibilities, and it is common knowledge that they do. (They do, they expect each other to, they expect each other to expect each other to, ...) Then—again, very defeasibly!—these generally ignored possibilities may properly be ignored. We are permitted, defeasibly, to adopt the usual and mutually expected presuppositions of those around us.

(It is unclear whether we need all four of these permissive rules. Some might be subsumed under others. Perhaps our habits of treating samples as representative, and of inferring to the best explanation, might count as normally reliable processes of transmission of information. Or perhaps we might subsume the Rule of Reliability under the Rule of Conservatism, on the ground that the reliable processes whereby we gain knowledge are familiar, are generally relied upon, and so are generally presupposed to be normally reliable. Then the only extra work done by the Rule of Reliability would be to cover less familiar—and merely hypothetical?—reliable processes, such as processes that relied on extrasensory faculties. Likewise, *mutatis mutandis*, we might subsume the Rules of Method under the Rule of Conservatism. Or we might instead think to subsume the Rule of Conservatism under the Rule of Reliability, on the ground that what is generally presupposed tends for the most part to be true, and the reliable processes whereby this is so are covered already by the Rule of Reliability. Better redundancy than incompleteness, though. So, leaving the question of redundancy open, I list all four rules.)

Our final rule is the *Rule of Attention*. But it is more a triviality than a rule. When we say that a possibility *is* properly ignored, we mean exactly that; we do not mean that it *could have been* properly ignored. Accordingly, a possibility not ignored at all is *ipso facto* not properly ignored. What is and what is not being ignored is a feature of the particular conversational context. No matter how far-fetched a certain possibility may be, no matter how properly we might have ignored it in some other context, if in *this* context we are not in fact ignoring it but attending to it, then for us now it is a relevant alternative. It is in the contextually determined domain. If it is an uneliminated possibility in which not-P, then it will do as a counter-example to the claim that P holds in every possibility left uneliminated by S's evidence. That is, it will do as a counter-example to the claim that S knows that P.

Do some epistemology. Let your fantasies rip. Find uneliminated possibilities of error everywhere. Now that you are attending to them, just as I told you to, you are no longer ignoring them, properly or otherwise. So you have landed in a context with an enormously rich domain of potential counter-examples to ascriptions of knowledge. In such an extraordinary context, with such a rich domain, it never can happen (well, hardly ever) that an ascription of knowledge is true. Not an ascription of knowledge to yourself (either to your present self or to your earlier self, untainted by epistemology); and not an ascription of knowledge to others. That is how epistemology destroys knowledge. But it does so only temporarily. The pastime of epistemology does not plunge us forevermore into its special context. We can still do a lot of proper ignoring, a lot of knowing, and a lot of true ascribing of knowledge to ourselves and others, the rest of the time.

What is epistemology all about? The epistemology we've just been doing, at any rate, soon became an investigation of the ignoring of possibilities. But to investigate the ignoring of them was *ipso facto* not to ignore them. Unless this investigation of ours was an altogether atypical sample of epistemology, it will be inevitable that epistemology must destroy knowledge. That is how knowledge is elusive. Examine it, and straightway it vanishes.

Is resistance useless? If you bring some hitherto ignored possibility to our attention, then straightway we are not ignoring it at all, so *a fortiori* we are not properly ignoring it. How can this alteration of our conversational state be undone? If you are persistent, perhaps it cannot be undone—at least not so long as you are around. Even if we go off and play backgammon, and afterward start our conversation afresh, you might turn up and call our attention to it all over again.

But maybe you called attention to the hitherto ignored possibility by mistake. You only suggested that we ought to suspect the butler because you mistakenly thought him to have a criminal record. Now that you know he does not—that was the *previous* butler—you wish you had not mentioned him at all. You knows as well as we do that continued attention to the possibility you brought up impedes our shared conversational purposes. Indeed, it may be common knowledge between you and us that we would all prefer it if this possibility could be dismissed from our attention. In that case we might quickly strike a tacit agreement to speak just as if we were ignoring it; and after just a little of that, doubtless it really would be ignored.

Sometimes our conversational purposes are not altogether shared, and it is a matter of conflict whether attention to some far-fetched possibility would advance them or impede them. What if some far-fetched possibility is called to our attention not by a sceptical philosopher, but by counsel for the defence? We of the jury may wish to ignore it, and wish it had not been mentioned. If we ignored it now, we would bend the rules of cooperative conversation; but we may have good reason to do exactly that. (After all, what matters most to us as jurors is not whether we can truly be said to know; what really matters is what we should believe to what degree, and whether or not we should vote to convict.) We would ignore the far-fetched possibility if we could—but can we? Perhaps at first our attempted ignoring would be make-believe ignoring, or self-deceptive ignoring; later, perhaps, it might ripen into genuine ignoring. But in the meantime, do we know? There may be no definite answer. We are bending the rules, and our practices of context-dependent attributions of knowledge were made for contexts with the rules unbent.

If you are still a contented fallibilist, despite my plea to hear the sceptical argument afresh, you will probably be discontented with the Rule of Attention. You will begrudge the sceptic even his very temporary victory. You will claim the right to resist his argument not only in everyday contexts, but even in those peculiar contexts in which he (or some other epistemologist) busily calls your attention to far-fetched possibilities of error. Further, you will claim the right to resist without having to bend any rules of cooperative conversation. I said that the Rule of Attention was a triviality: that which is not ignored at all is not properly ignored. But the Rule was trivial only because of how I had already chosen to state the *sotto voce* proviso. So you, the contented fallibilist, will think it ought to have been stated differently. Thus, perhaps: 'Psst!—except for those possibilities we *could* properly have ignored'. And then you will insist that those far-fetched possibilities of error that we attend to at the behest of the sceptic are nevertheless possibilities we could properly have ignored. You will say that no amount of attention can, by itself, turn them into relevant alternatives.

If you say this, we have reached a standoff. I started with a puzzle: how can it be, when his conclusion is so silly, that the sceptic's argument is so irresistible? My Rule of Attention, and the version of the proviso that made that Rule trivial, were built to explain how the sceptic manages to sway us—why his argument seems irresistible, however temporarily. If you continue to find it eminently resistible in all contexts, you have no need of any such explanation. We just disagree about the explanandum phenomenon.

I say S knows that P iff P holds in every possibility left uneliminated by S's evidence—Psst!—except for those possibilities that *we* are properly ignoring. 'We' means: the speaker and hearers of a given context; that is, those of us who are discussing S's knowledge together. It is our ignorings, not S's own ignorings, that matter to what we can truly say about S's knowledge. When we are talking about our own knowledge or ignorance, as epistemologists so often do, this is a distinction without a difference. But what if we are talking about someone else?

Suppose we are detectives; the crucial question for our solution of the crime is whether S already *knew*, when he bought the gun, that he was vulnerable to blackmail. We conclude that he did. *We* ignore various far-fetched possibilities, as hard-headed detectives should. But S does not ignore them. S is by profession a sceptical epistemologist. He never ignores much of anything. If it is our own ignorings that matter to the truth of our conclusion, we may well be right that S already knew. But if it is S's ignorings that matter, then we are wrong, because S never knew much of anything. I say we may well be right; so it is our own ignorings that matter, not S's.

But suppose instead that we are epistemologists considering what S knows. If we are well-informed about S (or if we are considering a well-enough specified hypothetical case), then if S attends to a certain possibility, we attend to S's attending to it. But to attend to S's attending to it is *ipso facto* to attend to it ourselves. In that case, unlike the case of the detectives, the possibilities we are properly ignoring must be among the possibilities that S himself ignores. We may ignore fewer possibilities than S does, but not more.

Even if S himself is neither sceptical nor an epistemologist, he may yet be clever at thinking up far-fetched possibilities that are uneliminated by his evidence. Then again, we well-informed epistemologists who ask what S knows will have to attend to the possibilities that S thinks up. Even if S's idle cleverness does not lead S himself to draw sceptical conclusions, it nevertheless limits the knowledge that we can truly ascribe to him when attentive to his state of mind. More simply: his cleverness limits his knowledge. He would have known more, had he been less imaginative.[17]

Do I claim you can know P just by presupposing it?! Do I claim you can know that a possibility W does not obtain just by ignoring it? Is that not what my analysis implies, provided that the presupposing and the ignoring are proper? Well, yes. And yet I do not claim it. Or rather, I do not claim it for any specified P or W. I have to grant, in general, that knowledge just by presupposing and ignoring *is* knowledge; but it is an *especially* elusive sort of knowledge, and consequently it is an unclaimable sort of knowledge. You do not even have to practise epistemology to make it vanish. Simply *mentioning* any particular case of this knowledge, aloud or even in silent thought, is a way to attend to the hitherto ignored possibility, and thereby render it no longer ignored, and thereby create a context in which it is no longer true to ascribe the knowledge in question to yourself or others. So, just as we should think, presuppositions alone are not a basis on which to *claim* knowledge.

In general, when S knows that P some of the possibilities in which not-P are eliminated by S's evidence and others of them are properly ignored. There are some that can be eliminated, but cannot properly be ignored. For instance, when I look around the study without seeing Possum the cat, I thereby eliminate various possibilities in which Possum is in the study; but had those possibilities not been eliminated, they could not properly have been ignored. And there are other possibilities that never can be eliminated, but can properly be ignored. For instance, the possibility that Possum is on the desk but has been made invisible by a deceiving demon falls normally into this class (though not when I attend to it in the special context of epistemology).

There is a third class: not-*P* possibilities that might either be eliminated or ignored. Take the far-fetched possibility that Possum has somehow managed to get into a closed drawer of the desk—maybe he jumped in when it was open, then I closed it without noticing him. That possibility could be eliminated by opening the drawer and making a thorough examination. But if uneliminated, it may nevertheless be ignored, and in many contexts that ignoring would be proper. If I look all around the study, but without checking the closed drawers of the desk, I may truly be said to know that Possum is not in the study—or at any rate, there are many contexts in which that may truly be said. But if I did check all the closed drawers, then I would know *better* that Possum is not in the study. My knowledge would be better in the second case because it would rest more on the elimination of not-*P* possibilities, less on the ignoring of them.[18,19]

Better knowledge is more stable knowledge: it stands more chance of surviving a shift of attention in which we begin to attend to some of the possibilities formerly ignored. If, in our new shifted context, we ask what knowledge we may truly ascribe to our earlier selves, we may find that only the better knowledge of our earlier selves still deserves the name. And yet, if our former ignorings were proper at the time, even the worse knowledge of our earlier selves could truly have been called knowledge in the former context.

Never—well, hardly ever—does our knowledge rest entirely on elimination and not at all on ignoring. So hardly ever is it quite as good as we might wish. To that extent, the lesson of scepticism is right—and right permanently, not just in the temporary and special context of epistemology.[20]

What is it all for? Why have a notion of knowledge that works in the way I described? (Not a compulsory question. Enough to observe that we do have it.) But I venture the guess that it is one of the messy short-cuts—like satisficing, like having indeterminate degrees of belief—that we resort to because we are not smart enough to live up to really high, perfectly Bayesian, standards of rationality. You cannot maintain a record of exactly which possibilities you have eliminated so far, much as you might like to. It is easier to keep track of which possibilities you have eliminated if you—Psst!—ignore many of all the possibilities there are. And besides, it is easier to list some of the propositions that are true in *all* the uneliminated, unignored possibilities than it is to find propositions that are true in *all and only* the uneliminated, unignored possibilities.

If you doubt that the word 'know' bears any real load in science or in metaphysics, I partly agree. The serious business of science has to do not with knowledge *per se*; but rather, with the elimination of possibilities through the evidence of perception, memory, etc., and with the changes that one's belief system would (or might or should) undergo under the impact of such eliminations. Ascriptions of knowledge to yourself or others are a very sloppy way of conveying very incomplete information about the elimination of possibilities. It is as if you had said:

The possibilities eliminated, whatever else they may also include, at least include all the not-P possibilities; or anyway, all of those except for some we are presumably prepared to ignore just at the moment.

The only excuse for giving information about what really maters in such a sloppy way is that at least it is easy and quick! But it *is* easy and quick; whereas giving full and precise information about which possibilities have been eliminated seems to be extremely difficult, as witness the futile search for a 'pure observation language'. If I am right about how ascriptions of knowledge work, they are a handy but humble approximation. They may yet be indispensable in practice, in the same way that other handy and humble approximations are.

If we analyse knowledge as a modality, as we have done, we cannot escape the conclusion that knowledge is closed under (strict) implication.[21] Dretske has denied that knowledge is closed under implication; further, he has diagnosed closure as the fallacy that drives arguments for scepticism. As follows: the proposition that I have hands implies that I am not a handless being, and *a fortiori* that I am not a handless being deceived by a demon into thinking that I have hands. So, by the closure principle, the proposition that I know I have hands implies that I know that I am not handless and deceived. But I don't know that I am not handless and deceived—for how can I eliminate that possibility? So, by *modus tollens*, I don't know that I have hands. Dretske's advice is to resist scepticism by denying closure. He says that although having hands *does* imply not being handless and deceived, yet knowing that I have hands *does not* imply knowing that I am not handless and deceived. I do know the former, I do not know the latter.

What Dretske says is close to right, but not quite. Knowledge *is* closed under implication. Knowing that I have hands *does* imply knowing that I am not handless and deceived. Implication preserves truth—that is, it preserves truth in any given, fixed context. But if we switch contexts midway, all bets are off. I say (1) pigs fly; (2) what I just said had fewer than three syllables (true); (3) what I just said had fewer than four syllables (false). So 'less than three' does not imply 'less than four'? No! The context switched midway, the semantic value of the context-dependent phrase 'what I just said' switched with it. Likewise in the sceptical argument the context switched midway, and the semantic value of the context-dependent word 'know' switched with it. The premise 'I know that I have hands' was true in its everyday context, where the possibility of deceiving demons was properly ignored. The mention of that very possibility switched the context midway. The conclusion 'I know that I am not handless and deceived' was false in *its* context, because that was a context in which the possibility of deceiving demons was being mentioned, hence was not being ignored, hence was not being properly ignored. Dretske gets the phenomenon right, and I think he gets the diagnosis of scepticism right; it is just that he misclassifies what he sees. He thinks it is a phenomenon of logic, when really it is a phenomenon of pragmatics. Closure, rightly understood, survives the test. If we evaluate the conclusion for truth not with respect to the context in which it was uttered, but instead with respect to the different context in which the premise was uttered, then truth is preserved. And if, *per impossibile,* the conclusion could have been said in the same unchanged context as the premise, truth would have been preserved.

A problem due to Saul Kripke turns upon the closure of knowledge under implication. *P* implies that any evidence against *P* is misleading. So, by closure, whenever you know that *P*, you know that any evidence against *P* is misleading. And if you know that evidence is misleading, you should pay it no heed. Whenever we know—and we know a lot, remember—we should not heed any evidence tending to suggest that we are wrong. But that is absurd. Shall we dodge the conclusion by denying closure? I think not. Again, I diagnose a change of context. At first, it was stipulated that *S* knew, whence it followed that *S* was properly ignoring all possibilities of error. But as the story continues, it turns out that there is evidence on offer that points to some particular possibility of error. Then, by the Rule of Attention, that possibility is no longer properly ignored, either by *S* himself or by we who are telling the story of *S*. The advent of that evidence destroys *S*'s knowledge, and thereby destroys *S*'s licence to ignore the evidence lest he be misled.

There is another reason, different from Dretske's, why we might doubt closure. Suppose two or more premises jointly imply a conclusion. Might not someone who is compartmentalized in his thinking—as we all are?—know each of the premises but fail to bring them together in a single compartment? Then might he not fail to know the conclusion? Yes; and I would not like to plead idealization-of-rationality as an excuse for ignoring such cases. But I suggest that we might take not the whole compartmentalized thinker, but rather each of his several overlapping compartments, as our 'subjects'. That would be the obvious remedy if his compartmentalization amounted to a case of multiple personality disorder; but maybe it is right for milder cases as well.[22]

A compartmentalized thinker who indulges in epistemology can destroy his knowledge, yet retain it as well. Imagine two epistemologists on a bushwalk. As they walk, they talk. They mention all manner of far-fetched possibilities of error. By attending to these normally ignored possibilities they destroy the knowledge they normally possess. Yet all the while they know where they are and where they are going! How so? The compartment in charge of philosophical talk attends to far-fetched possibilities of error. The compartment in charge of navigation does not. One compartment loses its knowledge, the other retains its knowledge. And what does the entire compartmentalized thinker know? Not an altogether felicitous question. But if we need an answer, I suppose the best thing to say is that *S* knows that *P* iff any one of *S*'s compartments knows that *P*. Then we can say what we would offhand want to say: yes, our philosophical bushwalkers still know their whereabouts.

Context-dependence is not limited to the ignoring and non-ignoring of far-fetched possibilities. Here is another case. Pity poor Bill! He squanders all his spare cash on the pokies, the races, and the lottery. He will be a wage slave all his days. We know he will never be rich. But if he wins the lottery (if he wins big), then he will be rich. Contrapositively: his never being rich, plus other things we know, imply that he will lose. So, by closure, if we know that he will never be rich, we know that he will lose. But when we discussed the case before, we concluded that we cannot know that he will lose. All the possibilities in which Bill loses and someone else wins saliently resemble the possibility in which Bill wins and the others lose; one of those possibilities is actual; so by the Rules of Actuality and of Resemblance, we may not properly ignore the possibility that Bill wins. But there is a loophole: the resemblance was required to be salient. Salience, as well as ignoring, may vary between contexts. Before, when I was explaining how the Rule of Resemblance applied to lotteries, I saw to it that the resemblance between the many possibilities associated with the many tickets was sufficiently salient. But this time, when we were busy pitying poor Bill for his habits and not for his luck, the resemblance of the many possibilities was not so salient. At that point, the possibility of Bill's winning was properly ignored; so then it was true to say that we knew he would never be rich. Afterward I switched the context. I mentioned the possibility that Bill might win, wherefore that possibility was no longer properly ignored. (Maybe there were two separate reasons why it was no longer properly ignored, because maybe I also made the resemblance between the many possibilities more salient.) It was true at first that we knew that Bill would never be rich. And at that point it was also true that we knew he would lose—but that was only true so long as it remained unsaid! (And maybe unthought as well.) Later, after the change in context, it was no longer true that we knew he would lose. At that point, it was also no longer true that we knew he would never be rich.

But wait. Don't you smell a rat? Haven't I, by my own lights, been saying what cannot be said? (Or whistled either.) If the story I told was true, how have I managed to tell it? In trendyspeak, is there not a problem of reflexivity? Does not my story deconstruct itself?

I said: S knows that P iff S's evidence eliminates every possibility in which not-P—Psst!—except for those possibilities that we are properly ignoring. That 'psst' marks an attempt to do the impossible—to mention that which remains unmentioned. I am sure you managed to make believe that I had succeeded. But I could not have done.

And I said that when we do epistemology, and we attend to the proper ignoring of possibilities, we make knowledge vanish. First we do know, then we do not. But I had been doing epistemology when I said that. The uneliminated possibilities were *not* being ignored—not just then. So by what right did I say even that we used to know?[23]

In trying to thread a course between the rock of fallibilism and the whirlpool of scepticism, it may well seem as if I have fallen victim to both at once. For do I not say that there are all those uneliminated possibilities of error? Yet do I not claim that we know a lot? Yet do I not claim that knowledge is, by definition, infallible knowledge?

I did claim all three things. But not all at once! Or if I did claim them all at once, that was an expository shortcut, to be taken with a pinch of salt. To get my message across, I bent the rules. If I tried to whistle what cannot be said, what of it? I relied on the cardinal principle of pragmatics, which overrides every one of the rules I mentioned: interpret the message to make it make sense—to make it consistent, and sensible to say.

When you have context-dependence, ineffability can be trite and unmysterious. Hush! [moment of silence] I might have liked to say, just then, 'All of us are silent'. It was true. But I could not have said it truly, or whistled it either. For by saying it aloud, or by whistling, I would have rendered it false.

I could have said my say fair and square, bending no rules. It would have been tiresome, but it could have been done. The secret would have been to resort to 'semantic ascent'. I could have taken great care to distinguish between (1) the language I use when I talk about knowledge, or whatever, and (2) the second language that I use to talk about the semantic and pragmatic workings of the first language. If you want to hear my story told that way, you probably know enough to do the job for yourself. If you can, then my informal presentation has been good enough.

NOTES

1. The suggestion that ascriptions of knowledge go false in the context of epistemology is to be found in Stroud 1989 and in Hetherington 1992. Neither of them tells the story just as I do, however it may be that their versions do not conflict with mine.

2. Unless, like some, we simply define 'justification' as 'whatever it takes to turn true opinion into knowledge' regardless of whether what it takes turns out to involve argument from supporting reasons.

3. The problem of the lottery was introduced in Kyburg 1961, and in Hempel 1962. It has been much discussed since, as a problem both about knowledge and about our everyday, nonquantitative concept of belief.

4. The case of testimony is less discussed than the others; but see Coady 1992, pp. 79–129.

5. I follow Unger 1975. But I shall not let him lead me into scepticism.

6. See Stalnaker 1984. pp. 59–99.

7. See Lewis 1979a; and Chisholm 1979.

8. Unger 1975, chap. II. I discuss the case, and briefly foreshadow the present paper, in Lewis 1979b, esp. pp. 353–355.

9. See Stalnaker 1973 and 1974. See also Lewis 1979b.
   The definition restated in terms of presupposition resembles the treatment of knowledge in Ferguson 1980.

10. See Dretske 1970 and 1981b; Goldman 1976; Stine 1976; and Cohen 1988.

11. Some of them, but only some, taken from the authors just cited.

12. Instead of complicating the Rule of Belief as I have just done, I might equivalently have introduced a separate Rule of High Stakes saying that when error would be especially disastrous, few possibilities are properly ignored.

13. Woozley 1953; Radford 1966.

14. See Gettier 1963. Diagnoses have varied widely. The four examples below come from: (1) Lehrer and Paxson 1969; (2) Russell 1948, p. 154; (3) Goldman 1976; (4) Harman 1973, p. 143.

Though the lottery problem is another case of justified true belief without knowledge, it is not normally counted among the Gettier problems. It is interesting to find that it yields to the same remedy.

15. See Goldman 1967; Armstrong 1973.

16. See Lewis 1980. John Bigelow has proposed to model knowledge-delivering processes generally on those found in vision.

17. See Elgin 1988. The 'efficacy' takes many forms; some to do with knowledge (under various rival analyses), some to do with justified belief. See also Williams 1991, on the instability of knowledge under reflection.

18. Mixed cases are possible: Fred properly ignores the possibility W_1 which Ted eliminates; however Ted properly ignores the possibility W_2 which Fred eliminates. Ted has looked in all the desk drawers but not the file drawers, whereas Fred has checked the file drawers but not the desk. Fred's knowledge that Possum is not in the study is better in one way, Ted's is better in another.

19. To say truly that X is known, I must be properly ignoring any uneliminated possibilities in which not-X; whereas to say truly that Y is better known than X, I must be attending to some such possibilities. So I cannot say both in a single context. If I say 'X is known, but Y is better known', the context changes in mid-sentence: some previously ignored possibilities must stop being ignored. That can happen easily. Saying it the other way around 'Y is better known than X, but even X is known' is harder, because we must suddenly start to ignore previously unignored possibilities. That cannot be done, really; but we could bend the rules and make believe we have done it, and no doubt we would be understood well enough. Saying 'X is flat, but Y is flatter' (that is, 'X has no bumps at all, but Y has even fewer or smaller bumps') is a parallel case. And again, 'Y is flatter, but even X is flat' sounds clearly worse-but not altogether hopeless.

20. Thanks here to Stephen Hetherington. While his own views about better and worse knowledge are situated within an analysis of knowledge quite unlike mine, they withstand transplantation.

21. A proof-theoretic version of this closure principle is common to all 'normal' modal logics: if the logic validates an inference from zero or more premises to a conclusion, then also it validates the inference obtained by prefixing the necessity operator to each premise and to the conclusion. Further, this rule is all we need to take us from classical sentential logic to the least normal modal logic. See Chellas 1980, p. 114.

22. See Stalnaker 1984, pp. 79–99.

23. Worse still: by what right can I even say that we used to be in a position to say truly that we knew? Then, we were in a context where we properly ignored certain uneliminated possibilities of error. Now, we are in a context where we no longer ignore them. If *now* I comment retrospectively upon the truth of what was said *then*, which context governs: the context now or the context then? I doubt there is an general answer, apart from the usual principle that we should interpret what is said so as to make the message make sense.

PART FIVE   Concessive
Responses

CHAPTER 13   Philosophical
Relativity

Peter Unger

THE HYPOTHESIS OF PHILOSOPHICAL RELATIVITY

It is generally believed that the traditional problems of philosophy have definite objective answers: It is not a matter of arbitrary convention what answer one is to give to these problems. This is a more widely held, more basic philosophical belief than any belief, more specific, as to where the right answers lie. In a limited way, I mean to question this widely held conviction: I do not intend to refute the belief, which may well be impossible anyhow; nor do I expect even to offer arguments against it so compelling that many will abandon the conviction. My aim really is more modest: to cast doubt, perhaps a considerable amount of doubt, upon this generally unquestioned view about philosophical problems.

1. Problems Without Solutions

The belief to be questioned is an extremely pervasive one. It is at work both with those traditional problems on which there is a great majority of philosophers on one side and also with those on which philosophers are more or less evenly divided. In each case, the belief that there is an objectively right answer is shared by those who dispute what that answer is.

　　An example of a problem with a fairly even division of advocates is the problem of determinism's consequences: If determinism is true, and everything that *happens* is the *inevitable outcome* of prior considerations, then what of presumed free action, of our ability to do otherwise, of moral responsibil-

Selections from *Philosophical Relativity* originally appeared in Peter Unger's *Philosophical Relativity* (University of Minnesota Press, 1984). © 1984 by Peter Unger. Reprinted by permission of the author and publisher.

ity? Many *compatibilists* all hold that we will still act freely and so on, while many *incompatibilists* hold the opposite. What both large groups have in common is the belief that there is a definite answer to the problem disputed; they disagree only on the more specific question as to what that objective answer is.

A problem on which a great majority stands on one side is the problem of knowledge. Almost all philosophers hold that we know quite a lot about the world, nearly all that we claim to know. The few skeptics about knowledge hold that we really do not know anywhere near that much, extreme skeptics in the matter holding that we know nothing at all to be the case. But, along with their unceasing dispute, the majority and the skeptics alike believe in an objectively right answer. It is just that, with regard to the question of whether or not we know, the former hold that (the right answer is that) we do while the latter hold that (it is that) we do not.

The belief in objectively right answers pertains to all, or to almost all, of the traditional philosophical problems. But the debates on these problems, as to where the answers lie, appear endless. And little solid progress toward a solution as satisfactory as it is definite ever seems made. Even in the case of problems on which there is (almost) always a great majority on a certain side, as in the problem of knowledge, we have this unfortunate situation. Indeed, majority philosophers are rarely long satisfied with any given justification, or set of considerations, for the positive answer favored. Each generation of positive advocates is, of course, disturbed by the force of opposing skeptical considerations. But, in addition, and unfortunately for the idea of solid progress, each group is largely dissatisfied with the attempts to meet this force offered by the preceding generations.

Why do these debates go on and on with so little in the way of results? In all likelihood, there is no single answer to this higher-level question that will serve well for all, or even for almost all, of the traditional philosophical problems. Rather, perhaps a number of different answers will divide the territory, with some overlap. Indeed, certain problems may require several partial explanations, each account appropriate to just one of the unyielding aspects of the problem in question.

In the case of some problems, the explanation of the lack of solid progress may be cruelly simple: The problems are just too hard for the likes of us, with our certainly finite, and even rather limited, intellectual capacities. In other cases, there may be no important lack in our abilities, but the state of our "general knowledge to date" may not be developed enough to point to the objective answer. Perhaps much later on, with many further scientific and other developments, we will be in a position to see the answer to these problems or at least to settle objectively one of their key aspects. Perhaps the traditional problem of mind and body, or one of its aspects, falls in this category.[1]

The explanations of failure so far suggested are perfectly compatible with the general belief in objective answers to philosophical problems. But we should also consider an answer to our higher-level question that is not compatible: For certain traditional problems, perhaps there really is no objective answer, neither positive nor negative, neither "commonsensical" nor "skeptical." I suspect that this might explain, at least in large measure, the unfortunate situation with the two problems on which I have been focusing, as well as with a number of other philosophical problems.

2. Philosophical Relativity and Semantic Relativity

On this suggestion, the answer one prefers for a certain philosophical problem will depend upon what assumptions one has adopted in relation to that problem. And, irrespective of the problem in question, assumptions crucial to one's answer will always be somewhat arbitrary, not determined by objective facts, including facts of logic and language. A certain set of assumptions yields one answer, another set another; whatever facts pertain to the problem fail to decide between the one set and the other.

Where such a situation exists, if it ever really does, we may say that there is *philosophical relativity.* One position on a philosophical problem is to be preferred only *relative to* assumptions involved in arriving at its answer to the problem; an opposed position is to be preferred only relative to alternative assumptions; there is nothing to determine the choice between the diverse assumptions and, hence, between the opposed positions.

How might there arise such a situation of philosophical relativity? One way it might arise is through considerations of language, through semantic considerations. A crucial aspect of a philosophical problem may depend on the meaning of, or on the semantic conditions of, certain linguistic expressions in terms of which the problem is directly and standardly formulated. For example, the problem of knowledge might thus turn upon the meaning of 'know' as it occurs in typical sentences of the form 'Someone knows that such and such is the case'. In much the same way, which answer one gives to the problem may turn on one's specification of the truth-conditions of such sentences. Even if there are other aspects of a given philosophical problem that are not undecidable, the existence of only one undecidable semantic aspect may be enough to lead to philosophical relativity in the case of that problem.

Suppose that there is no objectively right answer as to how a certain expression should be interpreted; no unique determinate meaning to be assigned. In such cases, if there really are any, we will have *semantic relativity:* One set of assumptions leads to one semantic interpretation, another set leads to another, and there is nothing to decide objectively in favor of either set. If this is the case with 'know', then there is no objectively right answer as to what 'know' means. And, if that is so, then there may be no objectively right answer to the problem of whether or not we *know* such and such to be so.

To develop the idea of philosophical relativity, we may look to developing the idea of semantic relativity. To make the latter thought plausible, we should suppose it to apply fairly generally to expressions of our language, and to those of related natural languages, and not only to terms that are of direct philosophical interest. Semantic relativity, thus developed generally, might then have specific application to various philosophically conspicuous expressions: 'know', 'certain', 'cause', 'explain', 'can', 'free', and others. From these applications, our strategy runs, there may arise cases of philosophical relativity.

3. Contextualism and Invariantism

In discussions of language, few things may be taken as even relatively basic: On the one hand, there are certain people (or other "users") making marks or sounds. On the other hand, there are certain effects achieved on people as regards their conscious thought, their experiences, and, most important, their behavior. Everything linguistic, in between, is an explanatory posit.

Where such posits are made, observable phenomena—and even all objective (concrete) facts—get left behind. Then, we might expect a certain latitude, or room for descriptive maneuver, where alternative formulations may have equal claims to propriety. This suggests the idea that, for a given group of speakers, there is no single semantics that is the unique, objectively real semantics of that group. Rather, we may formulate various explanations of the people's production of effects on each other, each formulation assigning a different semantics for the population. Different total explanations of behavior each allow for a different semantic approach.

We may argue for semantic relativity in terms of an apparent conflict between two semantic approaches: *contextualism* and *invariantism*. As we shall develop them, each of these views is only vaguely conceived. For example, we leave open the question of whether a person who is a contextualist with regard to a certain range of expressions will treat some other range in an analogous manner. Even with this vagueness, however, there are enough cases of apparently different treatment for the two approaches to serve as two "reference frames" for semantics. Our argument will be that these two frames are relativistically related.

For our argument to get going, we want a bit of background: Suppose that, in a normal context and manner, someone utters the words, or the sounds that we take to express the words, 'That field is flat'. Then, in the presence of a certain field and a certain audience, this speaker thus may get that audience to "focus upon" some such thought, idea, or proposition as this: that, according to the standards for surface shape most relevant in the audience's then current context, that field is flat. Now, intuitively, there is a certain "absolute character" to words like 'flat' and 'straight', which feature may be vaguely appreciated by a helpful visualization. Without being terribly contentious, I trust, we may build on this intuition so that we may specify the proposition the audience is gotten to focus on like this: that, *according to those contextually relevant standards*, that field is *sufficiently close* to being such that *nothing could ever be flatter* than it is. Perhaps using the adverb 'absolutely' somewhat as a term of art or of abbreviation, we may then conveniently refer to the proposition just specified in this way: that, according to those contextual standards, the field is sufficiently close to being *absolutely* flat.

The adaptation of induced behavior is as flexible as it is subtle. For example, a speaker may be aware or may strongly believe that his hearers want to play croquet and are discussing the surface shapes of various fields with such an end in view. Even so, he may say different things to different groups of hearers all sharing that end. He may do this even if, as we may further suppose, any decent croquet game requires a field that is, so to say, at least fairly flat as far as flatness for fields goes.

Suppose our speaker believes, correctly, that a certain group he is addressing consists of croquet duffers, or novices. Then, he may well say about a certain candidate field, "That field is flat." The duffers will, in normal circumstances, then think that the field indicated is sufficiently (close to being absolutely) flat for their sporting interests. They will, we may presume, proceed to use that field and have an enjoyable game.

Later on, suppose as well, our speaker addresses a different group; he correctly believes them to be croquet masters. About the field previously discussed, he may well say to them words to the opposite effect, "That field is not flat." Ordinarily, they will avoid that field that, we may suppose, had irregularities sufficient to interfere significantly with the high standard of play, precision stroking, that they require of themselves for sporting enjoyment. For *they* will think the indicated field *not* sufficiently (close to being absolutely) flat for *their* sporting needs. When things go well, the speaker will indicate to them some *other* field, less irregular and bumpy, and say about it the prompting words, "That field is flat." Then, they, too, will proceed to enjoy themselves. Each group of players behaves toward the environment in a way suitable for the satisfaction of its members.

On still another occasion, our speaker may address the masters differently, recognizing them to be mildly inebriated and wanting more in the way of jolly sporting fun than an enjoyably excellent game. They might want a field somewhat more level than the minimum suitable for the duffers even so, but not all that much more. In some such circumstances, the speaker might say to the masters, regarding the first field, "That field is flat." They will, presumably, then proceed to use it and have a suitably jolly time.

Our use of language allows us to modify each other's behavior so that, typically, we all have a somewhat better time of things; our goals are attained; at least certain desires are satisfied. Adaptive behavior, we theorize, proceeds from adaptive, contextually relevant thinking and belief. (For most purposes of this essay, it will be enough to mention the adaptive thought itself and to inquire how it manages to take hold. But, of course, we take the same attitude toward the relevant psychological states and processes as we take toward language: They are correctly attributed only to the extent that they serve to explain, however directly or obliquely, purposive behavior, actual and potential. So, implications for behavior, and its adaptation to context, will never be at any great remove.)

In understanding linguistic behavior, we employ a distinction, often appropriate and useful, between what, on the one hand, the agent actually said to be so and, on the other hand, what he merely suggested, informally implied, or whatever. Since it appears to have some very clear cases, this useful distinction seems about as well off, overall, as most that we employ. For example, one utters the words "He is closer to fifty years of age than to forty." Now, what one stated, or actually said to be so, is *perfectly consistent* with the proposition that his age is eighty-seven; for it is true of an eighty-seven-year-old man that his age *is* closer to fifty than to forty, indeed, by a good ten years. What one suggested or only implied, however, is that the man's age is *between* forty and fifty, which is *not* consistent with the statement that the man is eighty-seven. Since what one said to be so *is* consistent with this proposition of great age, while what one suggested is *not*, the two are clearly different in this case. As with almost all of our distinctions, however, there are various cases in which this present one does not admit of such clear-cut application. Let us see what possibilities for linguistic explanation might arise from the vagueness in this distinction.

Consider, again, the little conversation between our speaker and, say, the croquet duffers. As agreed before, the speaker did, in one way or another, get his audience to attend to, to have a belief in the truth of, a thought or proposition that *related to the context* of the conversation. Uncontentiously enough, we agreed, this was the proposition that, *according to contextually relevant standards*, a certain indicated field is *sufficiently close* to being such that *nothing could ever be flatter*, is *sufficiently close* to that logically absolute limit. So, our speaker got everyone involved to focus on, even to believe in, such a contextually sensitive and relevant thought. And he did this, we may also agree, by saying what he said. But, then, we may still ask this: *What was it* that the speaker *said to be so;* what *statement* did he *make;* what is the thought or proposition (attended to or not) that the speaker actually *expressed?* Even with quite a lot of agreed background, such a question, I suggest, might be equally well answered in two very different ways.

A certain sort of semanticist, whom we will call a *contextualist*, will hold that our speaker stated, or said to be so, the very thing on which he got his audience to focus. Presumably, he then achieved this effect in a *most simple manner*, by just saying the very thing on which the audience was to concentrate. But, in that case, the thing said, which will include an implicit reference to a contextual standard, will *not itself be any simple thing*. And, since the sounds and words uttered will be relatively simple in form, there will then be only a rather *complex relation* between these items and the complex "statement" made by way of them. So, this contextualist approach may have certain disadvantages along with its advantages. Whatever its credits and debits, most contemporary philosophers usually hold to such a contextualist line. For a contextualist interpretation fits well with the idea that, in the main, our *ordinary statements* are actually *true* or objectively correct.

Another philosopher may hold that what our speaker actually stated was nothing so contextual and so complex. Rather, the proposition he really expressed was a relatively simple one, without even implicit inclusion of any sensitive standards. On this view, which we will call *invariantism*, what is stated is more simply related to the speaker's sounds and words: that field is (perfectly, absolutely) *flat*. To emphasize the pristine severity of the invariant content, this might perhaps be put more elaborately as: that field is such that nothing could ever be flatter. There is no additional content about contextually relevant standards or sufficient closeness. This simplicity of semantics is itself all to the good. But, then, on this invariantist position, the way the speaker got his audience to light on the relevant thought will be far from simple or so would be its description in appropriately connecting terms.

If we put the matter in terms of reasoning, an appropriate description might run like this: By trading on suitable premises concerning the context, and understood by the conversational participants, the speaker gets his hearers to infer from an (obviously) irrelevant falsehood he expressed to a relevant (presumed) truth then attended. The attended proposition is just the one that the contextualist acknowledged: that, according to contextually relevant standards, that field is (sufficiently close to being absolutely) flat. On that (indirectly) achieved basis, the audience may then proceed to play croquet or to plant peanuts or perhaps to play baseball. Behavior adaptive to context is thus induced, serving salient purposes and goals.

When it involves (unconscious) pragmatic reasoning, but also even when it takes a less highly intellectual form, the associated psychology of invariantism should be worked out in more detail. There are, I suggest, no insuperable difficulties in spelling out some such plausible stories, to the extent that we ever do detail our accounts of purposive linguistic behavior. But the complexity required here, in the detailing of an appropriate psychology, is a notable disadvantage in the invariantist's total explanatory view. So, like contextualism, his approach has its debits as well as its credits. In all events, invariantism fits well with traditional skeptical positions about our ordinary statements; it will give the skeptic the demanding conditions he wants for the key terms of his negative arguments. Knowingly or not, in various skeptical writings I have been an invariantist.[2]

Both invariantists and contextualists agree on what may be taken as the basic facts of typical linguistic situations: the sounds employed by the speaker and, at the other end, the effects on behavior achieved by way of those sounds. Disagreement appears to occur only at some intermediate point and regarding only some "higher level" of description, where an aim at explanation is taken by way of posited items and processes. For terms, sentences, and statements posited for use in these explanations, the invariantist says that the semantics will be quite simple. Then, he must admit some other factors, at a substantial remove from semantics, that are correlatively complex. In apparent opposition, the contextualist says that it is the associated processes that are simple while the semantics is complicated.

Which position is the correct one; which incorrect? According to the *hypothesis of semantic relativity*, it is just a matter of how one chooses to distribute the acknowledged complexities. Either chosen distribution, this hypothesis says, is relevantly arbitrary, not fully determined by any objective facts of the matter. So, neither position is the more accurate; neither is correct to the exclusion of the other.

According to this thesis, there simply is no fact of the matter as to the (full) semantics of the relevant expressions. It is not that there is some very difficult discovery to be made, as to which position is right, a finding that will always remain beyond our all too limited reach. That other situation often obtains, of course: What was the blood type of Thales? Turning to matters of language and behavior: What was the thousandth to the last (Greek) word that Thales spoke? These questions, I presume, do have genuine answers; we will never, I also presume, have those answers. The difficulties are (rather purely) epistemological ones. In the case of these two questions, epistemological problems occur to an extremely great degree. As concerns the (full) semantics of 'flat', however, the problems are not (just) epistemological, however extreme. Rather, our hypothesis directs, there simply is nothing to discover, never was nor ever will be, as to whether the contextualist is correct or whether the invariantist is. That is the import of semantic relativity.

As I am understanding them, neither contextualism nor invariantism is an utterly extreme, absolutely sweeping semantic position: The invariantist allows that many sentences, and many terms, will be evaluated semantically according to context. How else, after all, could we explain the conditions of a typical use of 'She wasn't there last week'? And the contextualist allows that many (other) expressions will be evaluated without regard to their context of use, for example, 'At times in the history of the universe, stones exist'.

The apparent differences between these two approaches will concern a range of "intermediate" ordinary expressions. In this range, which we may regard as vaguely delimited, we find the ordinary predicate 'flat' and, thus, the containing sentence 'That field is flat'. Does the semantic evaluation of this sentence involve context only for the demonstrative subject term 'that field' or for the predicate as well? The contextualist says it is both; the invariantist says it is just the former. It is in regard to such intermediate expressions, and such aspects of their evaluation, that questions of apparent disagreement arise. It is in regard to these questions that, according to the hypothesis of semantic relativity, there is no unique, determinate answer. In that it may be thus considered as appropriately modest in scope, the envisioned relativity is not easy to dismiss.

Various distinctions commonly made in the philosophy of language, and usually rightly so, might be adduced now in an effort to dismiss invariantism and, with it, semantic relativity. But I suggest that this would involve a mis-application of these linguistic conceptions. For example, we may often distinguish between what a speaker means, in or by uttering a certain sentence, and what that sentence means; we may often distinguish, that is, between the speaker's meaning and the sentence's meaning. This is helpful in disambiguating utterances, in explaining various sorts of informal suggestions, including various figures of speech, in noticing successful communication by a speaker who is mixed up about vocabulary, and so on. But it will not serve to resolve our present problems: For the invariantist, as much as for anyone, when the speaker says "That field is flat," what he means is that a contextually indicated field is sufficiently close to being absolutely flat so as to satisfy contextually relevant purposes. But what the uttered sentence means, the invariantist maintains, is that such a field is absolutely flat (no matter about any purposes). This is the gap, or the difference, we have seen so often before, described now in somewhat different words.

The contextualist, for his part, will use the locutions of the distinction to insist that the offered gap does not exist, implying that any complexities in the situation must lie elsewhere. Therefore, he will say that, in such ordinary cases as our examples illustrate, the speaker's meaning and the sentence's meaning are relevantly the same or run in parallel or are as close as one pleases. The hypothesis of semantic relativity, confronting the same general point as before, says what is expected: In such ordinary cases, there is no objective fact of the matter, whether or not the speaker's meaning and the sentence's meaning significantly diverge.

We do not have the space here, of course, to canvass each of the numerous generally useful distinctions philosophers have drawn to discuss one or another of the indefinitely many aspects of linguistic behavior. But, as far as I can discern, none of these conceptions, however subtle, and however fruitful elsewhere, does anything much to resolve those matters that are our present object of study. Rather, each of the distinctions, it appears, is all too seminally vague. So, it seems, there are just more things to say *this* way, then more *that* way, and nothing, in the nature of the case, to decide between them.

4. Alternative Psychologies

This semantic relativity cannot be denied, I believe, by an attempt to locate some objectively telling psychological processes. For our two approaches to language can be contrasted in terms of how the psychological complexity, posited to explain adaptive behavior, enters a most appropriate explanatory story.

By making semantics itself a complex matter, the contextualist presents the acknowledged psychological complexity in a certain form. Just as sentences are sensitively complex, so grasping the meaning, or the truth-conditions, of a sentence is a suitably complex psychological act or process: Hearing only such a simple utterance as "That field is flat," the audience, in an appropriately complex mental act, grasps a complex meaning as thus offered. Typically, the hearer will then understand a complex statement to be made.

For the invariantist, such acts of grasping and understanding are simpler, no more complex than acts required by the simple linguistic items and properties that invariantism posits. In his explanatory description of the relevant mental activity, the invariantist has the complexity enter the story in a different way.

The alternative form for complexity is the key idea for the invariantist's psychological account. Within this leading conception, there is a fair amount of room for alternatives of detail. Some of the options are highly intellectual, stressing patterns of unconscious reasoning. The work of H. P. Grice on suggestion and inference in conversation shows that a good deal of unconscious reasoning is wanted by any account of our purposive linguistic behavior, even a contextualist account.[3] Of course, Grice's available writings do not give anything like a fully detailed account of these inferential situations. Insofar as such an account is available, however, it can be of particular use to an invariantist philosopher. He will just say that there is *more* such Gricean inference at work than has (usually) been suggested, outlining the additional areas, or levels, that his explanations would locate. Invariantism's use of unconscious pragmatic reasoning is only more extensive than the contextualist's, a difference in *degree*, not kind. And, as we have emphasized, this difference of degree is made up for by *other* such differences in the invariantist's explanations: He has a *less* complex semantics, and *less* complex psychological acts of semantic understanding performed, than does the contextualist.

Other psychological options for invariantism are less highly intellectual, describing the associated mental matters in terms of habits formed and followed. To a considerable extent, the recognition of such adaptive habits is appealing anyway, to be desired by any ambitious philosopher. Perhaps David Hume has done most to lead the way here. In our own day, Humean ideas have been developed by David Lewis, though, of course, here too much remains to be done.[4] Along these lines, we again have a difference that is only of degree, not kind. The invariantist posits *more* such adaptive habits than does the contextualist that are at a (further) *remove from* the population's semantic understanding. Again, such differences in degree can be compensated for elsewhere, and the invariantist does appear to pay back the debt.

Which of these psychological options should the invariantist more properly choose? We need not decide this matter. Indeed, compatible with our hypothesis, there might even be a further relativity here within the larger one that we are exploring.

ASPECTS OF SEMANTIC RELATIVITY

Our argument for semantic relativity requires that invariantism be a viable semantic approach. This approach, as we will increasingly observe, is less in accord with our commonsense ascriptions than is contextualism. In a limited sense or way, that makes it rational, as we will argue, to prefer our habitual contextualism to the invariantist view. But this limited rationality of preference will not be grounded in any greater truth of contextualism, only in its habitual employment. As far as any more objective considerations go, it is our hypothesis, the two views are on a par. This parity appears to hold across a wide domain of phenomena. Therefore, our hypothesis of semantic relativity, as we will observe, appears to have rather wide application.

5. Contrasting Groups of Expressions

Certain expressions in our language have one sort of semantic role; others have another. When examining one group of expressions, we may note contrasts between its members and those of another group. Then, it may be tempting to think that only one of our two approaches, say, invariantism, can adequately account for the differences. But, on our hypothesis of semantic relativity, that would be an erroneous judgment.

Alternatively, one may notice that, despite their interesting contrasts, there are important similarities between the two groups. When focusing on these similarities, one may be tempted to think that only one of our two approaches, say, contextualism, can adequately account for them. But, on that same relativity thesis, that would also be a mistaken inference, for, as the hypothesis will have things, there is enough room for accommodating psychological description so that either semantic approach can explain both the contrasts and the similarities.

Many of our predicates are typical *vague* terms. With many of these, their function is simply to express, vaguely, *to what degree* an object of our discourse has a certain property (in a suitably general sense of 'property').

With most words that appear to be of this sort, there is little room for alternative interpretation in this most general matter: 'red', 'short', 'bumpy', 'confident', 'doubtful'. But, with some apparently vague words, the situation is more complex: 'flat', 'empty', 'safe', 'dry', 'certain'. In some respects, these latter words are semantically similar to the previous group; in other ways, they are semantically unalike. How are we best to describe these differences and these similarities?

An invariantist may well emphasize the differences, apparently at the expense of the similarities: True enough, he says, we use 'flat' to get across the idea of how flat something is, but that is really the idea of *how close* to being absolutely flat it is. For 'flat', like 'certain', 'safe', and so on, always expresses an absolute limit beyond the various degrees of mere approximation to it. This is a very different matter from our use of 'bumpy'. When we are getting across the idea of how bumpy something is, that is all there is to the matter; for there is no (coherent) idea of how close something is to being absolutely bumpy, or even any idea of being absolutely bumpy. Words like 'bumpy' really are vague words, while words like 'flat' only appear to be vague but actually are not. The latter, which we will call *absolute terms*, perform (most of) the functions for us that the genuinely vague words do; but, not being vague, they do so only in a rather indirect fashion.

In line with this, the invariantist may continue, we may notice the contradictions we hear with sentences like 'That is flat, but that other is flatter' and 'He is certain of this, but more certain of that'. Once one is at the limit, the invariantist explains, there cannot be any going beyond. We notice no such logical discomfort with 'That is bumpy, but that other is bumpier' or with 'He is doubtful (confident) of this, but more doubtful (confident) of that'. Since no limit is at hand, there is no difficulty with going further.

There is not much doubt that 'flat' and fellows contrast with 'bumpy' and company. And the invariantist account just indicated as appropriate only for the first group is, I suggest, one way of describing this contrast. Along with that, the invariantist can say, too, some things about the similarities: Both sorts of expressions typically serve to bring to mind relevant matters of degree, vaguely expressed and conceived: the degree to which a field is close to being perfectly flat. The invariantist account is appropriate to the phenomena; it is relevantly complete. So, one might conclude, as I once did, that *only* such an account can be adequate.[5] But that would be, I now suggest, an erroneous conclusion, perhaps the result of taking too narrow a view.

A contextualist need not be insensitive to the contrasts between these two sorts of terms. But he will emphasize the similarities, apparently at the expense of those appreciated contrasts. The contextualist will then insist that *all* of the terms really are vague terms, the absolute terms included: It is just that, for a contextualist, these latter are a rather *special sort* of vague term, with special *context-sensitive* semantic features. By thinking along these lines, a contextualist may, as David Lewis has done, conclude that the *only* adequate semantics of 'flat' and 'certain' is a *contextualist* semantics:

> Peter Unger has argued that hardly anything is flat. Take something you claim is flat; he will find something else and get you to agree that it is even flatter. You think the pavement is flat—but how can you deny that your desk is flatter? But "flat" is an *absolute term:* it is inconsistent to say that something is flatter than something that is flat. . . .
>
> Some might dispute Unger's premise that "flat" is an absolute term; but on that score it seems to me that Unger is right. What he says is inconsistent does indeed sound that way. . . .
>
> The right response to Unger is that he is changing the score on you. When he says that the desk is flatter than the pavement, what he says is acceptable only under raised standards of precision. . . . Since what he says requires varied standards, the standards accommodatingly rise. Then it is no longer true enough that the pavement is flat. That does not alter the fact that it *was* true enough *in its original context.* "The desk is flatter than the pavement" said under varied standards does not contradict "The pavement is flat" said under unvaried standards, any more than "It is morning" said in the morning contradicts "It is afternoon" said in the afternoon. . . . Unger . . . can indeed create an unusual context in which hardly anything can acceptably be called "flat," but he has not thereby cast any discredit on the more usual contexts in which lower standards of precision are in force.
>
> In parallel fashion Unger observes, I think correctly, that "certain" is an absolute term; from this he argues that hardly ever is anyone certain of

anything. A parallel response is in order. . . . It is no fault in a context that we can move out of it.[6]

As regards such terms as 'flat' and 'certain', Lewis does note that there is *something distinctive* in their semantics. Against my (early) invariantist treatment of these terms, however, he holds that the special semantic features of these expressions are quite limited in scope: Even as 'bumpy' and 'doubtful' are *vague* terms, so, too, are 'flat' and 'certain'. The difference is just that the latter are a *special sort of vague term with contextually assigned limits for their temporary operation.*

Lewis holds that this contextualist treatment is supported by, perhaps even required by, the ability we have to accommodate our thought, and our attendant behavior, to many changes of context. In Lewis's terminology, this is our ability to alter, and to keep track of, the "conversational score." But does our "knowing the score" favor the idea that only a language with contextualist semantics is the one to be attributed to us? I do not think so.

Along the lines Lewis indicates, we may appropriately attribute such a language to us English speakers. Then, we will describe our knowing the score in the terms Lewis employs. But perhaps we may also attribute, just as appropriately, a language with invariantist semantics. Then, we will just have to employ correlative modes of semantic and psychological description.

For an invariantist, how do we keep track of how (nearly) flat something must be to be acceptably called 'flat' at a given stage in a conversation? We do this, the invariantist says, by keeping track of how close a thing must be to a certain absolute standard in order to be acceptably called 'flat'. That standard, unconsciously in mind, is the state of being such that nothing could possibly be flatter. True enough, at a given conversational stage, a surface is acceptably called 'flat' when it measures up to the temporary standard for flatness then relevant. But that temporarily relevant standard is reckoned in relation to the invariant absolute one, which is the only standard our word 'certain' itself directly expresses.

On the invariantist interpretation of our behavior, we will have ideas of these contextually relevant standards as *contextually acceptable departures* from absolute governing limits. Now, it is true that certain other contextually relevant standards, those in use for uncontroversially vague words, will be more directly employed, without reference to any absolute limits. That is, to be sure, a simpler business. But, then, both invariantists and contextualists admit that matters are *somehow* simpler with typical vague terms, like 'bumpy', for which no problematic contradictions ever even seem to be encountered.

The contextualist has the greater complexity of the facts about 'flat' accounted for by way of a more complex semantics for the term itself. It has all of the relevant complex features of typical vague terms and, in addition, the complexities involved in the assignment of temporarily operative limits on appropriate ranges. Along with this, there are quite complex psychological acts of understanding the semantics of these terms.

The invariantist also strives to account for the complexity of the facts about our absolute terms, but while always assigning a simple semantics to the terms themselves. Accordingly, he supposes there to be complex psychological processes that are not directly involved in the semantic understanding of words like 'flat'.

On the invariantist's account, apparently as good as any, it is by way of these associated processes that our complex uses of 'flat' and fellows are to be described and the adaptive sensitivity of our guiding thoughts to be accounted. What do our rules of accommodation do for us with these special expressions? They allow us to create, and to keep track of, the acceptability, and the unacceptability, of various departures from some simple, invariant semantic conditions.

The changing course of a conversation may be quite complex indeed; the participants move from context to context, creating or accepting new ones, destroying or ignoring the old. As our adaptive behavior attests, we keep track of all of this well enough. How so? Just as with less dynamic explanatory questions, there is, we hypothesize, no determinate answer. A contextualist description can be given in terms of which our linguistic and cognitive movement can be well enough explained. But there can also be given, apparently with equal explanatory propriety, an invariantist description.

6. The Relativity and the Rationality of Contextualism

As we noted, contextualism is a semantic approach that, more than its chief competitor, invariantism, is in accord with (the dominant aspects of) our commonsense view of things. Contextualism is more deeply involved with more of our developed intellectual habits. Now, we may take this as being, in *some* way, a point in favor of contextualism and against invariantism. But this is not the sort of point, or the sort of way, that undermines the hypothesis of semantic relativity.

The relativity thesis does not imply that these two approaches should be equally preferred by us. On the contrary, it fully allows that we might well prefer contextualism and even be rational in doing so, at least in some limited sense or way. What the hypothesis denies is that the basis of this preference will be that the one approach better accords with objective facts than does the other.

The fact that invariantist assignments of truth-values are so frequently surprising points to our habitual preference for contextualism over invariantism. But, as the relativity hypothesis implies, these assignments concern only *proposed* explanatory properties for *posited* explanatory entities—assignments of truth-values for statements. These are not objective predications for acknowledged things in the world. As far as objective reality goes, we are reasonably free to posit what statements we will, and then what truth-values we assign, providing that we make *compensatory psychological posits* elsewhere in our explanatory story. Now, owing to our contextualist habits of attribution, the psychological posits that the invariantist requires are also strange and surprising, just as are the semantic posits of his total view. But none of this strangeness need indicate any greater objective truth for the more habitual mode of attribution or for the more commonsensical judgments encouraged thereby.

Suppose that two procedures lead to different conclusions regarding matters of objective fact. One of the procedures might be our own, involved in our linguistic and cognitive practices; the other, if not hypothetical, will be peculiar to some quite alien society. Then, there arises the problem of justifying our own procedure as rational, at least as more rational for us to follow. One approach to this problem is to claim that it is simply the "entrenchment" of the first procedure in our society, the past and present employment of its terms and modes of attribution, that grounds the rationality of our preference for it. This is a sort of methodological conservatism. Such a conservatism does have some plausibility. But it is controversial that it can adequately account for, or justify, the presumed rationality of our own procedures and expectations in these matters of objective fact.

An outstanding example of such a controversial claim is in reference to Nelson Goodman's two languages with concomitant inference patterns: our own, with 'blue' and 'green', and an alien one, with "temporally indexed" 'grue' and 'bleen'.[7] In this situation, we and the presumed aliens have different expectations regarding certain matters of objective fact, even observable, concrete fact: They expect certain stones to be a certain color when observed at certain future times; we expect those objects to be otherwise. Intuitively, and very vaguely, we have the idea that the aliens are irrational in their procedures because they are counterinductive in them, while we, for being inductive, are rational in ours. Is this vague thought correct? Maybe it is, and maybe it is not. If it is, then there is more to our own personal rationality than just our sticking with that procedure we have already got. In situations like Goodman's, where there are disagreements as to objective facts, it is controversial that methodological conservatism can do much to explain our own expectations as being rational ones.

In the present case, however, there appears no disagreement as to objective facts at all. So says our hypothesis of semantic relativity. If that is so, then a very *mild* conservatism may, without much controversy, explain the rationality for us of our contextualist ways: If two equally coherent procedures lead to equivalent expectations concerning all (possible) objective facts and depart only as regards conventional assumptions used in explanation of the facts, then it is rational to prefer the one with which one is already comfortable, adept, and familiar. This relatively uncontroversial justification of contextualism, and of our associated commonsense thoughts about our statements, is, it seems to me, a point in favor of hypothesizing semantic relativity.

No doubt there are factors that explain why we are in fact contextualists, why we have accepted this approach and not the other. These are likely to involve considerations as to what habit patterns are more natural or more convenient for us, which will better foster improved social relations among beings like ourselves, and so on. Toward so many ends, it is productive for us to "take folks at their word," not to question their veracity; so that is how we treat each other. But however that may be, such socially helpful considerations do not, I think, confute semantic relativity. At least I cannot see how they undermine the hypothesis.

7. The Appeal of Invariantism

We have noted a key attraction of contextualism, which it retains even in the face of semantic relativity: On that view, but not on the approach of invariantism, the truth-values of ordinarily made statements come out the way we ordinarily believe them to do. And, in particular, they will usually come out as true, since, ordinarily, we believe such statements usually to be true. But, while most of the attraction is thus on the side of our habitual contextualism, not all of it is: Invariantism, too, has its own distinctive appeal for us.

The appeal of invariantism arises with its most definitive feature: On that approach, the semantics of the relevant expressions is as *simple* as might be supposed with any plausibility. All of us, I suggest, have the belief, or at least the tendency to believe, that the semantics of most ordinary expressions, including those discussed here, is a rather simple affair.

As regards certain expressions to which our relativity hypothesis seems to apply, our belief in simple semantics has a philosophically interesting consequence, also implicitly accepted. This is our belief that the semantics of these expressions is appropriately *independent*, that the conditions do not depend on the contextual interests of those happening to use the terms on a particular occasion. Let me illustrate with some examples; two will be reconsidered, one will be introduced.

First, we reconsider 'flat'. Now, whatever we may implicitly believe to the contrary, we think this term properly applies to a surface just in virtue of features of *that surface's shape, not* in virtue of quite *removed* features, such as the *interests in* the surface *taken by people* who happen to be talking and thinking about it in a *certain conversation*. We think, then, that it cannot be true to say of a given surface at *one* time that it *is* flat and at *another* that it is *not*, *unless there has occurred a change in the surface's shape itself*. And, at a given time, it cannot be true for *one* person to say of a certain surface that it *is* flat but *not* true for *another* person to say that about the surface. The truth-value of their statements cannot depend, we tend to think, on the interests of the people involved in two simultaneous but distant and unconnected conversations about the very same surface as it is at that particular time.

We turn to another familiar example, the expression of personal certainty. Whatever implicit beliefs we might harbor to the opposite effect, we do believe that it cannot be true of one person that he is certain of something, say, that twelve times twelve is one hundred and forty-four, but *not* true of another person unless there is some real difference in the psychological states of *those two people* or in the relations *they* bear to the proposition. The truth-values cannot depend, we presume, on the interests of some *third parties* who, on one occasion or another, may happen to converse about the people and the proposition in question.

Now for a new example to illustrate the same general point: Whatever else we may also believe, we tend to think that (almost all) singular causal judgments are independent of our specific conversational interests. Suppose, for example, that an auto accident has taken place and there are two conversations regarding it, each interchange removed from the other. In one conversation, the participants are road engineers; in the other, they are people in charge of issuing drivers' licenses. In the first interchange, someone says that what caused the accident was the inadequate banking of the road at the curve. In the other, someone else says that the drunken driving of the man at the convertible's wheel caused the accident. Well, which was it? From our external viewpoint, we seem pressured to adjudicate. That is, these judgments of causality *appear* to contradict each other. But suppose that, in fact, they do not. Then, the truth-conditions of each judgment will depend, not just on objective relations among events and objects on the highway, but also on the (temporary) interests of whomever happens to be discussing the events in question. Contrary to our presumption, our causal judgments will not then be relevantly independent propositions.

On an invariantist account of 'flat', 'certain', and 'cause', the semantics of these terms will be not only as simple as we generally suppose but also independent. This is quite in line with our commonsense beliefs about these terms and about the statements in which they enter. For a contextualist, however, none of this can be so. In these regards, then, it is invariantism, and not contextualism, that is in accord with common sense.

On many matters, common sense is inconsistent; we do not actually have our unreflective thoughts so perfectly in line all the time. So, in particular, it is with matters of semantics: On the one hand, we believe that most statements ordinarily made with 'flat' and fellows are true; on the other, we believe that the semantics of these terms and statements is not only relevantly simple but relevantly independent, or interest-free. Common sense would have it both ways, but that is impossible. This point, of which I am fairly confident, does not require any relativity hypothesis to hold.

In that common sense is ambivalent in these matters, it is an oversimplification to say, as we have done, that commonsense semantics is contextualist semantics. But it is not a harmful exaggeration. For the common beliefs favoring contextualism are much *stronger* than those favoring the opposite approach. We believe more strongly that most of our ordinary statements with these expressions are true, less strongly that their semantics is simple and independent. On the *whole*, then, our habitual modes of ascription are contextualist, not invariantist.

Nonetheless, insofar as it flies in the face of our belief in simple, independent semantics, contextualism engenders *something* of a paradox, even when viewed from within our commonsense perspective: How can the matter of whether a given surface is *flat,* in contradistinction to, say, whether it is suitable for our croquet game, depend upon the interests in that surface taken by those who happen to converse about it? This appears to go against our better judgment: If it does not go against the strongest, most influential aspect of common sense, perhaps it goes against its best or truest aspect.

Can such a paradox of contextualism undermine it as a tenable approach? If so, then we will be left with invariantism alone, and our hypothesis of semantic relativity will be jeopardized, at least for these expressions. But I do not think that contextualism, or relativity, will so easily fall.

Why do we believe that our ordinary locutions must, by and large, be semantically independent of our own interests and depend solely on features and items that are relevantly external? Partly because our own interests are so close to us that they go unnoticed unless explicitly mentioned, while in the cases at hand the (contextualist) reference to our perspective is only an implicit one. But most of the explanation, I think, can be traced to other sources.

As regards almost any genuine subject matter of our discussions, we must have *some* expressions available that *are* independent, whose conditions are free of the temporary interests of a particular user. Or, at least, we have a strong tendency to believe this to be so. So, in particular, we must have *some* objective way of describing the shapes of various surfaces and objects, *some* terms for independently indicating the "confidence level" of people with respect to propositions, *some* suitably independent terms for indicating the causal relations, if any, that obtain between certain events.

Let us suppose that this general claim, so appealing to our belief, is true. Even so, it may be that 'flat' is, despite appearances to the contrary, not among our independent terms for surface shape. And it may be that 'certain' is not part of our independent, interest-free vocabulary for confidence levels. Finally, despite appearances, it may even be that 'cause' is not one of our expressions for independently describing what passes as the causal order. Even if all of this is so, we may still have other expressions, of course, to do the job of interest-free description.

According to the contextualist, our actual situation is as follows: Either we have no interest-free expressions at all for these subject matters, or, as is somewhat more appealing, we do have some but they are not the terms that come to mind (perhaps they are only certain complex concatenations of common words, quite unobvious to us and possibly even inaccessible). According to the invariantist, that is not the situation; rather, we do have interest-free terms, as we seem to require, and, moreover, they are just the terms that come to mind as fitting the bill. According to semantic relativity, of course, there is no fact of the matter here as to what actually is our linguistic situation.

Intuitively, this present matter is as the invariantist claims, not as claimed by either the contextualist or the relativity hypothesis. For, as observed, 'flat', 'certain', and 'cause' do seem to be among our independent expressions. But, I suggest, this appearance need not be decisive.

We tend to think, perhaps even as a part of common sense, that the semantics of our ordinary words is, not only a rather simple affair, and often independent of interests, but also something *readily accessible*. We have an intuitive understanding of such familiar words; we just grasp their simple meanings and that is that. But it may well be, I suggest, that the understanding of semantic conditions is not nearly so simple as this part of common sense would have it.

The semantics to be assigned to an expression comes as part of an overall theory of the behavior of those speaking the language in which that expression has a place. Because an appropriate theory is not readily accessible, the semantics of many of our ordinary expressions is not, I suggest, so accessible. Among those familiar terms whose semantics is not accessible, we may conjecture, will be those to which our relativity hypothesis applies. So, even though the intuitive inclination toward the invariantist claim of independent treatments for 'flat', 'certain', and 'cause' is strong (whatever the details of the treatments), that inclination may be misleading.[8]

A RELATIVISTIC APPROACH TO SOME PHILOSOPHICAL PROBLEMS

We proceed to apply our relativistic approach to some philosophical problems. In each case, the treatment will proceed along the same general lines: First, look for some expressions that are important for a statement of the problem in question. Then, try to see how the thesis of semantic relativity might apply to the expressions encountered. We will argue that, for each problem studied, an invariantist can assign a semantics to the philosophically important terms that is comfortable to a skeptical view on the problem, and a contextualist can, with equal propriety, assign a semantics that is comfortable to the commonsense position on the problem, antithetical to the skeptic's position. On our hypothesis, since there is nothing to decide between the two assignments, the problems under review are insoluble: Although we might prefer one alleged solution to the other, that of common sense to that of skepticism, there is nothing to decide objectively in favor of either position.

8. A Problem of Knowledge

In the course of conversations, we claim to know many things about the world. The skeptic denies these claims, saying that we actually know nothing to be so or, at most, very little. These denials are motivated by arguments.

Many skeptical arguments take the following general form. The skeptic conjues up some propositions, each of which fairly obviously conflicts with what one claims to know to be true. If one really knows what one claims, the skeptic says, one must be in a position to rule out as untrue these logically conflicting propositions. But it seems that one cannot rule out those propositions noted by the skeptic. So, the skeptic concludes, one does not really know what one claims to know.

Arguments of this form have a considerable pull on almost everyone acquainted with them. Also, there is a considerable resistance to them that, almost always, eventually outweighs that pull. How is this to be accounted for?

In an ordinary conversation, when I say to you, "John knows there is milk on the rug," I get us to accept, among other things, some such complex contextually sensitive idea as this: Among the propositions logically conflicting with 'There is milk on the rug', John is in a position to rule out, according to standards for ruling out that are relevant to current context, all those conflictors that are *relevant* competitors. What competitors are relevant? Like the standards for ruling out taken as being in force, that, too, depends on the context and, thus, on our interests in the situation. Therefore, this thought, upon which we are brought to focus, is relevant to context in two ways. These ways are not wholly unrelated.

What I am proposing here must, I am afraid, remain somewhat vague even after my attempts at clarification, which follow.

To begin, I do not mean 'ruling out' to imply any articulation of reasons for regarding as untrue any proposition that may thus be so regarded. Nor does it imply, even, any ability to provide any such articulation, demonstration, proof, or whatever of the falsity of the ruled out proposition. Rather, the idea is that, when a proposition is ruled out, any chance at truth for that proposition may be (appropriately) discounted or ignored.

To further matters, we might say that, when one is experiencing (in the visual modality) only a homogeneous visual field of pure blue, one is in a position to rule out, and probably will have ruled out, the proposition 'I am now visually experiencing only phenomenal red'. And, typically, one will have done so even according to a very high standard for ruling out, one rarely used in, or required by, human conversations. Perhaps according to a higher standard than even that, one is in a position to rule out 'I do not exist', especially when one is consciously thinking, more especially when one knows that one is, most especially when one is aware that the falsity of that negative proposition follows, logically and immediately, from what one then knows so directly and so certainly. In contrast, only according to a very much lower standard than either just contemplated is one in a position to rule out the proposition 'My friend Frank is at the movies' when, earlier in the day, Frank had told one that he was going to spend the evening quietly at home. Ordinarily, the standard for ruling out appropriate to conversations about spilled milk and rugs (and about knowing) will be somewhat higher than the standard just contemplated, though quite a bit lower than the two standards contemplated previously to that one.

When I say to you, 'John knows there is milk on the rug', what competitors to 'There is milk on the rug' are *relevant* ones; which need ruling out? Like the standard in force for ruling out, that, too, will depend on context, so that our behavior may be contextually adaptive. In many ordinary contexts, though by no means all of them, a relevant competitor will be that there is only some whitish water on the rug that looks like milk but is not milk. In everyday contexts, certain other competitors will never be relevant, or at most scarcely ever: For example, that any experience as of milk and rugs is caused only by an evil demon who, in that way, gets one to believe falsely about such "external" matters.

In ordinary contexts, both standards for ruling out and ranges of relevant competitors are not as great as they might be. Thus, in at least two ways, complex thought and behavior can be adaptive to ordinary contexts. Now, even though these two ways are related, there is room for divergence: In some ordinary contexts, the standard may be relatively high even while the range is not all that great: Suppose that the rug is a rather valuable antique susceptible to damage by continued exposure to old milk. Suppose, also, that it is extremely expensive to clean the rug in order to prevent such exposure. Further, suppose that the only liquids anywhere on or near the premises, the only candidates with any significant chance of being spilled on the rug, are milk and harmless whitish water. In such a case, where John may have seen the spilling, the standards for his ruling out the whitish water will be quite high, while the range of competitors is quite minimal.

On the other hand, the standards for ruling out may be rather low even while the range of competitors is extensive. Suppose the rug is a rather cheap nylon thing, easily cleaned, and, to boot, not at all likely to be spoiled by exposure to milk or any other available substance. In addition, suppose that, on the premises, a combination drugstore and luncheonette, there are many liquids available that are of a similar whitish appearance. Again, John is the most likely witness. This time, for us to find 'John knows there is milk on the rug' acceptable, we will require that John be in a position to rule out quite a few competitors to 'There is milk on the rug', but rather low standards for ruling out will be those in force.

It almost goes without saying that, in everyday contexts, the remaining two alternatives are found: Often, we both impose high standards and consider large ranges; often, both the standards set are low and the ranges considered are narrow.

Finally, we may say this about our thought as to knowledge: As the standards for ruling out get higher, other things being equal, the relevant ranges become greater; as the ranges become greater, *ceteris paribus*, the standards become higher. At the very highest point for either, we must be at the highest point for the other; we are then, but only then, beyond *ceteris paribus* considerations. So, anywhere lower down, on either isolated dimension, we are not beyond such considerations. And this often happens in everyday life. Indeed, it often happens that other things are, not only relevant, but relevantly unequal. Our two examples about the milk and the rugs were two cases of such rather common divergence.

As we have been urging, the matter must be complex: For a limitation on the range of relevant competitors to be effective in allowing knowledge, the standards in force for ruling out must be sufficiently low. Otherwise, there would be this problem: According to the *very highest standards* for ruling out, not relevant to ordinary contexts, to *rule out*, say, 'There is milk only on the floor', one would have to be in a position to rule out, as well, 'There is an evil demon deceiving one into false belief as to whether or not there is milk only on the floor'. But, even according to fairly low standards for ruling out, one cannot, it seems, rule out this latter proposition; I cannot, you cannot, and, in particular, John cannot.[9] For adaptive thought, then, there must be an appropriate relationship between the two contextual features: It is only a certain (somewhat modest) range of competitors that is to be ruled out, and even they are to be ruled out only in a certain (somewhat modest) way, only according to a certain (somewhat modest) standard.

It is in this overall situation of adaptive thought that the skeptic about knowledge can make compelling arguments.[10] He may begin his negative moves in either of two main ways logically related to each other: He may start by bringing in competitors not usually deemed relevant or even envisioned at all. Or he may start by suggesting, quite compellingly, a movement toward higher standards for ruling out. Eventually, either of these will begin to involve the other; the skeptic may then seem to have things both ways at once. Although it means some repetition of certain points recently made, let me spell this out in just a bit of detail. For purposes of illustration, let a fledgling skeptic start by introducing novel competitors.

As is familiar, the competitors even a fledgling skeptic proposes are of the sort that, in ordinary conversations, we would (almost) never deem relevant. In relation to our examples, he might propose these conflicting propositions: There is, for John and perhaps for us, too, only part of a *perpetual* dream here, the part in which one dreams some milk is on a rug, while in reality there is nothing to it; there is only deceptive experience, induced by an evil demon, as of a real situation of milk on a rug but nothing real to answer.

When such "all-encompassing" competitors are at issue, the range of competitors will be at the maximum: all (rather obviously conflicting) competitors are fair game. And at that point, as we have said, the standards for ruling out are at their highest, too. So, the game is then set up for the skeptic to win overwhelmingly.

Suppose, contrary to our statement of convergence, that there are (sometimes) low standards for ruling out in force while the proposition to be ruled out is, for example, that an evil demon is deceiving in the matter (so that the range of competitors is at a maximum). Well, as we previously noted, even according to fairly low standards for ruling out, *such* a competitor is one the alleged knower *cannot* rule out. So, the supposition of low standards here will be to no avail in any case. We might as well suppose, as we did and as seems more intuitive, that when the range is so great the standards must be so high.

Now, let us take the skeptic's other main approach: The skeptic begins by urging us to raise the standards for ruling out; we go along, further and further, until the highest standards are in force. Does John know there is milk on the rug? With such high standards in force, it seems that, for John to know, he must be in a position to rule out (just about) any proposition conflicting with 'There is milk on the rug', in particular, even 'There is an evil demon deceiving me into false belief in the matter of whether or not there is milk on the rug'. But this proposition, it seemed, could not be ruled out even if standards for so doing were fairly low (which is not to say absolutely minimal). So, again, John does not know what was claimed for him.

A serious skeptic, no mere fledgling, says we never know anything about the world, or at least something nearly as sweeping. Is what he says true? That depends on, among other things, the meaning, or the semantics, of 'know': For the skeptic, an invariantist account of the semantics of 'know' will prove most congenial. On such a semantics, sentences of the form 'S knows that p' will have as a logically necessary condition some such severe proposition as this: S is in a position to rule out as untrue, according to a single invariant standard for ruling out that can never be transcended, *all propositions* that are (at least fairly obviously) logically incompatible with p (not just those competitors relevant for this or that person to consider, in this or that context).[11] Semantically, the invariantist thus contends, it makes no difference what alternatives to p are relevant for those involved with a given use of a given sentence of this form. The skeptic will embrace invariantism: If this sort of semantics gives the right account of such sentences, then, in particular, a claimed knower must always be in a position to rule out (according to the highest standard for so doing) various machinations of Cartesian demons, whether or not those involved with the making and the hearing of a particular knowledge claim take such considerations to be germane.

On a contextualist account of 'knows', in contrast, sentences for knowledge claims will have more complex, context-sensitive semantics: These sentences, the contextualist holds, will *directly express* contextually relevant thoughts or propositions. So, they will often, not never, express truths; they will do so depending not only on what (somewhat modest) standards for ruling out are relevant but also depending on what (restricted range of) competitors are relevant. Both the standards and the range, as regards their relevance, will vary with the context.

Now, it is very plausible to suppose that, *given* the falsity of such propositions as 'There's an evil demon deceiving in the matter', certain people can rule out, according to suitably modest standards for so doing, such competitors as 'There is only whitish water on the rug'. If a contextualist semantics for 'know' is right and the situation is as ordinarily presumed, then such a person might well know that there is milk on the rug. Contextualism hinders the skeptic and aids the commonsense epistemologist.

Invariantism favors skepticism about knowledge; contextualism favors the opposite, more commonsensical view. These are the main lines for us to notice. Still, within this large picture, there may well be certain smaller points that are worth noticing. It seems to be so.

An invariantist account of 'know' will *directly* give the day to skepticism about knowledge, at least to a fairly extreme form of that view. A contextualist account of 'know' will not, however, give the day to common sense *quite* so directly: Even if there is always an implicit reference to the *relevance* of alternatives, the skeptic can claim, for example, that, as a matter of fact, all (logically possible) alternatives always *are* relevant. Or, at least, he might claim that all those propositions are relevant that can be seen to be (logically imcompatible) alternatives by a reasonably good reasoner (if not the claimed knower). But, with nothing much to support it, even the less ambitious of these skeptical claims seems just something for the skeptic to say for want of anything more compelling or substantial.

Once it is thought that a contextualist account of 'know' does specify some contextually sensitive conditions that are fully determinate for the term, the skeptic has a very long and hard row to hoe. He must try to create contexts in which the very highest standards are enforced, and then he must sustain those contexts. Now, perhaps the skeptic can do this for some fleeting moments, in certain highly rarified philosophical discussions. David Lewis seems to think that this occurs frequently enough. Perhaps it does, but I am uncertain.

Even if he can sometimes create such effective philosophical contexts that high standards of exclusion will be temporarily in force for 'know' (and often for 'flat', too), the skeptic then has the problem of *maintaining* these contexts and of extending their standards to other, less rarified, situations in which more practical concerns affect matters of what is relevant. In an excellent recent paper on this subject, Jonathan Adler argues, in effect, that these extensions are always possible, or almost always.[12] Although the considerations Adler adduces are logically powerful, their psychological force is not greatly compelling. And, since Adler is neither our president nor our king, few will create contexts along the stringent lines he recommends. Hence, almost all of the contexts we do face daily, and the statements as to knowledge we make therein, will, if contextualism is accepted, be evaluated according to low standards for ruling out and, what amounts to the same, in relation to a restricted range of competitors. If contextualism provides the correct semantics for 'know', then most of our knowledge claims will, presumably, be evaluated as true, the position of common sense in the matter. Accordingly, even if the route to it is somewhat indirect, a contextualist semantics for 'know', and for related expressions, will almost certainly mean a widespread victory for commonsense epistemology. So, as we have said, the main lines of dispute are those already noted.

Here is a related way of noting the (apparent) disagreement over knowledge claims generated by our two semantic approaches: An invariantist appears to note many contradictions between ordinary statements about who knows what. In one context, someone says, "John knows there is milk on the rug; Fred told him there is." In another, someone says, "John doesn't know there is milk on the rug; for all he knows, Fred could have been lying." For the invariantist, these apparent contradictions are genuine ones. Not so for the contextualist: The context of the knowledge claim may have, and probably did have, lower standards for what alternatives must be excluded; those were the standards then relevant. The context of the knowledge denial had higher standards relevant. Because the different standards affect the statements made and affect the assignment of truth-values, both the earlier claim and the later denial may be true. The same point can be made, of course, just in a somewhat different way, in terms of the range, or ranges, of relevant competitors. However we choose to make the point, the question remains: Are we to grant truth for invariantism, and thus for skepticism, or are we to think only contextualism, and thus common sense, is correct in these matters?

Which semantics is correct? On our relativity hypothesis, neither is objectively more proper. The acknowledged facts are these: We do keep track well enough of which people are in what cognitive positions relative to which propositions and, in consulting, behave accordingly; moreover, our talk with 'know' and cognates appropriately alters our adaptive inventories of consultants. But, with apparently equal propriety, the two semantic approaches can variously explain, or account for, the relation between the useful noises and our tendencies toward consultant behavior. Because he helps himself to the appropriate pragmatic psychological complications, the invariantist can explain the relation via his simple semantics for 'know', so helpful to the skeptic. Without those complications, the contextualist can also explain the acknowledged relation, in a manner neither better nor worse, via the complex semantics so comfortable to common sense. Since neither semantics for 'know' is objectively more proper, neither epistemological position is correct at the expense of the other: There is no decidable issue between skepticism about knowledge and commonsense epistemology. Here, we conjecture, is a conspicuous instance of the hypothesis of philosophical relativity.

This is not, of course, our ordinary view of the matter. Commonly, we think there is a genuine issue here and, moreover, one that is overwhelmingly likely to be settled in favor of common sense, not skepticism. But a relativist can account for the popularity of these conceptions. Very briefly, he may do so as follows: Because of the simpler, more "independently aimed" semantics of invariantism, the skeptical arguments are recurrently appealing. They seem to present us with a *somewhat credible* position and, thus, with a genuine side of a decidable issue. But, because of the happily expected truth-values that it assigns to ordinary knowledge claims, contextualism has an even *greater* appeal, and so does commonsense epistemology. The latter thus appears to be the *correct* side of the matter; thus, again, and even more so, there appears to be a determinate matter before us. Such psychological facts as these, says the relativist, and not any "greater truth" of one of the traditional positions, will explain both the recurrent temptation of skepticism and the almost universal tendency to renounce it.

Within this large area of dispute, or of apparent disagreement, there are many finer points whose proper articulation is quite difficult to achieve.

Whether one is an invariantist or a contextualist, one would like a detailed account of which alternatives to which accepted propositions must be ruled out by an agent in which circumstances (so that we may most adaptively consult such an agent). In detail, how does our thinking proceed here, so that, in certain contexts, we may treat the agent as one who knows or, on the skeptical description, as one who departs from knowing to a (contextually determined) *acceptable* degree? Questions of when we count alternative hypotheses relevant and when not are subtle and difficult to articulate, whether the mechanisms of assessment are largely semantic, as the contextualist holds, or whether (almost) wholly psychological, as the invariantist skeptic would have it.[13] But the intricacies of these assessments, however challenging and intriguing, can be accommodated well enough by either of our general semantic approaches. Within the compass of either form of treatment, it appears, there is plenty of room to do so. So, in an inquiry of this generality, we need not enter into the intriguing details of our adaptive procedures.

As has been traditionally recognized, problems of knowledge and of certainty are related. This fits well with our contention that, with both problems, one or the other position is favored by this or that semantic approach: For example, as skepticism about certainty is aided by an invariantist semantics of 'certain', so skepticism about knowledge is favored by such an approach to 'know'. Perhaps the parallel can be explained by logical relations between the two terms.

In earlier writings, I argued that a logical (or necessary) condition of someone's *knowing* something to be so is that the person be *certain* of the thing. Despite some considerations that seem to go the other way, this claim still seems a likely one to me. But to others it is at least somewhat controversial.[14] What seems less controversial is this other claim: that a logical condition on the person's knowing the thing is that *the thing itself be certain.* If this is right, where does it take us?

If something is certain, then, I suggest, the situation is somewhat like this: Objective considerations exclude as being untrue any proposition incompatible with that thing; they do not rule out the thing itself but thus ensure its truth. When a person knows something, he has placed himself with respect to that thing so that he is in a position to do from his own perspective what those considerations have done from the larger objective perspective.

How certain is a particular thing? For the invariantist, the question is how close the thing is to an absolute limit, that of impersonal certainty. At this limit, objective considerations have excluded from being true, even according to a highest invariant standard, all propositions conflicting with the thing, not just those we might, in a given conversational context, consider to be relevant competitors.

Does someone know the thing? For the invariantist, he does know it only if he is at a similarly absolute limit, but one referenced from his own perspective. At this correlative limit, the person has "absolutely" excluded from being true, or is in a position to so exclude, all conflicting propositions (or at least all those he can learn about), not just those deemed relevant by people discussing his cognitive situation. In both of these related matters, the contextualist's approach is the obvious variant.

Perhaps our rough characterization of these epistemological issues gives a unified picture of them. Then, we might have a unified understanding of how our two semantic approaches contribute to the endless discussion of these traditionally related philosophical problems. (Whether or not a unified conception is at hand, there is the parallel of dialectics that encourages the search for some such idea.)

In all events, questions of knowledge and those of certainty are endlessly disputed by philosophers. It is our hypothesis (not, I think, a hopelessly implausible one) that the main reason for this lies not in the perverse confusions of the disputants but in the indeterminate nature of the questions themselves.

Although there is a lot more that could be said about problems of knowledge, and about closely related issues, we cannot here go on forever. And, anyway, from ruminative experience, my conjecture is that, however many strands we pursue and at whatever length, they will all take us back, eventually, to much the same ground as we have just gone over, ground fertile for relativity. Indeed, I will not spend even this much time or space on other problem areas, to which we shall turn almost immediately.

It is nonetheless useful, even in a work of a quite general character, to have at least one philosophical problem area treated in some detail and, so, at some length. But, also, one is probably enough. If so, then the author must make a choice.

9. The Skeptic and the Relativist

As is obvious enough, there is a certain broad similarity between the relativist and the traditional skeptic: Both hold that the truth-value situation of many things we say or express will be other than we ordinarily assume. But within this broad similarity crucial differences appear at once: What are we supposed to *do* about such troublesome words as 'flat', let alone those of greater philosophical importance, such as 'certain'? For the traditional skeptic, since the expression in question has a fully determinate semantics, there is nothing to do, except perhaps to change the subject of inquiry. For the relativist, however, the semantic conditions are not yet all laid down; there is still room for conventional stipulation, in one direction or in another.

Without violating the meaning of, say, 'flat', we may endow it with a more fully determinate sense than it yet has had. With any such indeterminate term, we may adopt certain conventions that will endow it with more exhaustive and articulate semantic conditions. For example, we may adopt such conventions as will have our 'flat' be evaluated semantically only in a contextually varying, sensitive fashion. Or, alternatively, we may impose such other conventions as will have the word be evaluated without any relation to context, thus always the same. Along with all of the conventions so far governing the use of any such word, it is our hypothesis, there is still ample room for either course of adopting conventions.

I will not attempt to spell out the details of either sort of additional conventions, nor will I try to detail how our behavior is to be regulated by either. But let me venture to sketch a broad difference between the propensities toward linguistic behavior that would be variously induced. The venture is, admittedly, speculative.

Should we adopt appropriate fully contextual conventions, a skeptical attempt to interrupt a conversation might have terribly little appeal, if any, and perhaps would be brushed aside as irrelevant, almost as an attempt to change the subject entirely. In other words, one who should "challenge" the claim of *flatness$_c$* for a road by pointing out with a magnifying glass many tiny irregularities might be taken, quite immediately, to be as far from the claimant's subject, or very nearly as far, as happens with the following: Someone "rebuts" a claim to the effect that it is raining by pointing out that in some area irrelevant to the context, perhaps the Sahara Desert, no rain is falling anywhere now. Likewise, a claim to *know$_c$* as "challenged" by reference to possible deceit by a Cartesian demon might be decisively felt to be, and declared to be, receiving no real challenge at all, not even one of theoretical interest. Thus, there might eventually occur some such broad shift in our linguistic behavior.

Through the adoption of invariantist conventions, there can occur, we might surmise, a broad shift to opposite effect. Such "challenges" as just discussed might, in such an event, be taken as absolutely genuine challenges and, indeed, as literally successful, but with respect to *flatness$_i$* and *knowing$_i$*. The people whose statements were challenged would, in this scenario, almost immediately acknowledge the falsity of their remarks and admit that they were speaking only very loosely, of course, much as though using figures of speech. They would admit that a road, or a field, was no more really *flat$_i$* than, as we now admit, a certain person was really going to *die of embarrassment*. They would admit that a person no more *knew$_i$* that another was angry, and do so just about as readily, as we now admit a certain angry person was never really about to *hit the ceiling*. There might, therefore, upon the adoption of certain other, "more stringent" conventions, eventuate some such quite different broad shift in our linguistic behavior.

As things stand, our hypothesis says, we have not yet adopted either sort of dimly envisaged additional conventions. Perhaps that is why, or is one of the reasons why, our actual linguistic behavior, covert as well as overt, is an uneasy mixture of the comfortably settled response patterns just sketched in outline. So much for my speculative venture.

In any event, let us suppose that, whatever their exact nature and behavioral import, we have gone ahead and adopted fully adequate contextual(ist) conventions for 'flat', 'certain', 'know', and other problematic expressions; in that way we will have resolved their problematic indeterminacy. As regards semantics, what will be the result? We will now have words that differ semantically from those we used before. Since the words in question remain numerically the same, we will have *changed the meaning* of many of our words. This we needed to do in order to use these words so commonly in sentences that express simple positive truths about the world.

According to traditional skeptics, we will have to do that, to change meaning, in order to use, say, 'know', to express such truths. In this general way, the relativist is like the traditional skeptic. But within the broad commonality an important difference arises: For the skeptic, since the old meaning gave fully determinate semantics, the new meaning will go against, or contradict, the old. For the relativist, in contrast, the new meaning will not contradict the old.

For the relativist, but not the skeptic, our newly determinate sentences will not be so very different, in their semantic conditions, from the old sentences disputed at such length. Viewed in this light, our relativity hypotheses can be seen to provide a compromise of sorts between more standard positions that are more directly opposed.

NOTES

1. But it may be that prospects of this sort are rather slight. Consider the problem of answering Zeno's challenge to (the belief in) objective motion. It often seems assume that modern mathematics, or perhaps mathematical physics, provides an adequate answer. But then, why do so many people keep thinking and writing variously on the problem, including so many that are sophisticated both scientifically and philosophically? Why is each writer so dissatisfied with the efforts of (almost all of) the others, feeling moved to make his own sophisticated efforts?

2. The most conspicuous instances of this are, I suppose, the second chapter of Unger 1975 and the chapter's ancestor, Unger 1971. There are many other instances.

3. As in Grice 1989.

4. See Lewis 1969.

5. See Unger 1971 and 1975.

6. Lewis 1979b, pp. 353–54.

7. See Goodman 1954, Part III, "The New Riddle of Induction."

8. The question of accessibility is treated at length in Unger 1984, chaps. IV and V.

9. Some philosophers dispute this: G.E. Moore seems to do so in various of his writings, and, much more recently, Klein 1981 seems to do it. Therefore the point is at least minimally controversial. But such philosophers seem more motivated by the thought that they must deny skepticism rather than by sensitivity to the phenomena. Therefore, I suggest, the point is also at most minimally controversial.

10. In this connection, see the antiskeptical writing of Lewis 1979b, and the skeptical writing of Adler 1981.

11. The note sentence contains the bracketed expressions "at least fairly obviously." Suppose, as is quite plausible, that, even on the invariantist account of "know," a person need not know all of the logical consequences of anything he knows to be so. Then, the bracketed expression, or one with similar meaning, must apply. Suppose, as is only somewhat less plausible, such a stringent condition on "know" is required by an adequate invariantist semantics for the term. In that case, no such expression need be used. Which is the right invariantist semantics; must we have such a modifying phrase or not? We need not decide the issue here; none of our main points depends upon its outcome.

12. Adler 1981.

13. Some of the complexities are discussed in Dretske 1981b. Further complexities are discussed in Sanford 1981.

14. For a couple of recent examples, see Blose 1980 and Andre 1982.

CHAPTER 14

The View from Nowhere

Thomas Nagel

1. SKEPTICISM

The objective self is responsible both for the expansion of our understanding and for doubts about it that cannot be finally laid to rest. The extension of power and the growth of insecurity go hand in hand, once we place ourselves inside the world and try to develop a view that accommodates this recognition fully.

The most familiar scene of conflict is the pursuit of objective knowledge, whose aim is naturally described in terms that, taken literally, are unintelligible: we must get outside of ourselves, and view the world from nowhere within it. Since it is impossible to leave one's own point of view behind entirely without ceasing to exist, the metaphor of getting outside ourselves must have another meaning. We are to rely less and less on certain individual aspects of our point of view, and more and more on something else, less individual, which is also part of us. But if initial appearances are not in themselves reliable guides to reality, why should the products of detached reflection be different? Why aren't they either equally doubtful or else valid only as higher-order impressions? This is an old problem. The same ideas that make the pursuit of objectivity seem necessary for knowledge make both objectivity and knowledge seem, on reflection, unattainable.

Objectivity and skepticism are closely related: both develop from the idea that there is a real world in which we are contained, and that appearances result from our interaction with the rest of it. We cannot accept those appearances uncritically, but must try to understand what our own consti-

Selection from *The View from Nowhere* originally appeared as Chapter 5 of Thomas Nagel's *The View from Nowhere* (Oxford University Press, 1986). © 1986 by Thomas Nagel. Reprinted by permission of the author and publisher.

tution contributes to them. To do this we try to develop an idea of the world with ourselves in it, an account of both ourselves and the world that includes an explanation of why it initially appears to us as it does. But this idea, since it is we who develop it, is likewise the product of interaction between us and the world, though the interaction is more complicated and more self-conscious than the original one. If the initial appearances cannot be relied upon because they depend on our constitution in ways that we do not fully understand, this more complex idea should be open to the same doubts, for whatever we use to understand certain interactions between ourselves and the world is not itself the object of that understanding. However often we may try to step outside of ourselves, something will have to stay behind the lens, something in us will determine the resulting picture, and this will give grounds for doubt that we are really getting any closer to reality.

The idea of objectivity thus seems to undermine itself. The aim is to form a conception of reality which includes ourselves and our view of things among its objects, but it seems that whatever forms the conception will not be included by it. It seems to follow that the most objective view we can achieve will have to rest on an unexamined subjective base, and that since we can never abandon our own point of view, but can only alter it, the idea that we are coming closer to the reality outside it with each successive step has no foundation.

All theories of knowledge are responses to this problem. They may be divided into three types: *skeptical, reductive,* and *heroic.*

Skeptical theories take the contents of our ordinary or scientific beliefs about the world to go beyond their grounds in ways that make it impossible to defend them against doubt. There are ways we might be wrong that we can't rule out. Once we notice this unclosable gap we cannot, except with conscious irrationality, maintain our confidence in those beliefs.

Reductive theories grow out of skeptical arguments. Assuming that we do know certain things, and acknowledging that we could not know them if the gap between content and grounds were as great as the skeptic thinks it is, the reductionist reinterprets the content of our beliefs about the world so that they claim less. He may interpret them as claims about possible experience or the possible ultimate convergence of experience among rational beings, or as efforts to reduce tension and surprise or to increase order in the system of mental states of the knower, or he may even take some of them, in a Kantian vein, to describe the limits of all possible experience: an inside view of the bars of our mental cage. In any case on a reductive view our beliefs are not about the world as it is in itself—if indeed that means anything. They are about the world as it appears to us. Naturally not all reductive theories succeed in escaping skepticism, for it is difficult to construct a reductive analysis of claims about the world which has any plausibility at all, without leaving gaps between grounds and content—even if both are within the realm of experience.

Heroic thories acknowledge the great gap between the grounds of our beliefs about the world and the contents of those beliefs under a realist inter-pretation, and they try to leap across the gap without narrowing it. The chasm below is littered with epistemological corpses. Examples of heroic theories are Plato's theory of Forms together with the theory of recollection, and Descartes' defense of the general reliability of human knowledge through an a priori proof of the existence of a nondeceiving God.[1]

I believe, first of all, that the truth must lie with one or both of the two realist positions—skepticism and heroism. My terminology reflects a realis-tic tendency: from the standpoint of a reductionist, heroic epistemology would be better described as quixotic. But I believe that skeptical problems arise not from a misunderstanding of the meaning of standard knowledge claims, but from their actual content and the attempt to transcend ourselves that is involved in the formation of beliefs about the world. The ambitions of knowledge and some of its achievements are heroic, but a pervasive skepti-cism or at least provisionality of commitment is suitable in light of our evi-dent limitations.

Though a great deal of effort has been expended on them recently, defi-nitions of knowledge cannot help us here. The central problem of epistemol-ogy is the first-person problem of what to believe and how to justify one's beliefs—not the impersonal problem of whether, given my beliefs together with some assumptions about their relation to what is actually the case, I can be said to have knowledge. Answering the question of what knowledge is will not help me decide what to believe. We must decide what our relation to the world actually is and how it can be changed.

Since we can't literally escape ourselves, any improvement in our beliefs has to result from some kind of self-transformation. And the thing we can do which comes closest to getting outside of ourselves is to form a detached idea of the world that includes us, and includes our possession of that con-ception as part of what it enables us to understand about ourselves. We are then outside ourselves in the sense that we appear inside a conception of the world that we ourselves possess, but that is not tied to our particular point of view. The pursuit of this goal is the essential task of the objective self. I shall argue that it makes sense only in terms of an epistemology that is signifi-cantly rationalist.

The question is how limited beings like ourselves can alter their concep-tion of the world so that it is no longer just the view from where they are but in a sense a view from nowhere, which includes and comprehends the fact that the world contains beings which possess it, explains why the world ap-pears to them as it does prior to the formation of that conception, and ex-plains how they can arrive at the conception itself. This idea of objective knowledge has something in common with the program of Descartes, for he attempted to form a conception of the world in which he was contained, which would account for the validity of that conception and for his capacity to arrive at it. But his method was supposed to depend only on propositions and steps that were absolutely certain, and the method of self-transcendence as I have described it does not necessarily have this feature. In fact, such a conception of the world need not be developed by proofs at all, though it must rely heavily on a priori conjecture.[2]

In discussing the nature of the process and its pitfalls, I want both to defend the possibility of objective ascent and to understand its limits. We should keep in mind how incredible it is that such a thing is possible at all. We are encouraged these days to think of ourselves as contingent organisms arbitrarily thrown up by evolution. There is no reason in advance to expect a finite creature like that to be able to do more than accumulate information at the perceptual and conceptual level it occupies by nature. But apparently that is not how things are. Not only can we form the pure idea of a world that contains us and of which our impressions are a part, but we can give this idea a content which takes us very far from our original impressions.

The pure idea of realism—the idea that there is a world in which we are contained—implies nothing specific about the relation between the appearances and reality, except that we and our inner lives are part of reality. The recognition that this is so creates pressure on the imagination to recast our picture of the world so that it is no longer the view from here. The two possible forms this can take, skepticism and objective knowledge, are products of one capacity: the capacity to fill out the pure idea of realism with more or less definite conceptions of the world in which we are placed. The two are intimately bound together. The search for objective knowledge, because of its commitment to a realistic picture, is inescapably subject to skepticism and cannot refute it but must proceed under its shadow. Skepticism, in turn, is a problem only because of the realist claims of objectivity.

Skeptical possibilities are those according to which the world is completely different from how it appears to us, and there is no way to detect this. The most familiar from the literature are those in which error is the product of deliberate deception by an evil demon working on the mind, or by a scientist stimulating our brain in vitro to produce hallucinations. Another is the possibility that we are dreaming. In the latter two examples the world is not totally different from what we think, for it contains brains and perhaps persons who sleep, dream, and hallucinate. But this is not essential: we can conceive of the possibility that the world is different from how we believe it to be in ways that we cannot imagine, that our thoughts and impressions are produced in ways that we cannot conceive, and that there is no way of moving from where we are to beliefs about the world that are substantially correct. This is the most abstract form of skeptical possibility, and it remains an option on a realist view no matter what other hypotheses we may construct and embrace.

2. ANTISKEPTICISM

Not everyone would concede either this skepticism or the realism on which it depends. Recently there has been a revival of arguments against the possibility of skepticism, reminiscent of the ordinary language arguments of the fifties which claimed that the meanings of statements about the world are revealed by the circumstances in which they are typically used, so that it couldn't be the case that most of what we ordinarily take to be true about the world is in fact false.

In their current versions these arguments are put in terms of reference rather than meaning.[3] What we refer to by the terms in our statements about the external world, for example—what we are really talking about—is said to be whatever *actually* bears the appropriate relation to the generally accepted use of those terms in our language. (This relation is left undefined, but it is supposed to be exemplified in the ordinary world by the relation between my use of the word 'tree' and actual trees, if there are such things.)

The argument against the possibility of skepticism is a *reductio.* Suppose that I am a brain in a vat being stimulated by a mischievous scientist to think I have seen trees, though I never have. Then my word "tree" refers not to what we now call trees but to whatever the scientist usually uses to produce the stimulus which causes me to think, "There's a tree." So when I think that, I am usually thinking something true. I cannot use the word "tree" to form the thought that the scientist would express by saying I have never seen a tree, or the words "material object" to form the thought that perhaps I have never seen a material object, or the word "vat" to form the thought that perhaps I am a brain in a vat. If I were a brain in a vat, then my word "vat" would not refer to vats, and my thought, "Perhaps I am a brain in a vat," would not be true. The original skeptical supposition is shown to be impossible by the fact that if it were true, it would be false. The conditions of reference permit us to think that there are no trees, or that we are brains in a vat, only if this is not true.

This argument is no better than its predecessors. First, I can use a term which fails to refer, provided I have a conception of the conditions under which it would refer—as when I say there are no ghosts. To show that I couldn't think there were no trees if there were none, it would have to be shown that this thought could not be accounted for in more basic terms which would be available to me even if all my impressions of trees had been artificially produced. (Such an analysis need not describe my *conscious* thoughts about trees.) The same goes for "physical object." The skeptic may not be able to produce on request an account of these terms which is independent of the existence of their referents, but he is not refuted unless reason has been given to believe such an account impossible. This has not been attempted and seems on the face of it a hopeless enterprise.

A skeptic does not hold that all his terms fail to refer; he assumes, like the rest of us, that those that do not refer can be explained at some level in terms of those that do. When he says, "Perhaps I have never seen a physical object," he doesn't mean (holding up his hand), "Perhaps *this,* whatever it is, doesn't exist!" He means, "Perhaps I have never seen anything with the spatiotemporal and mind-independent characteristics necessary to be a physical object—nothing of the kind that I take physical objects to be." It has to be shown that he couldn't have *that* thought if it were true. Clearly we will be pushed back to the conditions for the possession of very general concepts.

Nothing here is obvious, but it seems clear at least that a few undeveloped assumptions about reference will not enable one to prove that a brain in a vat or a disembodied spirit couldn't have the concept of mind-independence, for example. The main issue simply hasn't been addressed.

Second, although the argument doesn't work it wouldn't refute skepticism if it did. If I accept the argument, I must conclude that a brain in a vat can't think truly that it is a brain in a vat, even though others can think this about it. What follows? Only that I can't express my skepticism by saying, "Perhaps I'm a brain in a vat." Instead I must say, "Perhaps I can't even *think* the truth about what I am, because I lack the necessary concepts and my circumstances make it impossible for me to acquire them!" If this doesn't qualify as skepticism, I don't know what does.

The possibility of skepticism is built into our ordinary thoughts, in virtue of the realism that they automatically assume and their pretensions to go beyond experience. Some of what we believe must be true in order for us to be able to think at all, but this does not mean we couldn't be wrong about vast tracts of it. Thought and language have to latch onto the world, but they don't have to latch onto it directly at every point, and a being in one of the skeptic's nightmare situations should be able to latch onto enough of it to meet the conditions for formulating his questions.[4]

Critics of skepticism bring against it various theories of how the language works—theories of verifiability, causal theories of reference, principles of charity. I believe the argument goes in the opposite direction.[5] Such theories are refuted by the evident possibility and intelligibility of skepticism, which reveals that by "tree" I don't mean just anything that is causally responsible for my impressions of trees, or anything that looks and feels like a tree, or even anything of the sort that I and others have traditionally called trees. Since those things could conceivably not be trees, any theory that says they have to be is wrong.

The traditional skeptical possibilities that we can imagine stand for limitless possibilities that we can't imagine. In recognizing them we recognize that our ideas of the world, however sophisticated, are the products of one piece of the world interacting with part of the rest of it in ways that we do not understand very well. So anything we come to believe must remain suspended in a great cavern of skeptical darkness.

Once the door is open, it can't be shut again. We can only try to make our conception of our place in the world more complete—essentially developing the objective standpoint. The limit to which such development must tend is presumably unreachable: a conception that closes over itself completely, by describing a world that contains a being that has precisely that conception, and explaining how the being was able to reach that conception from its starting point within the world. Even if we did arrive at such a self-transcendent idea, that wouldn't guarantee its correctness. It would recommend itself as a possibility, but the skeptical possibilities would also remain open. The best we can do is to construct a picture that might be correct. Skepticism is really a way of recognizing our situation, though it will not prevent us from continuing to pursue something like knowledge, for our natural realism makes it impossible for us to be content with a purely subjective view.

3. SELF-TRANSCENDENCE

To provide an alternative to the imaginable and unimaginable skeptical possibilities, a self-transcendent conception should ideally explain the following four things: (1) what the world is like; (2) what we are like; (3) why the world appears to beings like us in certain respects as it is and in certain respects as it isn't; (4) how beings like us can arrive at such a conception. In practice, the last condition is rarely met. We tend to use our rational capacities to construct theories, without at the same time constructing epistemological accounts of how those capacities work. Nevertheless, this is an important part of objectivity. What we want is to reach a position as independent as possible of who we are and where we started, but a position that can also explain how we got there.

In a sense, these conditions could also be satisfied by a conception of the world and our place in it that was developed by other beings, different from us; but in that case the fourth element would not involve self-referential understanding, as it does in the understanding of ourselves. The closest we can come to an external understanding of our relation to the world is to develop the self-referential analogue of an external understanding. This leaves us in no worse position than an external observer, for any being who viewed us from outside would have to face the problem of self-understanding in its own case, to be reasonably secure in its pretensions to understand us or anything else. The aim of objectivity would be to reach a conception of the world, including one-self, which involved one's own point of view not essentially, but only instrumentally, so to speak: so that the form of our understanding would be specific to ourselves, but its content would not be.

The vast majority of additions to what we know do not require any advance in objectivity: they merely add further information at a level that already exists. When someone discovers a previously undetected planet, or the chemical composition of a hormone, or the cause of a disease, or the early influences on a historical figure, he is essentially filling in a framework of understanding that is already given. Even something as fruitful as the discovery of the structure of DNA is in this category. It merely extended the methods of chemistry into genetics. Discoveries like this may be difficult to make, but they do not involve fundamental alterations in the idea of our epistemic relation to the world. They add knowledge without objective advance.

An advance in objectivity requires that already existing forms of understanding should themselves become the object of a new form of understanding, which also takes in the objects of the original forms. This is true of any objective step, even if it does not reach the more ambitious goal of explaining itself. All advances in objectivity subsume our former understanding under a new account of our mental relation to the world.

Consider for example the distinction between primary and secondary qualities, the precondition for the development of modern physics and chemistry. This is a particularly clear example of how we can place ourselves in a new world picture. We realize that our perceptions of external objects depend both on their properties and on ours, and that to explain both their effects on us and their interactions with each other we need to attribute to them fewer types of properties than they may initially appear to have.

Colin McGinn has argued convincingly that this is in the first instance an a priori philosophical discovery, not an empirical scientific one. Things have colors, tastes, and smells in virtue of the way they appear to us: to be red simply *is* to be the sort of thing that looks or would look red to normal human observers in the perceptual circumstances that normally obtain in the actual world. To be square, on the other hand, is an independent property which can be used to explain many things about an object, including how it looks and feels. (McGinn, 1989)

Once this is recognized and we consider how the various perceptible properties of objects are to be explained, it becomes clear that the best account of the appearance of colors will not involve the ascription to things of intrinsic color properties that play an ineliminable role in the explanation of the appearances: the way in which the appearances vary with both physical and psychological conditions makes this very implausible. Objective shape and size, on the other hand, enter naturally into an account of variable appearance of shape and size. So much is evident even if we have only a very rough idea of how as perceivers we are acted upon by the external world— an idea having to do primarily with the type of peripheral impact involved. It is then a short step to the conjecture that the appearances of secondary qualities are caused by other primary qualities of objects, which we can then try to discover.

The pressure to make an objective advance comes, here as elsewhere, from the incapacity of the earlier view of the world to include and explain itself—that is, to explain why things appear to us as they do. This makes us seek a new conception that can explain both the former appearances and the new impression that it itself is true. The hypothesis that objects have intrinsic colors in addition to their primary qualities would conspicuously fail this test, for it provides a poorer explanation of why they appear to have colors, and why those appearances change under internal and external circumstances, than the hypothesis that the primary qualities of objects and their effects on us are responsible for all the appearances.

Consider another example. Not all objective advances have been so widely internalized as this, and some, like general relativity and quantum mechanics, are advances beyond already advanced theories that are not generally accessible. But one huge step beyond common appearance was taken by Einstein with the special theory of relativity. He replaced the familiar idea of unqualified temporal and spatial relations between events, things, and processes by a relativistic conception according to which events are not without qualification simultaneous or successive, objects are not without qualification equal or unequal in size, but only with respect to a frame of reference. What formerly seemed to be an objective conception of absolute space and time was revealed to be a mere appearance, from the perspective of one frame of reference, of a world whose objective description from no frame of reference is not given in a four-dimensional coordinate system of independent spatial and temporal dimensions at all. Instead, events are objectively located in relativistic space-time, whose division into separate spatial and temporal dimensions depends on one's point of view. In this case it was reflection on electrodynamic phenomena rather than ordinary perception that revealed that the appearances had to be transcended. There was also, as with the primary-secondary quality distinction, an important philosophical element in the discovery that absolute simultaneity of spatially separated events was not a well-defined notion, in our ordinary system of concepts.

These examples illustrate the human capacity to escape the limits of the original human situation, not merely by traveling around and seeing the world from different perspectives, but by ascending to new levels from which we can understand and criticize the general forms of previous perspectives. The step to a new perspective is the product of epistemological insight in each case.

Of course it is also the product in some cases of new observations that can't be accommodated in the old picture. But the satisfactoriness of a new external perspective depends on whether it can place the internal perspective within the world in a way that enables one to occupy both of them simultaneously, with a sense that the external perspective gives access to an objective reality that one's subjective impressions are impressions of. Experience is not the sole foundation of our knowledge of the world, but a place must be found for it as part of the world, however different that world may be from the way it is depicted in experience.

Only objectivity can give meaning to the idea of intellectual progress. We can see this by considering any well-established objective advance, like the examples discussed already, and asking whether it could be reversed. Could a theory which ascribed intrinsic colors, tastes, smells, feels, and sounds to things account for the appearance that these are to be explained as the effects on our senses of primary qualities? Could a theory of absolute space and time explain the appearance that we occupy relativistic space-time? In both cases the answer is no. An objective advance may be superseded by a further objective advance, which reduces it in turn to an appearance. But it is not on the same level as its predecessors, and may well have been essential as a step on the route to its successors.

Still, the fact that objective reality is our goal does not guarantee that our pursuit of it succeeds in being anything more than an exploration and reorganization of the insides of our own minds. On a realist view this always remains a possibility, at least in the abstract, even if one isn't thinking of a specific way in which one might be deceived. A less radical point is that whatever we may have achieved we are only at a passing stage of intellectual development, and much of what we now believe will be overthrown by later discoveries and later theories.

A certain expectation of further advance and occasional retreat is rational: there have been enough cases in which what was once thought a maximally objective conception of reality has been included as appearance in a still more objective conception so that we would be foolish not to expect it to go on. Indeed we should want it to go on, for we are evidently just at the beginning of our trip outward, and what has so far been achieved in the way of self-understanding is minimal.

4. EVOLUTIONARY EPISTEMOLOGY

Because self-understanding is at the heart of objectivity, the enterprise faces serious obstacles. The pursuit of objective knowledge requires a much more developed conception of the mind in the world than we now possess: a conception which will explain the possibility of objectivity. It requires that we come to understand the operations of our minds from a point of view that is not just our own. This would not be the kind of self-understanding that Kant aimed for, that is, an understanding from within of the forms and limits of all our possible experience and thought (though that would be amazing enough, and there is no reason to suppose that it could be arrived at a priori). What is needed is something even stronger: an explanation of the possibility of objective knowledge of the real world which is itself an instance of objective knowledge of that world and our relation to it. Can there be creatures capable of this sort of self-transcendence? We at least seem to have taken some steps in this direction, though it is not clear how far we can go. But how is even this much possible? In fact, the objective capacity is a complete mystery. While it obviously exists and we can use it, there is no credible explanation of it in terms of anything more basic, and so long as we don't understand it, its results will remain under a cloud.

Some may be tempted to offer or at least to imagine an evolutionary explanation, as is customary these days for everything under the sun. Evolutionary hand waving is an example of he tendency to take a theory which has been successful in one domain and apply it to anything else you can't understand—not even to apply it, but vaguely to imagine such an application. It is also an example of the pervasive and reductive naturalism of our culture. 'Survival value' is now invoked to account for everything from ethics to language. I realize that it is dangerous to enter into discussion of a topic on which one is not an expert, but since these speculations can't be ignored, and since even when they come from professional biologists they are in the nature of obiter dicta, let me try to say something about them.

The Darwinian theory of natural selection, assuming the truth of its historical claims about how organisms develop, is a very partial explanation of why we are as we are. It explains the selection among those organic possibilities that have been generated, but it does not explain the possibilities themselves. It is a diachronic theory which tries to account for the particular path evolution will take through a set of possibilities under given conditions. It may explain why creatures with vision or reason will survive, but it does not explain how vision or reasoning are possible.

These require not diachronic but timeless explanations. The range of biological options over which natural selection can operate is extraordinarily rich but also severely constrained. Even if randomness is a factor in determining which mutation will appear when (and the extent of the randomness is apparently in dispute), the range of genetic possibilities is not itself a random occurrence but a necessary consequence of the natural order. The possibility of minds capable of forming progressively more objective conceptions of reality is not something the theory of natural selection can attempt to explain, since it doesn't explain possibilities at all, but only selection among them.[6]

But even if we take as given the unexplained possibility of objective minds, natural selection doesn't offer a very plausible explanation of their actual existence. In themselves, the advanced intellectual capacities of human beings, unlike many of their anatomical, physiological, perceptual, and more basic cognitive features, are extremely poor candidates for evolutionary explanation, and would in fact be rendered highly suspect by such an explanation. I am not suggesting, as Kant once did (Kant 1785, pp. 395–6), that reason has negative survival value and could from that point of view be replaced by instinct. But the capacity to form cosmological and subatomic theories takes us so far from the circumstances in which our ability to think would have had to pass its evolutionary tests that there would be no reason whatever, stemming from the theory of evolution, to rely on it in extension to those subjects. In fact if, per impossible, we came to believe that our capacity for objective theory were the product of natural selection, that would warrant serious skepticism about its results beyond a very limited and familiar range. An evolutionary explanation of our theorizing faculty would provide absolutely no confirmation of its capacity to get at the truth. Something else must be going on if the process is really taking us toward a truer and more detached understanding of the world.

There is a standard reply to skepticism about evolutionary explanation of the intellect, namely that Darwinian theory doesn't require every feature of an organism to be separately selected for its adaptive value. Some features may be the side effects of others, singly or in combination, that have been so selected, and if they are not harmful they will survive. In the case of the intellect, a common speculation is that rapid enlargement of the human brain occurred through natural selection after the development of an erect posture and the capacity to use tools made brain size an advantage. This permitted the acquisition of language and the capacity to reason, which in turn conferred survival value on still larger brains. Then, like an adaptable computer, this complex brain turned out to be able to do all kinds of things it wasn't specifically "selected" to do: study astronomy, compose poetry and music, invent the internal combustion engine and the long-playing record, and prove Gödel's theorem. The great rapidity of civilized cultural evolution requires that the brains which took part in it have been developed to full capacity from its beginning.

Since this is pure speculation, not much can be said about its consistency with the empirical evidence. We know nothing about how the brain performs the functions that permitted our hunter-gatherer ancestors to survive, nor do we know anything about how it performs the functions that have permitted the development and understanding of the mathematics and physics of the past few centuries. So we have no basis for evaluating the suggestion that the properties which were necessary to fit the brain for the first of these purposes turned out to be sufficient for the second as well, and for all the cultural developments that have led to it.

Spinoza gives this description of the process of intellectual evolution:

> As men at first made use of the instruments supplied by nature to accomplish very easy pieces of workmanship, laboriously and imperfectly, and then, when these were finished, wrought other things more difficult with less labour and greater perfection; and so gradually mounted from the simplest operations to the making of tools, and from the making of tools to the making of more complex tools, and fresh feats of workmanship, till they arrived at making, with small expenditure of labour, the vast number of complicated mechanisms which they now possess. So, in like manner, the intellect, by its native strength, makes for itself intellectual instruments, whereby it acquires strength for performing other intellectual operations, and from these operations gets again fresh instruments, or the power of pushing its investigations further, and thus gradually proceeds till it reaches the summit of wisdom. (Spinoza 1951, p. 12)

The question is whether not only the physical but the mental capacity needed to make a stone axe automatically brings with it the capacity to take each of the steps that have led from there to the construction of the hydrogen bomb, or whether an enormous excess mental capacity, not explainable by natural selection, was responsible for the generation and spread of the sequence of intellectual instruments that has emerged over the last thirty thousand years. This question is unforgettably posed by the stunning transformation of bone into spaceship in Stanley Kubrick's *2001*.

I see absolutely no reason to believe that the truth lies with the first alternative. The only reason so many people do believe it is that advanced intellectual capacities clearly exist, and this is the only available candidate for a Darwinian explanation of their existence. So it all rests on the assumption that every noteworthy characteristic of human beings, or of any other organism, must have a Darwinian explanation. But what is the reason to believe that? Even if natural selection explains all adaptive evolution, there may be developments in the history of species that are not specifically adaptive and can't be explained in terms of natural selection.[7] Why not take the development of the human intellect as a probable counterexample to the law that natural selection explains everything, instead of forcing it under the law with improbable speculations unsupported by evidence? We have here one of those powerful reductionist dogmas which seem to be part of the intellectual atmosphere we breathe.

What, I will be asked, is my alternative? Creationism? The answer is that I don't have one, and I don't need one in order to reject all existing proposals as improbable. One should not assume that the truth about this matter has already been conceived of—or hold onto a view just because no one can come up with a better alternative. Belief isn't like action. One doesn't have to believe anything, and to believe nothing is not to believe something.

I don't know what an explanation might be like either of the possibility of objective theorizing or of the actual biological development of creatures capable of it. My sense is that it is antecedently so improbable that the only possible explanation must be that it is in some way necessary. It is not the kind of thing that could be either a brute fact or an accident, any more than the identity of inertial and gravitational mass could be; the universe must have fundamental properties that inevitably give rise through physical and biological evolution to complex organisms capable of generating theories about themselves and it. This is not itself an explanation; it merely expresses a view about one condition which an acceptable explanation should meet: it should show why this had to happen, given the relatively short time since the Big Bang, and not merely that it could have happened—as is attempted by Darwinian proposals. (I think an explanation of the original development of organic life should meet the same condition.) There is no reason to expect that we shall ever come up with such an explanation, but we are at such a primitive stage of biological understanding that there is no point in making any predictions.[8]

5. RATIONALISM

One image of self-reconstruction that has appealed to philosophers is Neurath's: that we are like sailors trying to rebuild our ship plank by plank on the high seas. This can be interpreted in more than one way. We might think of ourselves as simply rearranging and perhaps reshaping the planks, making small alterations one at a time, and using the materials we find ready to hand.[9] Such an image may fit the mundane case where knowledge is accumulated gradually and piecemeal, at a given objective level. But if we wish to depict the great objective advances on which real progress depends, we need a different image. Though we may incorporate parts of the original ship in the new one we are about to create, we call up out of ourselves most of the materials from which we will construct it. The place which we occupy for this purpose may be one we could not have reached except on the old ship, but it is really in a new world, and in some sense, I believe, what we find in it is already there. Each of us is a microcosm, and in detaching progressively from our point of view and forming a succession of higher views of ourselves in the world, we are occupying a territory that already exists: taking possession of a latent objective realm, so to speak.

I said earlier that the position to which I am drawn is a form of rationalism. This does not mean that we have innate knowledge of the truth about the world, but it does mean that we have the capacity, not based on experience, to generate hypotheses about what in general the world might possibly be like, and to reject those possibilities that we see could not include ourselves and our experiences. Just as important, we must be able to reject hypotheses which appear initially to be possibilities but are not. The conditions of objectivity that I have been defending lead to the conclusion that the basis of most real knowledge must be a priori and drawn from within ourselves. The role played by particular experience and by the action of the world on us through our individual perspectives can be only selective—though this is a very important factor, which makes the acquisition of such knowledge as we may have importantly subject to luck: the luck of the observations and data to which we are exposed and the age in which we live. Also important, for possession of the a priori component, are the possibilities and questions that are suggested to us and that we might not have formulated for ourselves— like the boy in Plato's *Meno*.

If the possibilities, or at least some of them, are available a priori to any mind of sufficient complexity, and if the general properties of reality are fairly uniform throughout, then the pursuit of objective knowledge can be expected to lead to gradual convergence from different starting points. But this limit of convergence is not the definition of truth, as Peirce suggests: it is a consequence of the relation between reality and the mind, which in turn must be explained in terms of the kind of part of reality the mind is. Obviously the capacities of different minds, and of different species of mind, differ. But in our case the capacities go far beyond the merely adaptive. A reasonably intelligent human being is capable of grasping, even if it cannot generate on its own, an extraordinary and rich range of conceptual possibilities, as we know from what has been learned already. There is no reason to think our mental capacities mirror reality completely, but I assume we all carry potentially in our heads the possibilities that will be revealed by scientific and other developments over the next few thousand years at least: we just aren't going to be around for the trip—perhaps it should be called the awakening.

This conception of knowledge is in the rationalist tradition, though without the claim that reason provides an indubitable foundation for belief. Even empirical knowledge, or empirical belief, must rest on an a priori base, and if large conclusions are derived from limited empirical evidence a large burden must be carried by direct a priori formulation and selection of hypotheses if knowledge is to be possible at all.[10]

This accounts for the extremely high ratio of rational to empirical grounds for great theoretical advances like Newton's theory of gravitation or the special and general theories of relativity: even though the empirical predictions of those theories are enormous, they were arrived at on the basis of relatively limited observational data, from which they could not be deduced. And I would maintain that even induction, that staple of empiricism, makes sense only with a rationalist basis. Observed regularities provide reason to believe that they will be repeated only to the extent that they provide evidence of hidden *necessary* connections, which hold timelessly. It is not a matter of assuming that the contingent future will be like the contingent past.

The capacity to imagine new forms of hidden order, and to understand new conceptions created by others, seems to be innate. Just as matter can be arranged to embody a conscious, thinking organism, so some of these organisms can rearrange themselves to embody more and more thorough and objective mental representations of the world that contains them, and this possibility too must exist in advance. Although the procedures of thought by which we progress are not self-guaranteeing, they make sense only if we have a natural capacity for achieving harmony with the world far beyond the range of our particular experiences and surroundings. When we use our minds to think about reality, we are not, I assume, performing an impossible leap from inside ourselves to the world outside. We are developing a relation to the world that is implicit in our mental and physical makeup, and we can do this only if there are facts we do not know which account for the possibility. Our position is problematic so long as we have not even a candidate for such an account.

Descartes tried to provide one, together with grounds for certainty that it was true, by proving the existence of the right sort of God. While he was not successful, the problem remains. To go on unambivalently holding our beliefs once this has been recognized requires that we believe that something—we know not what—is true that plays the role in our relation to the world that Descartes thought was played by God. (Perhaps it would be more accurate to say that Descartes' God is a personification of the fit between ourselves and the world for which we have no explanation but which is necessary for thought to yield knowledge.)

I have no idea what unheard-of property of the natural order this might be. But without something fairly remarkable, human knowledge is unintelligible. My view is rationalist and antiempiricist, not because I believe a firm foundation for our beliefs can be discovered a priori, but because I believe that unless we suppose that they have a basis in something global (rather than just human) of which we are not aware, they make no sense—and they do make sense. A serious rationalist epistemology would have to complete this picture—but our beliefs may rest on such a basis even if we cannot discover it. There is no reason to assume that even if we are so organized as to be capable of partly understanding the world, we can also gain access to these facts about ourselves in a way that will fill the blanks in our understanding.[11]

A theory of reality with pretensions to completeness would have to include a theory of the mind. But this too would be a hypothesis generated by the mind, and would not be self-guaranteeing. The point is made by Stroud with reference to Quine's proposal of naturalized epistemology, which is essentially an empiricist psychological theory of the formation of empirical theories (Stroud, 1984, ch. 6). It applies equally to a possible rationalist theory of the mind's capacity for a priori theorizing. But of course we have neither of these theories: we don't even have a hypothesis about our capacity to transcend the phenomena. The idea of a full conception of reality that explains our ability to arrive at it is just a dream.

Nevertheless, it's what we aim toward: a gradual liberation of the dormant objective self, trapped initially behind an individual perspective of human experience. The hope is to develop a detached perspective that can coexist with and comprehend the individual one.

6. DOUBLE VISION

To summarize, what we can hope to accomplish along these lines is bound to be limited in several ways. First, we are finite beings, and even if each of us possesses a large dormant capacity for objective self-transcendence, our knowledge of the world will always be fragmentary, however much we extend it. Second, since the objective self, though it can escape the human perspective, is still as short-lived as we are, we must assume that its best efforts will soon be superseded. Third, the understanding of the world of which we are intrinsically capable—leaving aside limitations of time and technology—is also likely to be limited. As I shall argue in the next chapter, reality probably extends beyond what we can conceive of. Finally, the development of richer and more powerful objective hypotheses does nothing to rule out the known and unknown skeptical possibilities which are the other aspect of any realist view.

None of this will deter us from the effort to make objective progress so far as our minds, our culture, and our epoch may permit. But there are other dangers in the pursuit of that goal, dangers not of failure but of ambition. These dangers are of three kinds: excessive impersonality, false objectification, and insoluble conflict between subjective and objective conceptions of the same thing.

The first comes from taking too literally the image of the true self trapped in the individual human perspective. This is a compelling image, and many have succumbed to its attractions. If the real me views the world from nowhere, and includes the empirical perspective and particular concerns of TN as merely one of myriad sentient flickers in the world so viewed, then it may seem that I should take as little interest in TN's life and perspective as possible, and perhaps even try to insulate myself from it. But the discovery and awakening of the objective self with its universal character doesn't imply that one is not also a creature with an empirical perspective and individual life. Objective advance produces a split in the self, and as it gradually widens, the problems of integration between the two standpoints become severe, particularly in regard to ethics and personal life. One must arrange somehow to see the world both from nowhere and from here, and to live accordingly.

The second danger, that of false objectification, is one I have already discussed in connection with the philosophy of mind—though it arises also in other areas. The success of a particular form of objectivity in expanding our grasp of some aspects of reality may tempt us to apply the same methods in areas where they will not work, either because those areas require a new kind of objectivity or because they are in some respect irreducibly subjective. The failure to recognize these limits produces various kinds of objective obstinacy—most notably reductive analyses of one type of thing in terms that are taken from the objective understanding of another. But as I have said, reality is not just objective reality, and objectivity itself is not one thing. The kinds of objective concepts and theories that we have developed so far, mostly to understand the physical world, can be expected to yield only a fragment of the objective understanding that is possible. And the detachment that objectivity requires is bound to leave something behind.

The third problem, that of insoluble subjective-objective conflict, arises when we succeed in constructing an objective conception of something and then don't know what to do with it because it can't be harmoniously combined with the subjective conception we still have of the same thing. Sometimes an internal conception can't acknowledge its own subjectivity and survive, nor can it simply disappear.

Often an objective advance will involve the recognition that some aspects of our previous understanding belong to the realm of appearance. Instead of conceiving the world as full of colored objects, we conceive it as full of objects with primary qualities that affect human vision in certain subjectively understandable ways. The distinction between appearance and objective reality becomes the object of a new, mixed understanding that combines subjective and objective elements and that is based on recognition of the limits of objectivity. Here there is no conflict.[12]

But it may happen that the object of understanding cannot be so cleanly divided. It may happen that something appears to require subjective and objective conceptions that cover the same territory, and that cannot be combined into a single complex but consistent view. This is particularly likely with respect to our understanding of ourselves, and it is at the source of some of the most difficult problems of philosophy, including the problems of personal identity, free will, and the meaning of life. It is also present in the theory of knowledge, where it takes the form of an inability to hold in one's mind simultaneously and in a consistent form the possibility of skepticism and the ordinary beliefs that life is full of.

What should be the relation between the beliefs we form about the world, with their aspirations to objectivity, and the admission that the world might be completely different from the way we think it is, in unimaginable ways? I believe we have no satisfactory way of combining these outlooks. The objective standpoint here produces a split in the self which will not go away, and we either alternate between views or develop a form of double vision.

Double vision is the fate of creatures with a glimpse of the view *sub specie aeternitatis*. When we view ourselves from outside, a naturalistic picture of how we work seems unavoidable. It is clear that our beliefs arise from certain dispositions and experiences which, so far as we know, don't guarantee their truth and are compatible with radical error. The trouble is that we can't fully take on the skepticism that this entails, because we can't cure our appetite for belief, and we can't take on this attitude toward our own beliefs while we're having them. Beliefs are about how things probably are, not just about how they might possibly be, and there is no way of bracketing our ordinary beliefs about the world so that they dovetail neatly with the possibility of skepticism. The thought "I'm a professor at New York University, unless of course I'm a brain in a vat" is not one that can represent my general integrated state of mind.[13]

The problems of free will and personal identity yield similarly unharmonious conclusions. In some respects what we do and what happens to us fits very naturally into an objective picture of the world, on a footing with what other objects and organisms do. Our actions seem to be events with causes and conditions many of which are not our actions. We seem to persist and change through time much as other complex organisms do. But when we take these objective ideas seriously, they appear to threaten and undermine certain fundamental self-conceptions that we find it very difficult to give up.

Earlier I said it was impossible fully to internalize a conception of one's own personal identity that depended on the organic continuity of one's brain. Ordinarily, an objective view of something with a subjective aspect does not require us simply to give up the subjective view, for it can be reduced to the status of an appearance, and can then coexist with the objective view. But in these cases that option seems not to be available. We cannot come to regard our ideas of our own agency or of the purity of our self-identity through time as mere appearances or impressions. That would be equivalent to giving them up. Though our intuitive convictions about these things emerge very much from our own point of view, they have pretensions to describe not just how we appear to ourselves but how we are, in some as yet unspecified sense which appears to conflict with the objective picture of what we are. This problem arises even if the objective picture does not claim to take in everything—for what it willingly omits is only subjective appearance, and that is not good enough. The claims of both the objective and the subjective self seem to be too strong to allow them to live together in harmony.

This problem will reappear in later chapters, but let me mention one further example: Wittgenstein's unacknowledged skepticism about deduction. I believe his view is rightly regarded by Kripke as a form of skepticism because the external account it gives of what is really going on when we apply a formula or a concept to indefinitely many cases—what the apparently infinite reach of meaning really rests on—is not an account we can take on internally. For example we can't think of the correct application of 'plus 2' as being determined by nothing more than the fact that a certain application is natural to those who share our language and form of life, or by anything else of the sort. In employing the concept we must think of it as determining a unique function over infinitely many cases, beyond all our applications and those of our community and independent of them, or else it would not be the concept it is. *Even if Wittgenstein is right,* we can't think of our thoughts this way while we have them. And even in the philosophical act of thinking naturalistically about how language and logic work, we can't take the Wittgensteinian stance toward *those* thoughts, but must think them straight.

I think a view deserves to be called skeptical if it offers an account of ordinary thoughts which cannot be incorporated into those thoughts without destroying them. One may be a skeptic about x no matter how sincerely one protests that one is not denying the existence of x but merely explaining what x really amounts to.[14]

NOTES

1. A fourth reaction is to turn one's back on the abyss and announce that one is now on the other side. This was done by G.E. Moore.

2. The idea is much closer to what Bernard Williams calls the absolute conception of reality, which is a more general description of Descartes' idea of knowledge. See Williams 1978.

3. See for example Putnam, in this volume.

4. There is perhaps one form of radical skepticism which could be ruled out as unthinkable, by an argument analogous to the *cogito:* skepticism about whether I am the kind of being who can have thoughts *at all.* If there were possible beings whose nature and relation to the world was such that nothing they did could constitute thinking, whatever went on inside them, then I could not wonder whether I was such a being, because if I were, I wouldn't be thinking, and even to consider the possibility that I may not be thinking is to think. But most forms of skepticism are not this extreme.

5. This is a theme of Clarke 1972 and Stoud 1984 on skepticism. See Stroud 1984, pp. 205–6. Stroud's book is a highly illuminating discussion and the inadequacy of most responses to it. He is nevertheless slightly more optimistic than I am about the possibility of finding something wrong with skepticism and with the desire for an objective or external understanding of our position in the world that leads to it.

6. Stephen Jay Gould reporters that Francis Crick once said to him, "The trouble with you evolutionary biologists is that you are always asking 'why' before you understand 'how'" (Gould 1983, p. 10).

7. See Gould 1980 for details.

8. It might be argued that the observation that the universe contains intelligent beings does not have to be explained in terms of fundamental principles which show it to be inevitable, because it has a much simpler explanation: if there were no such beings, there would be no observers and hence no observations. No general inferences can therefore be drawn from their existence. I am not persuaded by this argument. The fact that an observation can be predicted on this sort of ground does not mean that it needn't be explained by other, more fundamental principles as well.

It may be worth mentioning an analogy, the application of the anthropic principle in cosmology. The anthropic principle states that "what we can expect to observe must be restricted by the conditions necessary for our presence as observers" (Carter 1974, p. 291). A special case of this is the strong anthropic principle: "the Universe (and hence the fundamental parameters on which it depends) must be such as to admit the creation of observers within it at some stage" (p. 294). About this Carter says that "even an entirely rigorous prediction based on the *strong* principle will not be completely satisfying from the physicist's point of view since the possibility will remain of finding a deeper underlying theory explaining the relationships that have been predicted" (p. 295). In other words, predictability does not always eliminate the need for explanation.

9. As Neurath 1932–3 puts it, we are "never able to dismantle it in dry-dock and to reconstruct it there out of the best materials" (p. 201).

10. Both Chomsky 1980 and Popper 1972 have in very different ways rejected empiricist theories of knowledge and emphasized the incomprehensibility, at present, of our capacities to understand and think about the world. Chomsky in particular has argued that our innate capacity to learn languages is contrary to the empiricist conception of how the mind works. This is one aspect of his general attack on reductionism with respect to the mind. I believe that the scientific gaps between data and conclusions are of much greater importance to the theory of knowledge than the gap between the fragmentary linguistic data of early childhood and the grammar of the language that is learned from it, remarkable as that is. Somehow we call up whole worlds out of our heads, not just languages whose form has presumably evolved in part to suit our ability to learn them.

11. It may be that those areas of knowledge that are entirely a priori permit greater access to their sources in us than do other types of knowledge that we can develop a better understanding of how our thoughts can lead us to the truths of arithmetic than of how they can lead us to the truths of chemistry. It is possible to make discoveries about something a priori if our representation of the thing has so intimate a relation with the thing itself that the properties to be discovered are already buried in the representation. Thus we can think about mathematics because we are able to operate with a system of symbols whose formal properties make it capable of representing the numbers and all their relations. This system can itself be mathematically investigated. To that extent mathematics gives us a partial answer to the question of how the world that it describes can contain beings who will be able to arrive at some of its truths.

12. This is McGinn's point; the scientific image doesn't on reflection conflict with the manifest image over secondary qualities.

13. There is a further problem. In the course of arriving at a skeptical conclusion, we pass through thoughts to which we do not simultaneously take up a skeptical stance thoughts about the relation of the brain to experience, for example. These appear in the skeptic's reasoning in unqualified form. In order to draw skeptical conclusions from the objective standpoint, we have to engage in the kind of direct thought about the world that skepticism undermines. This is like the Cartesian circle in reverse: Descartes tried to prove the existence of God by the use of reasoning on which we can rely only if God exists; the skeptic reaches skepticism through thoughts that skepticism makes unthinkable.

14. See Kripke 1982, p. 65.

CHAPTER 15

Scepticism, 'Externalism', and the Goal of Epistemology

Barry Stroud

Scepticism has been different things at different times in the history of philosophy, and has been put to different uses. In this century it has been understood primarily as a position—or threat—within the theory of knowledge. It says that nobody knows anything, or that nobody has good reason to believe anything. That view must be of central significance in epistemology, given that the goal of the enterprise is to explain how we know the things we think we do. It would seem that any satisfyingly positive theory of knowledge should imply the falsity of scepticism.

Scepticism need not always be taken as completely general. It has more typically been restricted to this or that particular kind of alleged knowledge or reasonable belief: we have no reason to believe anything about the future, for example, even if we know a great deal about the past and the present; we know nothing about the world around us, although we know what the course of our own experience is like; or I know what the physical world and my own thoughts and experiences are like, but I know nothing about the minds of other persons. Scepticism is most illuminating when restricted to particular areas of knowledge in this way because it then rests on distinctive and problematic features of the alleged knowledge in question, not simply on some completely general conundrum in the notion of knowledge itself, or in the very idea of reasonable belief. It is meant to be a theory about human beings as they actually are, and about the knowledge we think we actually have in the circumstances in which we find ourselves.

"Scepticism 'Externalism', and the Goal of Epistemology" from the *Aristotelian Society Supplementary Volume* 68 (1994, pp. 291–307). Reprinted by courtesy of the Editor of the Aritotelian Society.

Scepticism in the theory of knowledge involves much more than the bare assertion that no one knows anything or has any reason to believe anything of a particular kind. If all animate life were suddenly (or even gradually) wiped off the face of the earth no one would then know anything or have any reason to believe anything about the world, but that would not make scepticism about the external world true. A philosophical theorist wants to understand human knowledge as it is, as human beings and the world they live in actually are. But again not just any denial of human knowledge in a certain domain counts as philosophical scepticism. Human beings as they are right now do not know the causes of many kinds of cancer, or of AIDS, or the fundamental structure of matter. But universal ignorance in a particular domain does not make scepticism true of that domain. Scepticism holds that people as they actually are fail to know or have good reason to believe the sorts of things we all think we already know right now. Anti-scepticism, or a positive theory of knowledge, holds the opposite. It would explain how human beings, equipped as they are and living in the world they live in, do in fact know the sorts of things they think they do.

Theories of knowledge which conflict in this way nevertheless typically share many assumptions about human beings and their cognitive and perceptual resources. It is agreed on all sides, for example, that if human beings know things about the world around them, they know them somehow on the basis of what they perceive by means of the senses. The dispute then turns on whether and how what the senses provide can give us knowledge or good reason to believe things about the world. Knowledge of matters which go beyond perception to the independent world is seen, at least temporarily, as problematic. A successful positive theory of knowledge would explain how the problem is solved so that we know the things we think we know about the world after all.

It must be admitted, I think, that what many philosophers have said about perceptual knowledge is pretty clearly open to strong sceptical objections. That is, *if* the way we know things about the world is the way many philosophers have said it is, *then* a good case can be made for the negative sceptical conclusion that we do not really know such things after all. That is why scepticism remains such a constant threat. If you don't get your description of the human condition right, if you describe human perception and cognition and reasoning in certain natural but subtly distorted ways, you will leave human beings as you describe them incapable of the very knowledge you are trying to account for. A sceptical conclusion will be derivable from the very description which serves to pose the epistemological problem. Thus did the ancient sceptics argue, conditionally, against the Stoics: 'if human knowledge is arrived at in the way you say it is, there could be no such thing as human knowledge at all'. Even if true, that does not of course show that scepticism is correct. It shows at most that human knowledge or the human condition must be understood in some other way. The threat of scepticism is what keeps the theory of knowledge going.

The point is that scepticism and its competitors among more positive theories of knowledge are all part of the same enterprise. They offer conflicting answers to what is for all of them a common question or set of questions. The task is to understand all human knowledge of a particular kind, or all reasonable belief concerning a certain kind of matter of fact. Scepticism is one possible outcome of that task. In that sense, scepticism, like its rivals, is a general theory of human knowledge. But it is not a satisfactory theory or outcome. It is paradoxical. It represents us as having none of the knowledge or good reasons we ordinarily think we've got. No other theory or answer is satisfactory either if it does not meet and dispel the threat of scepticism. I think many philosophical theories of knowledge have failed to do that, despite what their defenders have claimed for them.

In fact, I find the force and resilience of scepticism in the theory of knowledge to be so great, once the epistemological project is accepted, and I find its consequences to be so paradoxical, that I think the best thing to do now is to look much more closely and critically at the very enterprise of which scepticism or one of its rivals is the outcome: the task of the philosophical theory of knowledge itself. Its goal is not just any understanding of human knowledge; it seeks to understand knowledge in a certain way. Both scepticism and its opposites claim to understand human knowledge in that special way, or from that special philosophical point of view. I would like to inquire what that way of understanding ourselves and our knowledge is, or is supposed to be. I wonder whether there is a coherent point of view from which we could get a satisfactory understanding of ourselves of the kind we apparently aspire to. Many would dismiss scepticism as absurd on the grounds that there is no such point of view, or that we could never get ourselves into the position of seeing that it is true if it were true. But to adopt a more positive theory of knowledge instead is still to offer a description of the human condition from that same special position or point of view. If we cannot get into that position and see that scepticism is true, can we be sure that we can get into it and see that scepticism is false?

The coherence and achievability of what we aspire to in the epistemological enterprise tends to be taken for granted, or left unexplored. But that question is prior to the question whether scepticism or one or another of its positive competitors is the true theory of human knowledge. What does a true theory of knowledge do? What does a philosophical theorist of knowledge seek?

These are large and complicated questions to which we obviously cannot hope to get a definitive answer today. Distinguishing them from the question of the relative merits of scepticism and its competitors might nonetheless help to locate the target of Ernest Sosa's opposition to something he calls 'scepticism'. He gives that label to the view that 'there is no way to attain full philosophical understanding of our knowledge' or that 'a fully general theory of knowledge is impossible'.[1] That is obviously not what I have just called 'scepticism', which is itself a fully general theory of knowledge. Sosa considers a two-step argument for the view he has in mind which would show exhaustively that any general theory of knowledge possessing a certain feature would be what he calls 'impossible', and that any general theory lacking that feature would be 'impossible' too. So there couldn't be a fully general theory of knowledge. The conclusion certainly does follow from those two premisses, but Sosa doubts the second premiss. He thinks some theories which lack the feature in question have not been shown to be defective in the way the original argument was meant to show. The surviving theories are what he calls 'externalist'.[2]

Theories of the first type hold that a belief acquires the status of knowledge only by 'being based on some justification, argument, or reason'. That requirement is what makes them 'impossible', according to Sosa, because in order to succeed they would have to show that our acceptance of the things we think we know is justified in each case by good inferences or arguments which are not circular or infinitely regressive. That is what it would take to 'legitimate' those beliefs, and that cannot be done. Every inference has to start from something, so without circular or regressive reasoning there must always be something whose acceptance by us is left unsupported by inference, and so cannot be accounted for as knowledge by theories of this type. But a fully general theory of knowledge must account for everything we know. Sosa concludes that there could be no fully 'general, legitimating, philosophical understanding of all one's knowledge'.[3] This is equivalent, I believe, to saying that no such theory avoids the conclusion that we know nothing. What he is saying of theories of this first type is that if, in order to know things, we had to satisfy what those theories say are conditions of knowledge, then we would not know anything, since we cannot satisfy those conditions. So theories of the first type depict us as knowing nothing. They cannot be distinguished, in their consequences, from the view that I (but not Sosa) have called 'scepticism'.

I take it to be the main point of Sosa's paper to show that certain 'externalist, reliabilist' theories escape that fate. They can be fully general and still succeed where theories of other kinds fail. He thinks there is 'a very wide and powerful current of thinking [which] would sweep away externalism root and branch',[4] and he wants to resist that 'torrent of thought'.[5] He concentrates here on the reasons he thinks William Alston and I have given for thinking that, as he puts it, 'externalism will leave us ultimately dissatisfied'.[6] He appears to equate that charge with what he calls the 'unacceptability in principle'[7] of 'externalism'.

What exactly are these objections? For my part, I do think there is a way in which 'externalism' would leave us 'ultimately dissatisfied' as an answer to the completely general philosophical question of how any knowledge of the world is possible. I tried to indicate what I have in mind in the paper that Sosa refers to and discusses.[8] But I do not suggest that 'externalism' is unsatisfying because it cannot avoid depicting us as knowing nothing about the world and so is indistinguishable from the view that I call 'scepticism'. Nor would I argue that it is inconsistent or viciously circular or internally deficient in some other way which prevents it 'in principle' from being true or acceptable. Sosa says the objections are 'grounded in what seem to be demands inherent to the traditional epistemological project itself', and I think his efforts to meet the objections are intended to defend not only 'externalist' theories but also by implication that very epistemological project as well. My own doubts about 'externalism' could perhaps be said to be 'grounded in' or at least connected with demands inherent to that project, but that is because they are doubts not only about 'externalism' but about the coherence or feasibility of the general epistemological project itself.[9] That question is what I think should be our primary target, not just one or another of the answers offered to it. We need to examine more critically what we want or hope for from the traditional epistemological project of understanding human knowledge in general.

Alston's objections might well have a different source. I suspect that in opposing 'externalism' as he does he is working towards what he sees as a more adequate theory of knowledge, perhaps one which would recognize some beliefs as 'evident' or *prima facie* justified' in a way that 'externalism' cannot explain. But to support a theory that competes with pure 'externalism' as the right answer to the philosophical question is not to bring that whole philosophical project itself into question. Although I think there are many points on which we would agree, I shall therefore leave Alston to one side. That leaves me with the question: does Sosa's defence of 'externalism' show that it does not have that feature which I think means it must always leave us dissatisfied, and so by implication that the goal of epistemology must always leave us dissatisfied as well, or does he really accept the point and not regard it as a deficiency in his 'externalist' theory?

The question is complicated because Sosa sees opposition to 'externalism' as coming from some competing philosophical conception or theory of knowledge. His defence amounts to arguing that any theory from which the objections could come must be a theory of his first general type, and so can be discredited 'for simple, demonstrable logical reasons'.[10] If it is a conflict between competing theories of knowledge, 'externalism' must win, since it does not have the fatal defect those other theories have. In order to bring out my doubts about the kind of satisfaction offered by 'externalism' I can grant that point. I would like to reveal something that I think remains unsatisfying about 'externalism' even if it is the best philosophical theory of knowledge there is or could be. I do not want to put a better theory in its place; I want to ask what a philosophical theory of knowledge is supposed to be, even at its best. Revealing the unsatisfactoriness of even the best 'answer' to the philosophical question can perhaps help draw attention to its unsatisfiable demands.

We aspire in philosophy to see ourselves as knowing all or most of the things we think we know and to understand how all that knowledge is possible. We want an explanation, not just of this or that item or piece of knowledge, but of knowledge, or knowledge of a certain kind, *in general*. Take all our knowledge of the world of physical objects around us, for example. A satisfactory 'theory' or explanation of that knowledge must have several features. To be satisfyingly positive it must depict us as knowing all or most of the things of that sort that we think we know. It must explain, given what it takes to be the facts of human perception, how we nonetheless know the sorts of things we think we know about that world. To say simply that we see, hear, and touch the things around us and in that way know what they are like, would leave nothing even initially problematic about that knowledge. Rather than explaining how, it would simply state that we know. There is nothing wrong with that; it is true, but it does not explain how we know even in those cases in which (as we would say) we are in fact seeing or hearing or touching an object. That is what we want in a philosophical explanation of our knowledge. How, given what perception provides us with even in such cases, do we thereby know what the objects in question are like? What needs explanation is the connection between our perceiving what we do and our knowing the things we do about the physical objects around us. How does the one lead to, or amount to, the other?

Suppose there is an 'externalist, reliabilist' theory of the kind Sosa has in mind which accounts for this. I mean suppose there are truths about the world and the human condition which link human perceptual states and cognitive mechanisms with further states of knowledge and reasonable belief, and which imply that human beings acquire their beliefs about the physical world through the operation of belief-forming mechanisms which are on the whole reliable in the sense of giving them mostly true beliefs. Let us not pause over details of the formulation of such truths, although they are of course crucial and have not to this day been put right by anybody, as far as I know. If there are truths of this kind, although no one has discovered them yet, that fact alone obviously will do us no good as theorists who want to understand human knowledge in this philosophical way. At the very least we must believe some such truths; their merely being true would not be enough to give us any illumination or satisfaction. But our merely happening to believe them would not be enough either. We seek understanding of certain aspects of the human condition, so we seek more than just a set of beliefs about it; we want to know or have good reason for thinking that what we believe about it is true. This is why I say, as Sosa quotes me: 'we need some reason to accept a theory of knowledge if we are going to rely on that theory to understand how our knowledge is possible'.[11]

Sosa does not dispute that as a condition of success for understanding human knowledge. He disputes my going on to say that 'no form of 'externalism' can give a satisfactory account'[12] of our having such a reason to accept it and so understanding our knowledge of the world in purely 'externalist' terms. He thinks my only support for that second claim comes from what he calls a 'metaepistemic requirement'[13] which does not follow from the conditions of success admitted so far. It comes, he thinks, from 'a deeply held intuition that underlies a certain way of thinking about epistemology'.[14] He thinks I have an 'anti-externalist' conception of knowledge according to which 'what is important in epistemology is justification', which in turn requires 'appeal to *other* beliefs that constitute one's reasons for holding the given belief'.[15] That is what can only lead in a circle or down an infinite regress, and so in Sosa's terms it is an 'impossible' theory of knowledge. Without that requirement, he thinks, the objection vanishes.

Now I want to say that I do not accept any of that. As far as I know, I do not hold an 'anti-externalist' theory of knowledge with which I seek to oppose 'externalism'. I do not think that everything a person knows requires justification which involves appeal to other beliefs, and so on. I think that what I am drawing attention to about 'externalism' is something that can be recognized by anyone who has a good idea of what the general epistemological project is after. Of course, it could be that I am unwittingly imposing the 'anti-externalist' requirement that Sosa's diagnosis says I am. He thinks I must be; I don't think I am. But rather than searching my soul, which I am sure would be of limited general interest, let me again present for public assessment the way I think 'externalism' must leave us dissatisfied. I find in any case that Sosa has not really considered the reasons I actually gave.

We agree that an 'externalist' theorist of knowledge must know or have good reason to believe that his explanation of our knowledge of the physical world around us is correct in order to understand in that way how that knowledge is possible. How will he know or have good reason to believe that? Well, his theory is in part a theory of the conditions under which people in fact know or have good reasons to believe things about the world. If that theory is true in particular of the theorist's own acceptance of that theory, then the theorist has what his own theory says is knowledge of or reasonable belief in the truth of that theory. I believe this is the situation Sosa is describing when he says: 'We can legitimately and with rational justification arrive at a belief that a certain set of faculties or doxastic practices are those that we employ *and* are reliable'.[16] He thinks there is 'no obstacle in principle'[17] to our achieving such a state. I do not disagree with that.

That Sosa thinks the resistance to 'externalism' must be based on some such 'obstacle in principle' is suggested by his immediately going on to ask 'why could we not conceivably attain thereby a general understanding of how we know whatever we do know?'.[18] It is clear that his question at that point is rhetorical. His idea is that if we can have what an 'externalist' theory calls good reason to believe our 'externalist' theory, it could thereby give us a satisfactory general understanding of our knowledge. For me his question is not rhetorical. I think we can see why, even with what counts for an 'externalist' as good reason to believe his theory, there would remain something ineliminably unsatisfactory about the position a theorist would then be in for gaining a philosophical understanding of his knowledge of the physical world in general.

The difficulty I have in mind does not show up in understanding the knowledge which other people, not myself, have about the world. I understand others' knowledge by connecting their beliefs in the right way with what I know to be true in the world they live in. I can discover that others get their beliefs through the operation of belief-forming mechanisms which I can see to be reliable in the sense of producing beliefs which are largely true. But each of us as theorists of knowledge is also a human being to whom our theory of knowledge is meant to apply, so we must understand ourselves as knowers, just as we understand others. *All* human knowledge of the world is what we want to understand.

If I ask of my own knowledge of the world around me how it is possible, I can explain it along 'externalist' lines by showing that it is a set of beliefs I have acquired through perception by means of belief-forming mechanisms which are reliable. Suppose that is what I believe about the connection between my perceptions and the beliefs I acquire about the world. As we saw, my merely happening to believe such a story would not be enough for me to be said to understand in that way how that knowledge is possible. I must know or have good reason to believe that that story is true of me. As a good 'externalist', I do of course believe that I do. I think that I acquired my belief in my 'externalist' explanation of human knowledge by means of perception and of the operation of the same reliable belief-forming mechanisms which give me and others all our other knowledge of the world around us. So I think I do know or have good reason to believe my theory; I believe that I fulfil the conditions which that very theory says are sufficient for knowing or having good reason to believe it. Do I now have a satisfactory understanding of my knowledge of the world? Have I answered to my own satisfaction the philosophical question of how my knowledge of the world is possible? I want to say No.

It is admittedly not easy to describe the deficiency in a few words. It is not that there is some internal defect or circularity in the 'externalist' theory that I believe. Nor is there any obstacle to my believing that theory or even to my having good reasons in the 'externalist' sense to believe it. *If* the theory is true, and *if* I did acquire my belief in it in the way I think I did, *then* I do know or have good reason to believe it to be true. To appreciate what I still see as a deficiency, or as less than what one aspires to as a philosophical theorist of knowledge, let us consider the merits of a different and conflicting, but still 'externalist', account of our knowledge of the world.

I have in mind a fictional 'externalist' whom I shall call 'Descartes'. The theory of our knowledge of the world which he accepts says that there is a beneficent, omnipotent, and omniscient God who guarantees that whatever human beings carefully and clearly and distinctly perceive to be true is true. The real René Descartes held a closely similar theory, but he tried to prove demonstratively that it is true. He was accused of arguing in a circle. My 'externalist' Descartes offers no proofs. He believes that when people carefully and clearly and distinctly perceive things to be true, they are true; God makes sure of that. That is how people come to know things. He also acknowledges that what he himself needs in order to know or have good reason to believe his own theory of knowledge is to fulfil the conditions it says are sufficient for knowing or having good reason to believe something: to acquire belief in it by carefully and clearly and distinctly perceiving it to be true while God guarantees that it is true. Suppose he examines the origins of his own theory and carefully and clearly and distinctly perceives that he did acquire his belief in it in just that way. Does he now have a satisfactory understanding of his knowledge of the world? Has he got what he can see to be a satisfactory answer to the philosophical question of how his knowledge of the world is possible? I want to say No.

Your seeing and sharing my reservations about the adequacy of 'externalism' and so about the feasibility of the epistemological project depend on your finding the position of this 'externalist' Descartes unsatisfactory in a certain way as an understanding of his knowledge. The question is what is wrong with it. I think most of us will say first that what is wrong is that his theory is simply not true; there is no divine guarantor of the truth of even our most carefully arrived-at beliefs, and he is therefore wrong to think that he acquired his belief in his theory in that way. Even if that is so, is it the only deficiency in his position? I think it is not.

We cannot deny that he does believe his explanation of human knowledge, and does believe that he came to believe that theory by a procedure which his theory says is reliable, so we have to admit that *if* his theory and his account of how he came to believe it were true, *then* he would know or have good reason to believe his explanation of knowledge. But if we say that the falsity of his theory is the only deficiency in his position we would have to admit that if his theory and his belief about how he came to believe it were true, then he would have a satisfactory understanding of all of his knowledge of the world. That implies that whether he understands how his knowledge is possible or not depends only on whether the theory which he holds about how he came to believe it is true or not. If it is true, he does understand his knowledge; if it is not, he does not. An 'externalist' theorist of this fictional kind who reflects on his position could still always ask: 'I wonder whether I understand how my knowledge of the world is possible? I have a lot of beliefs about it. If what I believe about it is true, I do; if it is not, I don't. Of course, I believe all of it is true, so I believe that I do understand my knowledge. But I wonder whether I do'. I think anyone who can get into only that position with respect to his alleged knowledge of the world has not achieved the kind of satisfaction which the traditional epistemological project aspires to. He has not got into a position from which he can see all of his knowledge of the world all at once in a way that accounts for it as reliable or true.

Sosa's 'externalist, reliabilist', I believe, can get himself into no better position for understanding himself. If what distinguishes his position from that of my 'externalist' Descartes is only that his theory is in fact true while that fictional character's theory is false, then he too will be in a position to say no more about himself than 'If what I believe about my knowledge is true, I do understand it; if it is not, I do not. I think I do, but I wonder whether I understand my knowledge or not?'. This is where the difficulty of describing the deficiency in his position comes in. It will not be true to say simply that although he believes his theory, he has no reason to believe it. If we imagine that his 'externalist' theory and his account of how he came to believe it are in fact true, as I have been conceding, then in that sense he does have good reason to believe his explanation of human knowledge. But still his own view of his position can look no better to him than the fictional 'externalist' Descartes's position looks to him.

It would be to no avail at this point for him to try to improve his position by asking himself whether he knows or has good reason to believe that he does know or have good reason to believe his theory. Answering that question would be a matter of coming by what he believes is a procedure that his theory says is reliable to the belief that he knows or has good reason to believe his theory. Again, if he did come to believe that in that way, and his theory is in fact true, he will in fact know or have good reason to believe a second-order claim about the goodness of his reasons for believing his theory. But still he could then make only the same sort of conditional assertion about his position one level up, as it were, as he made earlier. The 'externalist' Descartes could do the same. He could carefully and clearly and distinctly perceive that he came to believe his theory to be true of himself by what that very theory says is a way of coming to know or have good reason to believe. He could then come to a similarly true conditional verdict about his position. Both he and Sosa's 'externalist' could say at most: 'If the theory I hold is true, I do know or have good reason to believe that I know or have good reason to believe it, and I do understand how I know the things I do'. I think that in each case we can see a way in which the satisfaction the theorist seeks in understanding his knowledge still eludes him. Given that all of his knowledge of the world is in question, he will still find himself able to say only 'I might understand my knowledge, I might not. Whether I do or not all depends on how things in fact are in the world I think I've got knowledge of'.

Those of us who are inclined to think that Sosa's 'externalist's' theory is in fact true and the fictional Descartes's theory false will say that he does know and perhaps that he does understand his knowledge and that the fictional Descartes does not. But that does not show that that theorist's position gives him a satisfactory understanding of his own knowledge. As I said, the difficulty does not show up in one's understanding all of someone else's knowledge of the world; it is only when each of us seeks to understand our own knowledge of the world in general that we reach this unsatisfactory position.

If we do recognize a certain ineliminable dissatisfaction in any such 'externalist' attempt at self-understanding I do not think it is because of hidden attachment to an opposing 'internalist' theory which requires that everything we know must be justified by reasonable inference from something else we believe. We can be 'externalists' and still reach at best what I think is an unsatisfactory position, even if we do in fact have what 'externalism' regards as knowledge of or reasonable belief in that 'externalist' theory. I think the dissatisfaction, if we recognize it, is felt to come from the demands of the epistemological project itself, or perhaps we could say from the complete generality of the project. Whatever we seek, and what the theorists I have imagined appear to lack, is something that 'externalism' alone seems unable to explain or to account for.

Sosa grants that the epistemological goal can never be reached if the successful theory is expected to provide what he calls a 'legitimating' account. He means by that an account which 'specifies the reasons favouring one's beliefs',[19] and he thinks no theory that is 'internalist' in his sense can do that without circularity or regress. But surely the goal of understanding how we know what we do does require that the successful account be 'legitimating' at least in the sense of enabling us to understand that what we have got *is* knowledge of, or reasonable belief in, the world's being a certain way. We should be able to see that the view that I call 'scepticism' is not true of us, and we want to understand how we get the knowledge we can see that we've got. 'Externalism' implies that *if* such-and-such is true in the world, *then* human beings do know things about what the world is like. Applying that conditional proposition to ourselves, to our own knowledge of the world, to our own knowledge of how that knowledge is acquired, and so on, even when the antecedent and so the consequent are in fact both true, still leaves us always in the disappointingly second-best position I have tried to illustrate, however far up we go to higher and higher levels of reiterated knowledge or reasonable belief. We want to be in a position knowingly to detach that consequent about ourselves, and at the same time to know and so to understand how any or all of that knowledge of the world comes to be. And that would require appealing to or relying on part of our knowledge of the world in the course of explaining to ourselves how we come to have any knowledge of the world at all.

There are indications that Sosa acknowledges and accepts the situation I have tried to describe. Believing that our belief-forming mechanisms are reliable when they are in fact reliable, and coming by what are in fact those very mechanisms to believe that they are reliable, he says, is 'the very best conceivable outcome'[20] of the epistemological project. 'How could we possibly improve our epistemic situation?', he asks.[21] The thought that someone else could find his own 'epistemic situation' equally good on the basis of a competing theory of knowledge, he admits, might cause some dissatisfaction or discomfort, but he thinks that is 'discomfort we must learn to tolerate'.[22] He concedes that in explaining, even to ourselves, how we know our 'externalist' theory of knowledge to be true, we must appeal to that very theory, and so cannot avoid, as he puts it, 'begging the question' or 'arguing circularly'[23] in our attempts to account for our knowledge. But again, he asks, 'once we understand this, what option is left to us except to go ahead and 'beg' that question?'.[24] I think his thought is that without doing that, we would have no chance of answering the epistemological question at all. We have to 'tolerate' the 'discomfort' of relying on a 'self-supporting argument'[25] for our theory simply because we could not arrive at a 'successful and general theory of knowledge'[26] in any other way.

Here, perhaps, we approach something that Sosa and I can agree about. What I have tried to identify as a dissatisfaction that the epistemological project will always leave us with is for him something that simply has to be accepted if we are going to have a fully general theory of knowledge at all. He appears to think, as I do, that it is endemic to the epistemological project itself. We differ in what moral we draw from that thought.

I want to conclude that we should therefore re-examine the source of, and so perhaps find ourselves able to resist, the not-fully-satisfiable demand embodied in the epistemological question. I think its source lies somewhere within the familiar and powerful line of thinking by which all of our alleged knowledge of the world gets even temporarily split off all at once from what we get in perception, so we are presented with a completely general question of how perception so understood gives us knowledge of anything at all in the physical world. If that manoeuvre cannot really be carried off successfully, we have no completely general question about our knowledge of the world to answer. We could still ask how we know one sort of thing about the physical world, given that we know certain other things about it, but there would be no philosophical problem about all of our knowledge of the world in general. What then would 'externalism' or any other fully general theory of knowledge be trying to do?

Sosa wants his 'externalism', even with its admitted 'discomfort', to serve as a bulwark against the 'relativism', 'contextualism', and 'scepticism' which he sees as rampant in our culture. I share his dark view of our times, but if those widely-invoked 'isms' are thought of as competing answers to a fully general question about our 'epistemic situation' in the world, I think the resistance has to start farther back. It is what all such theories purport to be about, and what we expect or demand that any such theory should say about the human condition, that we should be examining, not just which one of them comes in first in the traditional epistemological sweepstake. In that tough competition, it still seems to me, scepticism will always win going away.

NOTES

1. Sosa, this volume, p. 93.
2. Sosa, this volume, p. 100.
3. Sosa, this volume, p. 96.
4. Sosa, this volume, p. 95.
5. Sosa, this volume, p. 95.
6. Sosa, this volume, p. 95.
7. Sosa, this volume, p. 95.
8. Stroud 1989.
9. Sosa, this volume, p. 95.
10. Sosa, this volume, p. 109.
11. Sosa, this volume, p. 99, quoting from Stroud 1989, p. 43.
12. Stroud 1989.
13. Sosa, this volume, p. 99.
14. Sosa, this volume, p. 100.
15. Sosa, this volume, p. 100.
16. Sosa, this volume, p. 108.

17. Sosa, this volume, p. 108.
18. Sosa, this volume, p. 108.
19. Sosa, this volume, p. 100.
20. Sosa, this volume, p. 106.
21. Sosa, this volume, p. 106.
22. Sosa, this volume, p. 107.
23. Sosa, this volume, p. 111.
24. Sosa, this volume, p. 111.
25. Sosa, this volume, p. 111.
26. Sosa, this volume, p. 111.

BIBLIOGRAPHY

Adams, E. 1976. *The Logic of Conditionals*. Dodrecht: Reidel.

Adler, J. 1981. Skepticism and Universalizability. *The Journal of Philosophy*. 78: 143–156.

Almog, J. 1981. Dthis and Dthat: Indexicality Goes beyond That. *Philosophical Studies*. 39: 347–81.

Alston, W. 1991. *Perceiving God: The Epistemology of Religious Experience*. Ithaca: Cornell University Press.

Alston, W. 1993a. *The Reliability of Sense Perception*. Ithaca: Cornell University Press.

Alston, W. 1993b. Review of Sosa 1991. *Mind* 102: 199–203.

Andre, S. 1982. Unger's Defense of Skepticism: New Wine in Old Bottles. *Canadian Journal of Philosophy* 12: 453–465.

Antony, M. 1993. Social Relations and the Individuation of Thought. *Mind* 102: 247–61.

Armstrong, D.M. 1973. *Belief, Truth and Knowledge*. Cambridge: Cambridge University Press.

Audi, R. 1988. *Belief, Justification, and Knowledge*. Belmont: Wadsworth.

Audi,R. 1995. Deductive Closure, Defeasibility and Scepticism: A Reply to Feldman. *Philosophical Quarterly* 45: 494–9.

Austin, J. 1961. Other Minds. In *Philosophical Papers*. Oxford: Oxford University Press.

Austin, J. 1962. *Sense and Sensibilia*. Oxford: Clarendon Press.

Benacerraf, P. 1973. Mathematical Truth. *Journal of Philosophy* 70: 661–79.

Bennett, J. 1974. Review of Lewis: Counterfactuals and Possible Worlds. *Canadian Journal of Philosophy* 4: 381–402.

Blose, B.L. 1980. The 'Really' of Emphasis and 'Really' of Restriction. *Philosophical Studies* 38: 183–188.

Boghossian, P. 1989. Content and Self-Knowledge. *Philosophical Topics* 17: 5–26.

Bonjour, L. 1985. *The Structure of Empirical Knowledge*. Cambridge, MA: Harvard University Press.

Bouwsma, O.K. 1949. Descartes' Evil Genius. *Philosophical Review*. 58: 141–51.

Brown, J. 1995. The Incompatibility of Anti-individualism and Privileged Access. *Analysis* 55: 149–56.

Brueckner, A. 1985. Skepticism and Epistemic Closure. *Philosophical Topics* 13: 89–117.

Brueckner, A. 1986a. Brains in a Vat. *Journal of Philosophy* 83: 148–67.

Brueckner, A. 1986b. Charity and Skepticism. *Pacific Philosophical Quarterly* October: 264–268.

Brueckner, A. 1986c. Review of Unger's *Philosophical Relativity*. *Journal of Philosophy* 83: 509–17.

Brueckner, A. 1987. Begging the Skeptic's Question. *Philosophia* 17: 523–529.

Brueckner, A. 1990. Skepticism about Knowledge of Content. *Mind,* 99: 447–51.

Brueckner, A. 1991. The Omniscient Interpreter Rides Again. *Analysis* 51: 199–205.

Bibliography

Brueckner, A. 1992a. Semantic Answers to Skepticism. *Pacific Philosophical Quarterly* 73: 200–19. Reprinted in this volume.

Brueckner, A. 1992b. What An Anti-Individualist Knows A Priori. *Analysis* 52: 111–8.

Brueckner, A. 1993. Skepticism and Externalism. *Philosophia* 22: 169–171.

Brueckner, A. 1994. Knowledge of Content and Knowledge of the World. *Philosophical Review* 103: 327–43.

Brueckner, A. 1995. The Characteristic Thesis of Anti-individualism. *Analysis* 55: 146–8.

Brueckner, A. 1996. Trying To Get Outside Your Own Skin. *Philosophical Topics*. 23: 79–111.

Burge, T. 1979. Individualism and the Mental. *Midwest Studies in Philosophy* 4: 73–121.

Burge, T. 1982. Other Bodies. In *Thought and Object: Essays on Intentionality*, ed. A. Woodfield. Oxford: Oxford University Press.

Burge, T. 1986. Individualism and Psychology. *Philosophical Review* 95: 3–45.

Burge, T. 1988. Individualism and Self-Knowledge. *Journal of Philosophy* 85: 649–63.

Cargile, J. 1973. Knowledge and Deracination. Presented at the Annual Philosophy Colloquium, University of Cincinnati.

Carrier, L.S. 1971. An Analysis of Empirical Knowledge. *Southern Journal of Philosophy* 9: 3–11.

Carter, B. 1974. Large Number Coincidences and the Anthropic Principle in Cosmology. In *Confrontation of Cosmological Theories with Observational Data*, ed. M. Longair. Dordrecht: Reidel.

Cavell, S. 1979. *The Claim of Reason*. Oxford: Oxford University Press.

Chellas, B. 1980. *Modal Logic: An Introduction*. Cambridge: Cambridge University Press.

Chisholm, R.M. 1979. The Indirect Reflexive. In *Intention and Intentionality: Essays in Honour of G.E.M. Anscombe*, ed. C. Diamond and J. Teichman. Brighton: Harvester.

Chomsky, N. 1980. *Rules and Representations*. New York: Columbia University Press.

Christensen, D. 1993. Skeptical Problems, Semantical Solutions. *Philosophy and Phenomenological Research* 53: 301–21.

Clarke, T. 1972. The Legacy of Skepticism. *Journal of Philosophy*. 69: 754–69.

Coady, C.A.J. 1992. *Testimony: A Philosophical Study*. Oxford: Clarendon Press.

Cohen, S. 1987. Knowledge, Context, and Social Standards. *Synthese* 73: 3–26.

Cohen, S. 1988. How to be A. Fallibilist. *Philosophical Perspectives* 2: 91–123.

Davidson, D. 1983. A Coherence Theory of Truth and Knowledge. In *Kant oder Hegel*, ed. D. Henrich. Stuttgart: Klett-Cotta.

Davidson, D. 1986a. A Coherence Theory of Truth and Knowledge. In *Truth and Interpretation: Essays on the Philosophy of Donald Davidson*, ed. E. LePore. Oxford: Basil Blackwell.

Davidson, D. 1986b. Empirical Content. In *Truth and Interpretation: Essays on the Philosophy of Donald Davidson*, ed. E. LePore. Oxford: Basil Blackwell.

Davidson, D. 1988. Reply to Burge. *Journal of Philosophy* 85: 664–665.

DeRose, K. 1989. Reid's Anti-Sensationalism and His Realism. *Philosophical Review* 98: 313–48.

DeRose, K. 1990. *Knowledge, Epistemic Possibility, and Scepticism*. Ph.D. dissertation UCLA.

DeRose, K. 1991. Epistemic Possibilities. *Philosophical Review* 100: 581–605.

DeRose, K. 1992. Contextualism and Knowledge Attributions. *Philosophy and Phenomenological Research* 52: 913–29.

Bibliography

Descartes, R. 1960. *Meditations on First Philosophy*. New York: Liberal Arts Press.

Descartes, R. 1980. *Discourse on Method and Meditations on First Philosophy*, trans. D. Cress. Indianapolis: Hackett.

DeSousa, R. 1970. Knowledge, Consistent Belief, and Self-Consciousness. *Journal of Philosophy* 67: 66–73.

Dretske, F. 1968. Reasons and Consequences. *Analysis* April: 28: 166–168.

Dretske, F. 1969. *Seeing and Knowing*. Chicago: University of Chicago Press.

Dretske, F. 1970. Epistemic Operators. *Journal of Philosophy* 67: 1007–1023. Reprinted in this volume.

Dretske, F. 1971. Conclusive Reasons. *Australasian Journal of Philosophy* 49: 1–22.

Dretske, F. 1972. Contrastive Statements. *Philosophical Review* 81: 411–30.

Dretske, F. 1981a. *Knowledge and the Flow of Information*. Cambridge: MIT Press, Bradford Books.

Dretske, F. 1981b. The Pragmatic Dimension of Knowledge. *Philosophical Studies* 40: 363–378.

Dretske, F. 1993. The Nature of Thought. *Philosophical Studies* 70: 185–99.

Elgin, C. 1988. The Epistemic Efficacy of Stupidity. *Synthese* 74: 297–311.

Elugardo, R. 1993. Burge on Content. *Philosophy and Phenomenological Research* 53: 367–84.

Empiricus, Sextus. *Writings*. Cambridge: Harvard University Press, Loeb Classical Library.

Evans, G. 1982. *The Varieties of Reference*. New York: Oxford University Press.

Falvey, K., and J. Owens. 1994. Externalism, Self-Knowledge, and Skepticism. *The Philosophical Review* 103: 107–37.

Feldman, R. 1995. In Defense of Closure. *Philosophical Quarterly* 45: 487–94.

Ferguson, K.S. 1980. *Philosophical Scepticism*. Cornell University doctoral dissertation.

Firth, R. 1967. The Anatomy of Certainty. *Philosophical Review,* 76: 3–27.

Foley, R. 1993. *Working Without a Net: A Study of Egocentric Epistemology*. New York: Oxford University Press.

Forbes, G. 1984. Nozick on Skepticism. *Philosophical Quarterly* 34: 43–52.

Forbes, G. 1995. Realism and Skepticism: Brains in a Vat Revisited. *Journal of Philosophy* 92: 205–22. Reprinted in this volume.

Gettier, E. 1963. Is Justified True Belief Knowledge? *Analysis* 23: 121–3.

Gewirth, A. 1960. Positive "Ethics" and Normative "Science". *The Philosophical Review* 69: 311–330.

Goldman, A. 1967. A Causal Theory of Knowing. *Journal of Philosophy* 64: 357–72.

Goldman, A. 1976. Discrimination and Perceptual Knowledge. *The Journal of Philosophy* 73: 771–91.

Goldman, A. 1979. What is Justified Belief? In *Justification and Knowledge*, ed. G.S. Pappas. Dordrecht: D. Reidel.

Goodman, N. 1995. The New Riddle of Induction. In *Fact, Fiction and Forecast*. Cambridge: Harvard University Press.

Gould, S.J. 1980. Is a New and General Theory of Evolution Emerging? *Paleobiology*.

Gould, S.J. 1983. Genes and the Brain. *New York Review of Books* June 30.

Grice, H.P. 1961. The Causal Theory of Perception. *Proceedings of the Aristotelian Society* Supp. 35.

Grice, H.P. 1975. Logic and Conversation. In *Studies in the Way of Words;* H.P. Grice. Cambridge, Mass.: Harvard University Press.

Bibliography

Harman, G. 1973. *Thought.* Princeton University Press.
Heil, J. 1988a. The Epistemic Route to Anti-Realism. *The Australasian Journal of Philosophy* 66: 161–73.
Heil, J. 1988b. Privileged Access. *Mind* 97: 238–251.
Heil, J. 1992. *The Nature of True Minds.* Cambridge: Cambridge University Press.
Hempel, C. 1962. Deductive-Nomological vs. Statistical Explanation. In *Minnesota Studies in the Philosophy of Science,* ed. H. Feigl and G. Maxwell, Vol. 2. Minneapolis: University of Minnesota Press.
Hetherington, S. 1992. Lacking Knowledge and Justification by Theorizing About Them. Lecture at the University of New South Wales, August.
Hill, C. 1991. *Sensations.* Cambridge: Cambridge University Press.
Hill, C. 1994. Two Cheers For Process Reliabilism. *Pacific Philosophical Quarterly* 75: 12–28.
Hintikka, J. 1962. *Knowledge and Belief.* Ithaca: Cornell University Press.
Johnston, M. 1993. Objectivity Refigured: Pragmatism without Verificationism. In *Reality: Representation and Projection,* ed. J. Haldane and C. Wright. New York: Oxford.
Kant, I. 1785. *Foundations of the Metaphysics of Morals.* Prussian Academy ed., vol. IV.
Kaplan, D. 1989. Demonstratives. In *Themes from Kaplan.* ed. J. Almog, J. Perry, and H. Wettstein. New York: Oxford.
Klein, P. 1981. *Certainty: A Refutation of Scepticism.* Minneapolis: University of Minnesota Press.
Klein, P. 1985. The Virtue of Inconsistency. *Monist* 68: 105–35.
Klein, P. 1995. Skepticism and Closure: Why the Evil Genius Argument Fails. *Philosophical Topics* 23: 213–236.
Kripke, S. 1982. *Wittgenstein on Rules and Private Language.* Cambridge: Harvard University Press.
Kyburg, H. 1961. *Probability and the Logic of Rational Belief.* Middletown: Wesleyan University Press.
Kyburg, H. 1970. Conjunctivitis. In *Induction, Acceptance, and Rational Belief,* ed. by M. Swain. Dordrecht: Reidel.
Lehrer, K. 1968. Belief and Knowledge. *Philosophical Review* 77: 491–499.
Lehrer, K. 1970. Justification, Explanation, and Induction. In *Induction, Acceptance, and Rational Belief,* ed. by M. Swain. Dordrecht: Reidel.
Lehrer, K. 1974. *Knowledge.* Oxford: Oxford University Press.
Lehrer, K. 1978. Why Not Skepticism? In *Essays on Knowledge and Justification,* ed. M. Swain and G. Pappas. Ithaca: Cornell University Press.
Lehrer, K. and T. Paxson. 1969. Knowledge: Undefeated True Belief. *The Journal of Philosophy* 66: 225–37.
Levi, I. 1967. *Gambling With Truth.* Cambridge: MIT Press.
Lewis, D.K. 1969. *Convention.* Cambridge: Harvard University Press.
Lewis, D.K. 1973. *Counterfactuals.* Cambridge: Harvard University Press.
Lewis, D.K. 1979a. Attitudes *De Dicto* and *De Se.* The Philosophical Review 88: 513–43.
Lewis, D.K. 1979b. Scorekeeping in a Language Game. *Journal of Philosophical Logic* 8: 339–59.
Lewis, D.K. 1980. Veridical Hallucination and Prosthetic Vision. *Australasian Journal of Philosophy* 58: 239–249.
Ludwig, K. 1992. Brains in a Vat, Subjectivity, and the Causal Theory of Reference. *Journal of Philosophical Research* 17: 313–45.

Bibliography

Luper-Foy, S. 1987. ed. *The Possibility of Knowledge: Nozick and His Critics*. Totowa: Rowman and Littlefield.

Malcolm, N. 1952. Knowledge and Belief. *Mind* 51: 178–89.

Malcolm, N. 1963. The Verification Argument. In *Knowledge and Certainty*. Englewood Cliffs: Prentice-Hall.

McDowell, J. 1992. Putnam on Mind and Meaning. *Philosophical Topics* 20: 35–48.

McGinn, C. 1989. *Mental Content*. Oxford: Basil Blackwell.

McKinsey, M. 1991. Anti-Individualism and Privileged Access. *Analysis* 51: 9–16.

McKinsey, M. 1993. Curing Folk Psychology of 'Arthritis'. *Philosophical Studies* 70: 323–36.

McKinsey, M. 1994. Accepting the Consequences of Anti-Individualism. *Analysis* 54: 124–28.

Moore, G.E. 1959. *Philosophical Papers*. London: George Allen and Unwin.

Moser P. 1991. Review of Sosa 1991. *Canadian Philosophical Reviews* 11: 425–7.

Naess, A. 1968. *Skepticism*. New York: Humanities Press.

Neurath, O. 1932–33. Protokollsatze. *Erkenntis*. In A.J. Ayer, ed. 1980. *Logical Positivism*, trans. F. Shick. New York: The Free Press.

Noonan, H. 1993. Object Dependent Thoughts. In *Mental Causation* ed. J. Heil and A. Mele. Oxford: Oxford University Press.

Nozick, R. 1980. Fiction. *Ploughshares*, vol. 6, no. 3.

Nozick, R. 1981. *Philosophical Explanations*. Cambridge: Harvard University Press.

Peacocke, C. 1983. *Sense and Content*. New York: Oxford.

Popkin, R. 1964. *History of Skepticism from Erasmus to Descartes*, rev. ed. New York: Humanities Press.

Popper, K. 1972. *Objective Knowledge*. Oxford: Oxford University Press.

Putnam, H. 1975. The Meaning of Meaning. In *Mind, Language and Reality: Philosophical Papers, Volume II*. New York: Cambridge.

Putnam, H. 1977. Realism and Reason. *Procedings and Addresses of the American Philosophical Association* 50: 483–9.

Putnam, H. 1981. *Reason, Truth and History*. New York: Cambridge University Press.

Putnam, H. 1992. Replies. *Philosophical Topics*, 20: 347–408.

Radford, C. 1966. Knowledge-By Examples. *Analysis* 27: 1–11.

Ramsey, F.P. 1931. *The Foundations of Mathematics and Other Logical Essays*. London: Routledge and Kegan Paul.

Reid, T. 1985. *The Works of Thomas Reid*. 8th ed., ed. W. Hamilton. Edinburgh: James Thin.

Robinson, R. 1971. Begging the Question. *Analysis* 31: 113–7.

Rorty, R. 1979. *Philosophy and the Mirror of Nature*. Princeton: Princeton University Press.

Rorty, R. 1989. *Contingency, Irony, and Solidarity*. Cambridge: Cambridge University Press.

Russell, B. 1948. *Human Knowledge: Its Scope and Limits*. London: Allen and Unwin.

Salmon, N. 1986. *Frege's Puzzle*. Cambridge, MA: MIT.

Sanford, D. 1981. Knowledge and Relevant Alternatives: Comments on Dretske. *Philosophical Studies* 40: 379–388.

Schiffer, S. 1996. Contextualist Solutions to Scepticism. *Proceedings of the Aristofelian Society* 96: 317–333.

Skyrms, B. 1967. The Explication of 'X Knows that P'. *Journal of Philosophy* 64: 373–89.

Slote, M. 1970. *Reason and Skepticism*. London: Allen and Unwin.

Sorensen, R. 1996. Unbeggable Questions. *Analysis* 56: 51–5.

Bibliography

Sosa, E. 1994. Philosophical Scepticism and Epistemic Circularity. *Aristotelian Society* Supplementary Volume 68. Reprinted in this volume.

Sosa, E. 1989. Understanding Human Knowledge in General. In *Knowledge and Scepticism*, ed. M. Clay and K. Lehrer. Boulder: Westview.

Sosa, E. 1991. *Knowledge in Perspective* Cambridge: Cambridge University Press.

Sosa, E. 1993. Knowledge in Perspective. *Mind* 102: 199–203.

Spinoza, B. 1951. *On the Improvement of the Understanding;* tr. R.H.M. Elwes. In *The Chief Works of Benedict de Spinoza,* vol. II. New York: Dover.

Stalnaker, R. 1968. A Theory of Conditionals. In *Studies in Logical Theory,* ed. N. Rescher. Oxford: Basil Blackwell.

Stalnaker, R. 1972. Pragmatics. In *Semantics of Natural Language,* ed. D. Davidson and G. Harman. Dordrect: Reidel.

Stalnaker, R. 1973. Presuppositions. *Journal Philosophical Logic* 2: 447–57.

Stalnaker, R. 1974. Pragmatic Presuppositions. In *Semantics and Philosophy,* ed. M. Munitz and P. Unger. New York: New York University Press.

Stalnaker, R. 1984. *Inquiry.* Cambridge: MIT Press.

Stalnaker, R. 1990. Narrow Content. In *Propositional Attitudes: The Role of Content in Logic, Language, and Mind,* ed. C.A. Anderson and J. Owens. Stanford: CSLI.

Steiner, M. 1975. *Mathematical Knowledge.* Ithaca: Cornell University Press.

Stine, G.C. 1973. Essentialism, Possible Worlds, and Propositional Attitudes. *Philosophical Review* 82: 471–82.

Stine, G.C. 1974. Quantified Logic for Knowledge Statements. *Journal of Philosophy* 71: 127–140.

Stine, G.C. 1976. Skepticism, Relevant Alternatives, and Deductive Closure. *Philosophical Studies* 29: 249–61.

Stroud, B. 1984. *The Significance of Philosophical Scepticism.* Oxford: Clarendon Press.

Stroud, B. 1989. Understanding Human Knowledge in General. In *Knowledge and Scepticism,* ed. by M. Clay and K. Lehrer. Boulder: Westview.

Swain, M. 1970. The Consistency of Rational Belief. In *Induction, Acceptance, and Rational Belief,* ed. M. Swain. Dordrecht: Reidel.

Turing, A.M. 1950. Computing Machinery and Intelligence. In *Minds and Machines,* ed. A.R. Anderson.

Tymoczko, T. 1990. Brains Don't Lie: They Don't Even Make Many Mistakes. In *Doubting* ed. M. Roth and G. Ross. Dordrecht: Kluwer.

Unger, P. 1968. An Analysis of Factual Knowledge. *Journal of Philosophy* 65: 157–70.

Unger, P. 1971. A Defense of Skepticism. *Philosophical Review* 80: 198–219.

Unger, P. 1975. *Ignorance: A Case for Scepticism.* Oxford: Oxford University Press.

Unger, P. 1984. *Philosophical Relativity.* Minneapolis: University of Minnesota Press.

Unger, P. 1986. The Cone Model of Knowledge. *Philosophical Topics* 14: 125–78.

van Fraassen, B. 1966. Singular Terms, Truth Value Gaps, and Free Logic. *Journal of Philosophy* 63: 481–95.

van Fraassen, B. 1968. Presupposition, Implication, and Self Reference. *Journal of Philosophy* 65: 136–51.

Vogel, J. 1990. Cartesian Skepticism and Inference to the Best Explanation. *Journal of Philosophy* 87: 658–666.

Warfield, T. 1992. Privileged Access and Externalism are Compatible. *Analysis* 52: 232–7.

Warfield, T. 1994. Knowing the World and Knowing Our Minds. *Philosophy and Phenomenological Research* 55: 525–45.

Warfield, T. 1995. *Privileged Access and Externalism.* Ph.D. Thesis, Rutgers.

Bibliography

Wilkerson, T. 1992. Review of *Knowledge in Perspective*. *Philosophical Books* 33: 159–61.

Williams, B. 1978. *Descartes: The Project of Pure Inquiry.* Harmondsworth: Penguin.

Williams, M. 1988. Epistemological Realism and the Basis of Scepticism. *Mind* 97: 415–439.

Williams, M. 1991. *Unnatural Doubts: Epistemological Realism and the Basis of Scepticism.* Oxford: Blackwell.

Wittgenstein, L. 1969. *On Certainty.* Oxford: Basil Blackwell.

Woozley, A.D. 1953. Knowing and Not Knowing. *Proceedings of the Aristotelian Society* 53: 151–72.

Wright, C. 1992a. *Truth and Objectivity.* Cambridge: Harvard.

Wright, C. 1992b. On Putnam's Proof that We are not Brains-in-a-Vat. *Proceedings of the Aristotelian Society.* 92: 67–94.

NAME INDEX

Page numbers in bold indicate a complete chapter by author

Index